Land Law

L B Curzon
Barrister

Sixth Edition

THE M & E HANDBOOK SERIES

Pitman Publishing
128 Long Acre, London WC2E 9AN

A Division of Pearson Professional Limited

First published in Great Britain 1968
Second edition 1975
Third edition 1979
Fourth edition 1982
Fifth edition 1989
Sixth edition 1993
Reprinted 1994, 1995

© Macdonald & Evans Ltd 1968, 1975, 1979, 1982
© Longman Group UK Limited 1989, 1993

British Library Cataloguing in Publication Data
Curzon, L.B. (Leslie Basil)
    Land law.- 6th ed. - (The M & E Handbook
    series)
    1. England. Real property. Law
    I. Title
    344.2064'3

ISBN 0 7121 1047 X

Founding Editor: P W D Redmond

Typeset by FDS Ltd, Penarth
Printed and bound in Singapore

Contents

Preface   vii
List of abbreviations   ix
Table of cases   xi
Table of statutes   xxiii

Part one   Preliminary matters

1   Introduction to land law   3
General considerations; Land and land law in legal history;
Principal sources of land law; The legal concept of land; The
concept of property; Tenures and estates; The significance of
equitable interests in land; Equitable interests and the doctrine
of notice; Fixtures

2   The property legislation of the 1920s   25
The legislation of 1925; The abolition of anachronisms; The
reduction in tenures; The converging of rules concerning real
and personal property; The simplifying of conveyancing

Part two   The fee simple and the term of years

3   The fee simple absolute in possession   37
Meaning of the phrase; Types of fee simple; Creation of the
fee simple absolute in possession; Rights of the fee simple
owner; Limitations of the rights of a fee simple owner

4   The term of years (1)   50
General terminology; The term of years absolute under LPA
1925; General background; The essence of the lease; Modes of
creation of a leasehold; The doctrine of *Walsh* v. *Lonsdale*:
leases in equity; Types of leases and tenancies; Modes of
determination of tenancies and leases

5 The term of years (2) 71

Rights and obligations of lessor and lessee; Implied rights of the lessee; Implied obligations of the lessee; Implied obligations of the lessor; Express covenant not to assign or underlet, etc.; Express covenant to repair; Express covenant to insure against fire; Express covenant to pay rent; Remedies concerning a covenant for rent; Remedies concerning other covenants; The problem of the running of covenants affecting land; Recent legislation affecting regulation of leases

6 The term of years (3) 93

Preliminaries; Licences; Licences and leases; An attempted resolution of the problem — *Street* v. *Mountford* (1985)

7 Statutory protection of the residential tenant (1) 105

Preliminaries; Protection against harassment, eviction, etc.; Tenancies affording a measure of protection (1); Tenancies affording a measure of protection (2)

8 Statutory protection of the residential tenant (2) 114

The 'new-style' assured tenancy under HA 1988; Security under the assured tenancy; Rent and other matters; The assured shorthold tenancy

9 Housing associations, housing trust areas, and change of landlord 122

Housing associations; Housing action trust areas; Public sector tenants' right to buy

Part three Strict settlements and trusts for sale

10 Strict settlements 129

The nature of a settlement; Settled Land Act 1925; Creation of a strict settlement under SLA 1925; What constitutes a strict settlement; Other types of settlement; The tenant for life under SLA; Trustees of the strict settlement and their duties; Powers conferred by SLA on tenant for life; Overreaching under SLA; Change of ownership and protection of purchasers under SLA; Determination of a settlement

11   Trusts for sale   **147**
Nature of a trust for sale; Definition of a trust for sale;
Creation of a trust for sale; Beneficiaries under a trust for sale;
Trustees for sale; Overreaching under a trust for sale; The *ad
hoc* trust for sale

Part four   Life, concurrent, and other interests

12   Life and concurrent interests   **159**
The essence of life interests; Some general rights and
liabilities of the tenant for life at common law; The nature of
concurrent interests; Essence of the joint tenancy; Creation of
a joint tenancy; Determination of a joint tenancy; Essence of
the tenancy in common; Creation of a tenancy in common;
Determination of a tenancy in common; The tenancy by
entireties; Coparcenary; Party-walls

13   Future, determinable and conditional interests   **173**
The nature of future interests; Categories of future interests;
Future interests following the legislation of 1925; Rules
concerning remoteness; Rule against accumulations; Rule
against perpetuities; The rule in operation; Exceptions to the
perpetuity rule; Determinable interests; Conditional interests;
A note on entailed interests

Part five   Incumbrances on land

14   Mortgages (1)   **189**
Fundamentals; The legal mortgage; The equitable mortgage;
The equity of redemption; Priorities of mortgages; Discharge
of mortgages

15   Mortgages (2)   **202**
Rights of the mortgagor; Rights of the legal mortgagee; Rights
of the equitable mortgagee; Mortgages and the Consumer
Credit Act 1974; Proposals for reform of mortgage law

16   Restrictive covenants   **219**
Nature of restrictive covenants; General position at common
law; General position in equity; Restrictive covenants after
1925; Modification and discharge of restrictive covenants;
A note on rentcharges

17 Easements and profits   **234**
Terminology; Nature of an easement; Examples of easements;
Easements and other rights; Nature of *profits à prendre*; Profits
and other rights; The creation and acquisition of easements
and profits; The Prescription Act 1832; Modes in which
easements and profits may be extinguished

18 The registration of land charges   **254**
Preliminaries; The Land Charges Acts; Register of pending
actions; Register of annuities; Register of writs and orders
affecting land; Register of deeds of arrangement; Register of
land charges; Priority notices, overreaching powers and
general effect of registration; Local land charges; The
problem of land charges registration and 'good faith'

**Part six Transfer of land, limitation of actions, and
adverse possession**

19 The transfer by sale of unregistered land   **269**
Preliminaries; Disabilities in relation to the transfer of
interests in land; Sequence of events leading to completion;
Essentials of deed of conveyance

20 The transfer of registered land   **281**
Preliminaries; Nature of registration of title; Registration;
Titles and conversion of titles; Rights against registered land;
Modes of transfer of registered land; Rectification and
indemnity; Registration and notice: recent developments

21 Limitation of actions, and adverse possession   **298**
Preliminaries; Actions to recover land and rent; Actions
relating to recovery of money secured by mortgage, charge,
proceeds of sale of land; Extension in case of disability, fraud,
etc.; Accrual of rights of action to recover land; Adverse
possession

Appendices   **307**
1 Bibliography; 2 Examination technique; 3 Specimen test
paper

Index   **315**

Preface to the sixth edition

This *Handbook* is designed so as to provide a *structured sequence of study notes* intended for the use of those who are preparing or revising for first examinations in English land law. It is not intended as a substitute for any one of the standard texts (see Appendix 1), an intensive study of which is *essential* for examination success; rather is it a guide and supplement.

The nature and logic of land law demand an appropriate method of learning. First, it is advisable that no attempt be made to plan a scheme of work based on fragmenting the subject area; *it must be studied as a whole*. Secondly, *the learning of principles and their application is essential*. Rote-learning, in which repetitive memorisation drills take the place of comprehension, is an ineffective learning strategy for the law student; it tends to preclude the acquisition of real knowledge of the fundamental structures of the law. *Analysis and problem solving* must be seen, therefore, as necessary skills for the learning of land law.

The following scheme for using this text is suggested for the beginner.

(a) The *first reading* of the text should be undertaken methodically with the object of obtaining *a general picture of the scope and pattern of land law*. It need not include the progress tests.

(b) The *second reading* is the most important part of this scheme of work. It is likely to be a lengthy process, since it necessitates a *close and detailed study of the text*. Principles must be identified and analysed, applications of principles in leading cases must be comprehended. (This is perhaps the most effective technique for remembering the essentials of land law. Coke reminded law students some three and a half centuries ago: 'If by your study and industry you make not the reason of the law your own, it is not possible for you long to retain it in your memory.') The progress test at the end of each chapter should be completed and checked before moving on to a further study of the text.

(c) The *third reading* should have as its objective a *general revision of* principles.

(d) Finally, the *test paper* constituting Appendix 3 should be attempted under examination conditions.

Property Statutes (Sweet and Maxwell) or *Property Statutes* (Blackstone Press) will be found extremely useful. No student should be without a copy of the Law of Property Act 1925.

This sixth edition owes much to the constructive comments of law lecturers and LL.B. students, to whom I express my thanks. Some chapters that had appeared in previous editions have been recast so as to include references to recent legislation and decisions. The sections of the text dealing with priority of mortgages and adverse possession have been rewritten. The Law of Property (Miscellaneous Provisions) Act 1989 is discussed in detail, and the Town and Country Planning Act 1990 and the Charities Act 1992 are among new legislative measures that are recorded. The extension of land registration to cover the entire country is noted, and additional material concerning the Land Registration Act 1925, s. 70(1)(g), is provided. Attention is drawn to the far-ranging Law Commission Report No. 204 (1991) on Land Mortgages. Significant decisions of the House of Lords are recorded: these include *Westminster CC* v. *Clarke* (1992) — a further development of the 'lease or licence' controversy, and *Prudential Assurance Co. Ltd*. v. *London Residuary Body* (1992) — a reaffirmation of the principle that a lease is not created by an agreement for an uncertain term or duration. The tables of statutes and cases have been brought up to date.

The questions forming the test paper in Appendix 3 are reprinted by kind permission of the Senate of the University of London.

I am grateful to the staff of Pitman Publishing for their help.

LBC
1992

List of abbreviations

The following abbreviations are used in the text:

AEA	Administration of Estates Act
HA	Housing Act
LA	Limitation Act
LCA	Land Charges Act
LPA	Law of Property Act
LP(Misc. Provs.)A	Law of Property (Miscellaneous Provisions) Act
LRA	Land Registration Act
LRR	Land Registration Rules
P & AA	Perpetuities and Accumulations Act
RA	Rent Act
SLA	Settled Land Act

(The cross references in the text consist of the relevant chapter number followed by the section number in bold type.)

Table of cases

Abbey Homesteads v.
Northamptonshire CC (1986) 278 EG
1249 *229*
Abbey National BS v. Cann [1990] 2
WLR 832 *287*
Abbey National BS v. Maybeech [1985]
Ch. 190 *85*
Aberconway's ST *Re* [1953] Ch. 647
141
Acklom, *Re* [1929] 1 Ch. 195 *142*
Ackroyd v. Smith (1850) 10 CB 164
236, 239
A'Court v. Cross (1825) 3 Bing 329
298
Addis v. Burrows [1948] 1 KB 444 *66*
Adeane v. Mortlock (1839) 5 Bing NC
236 *243*
Adler v. Blackman [1953] 1 QB 146 *64*
AG Securities v. Vaughan [1988] 3
WLR 1205 *100*
Aldin v. Latimer Clark, Muirhead & Co.
[1894] 2 Ch. 437 *75*
Aldred's Case (1610) 9 Co. Rep. 57b
237
Alefounder's WT, *Re* [1927] 1 Ch. 360
132, 145
Allen v. Greenwood [1980] Ch. 119
250
Allison v. Scargall [1920] 3 KB 443 *61*
American Express Corp. v. Hurley
[1985] 3 All ER 564 *209*
Ames, *Re* [1893] 2 Ch. 479 *141*
Anchor Brewhouse Developments v.
Berkley House (1987) 284 E6 625 *47*
Anderson v. Bostock [1976] Ch. 312
235, 241
Andrews v. Partington (1791) 3 Bro. CC
401 *181*
Andrews v. Schooling [1991] 1 WLR
783 *77*
Anon. (1575), 3 Dy. 345a *61*
Antoniades v. Villiers [1988] 3 WLR
1025 *101*
Appah v. Parncliffe Investments Ltd
[1964] 1 WLR 1064 *55*
Archbold v. Scully (1861) 9 HLC 360
82
Argyle BS v. Hammond (1985) 49
P&CR 148 *294*
Armstrong v. Sheppard & Short Ltd
[1959] 2 QB 384 *84, 241*

Ashburn Anstalt v. Arnold (No 2) [1989]
Ch. 1 *62*
Ashby v. Tolhurst [1937] 2 KB 242 *95*
Aslan v. Murphy [1990] 1 WLR 766
102
Associated British Ports v. C. H. Bailey
plc [1990] 2 WLR 812 *81*
Atkinson and Horsell's Contract, *Re*
[1912] 2 Ch. 1 *303*
A.-G. v. Lonsdale (1868) LR 7 Eq. 377
47
A.-G. v. Moore [1893] 1 Ch. 678 *46*
A.-G. v. Morgan [1891] 1 Ch. 432 *45*
A.-G. v. Terry (1874) LR 9 Ch. App.
423 *48*
A.-G. of Duchy of Lancaster v. Overton
Farms Ltd [1980] 3 All ER 503 *46*
A.-G. of S. Nigeria v. James Holt [1915]
AC 599 *239*
Austen, *Re* [1929] 2 Ch. 155 *132*
Austerberry v. Oldham Corp. (1885) 29
Ch. D 750 *223*
Avon Finance v. Bridger [1985] 2 All
ER 281 *201*

Bagot's Settlement, *Re* [1894] 1 Ch.
177 *151*
Bailey v. Stephens (1862) 12 CB (NS)
99 *237*
Bailey (CH) Ltd v. Memorial
Enterprises Ltd [1974] 1 All ER
1003 *74*
Balchin v. Buckle (1982) 126 SJ 412
229
Ballard v. Tomlinson (1885) 29 Ch. D
115 *47*
Ballard's Conveyance, *Re* [1937] Ch.
473 *226*
Bank of Scotland v. Grimes [1985] QB
1179 *208*
Barclays Bank v. Taylor [1974] Ch.
137 *293*
Barclays Bank v. Walters (1988) *The
Times*, 20 October *300*
Barnett v Hassett [1982] 1 All ER 80
260
Barnhart v. Greenshields (1853) 9 Moo
PCC 18 *19*
Barrett v. Lounova Ltd [1989] 1 All ER
351 *73*

Barry v. Hasseldine [1952] Ch. 835
  246
Barwick's Case (1597) 5 Co. Rep. 93b
  175
Basham, Re [1986] 2 WLR 1498 96
Bass v. Gregory (1890) 25 QBD 481
  237
Bassett v. Nosworthy (1673) Rep. t.
  Finch 102 18
Bathe, Re [1925] Ch. 377 3, 40, 185
Baxendale v. McMurray (1867) 2 Ch.
  App. 508 238
Baxter v. Four Oaks Properties Ltd
  [1965] Ch. 876 227
Baynes & Co. v. Lloyd & Sons [1895] 2
  QB 610 75
Beachway Management Ltd v. Wisewell
  [1971] Ch. 610 178
Beckett v. Lyons [1967] Ch. 449 250
Bedford (Duke of) v. Dawson (1875) LR
  20 Eq. 353 251
Bedson v. Bedson [1965] 2 QB 666
  153, 170
Beech, Re (1990) 59 P & CR 502 229
Belgravia Insurance Co. v. Meah [1963]
  3 All ER 828 84
Benn v. Hardinge (1992) The Times, 13
  October 252
Berkeley Road (No. 88), Re [1971] Ch.
  648 166
Berkley v. Poulett (1976) 241 EG 911
  23
Bernards v. Josephs [1982] Ch. 391
  153
Bernstein v. Skyviews [1978] QB 479
  3, 8, 46
Berry v. Green [1938] AC 575 178
Beswick v. Beswick [1968] AC 58 228
Biggs v. Hoddinott [1898] 2 Ch. 307
  193
Billson v. Residential Apartments [1992]
  2 WLR 15 86
Binions v. Evans [1972] Ch. 359 95
Birmingham, Re [1959] Ch. 523 16
Bisco v. Banbury (1676) 1 Ch. Cas.
  287 19
Bishop v. Bonham [1988] 1 WLR 742
  206
Bladder v. Phillips [1991] EGCS 109
  304
Blades v. Higgs (1865) HL Cas. 621
  46
Bland v. Yates (1914) 58 SJ 612 44
Bolton v. Buckenham [1891] 1 QB
  278 204
Booker v. Palmer [1942] 2 All ER 674
  94
Boosey v. Davies (1988) 55 P&CR 83
  304
Boyle's Claim, Re [1961] 1 All ER 620
  287, 294
BP Properties v. Buckle (1987) 55
  P&CR 337 299

Bradley v. Carritt [1903] AC 253 195
Bradshaw v. Pawley [1979] 3 All ER
  273 54
Brady v. Warren [1900] 2 IR 44
Braythwayte v. Hitchcock (1842) 10
  M&W 494 63
Brent LBC v. O'Bryan (1992) The
  Times, 16 July 64
Bretherton v. Paton [1986] 278 EG
  615 99
Brickfield Properties v. Hughes (1988)
  20 HLR 108 112
Bridges v. Mees [1957] Ch. 475 287
Bridle v. Ruby [1988] 3 WLR 191 247
Brighty v. Norton (1862) 3 B&S 305
  204
Brinnand v. Ewens (1987) 19 HLR
  415 96
Bristol & West Building Society v.
  Henning [1985] 1 WLR 778 95
British Anzani Ltd v. International
  Marine Management [1979] 2 All ER
  1063 80
British Railways Board v. Bodywright
  (1971) 220 EG 651 63
Brocklebank v. Thompson [1903] 2 Ch.
  344 240
Bromley Park Garden Estates v. George
  [1991] 37 EG 139 113
Browne v. Flower [1911] 1 Ch. 219 75
Browne v. Perry (1991) 135 SJ 173 303
Brunner v. Greenslade [1971] Ch. 993
  226
BTE v. Merseyside Rent Assessment
  Committee [1992] 16 EG 111 108
Buchanan-Wollaston's Conveyance, Re
  [1939] Ch. 738 153
Buckland v. Butterfield (1820) 2 Brod.
  & B 54 21
Bucks CC v. Moran [1989] 3 WLR
  152 304
Bull v. Bull [1955] 1 QB 234 151, 162
Burgess v. Rawnsley [1975] Ch. 429
  166
Burnett (Marjorie) v. Barclay (1981)
  125 SJ 99 64

Campbell v. Holyland (1877) 7 Ch. D
  166 205
Cargill v. Gotts [1981] 1 WLR 441 251
Carne v. Debono [1988] 1 WLR 1107
  277
Carr-Saunders v. McNeil [1986] 1 WLR
  922 250
Casborne v. Scarfe (1738) 1 Atk. 603
  193
Cassel, Re [1926] Ch. 358 178
Catling, Re [1931] 2 Ch. 359 135
Cave v. Cave (1880) 15 Ch.D 639 18
Cayley & Evans' Contract, Re [1930] 2
  Ch. 143 132
Celsteel v. Alton House [1985] 1 WLR
  204 7, 286

Celsteel *v.* Alton House (No.2) [1987] 1 WLR 291   *75*

Centaploy *v.* Matlodge [1974] Ch. 1   *62*

Central Estates (Belgravia) Ltd *v.* Woolgar (No.2) [1972] 1 WLR 1048   *84*

Centrax Trustees Ltd *v.* Ross [1979] 2 All ER 952   *208*

Chandler *v.* Bradley [1897] 1 Ch. 315   *142*

Chaplin *v.* Young (1864) 33 Beav. 330   *208*

Chatsworth Estates *v.* Fewell [1931] 1 Ch. 224   *229*

Chatsworth Properties Ltd *v.* Effiom [1971] 1 WLR 144   *209*

Chester *v.* Buckingham Travel Ltd [1981] 1 All ER 386   *72*

Chesterfield (Lord) *v.* Harris [1908] 2 Ch. 397   *241*

Chhokar *v.* Chhokar [1984] FLR 313   *153*

China South Sea Bank Ltd *v.* Tan Soon Gin [1990] 1 AC 536   *205*

Chowood's Registered Land, *Re* [1933] Ch. 574   *294*

Chrisdell Ltd *v.* Johnson (1987) 19 HLR 406   *78, 84*

Church of England BS *v.* Piskor [1954] Ch. 553   *65*

Citibank Trust *v.* Agivor [1987] 1 WLR 1157   *209*

Cityland and Property Holdings *v.* Dabrah [1968] Ch. 186   *195*

City of London BS *v.* Flegg [1988] AC 54   *32, 154, 288*

City Permanent BS *v.* Miller [1952] Ch. 840   *287*

Clark *v.* Chief Land Registrar (1992) *The Times*, 14 October   *292*

Clark (W.G.) Ltd *v.* Dupre Properties [1991] EGCS 64   *69*

Clayhope Properties *v.* Evans [1986] 2 All ER 795   *292*

Clayton's Deed Poll, *Re* [1980] Ch. 99   *174*

Cleaver *v.* Mutual Reserve Fund Life Assoc. [1892] 1 QB 147   *167*

Cogan *v.* Cogan (1596) Cro.Eliz. 360   *175*

Colchester BC *v.* Smith [1992] 2 WLR 728   *305*

Coldunell *v.* Gallon [1986] 2 WLR 466   *201*

Cole *v.* Kelly [1920] 2 KB 106   *62*

Collins' Application, *Re* (1975) 30 P&CR 527   *229*

Colls *v.* Home & Colonial Stores Ltd [1904] AC 179   *250*

Commercial General Administration *v.* Thomsett (1979) 250 EG 547   *86*

Commissioners of Income Tax *v.* Pemsel [1891] AC 531   *273*

Commissioners of Sewers *v.* Glasse (1874) LR 19 Eq. 134   *242*

Congleton Corp. *v.* Patterson (1808) 10 East 130   *87*

Constable *v.* Nicholson (1863) 14 CBNS 230   *241*

Cook, *Re* [1948] Ch. 212   *151*

Cook *v.* Mayor & Corp. of Bath (1868) LR 6 Eq. 177   *252*

Cook *v.* Taylor [1942] Ch. 349   *277*

Coomber *v.* Howard (1845) 1 CB 440   *81*

Copeland *v.* Greenhalf [1952] Ch. 488   *238, 240*

Corbet *v.* Stone (1653) T.Raym. 140   *175*

Cornish *v.* Brook Green Laundry Ltd [1959] 1 QB 394   *59*

Corpus Christi College *v.* Gloucestershire CC [1982] 3 WLR 849   *251*

Cousens *v.* Rose (1871) LR 12 Eq. 366   *238*

Cousins, *Re* (1886) 31 Ch.D. 671   *20*

Cowcher *v.* Cowcher [1972] 1 WLR 425   *168*

Crabb *v.* Arun DC [1976] Ch. 179   *96*

Crago *v.* Julian [1992] 1 All ER 744   *56*

Cricklewood Property & Investment Trust Ltd *v.* Leighton's Investment Trust Ltd [1945] AC 221   *4, 69*

Crow *v.* Wood [1971] 1 QB 77   *236, 238*

Crown Estate Commissioners *v.* Wordsworth (1982) 6 HLR 99   *108*

Crown Land Commissioners *v.* Page [1960] 3 QB 274   *81*

Cuckmere Brick Co. *v.* Mutual Finance Ltd [1971] Ch. 949   *206*

Culling *v.* Tufnal (1694) Bull NP 34   *21*

Cunliffe *v.* Goodman [1950] 2 KB 237   *80*

Curtis *v.* Lutkin (1842) 5 Beav. 147   *177*

D. *Re* [1982] Ch. 237   *273*

Dalton *v.* Angus & Co. (1881) 6 App.Cas. 740   *4, 238, 247*

Damon *v.* Hapag-Lloyd [1983] 3 All ER 510   *274*

Dance *v.* Triplow [1992] 17 EG 103   *250*

Dances Way, *Re* [1962] Ch. 490   *290*

Darby *v.* Harris (1841) 1 QB 895   *23*

Dare *v.* Heathcote (1856) 25 LJ Ex. 245   *246*

Darling *v.* Clue (1864) 4 F&F 329   *247*

Darlington BC *v.* Denmark Chemists Ltd (1992) *The Times*, 12 August   *84*

Dartstone Ltd *v.* Cleveland Petroleum Co. Ltd [1969] 1 WLR 1807   *228*

Dashwood *v.* Magniac [1891] 3 Ch. 306   *160*

Davies v. Benyon-Harris (1931) 47 TLR 424 *272*

Davies v. Davies (1888) 38 Ch.D. 499 *74*

Davies v. Direct Loans Ltd [1986] 1 WLR 823 *214*

Davies v. Du Paver [1953] 1 QB 184 *249*

Davis v. Johnson [1979] AC 264 *162*

Davis v. Symons [1934] Ch. 442 *194*

Davis v. Whitby [1973] 1 WLR 629 *249*

Deanplan Ltd v. Mahmoud [1992] 16 EG 100 *67*

Dearle v. Hall (1828) 3 Russ. 1 *28, 198, 292*

Deen v. Andrews (1986) 52 P&CR 17 *21*

Dellneed v. Chin (1987) 53 P&CR 172 *100*

Dennis v. Malcolm [1934] Ch. 244 *284*

Dewar v. Goodman [1909] AC 72 *88*

D'Eyncourt v. Gregory (1866) LR 3 Eq. 382 *22*

Diment v. N H Foot Ltd [1974] 2 All ER 785 *247*

Dimsdale Development v. De Haan (1984) 47 P&CR 1 *275*

Di Palma v. Victoria Square Property Co. [1986] Ch. 150 *83*

Diplock, *Re* [1948] Ch. 465 *17*

Dixon v. Allgood [1987] 1 WLR 1689 *91*

Dodd v. Acklom (1843) 6 Man. & G 672 *67*

Dodds v. Walker [1981] 1 WLR 1027 *66*

Dodwell & Co.'s Trust Deed, *Re* [1979] Ch. 301 *177*

Doherty v. Allman (1878) 3 App.Cas. 709 *73*

Domb v. Isoz [1980] Ch. 548 *274*

Dougal v. McCarthy [1893] 1 QB 736 *64*

Dowty Boulton Paul Ltd v. Wolverhampton Corporation (No. 2) [1976] Ch. 13 *239*

Draper's Conveyance, *Re* [1969] 1 Ch. 486 *166, 170*

Dresden Estates v. Collinson (1987) 281 EG 1321 *100*

Drummond, *Re* [1988] 1 WLR 234 *178, 181*

Duce's Contract, *Re* [1937] Ch. 642 *279*

Dunning Ltd v. Sykes & Son Ltd [1987] Ch. 287 *41*

Dunsany (Lady) v. Bedworth (1979) 38 P&CR 546 *243*

Duppa v. Mayo (1669) 1 Wms Saund. 275 *83*

Dyce v. Lady James Hay (1852) 1 Macq. 305 *239*

Ecclesiastical Commissioners for England's Conveyance, *Re* [1936] Ch. 430 *228*

Eckroyd v. Coulthard [1898] 2 Ch. 358 *48*

Edgington v. Clark [1967] 1 QB 367 *303*

Elias v. Mitchell [1972] 2 WLR 740 *292*

Elite Investments v. Bainbridge Silencers (1986) 280 EG 1001 *80*

Ellenborough Park, *Re* [1956] Ch. 131 *239*

Elliot v. Bishop (1854) 10 Ex. 496 *23*

Elliston v. Reacher [1908] 2 Ch. 374 *226*

Elsden v. Pick [1980] 1 WLR 899 *62*

Embrey v. Owen (1851) 6 Ex. 353 *47*

Entick v. Carrington (1765) 19 St Tr. 1029 *9, 94*

Epps v. Esso Petroleum [1973] 2 All ER 465 *288*

Equity and Law Home Loans v. Prestidge [1991] 1 WLR 137 *197*

Errington v. Errington [1952] 1 KB 290 *95*

Esso Petroleum Co. Ltd v. Harper's Garage Ltd [1968] AC 269 *197*

Esso Petroleum Co. Ltd v. Kingswood Motors Ltd [1974] QB 142 *197*

Evans v. Walker (1876) 3 Ch.D. 211 *173*

EWP v. Moore [1992] 2 WLR 184 *60*

Expert Clothing Ltd v. Hillgate House Ltd [1986] Ch. 340 *84, 86*

Facchini v. Bryson [1952] 1 TR 1368 *93, 97, 99*

Fairclough v. Swan Brewery Co. Ltd [1912] AC 565 *193*

Family Management v. Gray (1979) 253 EG 369 *80*

Farnol Eades Irvine & Co. Ltd, *Re* [1915] 1 Ch. 22 *205*

Faruqui v. English Real Estates [1979] 1 WLR 963 *275*

Federated Homes v. Mill Lodge Properties [1980] 1 WLR 594 *222*

Field v. Barkworth [1986] 1 WLR 137 *77*

First National Bank v. Syed [1991] 2 All ER 250 *209*

Fletcher v. Ashburner (1779) 1 Bro.CC 497 *148*

Flexman v. Corbett [1930] 1 Ch. 672 *72*

Ford, *Re* [1879] 10 Ch.D. *276*

Formby v. Barker [1903] 2 Ch. 539 *225*

Foster v. Wright (1878) LR 4 CPD 438 *242*

Four-Maids Ltd v. Dudley Marshall (Properties) Ltd [1957] Ch. 317 *4, 207*

Francke v. Hakmi [1984] CLY 1906
    108
Freer v. Unwins [1976] 2 WLR 609
    294
Frewen, Re [1926] Ch. 580   135
Fuller v. Judy Properties [1992] 14 EG
    106   78, 86
Furness v. Bond (1888) 4 TLR 457   53

Gallenga, Re [1938] 1 All ER 106   130
Gardner v. Ingram (1889) 61 LT 729
    66
Gateward's Case (1607) 6 Co.Rep. 59b
    242
Georgiades v. Edward Wolfe & Co.
    [1965] Ch. 487   259
Gilbert v. Spoor [1983] Ch. 27   229
GMS Syndicate Ltd v. Gary Elliot Ltd
    [1982] Ch. 1   86
Gold v. Jacques Amand (1992) 63
    P & CR 1   60
Goldberg v. Edwards [1950] Ch. 247
    238
Goldsmith v. Burrow Construction Co.
    (1987) The Times, 31 July   249
Goldsworthy v. Brickell [1987] 2 WLR
    133   209
Goodman v. Gallant [1986] 1 All ER
    311   167
Goodman v. Mayor of Saltash (1882) 7
    App.Cas. 623   250
Gordon v. Holland (1913) 82 LJPC 81
    18
Gorman, Re [1990] 1 WLR 616   167
Graham v. Pitkin [1992] 2 All ER 235
    277
Gran Gelato v. Richcliff [1992] 1 All ER
    865   277
Grangeside Properties v. Collingwood
    Securities [1964] 1 WLR 139   193
Grant v. Edwards [1986] Ch. 638   168
Gratton-Story v. Lewis (1987) 283 EG
    1562   90
Graves v. Dolphin (1826) 1 Sim. 66
    72, 185
Graves v. Weld (1833) 5 B&Ad. 105   72
Greater London Council v. Connolly
    [1970] 2 QB 100   82
Greenhi Builders v. Allen [1979] 1 WLR
    156   255
Green's WT, Re [1985] 3 All ER 455
    179
Greenwood, Re [1903] 1 Ch. 749   39
Griffiths v. Ricketts (1849) 19 LJ Ch.
    100   148
Griffiths v. Vere (1803) 9 Ves. 127   177
Grigsby v. Melville [1973] 3 All ER
    455   238
Grimthorpe, Re [1908] 2 Ch. 675   149
Grosvenor Estates v. Amberton (1983)
    265 EG 693   107
Guppys Ltd v. Brookling (1984) 269 EG
    846   76

Habib Bank v. Taylor [1982] 1 WLR
    1218   208
Hagee v. Co-operative Insurance
    Society [1992] 7 EG 122   63
Hagee Ltd v. Erikson & Larson [1976]
    QB 209   85
Halifax BS v. Keighley [1931] 2 KB
    248   212
Hall v. King (1987) 19 HLR 440   260
Halsall v. Brizell [1957] Ch. 169   223
Hammersmith and Fulham LBC v.
    Monk [1991] 3 WLR 1144   62
Hammond v. Allen (1992) The Times, 21
    July   80
Hampshire v. Wickens (1878) 7 Ch. D
    555   71
Hampstead Way Investments v.
    Lewis-Weare [1985] 1 WLR 164   112
Hanbury v. Jenkins [1901] 2 Ch. 401
    48
Hansford v. Jago [1921] 1 Ch. 322   245
Harris v. De Pinna (1886) 33 Ch. D
    238   237
Harris v. Goddard [1983] 1 WLR 1203
    165, 167
Harrison v. Hammersmith & Fulham
    LBC [1981] 1 WLR 650   106
Harvey v. Pratt [1965] 1 WLR 1025
    51, 53
Haskell v. Marlow [1928] 2 KB 45   80
Haslemere Estates v. Baker [1982] 1
    WLR 1109   255
Haviland v. Long [1952] 1 All ER 463
    80
Hayward v. Challoner [1968] 1 QB
    107   305
Haywood v. Brunswick BS (1881) 8
    QBD 603   225
Healey v. Hawkins [1968] 1 WLR
    1967   246
Heasman v. Pearse (1871) 7 Ch. App.
    275   182
Heath v. Elliot (1838) 4 Bing NC 388
    242
Hembry v. Henry Smith's Charity
    Trustees (1987) 284 EG 369   91
Hepworth v. Pickles [1900] 1 Ch. 108
    229
Herklot's WT, Re [1964] 1 WLR 583
    150, 152
Heslop v. Burns [1974] 1 WLR 1241
    98
Heywood v. Mallalieu (1883) 25 Ch. D
    357   239
Hill v. Tupper (1863) 2 H&C 121   237
Hodgson v. Marks [1971] Ch. 892
    288, 289, 294
Hodgson v. Salt [1936] 1 All ER 95
    201
Hodson & Howe's Contract, Re (1887)
    35 Ch. D 668   212
Hoggett v. Hoggett (1979) 39 P&CR
    121   67

Holdom v. Kidd [1991] 2 EG 163   *229*
Holland v. Hodgson (1872) LR 7 CP
    328   *22*
Holland v. Tolley [1952] CPL 34   *270*
Holmes, Re (1885) 29 Ch. D 786   *198*
Holmes v. Cowcher [1970] 1 WLR
    834   *200, 300*
Home Brewery Co. v. Davis & Co.
    [1987] 2 WLR 117   *48*
Honywood v. Honywood (1874) LR 18
    Eq. 306   *73*
Hopkins' Lease, Re [1972] 1 All ER
    248   *64*
Hopkinson v. Rolt (1861) 9 HLC 514
    199
Hopper v. Liverpool Corp. (1944) 88 SJ
    213   *183*
Horford Investments Ltd v. Lambert
    [1976] Ch. 39   *105*
Horn v. Hiscock (1972) 223 EG 1437
    245
Horrocks v. Forray [1976] 1 WLR 230
    95
Hounslow LBC v. Twickenham Garden
    Developments [1971] Ch. 233   *94*
Howard v. Shaw (1841) 8 M & W 118
    63
Hulme v. Brigham [1943] KB 152   *3,
    21*
Hulme v. Langford (1985) 50 P&CR
    199   *67*
Hunt v. Luck [1902] 1 Ch. 428   *19*
Hurst v. Picture Theatres Ltd [1915] 1
    KB 1   *95*
Hyde v. Pearce [1982] 1 All ER 1029
    303

IDC Group Ltd v. Clark (1992) *The
    Times*, 23 July   *238*
Ilkley and Burley Moors, Re [1984] 47
    PLCR 121   *242*
International Drilling Fluids Ltd v.
    Louisville Investments Ltd [1986] 1
    All ER 321   *78*
International Tea Stores Co. v. Hobbs
    [1903] 2 Ch. 165   *239, 244*
Inwards v. Baker [1965] 2 QB 29   *95*
Irani Finance Ltd v. Singh [1971] Ch.
    59   *148*
Ironside & Crabb v. Cook & Barefoot
    [1981] 41 P&CR 326   *246*
Irvine v. Moran [1991] 24 HLR 1   *77*
Ives Ltd v. High [1967] 2 QB 379   *260*

Jackson's Settled Estates, Re [1902] 1
    Ch. 258   *150*
Jacobs v. Seward (1872) LR 5 HL 464
    168
James v. Dean (1805) 11 Ves. 383   *63*
Javad v. Aquil [1991] 1 WLR 1007   *63*
Jee v. Audley (1787) 1 Cox. Eq. Cas.
    324   *179*
Jefferys, Re [1939] Ch. 205   *134*

Jenkins v. Jackson (1888) 40 Ch. D 71
    75
Jennings v. Jordan (1880) 6 App. Cas.
    698   *210*
Jessamine Investments v. Schwartz
    [1978] QB 264   *112*
Jeune v. Queen's Cross Properties
    [1973] 3 WLR 378   *80*
Johnson v. Moreton [1980] AC 37   *105*
Johnstone v. Holdway [1963] 1 QB
    601   *243*
Jones, Re [1953] 1 All ER 357   *185*
Jones v. Challenger [1961] 1 QB 176
    153
Jones v. Jones [1977] 1 WLR 438   *153,
    168*
Jones v. Smith (1841) 1 Hare 43   *19*
Jones & Sons Ltd v. Tankerville [1909]
    2 Ch. 440   *240*
Jordan v. May [1947] KB 427   *21*

K., Re [1985] 3 WLR 234   *167*
Kaur v. Gill [1988] 2 All ER 288   *260*
Kelly v. Barrett [1924] 2 Ch. 379   *225*
Kelly v. Monck (1795) 3 Ridg PR 205
    40
Kempthorne, Re [1930] 1 Ch. 268   *148*
Kennedy v. Green (1834) 3 My.&K
    699   *20*
Kenny v. Preen [1963] 1 QB 499   *75*
Kenworthy v. Ward (1853) 11 Hare
    196   *162*
Keppell v. Bailey (1834) 2 My.&K 517
    239
Ketley Ltd v. Scott [1981] ICR 241   *214*
Killick v. Roberts [1991] 4 All ER 289
    112
King v. David Allen Ltd [1916] 2 AC
    54   *95*
King v. S. Northants DC [1992] 6 EG
    152   *77*
King's Leasehold Estate, Re (1873) LR
    16 Eq. 521   *18*
Kingsnorth Trust v. Bell [1986] 1 WLR
    119   *201*
Kingsnorth Trust v. Tizard [1986] 2 All
    ER 54   *19*
Kinnaird v. Trollope (1889) 39 Ch. D
    638   *204*
Kitney v. MEPC [1977] 1 WLR 981
    259
Kling v. Keston Properties (1985) 49
    P&CR 212   *289*
Knightsbridge Estates Trust Ltd v.
    Byrne [1940] AC 613   *183, 194*
Kreglinger v. New Patagonia Meat Co.
    [1914] AC 25   *192, 195*
Kumar v. Dunning [1987] 2 All ER
    801   *88*

Lace v. Chantler [1944] KB 368   *54*
Lake v. Craddock (1732) 3 PW 158
    163

Lake v. Gibson (1729) 1 Eq. Cas. Ab. 294 *163*

Land Securities v. Receiver for MPD [1983] 1 WLR 439 *81*

Langbrook Properties v. Surrey CC [1970] 1 WLR 161 *47*

Lavender v. Betts [1942] 2 All ER 72 *75*

Leach, Re [1912] 2 Ch. 433 *183*

Leach v. Thomas (1835) 7 C&P 327 *23*

Leicester (Earl of) v. Wells UDC [1973] Ch. 110 *227*

Leigh v. Taylor [1902] AC 157 *22*

Leigh's Settled Estates (No 1), Re [1926] Ch. 852 *150*

Lemon v. Lardeur [1946] 2 All ER 329 *62*

Lever Finance Ltd v. Needleman's Trustee [1956] Ch. 375 *210*

Lewis v. Baker [1905] 1 Ch. 46 *54*

Lewis v. Frank Love Ltd [1961] 1 WLR 261 *193*

Lewis-Graham v. Conacher [1922] EG 171 *108*

Lim v. Ang [1991] NPC 129 *96*

Liverpool CC v. Irwin [1977] AC 239 *76, 245*

Lloyd v. Sadler [1978] QB 774 *112*

Lloyds Bank v. Rossett [1988] 3 WLR 1301 *287*

L&NW Railway v. Evans [1893] 1 Ch. 16 *43*

Lobb (Alec) Garages Ltd v. Total Oil Ltd [1985] 1 WLR 173 *197*

London & County Ltd v. Wilfred Sportsman Ltd [1971] Ch.23 764 *84*

London and Suburban Land Co. v. Carey (1991) 62 P & CR 480 *234, 245*

Longrigg Burrough & Trounson v. Smith (1979) 251 EG 847 *63*

Lonsdale (Earl) v. A-G [1982] 1 WLR 887 *45*

Lord Advocate v. Lord Lovat (1880) 5 App. Cas. 273 *303*

Lotus Ltd v. British Soda Ltd [1972] Ch. 123 *238*

Lowe v. Ashmore Ltd [1971] Ch. 545 *242*

Lund v. Taylor & Co. (1975) 31 P&CR 167 *227*

Lyon & Co. v. London City & Midland Bank [1903] 2 KB 135 *22*

Lyus v. Prowsa Developments Ltd [1982] 1 WLR 1044 *296*

Macleay, Re (1875) LR 20 Eq. 186 *39, 184*

Malayan Credit v. Jack Chia MPH [1986] AC 549 *163*

Malpas v. St Ermin's Properties [1992] RVR 68 *90*

Mancetter Developments Ltd v. Garmanson Ltd [1986] QB 1212 *23*

Manchester Brewery Co. v. Coombs [1901] 2 Ch. 608 *59*

Marcroft Wagons Ltd v. Smith [1951] 2 KB 496 *63*

Markham v. Paget [1908] 1 Ch. 697 *75*

Markou v. Da Silvaesa (1986) 52 P&CR 204 *108*

Marks v. Warren [1979] 1 All ER 29 *77*

Marsden v. Edward Heyes Ltd [1927] 2 KB 1 *73*

Marshall v. Green (1875) 1 CPD 935 *94*

Martin, Re [1989] 5 EG 85 *229*

Martin v. Martin (1987) 54 P&CR 238 *168*

Maryon-Wilson's Instruments, Re [1971] Ch. 789 *142*

Mason v. Clarke [1955] AC 778 *242, 243*

Mason v. Hill (1833) 5 B&Ad. 1 *47*

Mason v. Skilling [1974] 1 WLR 1437 *108*

Mather v. Barclays Bank [1987] 2 EGLR 254 *80*

Matthews v. Goodday (1861) 31 LJ Ch. 282 *16, 192*

Matthews v. Smallwood [1910] 1 Ch. 777 *84*

Matthey v. Curling [1922] 2 AC 180 *68, 81*

Maugham, Re (1885) 14 QBD 956 *59*

May v. Platt [1900] 1 Ch. 616 *280*

Mayho v. Buckhurst (1617) Cro. Jac. 438 *88*

Mayo, Re [1943] Ch. 302 *152, 153*

McAuley v. Bristol CC (1991) 23 HLR 586 *77*

McCall v. Abelesz [1976] QB 585 *75*

McGrath v. Shah (1987) *The Times*, 22 October *274*

McHugh v. Union Bank of Canada [1913] AC 299 *206*

McManus v. Cooke (1887) 35 Ch. D 681 *243*

McNerny v. Lambeth LBC (1988) *The Times*, 10 December *77*

Meaden v. Sealey (1849), 6 Hare 620 *213*

MEPC v. Christian-Edwards [1979] 3 WLR 713 *275*

Mercer v. Denne [1905] 2 Ch. 538 *240*

Meretune Investments v. Martin [1984] CLY 1917 *67*

Midland Bank v. Chart Enterprises [1990] 44 EG 68 *79*

Midland Bank v. Farmpride Hatcheries (1981) 260 EG 493 *20*

Midland Bank v. Shephard [1988] 3 All ER 17 *20, 209*

Midland Bank Trust Co. Ltd v. Green [1981] AC 513   *18, 263*

Midland Bank Trust Co. v. Green (No. 3) [1982] 2 WLR 1   *264*

Midland Bank Trust Co. v. Hett, Stubbs and Kemp [1979] Ch. 384   *264*

Midland Railway Co's Agreement, *Re* [1971] Ch. 725   *62*

Mills v. Silver [1991] 2 WLR 324   *248*

Mines, Case of (1568) 1 Plowd. 310   *45*

Mint v. Good [1951] 1 KB 517   *74*

Moffatt v. Kazana [1969] 2 QB 152   *23*

Molton Finance Ltd, *Re* [1968] Ch. 325   *212*

Moody v. Steggles (1879) 12 Ch. D 261   *237, 239*

Moore v. Rawson (1824) 3 B&C 332   *252*

Morgan, *Re* [1914] 1 Ch. 910   *160*

Morgan v. Fear [1907] AC 425   *249*

Morgan v. Liverpool Corp. [1927] 2 KB 131   *80*

Morgan's Lease, *Re* [1972] Ch. 1   *139, 144*

Morley v. Rennoldson (1843) 2 Hare 570   *40*

Morrice v. Evans (1989) *The Times*, 27 February   *304*

Morris v. Edgington (1810) 3 Taunt. 24   *236*

Mortgage Corporation Ltd v. Nationwide Credit Corporation Ltd (1992) *The Times*, 27 July   *293*

Mount Carmel Investments v. Thurlow [1988] 1 WLR 1078   *305*

MRA Engineering v. Trimster Co. [1988] 56 P & CR 1   *280*

Mulliner v. Midland Railway Co. (1879) 11 Ch. D 611   *238*

Multiservice Bookbinding v. Marden [1979] Ch. 84   *196*

Mundy & Roper's Contract, *Re* [1899] 1 Ch. 275   *138*

Murray v. Two Strokes [1973] 1 WLR 823   *290*

Musgrave v. Brooke (1884) 26 Ch. D 792   *175*

N. & D. v. Gadsdon [1992] 2 EG 176   *119*

National Carriers Ltd v. Panalpina Ltd [1981] AC 675   *3, 4, 68*

National Guaranteed Manure Co. Ltd v. Donald (1859) 4 H&N 8   *238, 252*

National Provincial Bank v. Hastings Car Mart [1964] Ch. 665   *288*

National Westminster Bank v. Morgan [1985] AC 686   *201, 209*

Neaverson v. Peterborough RDC [1902] 1 Ch. 557   *247*

Nelson Developments v. Taboada [1992] 34 EG 72   *108*

Ness v. O'Neill [1916] 1 KB 706   *205*

Newberry v. Turngiant [1991] EGCS 103   *77*

Newbould, *Re* (1913) 110 LT 6   *148*

Newman v. Bennett [1981] QB 726   *242*

Newnham v. Willison [1988] 56 P & CR 8   *248*

Newton Abbott Co-op Soc. v. Williamson & Treadgold Ltd [1952] 2 Ch. 286   *227*

New Zealand Government Property Corp. v. HM&S Ltd [1982] 1 All ER 624   *22*

Nickerson v. Barraclough [1981] 2 WLR 773   *244, 245*

Noakes v. Rice [1902] AC 24   *195*

Nokes v. Doncaster Amalgamated Collieries [1940] AC 1014   *9*

Norfolk's (Duke of) Case (1681) 2 Swans. 454   *176*

Norris v. Checksfield [1992] 1 EG 97   *67*

Norton, *Re* [1929] 1 Ch. 84   *150*

Norwich and Peterborough BS v. Steed (1992) *The Independent*, 10 March   *294*

Nottingham Brick Co. v. Butler (1886) 16 QBD 778   *276*

Oak Co-operative BS v. Blackburn [1968] Ch. 730   *258*

O'Brien v. Robinson [1973] 2 WLR 393   *80*

Official Custodian of Charities v. Parway Estates (1984) 270 EG 1077   *84*

Ogle, *Re* [1927] 1 Ch. 229   *134*

Ogwr BC v. Dykes [1989] 1 WLR 295   *101*

Otter v. Norman [1988] 3 WLR 321   *108*

Owen v. Gadd [1956] 2 All ER 28   *75*

Paddington BS v. Mendelsohn [1987] Fam. Law 121   *289*

Palk v. Mortgage Services Funding plc (1992) *The Times*, 7 August   *205*

Palmer v. Barclays Bank (1971) 23 P&CR 30   *207*

Parker v. BA Board [1982] QB 1004   *9, 46*

Parker's Settled Estates, *Re* [1928] Ch. 247   *150*

Parker-Tweedale v. Dunbar [1990] 3 WLR 780   *206*

Parkus v. Greenwood [1950] 1 All ER 436   *65*

Pearks v. Moseley (1880) 5 App. Cas. 714   *181*

Pearson v. IRC [1981] AC 753   *38, 173*

Peffer v. Rigg [1978] 3 All ER 745   *296*

Pelly's WT, *Re* [1957] Ch. 1   *143*

Pennant's WT, *Re* [1970] Ch. 75   *142*

Penniall *v.* Harborne (1848) 11 QB 368 *81*
Perez-Adamson *v.* Perez-Rivas [1987] 2 WLR 500 *255*
Perham *v.* Kempster [1907] 2 Ch. 596 *18*
Perry *v.* Phoenix Assurance [1988] 1 WLR 940 *147*
Peto *v.* Hammond (1861) 30 Beav. 495 *19*
Phillips *v.* Lamdin [1949] 2 KB 33 *23*
Phillips *v.* Mobil Oil Ltd [1989] 1 WLR 888 *259*
Phipps *v.* Pears [1965] 1 QB 76 *240*
Pilcher *v.* Rawlins (1872) 25 LT 921 *18*
Pirelli Cables *v.* Faber [1983] 2 WLR 6 *77*
Pledge *v.* White [1896] AC 187 *211*
Poland *v.* Earl of Cadogan [1980] 3 All ER 544 *91*
Poole's Case (1703) 1 Salk. 368 *23*
Powell *v.* McFarlane (1977) 38 P&CR 452 *304*
Powys *v.* Blagrave (1854) 4 De GM&G 448 *73*
Precious *v.* Reedie [1924] 2 KB 149 *62*
Price *v.* Bouch (1986) 279 EG 1226 *229*
Pritchard *v.* Briggs [1980] Ch. 338 *259*
Proudfoot *v.* Hart (1890) 25 QBD 42 *80*
Prudential Assurance Co. Ltd *v.* London Residuary Body [1992] 3 WLR 279 *54, 61*
Prudential Assurance Co. Ltd *v.* Salisbury's Handbags [1992] 23 EG 17 *108*
Pugh *v.* Savage [1970] 2 All ER 253 *237, 246, 249*
Purnell, *Re* (1988) 55 P&CR 133 *229*
Purser *v.* Bailey [1967] WLR 146 *90*
Pwllbach Colliery Co. Ltd *v.* Woodman [1915] AC 634 *244*

Queensway Marketing *v.* Associated Restaurants (1984) 271 EG 1106 *75*
Quennell *v.* Maltby [1979] 1 All ER 568 *209*

R. *v.* Plymouth CC *ex. p.* Freeman (1987) 19 HLR 328 *110*
R. *v.* Secretary of State for the Environment *ex. p.* Davies (1990) 61 P & CR 487 *304*
R. *v.* Townley (1871) LR 1 CC 315 *46*
R. *v.* Welwyn Hatfield DC (1982) 80 LGR 727 *240*
R. *v.* Westminster CC *ex. p.* Leicester Square Coventry Street Association (1989) 87 LGR 675 *225*
Radnor's (Earl of) WT (1890) 45 Ch. D 402 *142*

Raikes *v.* Lygon [1988] 1 WLR 281 *141*
Raineri *v.* Miles [1980] 2 All ER 145 *277*
Ramsden *v.* Dyson (1866) LR 1 HL 129 *95*
Rance *v.* Elvin (1985) 50 P&CR 9 *238*
Rangeley *v.* Midland Railways (1868) 3 Ch. App. 306 *236*
Ransome's WT, *Re* [1957] Ch. 348 *177*
Rawlings *v.* Rawlings [1964] P 398 *153*
Rawlins *v.* Turner (1699) 1 Ld Raym 736 *59*
RB Policies at Lloyd's *v.* Butler [1950] 1 KB 76 *298*
Redland Bricks Ltd *v.* Morris [1970] AC 652 *44*
Reeve *v.* Lisle [1902] AC 461 *196*
Reeves *v.* Pope [1914] 2 KB 284 *19*
Regan Ltd *v.* Rogers [1985] 1 WLR 870 *255*
Regent Oil Co. *v.* Gregory Ltd [1966] Ch. 402 *87*
Regis Property *v.* Dudley [1959] AC 370 *80*
Regis Property *v.* Redman [1956] 2 QB 612 *236, 240*
Reid *v.* Bickerstaff [1909] 2 Ch. 305 *227, 228*
Renals *v.* Cowlishaw (1878) 9 Ch. D 125 *221*
Reynolds *v.* Ashby & Son [1904] AC 466 *22*
Rhodes *v.* Dalby [1971] 1 WLR 1325 *203*
Richards *v.* Richards [1984] AC 174 *260*
Richardson *v.* Langridge (1811) 4 Taunt. 128 *63*
Ricketts *v.* Enfield Churchwardens [1909] 1 Ch. 544 *87*
Rignall Developments *v.* Halil [1988] Ch. 190 *276*
Rimmer *v.* Liverpool CC [1985] QB 1 *77*
Roake *v.* Chadha [1984] 1 WLR 40 *222*
Robins, *Re* [1928] Ch. 721 *164*
Rochford's ST, *Re* [1965] Ch. 111 *177*
Rock Permanent BS *v.* Kettlewell (1956) 168 EG 397 *20*
Rogers *v.* Hosegood [1900] 2 Ch. 388 *220*
Rogers *v.* Longsdon [1967] 2 WLR 861 *8*
Rooke, *Re* [1953] Ch. 716 *152*
Rose *v.* Page (1829) 2 Sim. 471 *205*
Rous *v.* Mitchell [1991] 1 WLR 469 *67, 90*
Rouse *v.* Gravelworks Ltd [1940] 1 KB 489 *43*
Rowhook Mission Hall, *Re* [1985] Ch. 62 *39, 174*

Royco Homes v. Eatonwill Construction [1978] 2 All ER 821   *21*
Rugby Joint Water Board v. Walters [1966] 3 All ER 497   *47*
Russel v. Russel (1783) 1 Bro.CC 269   *191*
Russell Road Purchase Money, *Re* (1871) LR 12 Eq. 78   *52*
Rycroft's Settlement, *Re* [1962] Ch. 263   *141*
Rylands v. Fletcher (1868) LR 3 HL 330   *44*
Rymer Investments v. Waite [1958] Ch. 831   *288*

St Edmundsbury & Ipswich Diocesan Board of Finance v. Clark (No 2) [1973] 1 WLR 1572   *243*
St Marylebone Property Co. v. Tesco [1988] 27 EG 72   *85*
Saleh v. Robinson [1988] 36 EG 180   *107*
Salih v. Atchi [1961] AC 778   *18*
Salmon, *Re* [1903] 1 KB 147   *211*
Salt v. Northampton [1892] AC 1   *194*
Sampson v. Hodson-Pressinger [1981] 3 All ER 710   *75*
Samuel v. Jarrah Timber & Wood Paving Corp. [1904] AC 323   *193, 194*
Sandbrook, *Re* [1912] 2 Ch. 471   *184*
Santley v. Wilde [1899] 2 Ch. 474   *189, 193*
Sarson v. Roberts [1895] 2 QB 395   *76*
Saunders v. Vautier (1841) 4 Beav. 115   *178*
Scarfe v. Adams [1981] 1 All ER 843   *280*
Scott v. Martin [1987] 1 WLR 841   *238*
Scott-Whitehead v. NCB (1987) 53 P&CR 263   *47*
Searle, *Re* [1912] 1 Ch. 610   *60*
Secretary of State for the Environment v. Cambridge CC (1992) *The Times*, 12 February   *48*
Selim v. Bickenhall Engineering [1981] 3 All ER 210   *255*
Selkirk v. Romar Investments [1963] 1 WLR 1415   *276*
Seton v. Slade (1802) 7 Ves. 265   *193*
Shamji v. Johnson Matthey [1991] BCLC 36   *210*
Sharpe v. Duke Street Securities (1987) 283 EG 1558   *90*
Sharpe v. Manchester CC (1977) 5 HLR 71   *76*
Shaw v. Applegate [1977] 1 WLR 970   *96, 220*
Sheehy, *Re* (1992) 63 P & CR 95   *229*
Shelfer v. City of London Electric Lighting Co. [1895] 1 Ch. 287   *222*

Shelley's Case (1581) 1 Co. Rep. 88b   *26*
Sherry v. Sherry [1991] 1 FLR 307   *170*
Shiloh Spinners v. Harding [1973] 2 WLR 28   *85, 259*
Shirley v. Newman (1795) 1 Esp. 266   *60*
Short Bros. v. Edwards (1978) 249 EG 539   *67*
Shrewsbury's (Countess of) Case (1600) 5 Co. Rep. 13b   *63, 74*
Shropshire CC v. Edwards (1983) 46 P&CR 270   *225*
Simmons v. Dobson [1991] 1 WLR 720   *248*
Simmons v. Midford [1969] 2 Ch. 415   *22*
Simpson v. Weber (1925) 133 LT 46   *239*
Smith v. City Petroleum Ltd [1940] 1 All ER 260   *23*
Smith v. Marrable (1943) 11 M&WS   *76*
Smith v. Scott [1973] Ch. 314   *45*
Smith v. Thackerah (1866) LR 1 CP 564   *44*
Smith and Snipes Hall Farm Ltd v. River Douglas CB [1949] 2 KB 500   *220*
Somma v. Hazelhurst [1978] 1 WLR 1014   *73, 93, 98, 99*
Soper v. Arnold (1889) 14 App. Cas. 429   *275*
South of England Dairies Co. v. Baker [1906] 2 Ch. 631   *89*
Specialised Plant Services v. Braithwaite [1987] BCLC 1   *260*
Spectrum Investment Co. v. Holmes [1981] 1 All ER 6   *285*
Spencer's Case (1583) 5 Co. Rep. 16   *88*
Spyer v. Phillipson [1931] 2 Ch. 183   *22*
Standard Chartered Bank v. Walker [1982] 1 WLR 1410   *206*
Standard Property Investment v. British Plastics Federation (1987) 53 P&CR 25   *258*
Stannard v. Issa [1987] 2 WLR 188   *229*
Stearn v. Twitchell [1985] 1 All ER 631   *270*
Steeds v. Steeds (1889) 22 QBD 537   *163*
Steel v. Wellcome Custodian Trustees Ltd [1988] 1 WLR 167   *140*
Stent v. Monmouth DC (1987) 19 HLR 269   *80*
Stephens v. Anglian Water Authority (1988) 86 LGR 48   *47*
Stevens v. Hutchinson [1953] Ch. 299   *152*
Stokes v. Anderson [1991] 1 FLR 391   *170*
Strand & Savoy Properties Ltd, *Re* [1960] Ch. 582   *65*

Strand Securities Ltd *v.* Caswell [1965] 1 All ER 820 *287, 289, 295*

Street *v.* Mountford [1985] AC 809 *55, 94, 98, 99, 100, 101, 102, 104*

Strover *v.* Harrington [1988] 2 WLR 572 *274*

Stuart's Contract, *Re* [1896] 2 Ch. 328 *275*

Suffield *v.* Brown (1864) 4 De GJ&S 185 *245*

Suleman *v.* Shahsavari [1988] 1 WLR 118 *277*

Surplice *v.* Farnworth (1844) 13 LJCP 215 *80*

Surtees *v.* Surtees (1871) LR 12 Eq. 400 *168*

Sutherland *v.* Heathcote [1892] 1 Ch. 484 *235*

Sutton *v.* Moody (1697) 1 Ld.Raym. 250 *46*

Swans, Case of (1592) 7 Co. Rep. 15b *46*

Swift *v.* Macbean [1942] 1 KB 375 *53*

Swift Investments *v.* Combined English Stores Group [1988] 3 WLR 313 *53, 88*

Swindon Waterworks Co. *v.* Wilts & Berks Canal Navigation Co. (1875) LR 7 HL 697 *47*

Swiss Bank Corp. *v.* Lloyds Bank [1982] AC 584 *192*

Symons *v.* Leaker (1885) 15 QBD 629 *249*

Tagro *v.* Cafane [1991] 1 WLR 378 *107*

Taylor *v.* Russell [1892] AC 244 *18*

Taylor *v.* Taylor [1968] 1 All ER 843 *255*

Taylors Fashions *v.* Liverpool Victoria Friendly Soc. [1982] QB 133 *96*

Tebb *v.* Hodge (1869) LR 5 CP 73 *192*

Tecbild *v.* Chamberlain (1969) 20 P&CR 633 *304*

Tehidy Minerals *v.* Norman [1971] 2 WLR 711 *248*

Texaco Antilles *v.* Kernochan [1973] 2 WLR 381 *227*

Thames Guaranty Ltd *v.* Campbell [1985] 2 QB 210 *192*

Thomas *v.* Hayward (1869) LR 4 Ex. 311 *88*

Thomas *v.* Sorrell (1673) Vaugh. 330 *94*

Thornborough *v.* Baker (1675) 3 Swans. 628 *190*

Thorndike *v.* Hunt (1859) 3 De G&J 563 *18*

Thornley *v.* Thornley [1893] 2 Ch. 229 *169*

Threlfall, *Re* (1880) 16 Ch. D 274 *62*

Tickner *v.* Buzzacott [1965] Ch. 426 *60*

Tiltwood, *Re* [1978] Ch. 269 *229*

Tithe Redemption Commissioner *v.* Runcorn UDC [1954] Ch. 383 *38*

Tito *v.* Waddell (No 2) [1977] Ch. 106 *223*

Todrick *v.* Western National Omnibus Co. [1934] Ch. 561 *237*

Tootal Clothing Ltd *v.* Guinea Properties Management Ltd (1992) *The Times*, 8 June *42*

Toplis *v.* Green [1992] EGCS 20 *280*

Torrens *v.* Walker [1906] 2 Ch. 166 *80*

Tower Hamlets LBC *v.* Miah [1992] 2 WLR 761 *110*

Town and Country BS *v.* Julien (1991) 24 HLR 312 *208*

Tredegar (Viscount) *v.* Harwood [1929] AC 72 *81*

Treloar *v.* Nute [1977] 1 All ER 230 *304*

Tremayne *v.* English Clays Co. [1972] 1 WLR 657 *248*

Tse Kwong Lam *v.* Wong Chit Sen [1983] 1 WLR 1349 *207*

Tucker *v.* Hutchinson (1987) *The Times*, 17 January *292*

Tulk *v.* Moxhay (1848) 2 Ph 774 *223, 224*

Turner *v.* Wright (1860) 2 De SF&J 234 *73*

Twentieth Century Banking Corp. *v.* Wilkinson [1977] Ch. 99 *206*

Tyler, *Re* [1891] 3 Ch. 252 *182*

Ungurian *v.* Lesnoff [1989] 3 WLR 840 *131*

United Dominions Trust *v.* Shellpoint Trustees (1992) *The Times*, 27 July *83*

United Scientific Holdings *v.* Burnley BC [1977] 2 All ER 62 *74*

Uniting Church in Australia *v.* Immer [1992] ALMD 2318 *47*

Universal Corporation *v.* Five Ways Properties [1979] 1 All ER 552 *275*

Vane *v.* Lord Barnard (1716) 2 Vern. 738 *73*

Vaudeville Electric Co. *v.* Muriset [1923] 2 Ch. 74 *22*

Vernon *v.* Bethell (1762) 2 Eden 110 *193*

Verrall *v.* Great Yarmouth BC [1981] QB 202 *95*

Villar, *Re* [1928] Ch. 471 *179*

Viner *v.* Vaughan (1840) 2 Beav. 466 *160*

Wakeham *v.* Wood (1981) 43 P & CR 40 *231*

Walker *v.* Linom [1907] 2 Ch. 104 *19*

Walpole, *Re* [1933] Ch. 431 *149*

Walsh v. Lonsdale (1882) 21 Ch. D 9
  17, 58, 59, 192, 213
Walsingham's Case (1573) 2 Plowd.
  547   *13, 14, 185*
Waltham Forest LBC v. Thomas (1992)
  NLJ 1005   *111*
Ward v. Day (1864) 5 B&S 359   *84*
Ward v. Kirkland [1967] Ch. 194   *75*
Ward v. Van der Leoff [1924] AC 653
  180
Ward v. Warnke (1990) 22 HLR 496
  102
Ware v. Cann (1830) 10 B&C 433   *185*
Warner v. Sampson [1959] 1 QB 297
  69
Warren v. Keen [1954] 1 QB 15   *73, 74*
Waterlow v. Bacon (1866) LR 2 Ch.
  514   *252*
Watson v. Gray (1880) 14 Ch. D 192
  170
Webb v. Pollmount Ltd [1966] Ch.
  584   *288, 290*
Webb v. Russell (1789) 3 TR 393   *222*
Webb's Lease, Re [1951] Ch. 808   *246*
Weg Motors Ltd v. Hales [1961] Ch.
  176   *65, 87*
Weld-Blundell v. Wolseley [1903] 2 Ch.
  664   *73*
Wells, Sir Thomas Spencer, Re [1933]
  Ch. 29   *193*
Wellsted's WT, Re [1949] Ch. 296   *152,
  154*
Wembley Park Estate Co. Ltd's
  Transfer, Re [1968] 1 All ER 457
  227
Western Bank v. Schindler [1977]
  Ch. 1   *207*
Westhoughton UDC v. Wigan Coal &
  Iron Co. Ltd [1919] 1 Ch. 159   *222*
Westminster Bank Ltd v. Residential
  Properties Improvement Co. Ltd
  [1938] Ch. 639   *205*
Westminster CC v. Basson (1990) 23
  HLR 225   *103*
Westminster CC v. Clarke [1992] 2WLR
  229   *103*
Westminster (Duke of) v. Guild [1985]
  QB 688   *244*
Weston v. Henshaw [1950] Ch. 510
  292
Wetherall v. Smith [1980] 2 All ER
  530   *61*
Whaley, Re [1908] 1 Ch. 615   *23*
Wheeldon v. Burrows (1879) 12 Ch. D
  31   *237, 244, 245*
Wheeler v. Mercer [1957] AC 416   *64*
Wheelwright v. Walker (1883) 23 Ch. D
  752   *137*

Whitby v. Mitchell (1890) 44 Ch. D 85
  26
White v. City of London Brewery
  (1889) 42 Ch. D 237   *207*
White v. Taylor [1969] 1 Ch. 150   *252*
White Rose Cottage, Re [1965] Ch.
  940   *32, 212*
Whittingham v. Murdy (1889) 60 LT
  956   *272*
Whittingham v. Whittingham [1979]
  Fam. 9   *255*
Wigg v. Wigg (1739) 1 Atk. 382   *18*
Wiles v. Bank (1985) 50 P&CR 81   *243*
Wilford's Estate, Re (1879) 11 Ch. D
  267   *166*
Wilks, Re [1891] 3 Ch. 59   *166*
Williams v. Earle (1868) LR 3 QB 739
  87
Williams v. Hensman [1861] 30 LJ Ch.
  878   *166*
Williams v. Usherwood (1983) 45
  P & CR 235   *303*
Williams & Glyn's Bank v. Boland
  [1981] AC 487   *288, 296*
Wilson v. Waddell (1876) 2 App. Cas.
  95   *44*
Wimpey Ltd v. Sohn [1967] Ch. 487
  304
Windsor Hotel v. Allan (1981) JPL
  274   *226*
Winter Garden Theatre Ltd v.
  Millenium Productions [1948] AC
  173   *95*
Wong v. Beaumont Property Trust Ltd
  [1965] 1 QB 173   *244*
Wood v. Leadbitter (1845) 13 M&W
  838   *95*
Woodstead Finance Ltd v. Petrou
  (1986) *The Times*, 23 January   *215*
Woolworth v. Charlwood Properties
  (1987) 282 EG 585   *78*
Wright v. Macadam [1949] 2KB 744
  239
Wrotham Park Estate Co. v. Parkside
  Homes Ltd [1974] 1 WLR 798   *231*
Wyatt v. Harrison (1832) 3 B&Ad. 871
  44

Yarmarine, Re [1992] BCC 28   *69*
Yately Common, Re [1977] 1 All ER
  505   *252*
Young v. Dalgely (1987) 281 EG 427
  22
Young (John) & Co. v. Bankier
  Distillery Co. [1893] AC 691   *47*

Zetland (Marquess of) v. Driver [1939]
  Ch. 1   *226*

Table of statutes

Access to Neighbouring Land Act
  1992 *44*
Accumulations Act 1800 *176*
Administration of Estates Act 1925
  s. 33(1) *150, 170*
  s. 34 (3) *28*
  s. 36(4) *150*
  s. 45 *26, 27*
  s. 45(1) *29, 135, 170*
  s. 45(1)(a) *12*
  s. 46 *29*
  s. 51 *273*
  Sch. 2 *27*
Administration of Justice Act 1970
  s. 36 *205, 208*
Administration of Justice Act 1973
  s. 8 *205, 208*
Administration of Justice Act 1977
  s. 24 *294*
  s. 26 *292, 293*
Administration of Justice Act 1985
  s. 11 *277*
  s. 12 *277*
  s. 55(2) *83*
Agricultural Holdings Act 1986 *48, 66,
  90*
  s. 2(1) *60*
  s. 10 *23*
  s. 16 *83*
  s. 23 *74*
  s. 25(1) *61*
  s. 26 *90*
  s. 27 *90*
  s. 27(2) *90*
  s. 60 *72*
  s. 86 *258*
  s. 87 *258*
  Sch. 14 *140, 203*
Agricultural Holdings (Amendment) Act
  1990 *90*

Building Act 1984
  s. 76 *77*
Building Societies Act 1986
  Sch. 4, para. 1(1) *206*
  Sch. 4, para. 2 *201*
Charging Orders Act 1979 *147, 292*
Charities Act 1960
  s. 38 *273*
  s. 48.0 *273*
Charities Act 1992
  s. 31 *174*
  s. 32(1) *274*
  s. 32(2) *274*
  s. 32(3) *274*
  s. 32(5) *274*
  Sch. 2 *274*
Civil Aviation Act 1982
  s. 61 *46*
  s. 62 *46*
  s. 76 *46*
  s. 81 *46*
Coal Industry Act 1987
  s. 1(1) *45*
Coal Industry Nationalisation Act
  1946 *45*
Common Law Procedure Act 1852 *84*
  s. 210 *83*
  s. 212 *83*
Commons Registration Act 1965 *251*
Community Land Act 1975 *48*
Companies Act 1985
  s. 193 *195*
  s. 395 *260*
  s. 396 *260*
Consumer Credit Act 1974 *213*
  s. 16 *213*
  s. 58(1) *214*
  s. 58(2) *214*
  s. 61(1) *214*
  s. 65 *214*

s. 87   *215*
s. 93   *213*
s. 94   *213*
s. 113   *215*
s. 129   *215*
s. 138   *214*
s. 138(1)   *214*
s. 139(1)   *214*
s. 171   *214*
s. 189(1)   *213*
County Courts Act 1984
s. 138(2)   *83*
Courts and Legal Services Act 1990
s. 104   *196*
s. 107   *196*
s. 119(1)   *277*
Criminal Law Act 1977
s. 6   *64, 83*
s. 7   *83, 305*
De Donis Conditionalibus 1285   *4*
Deeds of Arrangement Act 1914
s. 1   *257*
Defective Premises Act 1972
s. 4   *77*
Distress for Rent Act 1689   *82*
Distress for Rent Act 1737   *64*
Domestic Violence and Matrimonial
     Proceedings Act 1976
s. 1(2)   *162*
s. 2(1)   *162*
s. 2(2)   *162*
Environmental Protection Act 1990   *7*
s. 143   *263*
Sch. 13   *49*
Estate Agents Act 1979
s. 13   *275*
Family Law Reform Act 1969
s. 1   *177, 271*
s. 9   *271*
Finance Act 1977
s. 56   *286*
Finance Act 1982
Sch. 7, para. 14   *215*
Finance Act 1983
s. 17   *215*
Finance Act 1986   *258*
Financial Services Act 1986   *42*
Fines and Recoveries Act 1833   *186*
Forfeiture Act 1982   *167*
Housing Act 1980   *49, 106*
s. 56   *109*

s. 65   *108*
s. 67   *112*
s. 73(1)   *108*
s. 76(1)   *113*
Sch. 21   *91*
Housing Act 1985   *49*
s. 1   *124*
s. 4(b)   *124*
s. 24   *111*
s. 65(3)   *101*
s. 80   *110*
s. 80(1)   *110*
s. 87   *111*
s. 93   *78*
s. 94   *78*
s. 118   *111*
s. 129   *111*
s. 621   *50*
Sch. 2   *67, 110*
Housing Act 1988   *49, 106*
s. 1(1)   *114*
s. 1(3)   *109*
s. 2(3)   *114*
s. 3(1)   *114*
s. 3(3)   *114*
s. 5(1)   *115*
s. 5(2)   *115*
s. 5(3)   *116*
s. 5(5)   *116*
s. 6   *116*
s. 7(1)   *116*
s. 7(6)   *117*
s. 8   *117*
s. 8(1)   *118*
s. 8(3)   *118*
s. 9(2)   *118*
s. 9(3)   *118*
s. 9(4)   *118*
s. 10   *118*
s. 12   *118*
s. 13   *118*
s. 13(3)   *118*
s. 13(5)   *118*
s. 14   *118*
s. 14(1)(a)   *118*
s. 14(2)(b)   *119*
s. 15(1)   *119*
s. 16   *119*
s. 19   *107*
s. 20(1)   *119*
s. 20(2)   *119, 120*

s. 20(3) *119*
s. 21 *120*
s. 22(1) *120*
s. 22(2) *120*
s. 22(3) *120*
s. 22(4) *120*
s. 24 *90*
s. 25 *90*
s. 27(3) *107*
s. 28 *107*
s. 29(1) *106*
s. 29(2) *107*
s. 32(1) *62*
s. 34 *108*
s. 34(1)(c)*108*
s. 35 *112*
s. 35(2) *110*
s. 36(1) *109*
s. 37(1) *109*
s. 38 *112*
s. 38(1) *109*
s. 38(3) *109*
s. 38(4) *109*
s. 39 *113*
s. 46 *122*
s. 48(1) *122*
s. 49 *122*
s. 50 *122*
s. 60(1) *122*
s. 60(3) *123*
s. 63(1) *123*
s. 63(3) *123*
s. 64(1) *123*
s. 67 *123*
s. 71 *123*
s. 74 *123*
s. 77 *123*
s. 79 *123*
s. 81 *110*
s. 84 *123*
s. 85(1) *123*
s. 85(2) *123*
s. 86(2) *123*
s. 86(3) *123*
s. 93(1) *124*
s. 93(4) *124*
s. 94 *124, 125*
s. 94(3) *125*
s. 95 *125*
s. 96(1) *125*
s. 97(2) *125*

s. 99 *125*
s. 100 *125, 126*
s. 100(3) *125*
s. 102 *125*
s. 103(1) *125*
s. 103(2) *125*
s. 104(1) *126*
s. 105(1) *126*
s. 105(7) *126*
s. 105(8) *126*
s. 116 *76*
Sch. 1 *114. 115. 117, 118*
Sch. 2 *116, 117*
Sch. 4 *113*
Sch. 7 *123*
Sch. 10 *251*
Sch. 11 *123*
Sch. 15 *77*
Sch. 17 *108, 109, 213, 205*
Sch. 18 *109*
Housing Associations Act 1985
  s. 1 *122*
  s. 4(3) *122*
  s. 5 *122*
  s. 36A *122*
Increase of Rent and Mortgage Interest
    (War Restriction) Act 1915 *105*
Inheritance (Provision for Family and
    Dependants) Act 1975 *45*
Inheritance Tax Act 1984 *258*
Insolvency Act 1986
  s. 315 *69*
  s. 337(2) *260*
Interpretation Act 1978
  Sch. 1 *8*
Intestates' Estates Act 1952 *29*
Judicature Acts 1873–5 *17, 59*
Judicature Act 1873 *58*
  s. 25(11) *17*
Land Charges Act 1925 *31, 254*
Land Charges Act 1972 *31, 95, 228,
    254, 263*
  s. 1 *255, 261*
  s. 1(1) *143*
  s. 1(4) *143*
  s. 2(3) *258*
  s. 2(4) *59*
  s. 2(4)(i) *258*
  s. 2(4)(ii) *259*
  s. 2(4)(iii) *259*
  s. 2(4)(iv) *259*

s. 2(5)   *259*
s. 2(6)   *260*
s. 2(7)   *260*
s. 3(1)   *258*
s. 4(1)   *260*
s. 4(2)   *260*
s. 4(3)   *260*
s. 4(5)   *260*
s. 4(6)   *260*
s. 4(7)   *260*
s. 4(8)   *260*
s. 5   *255, 257*
s. 5(7)   *255*
s. 5(8)   *255*
s. 5(10)   *255*
s. 6   *257*
s. 6(1)   *256*
s. 6(2)   *257*
s. 6(4)   *257*
s. 6(5)   *257*
s. 6(6)   *257*
s. 7   *257*
s. 7(1)   *257*
s. 7(2)   *257*
s. 8   *257*
s. 10(4)   *255*
s. 11   *261*
s. 13(1)   *261*
s. 13(2)   *262*
s. 17(1)   *18, 255, 256*
Sch. 1   *256*
Landlord and Tenant Act 1927
s. 18   *80*
s. 19(1)   *78*
s. 23   *79*
Landlord and Tenant Act 1954   *67, 115, 120*
s. 23   *120*
s. 52   *229*
Landlord and Tenant Act 1985
s. 1(1)   *71*
s. 4(1)   *71*
s. 8(1)   *76*
s. 8(5)   *76*
s. 10   *76*
s. 11   *76*
Landlord and Tenant Act 1987   *111*
s. 59(1)   *50*
Landlord and Tenant Act 1988   *78*
s. 1   *78, 79*
s. 1(a)   *78*

s. 1(b)   *78*
s. 1(3)   *79*
s. 1(4)   *79*
s. 1(5)   *79*
s. 1(6)   *79*
s. 4   *79*
s. 5(2)   *79*
s. 5(3)   *79*
s. 5(4)   *79*
s. 6   *79*
Land Registration Act 1925   *32, 269*
s. 1   *282, 283*
s. 3(xv)   *290*
s. 3(xvi)   *286*
s. 3(xxi)   *296*
s. 4   *284*
s. 5   *284*
s. 6   *285*
s. 7(1)   *285*
s. 8   *285*
s. 8(1A)   *283*
s. 8(2)   *284*
s. 9   *285*
s. 10   *285*
s. 11   *285*
s. 20   *293, 296*
s. 20(1)   *295*
s. 23   *293*
s. 29   *198*
s. 35   *201*
s. 40(1)   *228*
s. 40(3)   *229*
s. 41   *293*
s. 48   *291*
s. 49   *291, 293*
s. 50   *291*
s. 50(1)   *229*
s. 51   *291*
s. 52   *291*
s. 53   *292*
s. 54   *292, 293*
s. 56   *292*
s. 56(3)   *292*
s. 57   *291, 292*
s. 58(1)   *292*
s. 58(2)   *292*
s. 59(6)   *295*
s. 61(1)   *293*
s. 61(3)   *293*
s. 63(1)   *283*
s. 66   *292*

s. 70 *290*
s. 70(1) *286, 289*
s. 70(1)(a)–(f) *97, 251, 286, 287, 303*
s. 70(1)(g) *97, 112, 155, 287, 288, 289, 296*
s. 70(1)(h)–(l) *287*
s. 70(2) *251*
s. 70(3) *289*
s. 74 *296*
s. 75(1) *294, 298, 302*
s. 75(2) *294, 303*
s. 75(3) *303*
s. 77 *285*
s. 82(1) *294*
s. 82(3) *294*
s. 83 *294*
s. 84 *229, 295*
s. 86(2) *289*
s. 102(2) *292*
s. 106 *292, 293*
s. 112 *283*
s. 123(1) *283, 284*
Land Registration Act 1986 *32*
  s. 1(1) *285*
  s. 2 *283*
  s. 2(1) *284*
  s. 2(2) *283*
  s. 4 *287*
  s. 5(1)(a) *198, 292*
Land Registration Act 1988 *32, 281*
Land Registration and Land Charges
    Act 1971
  s. 3 *295*
Land Registry Act 1862 *281*
Land Transfer Act 1897 *281*
Latent Damage Act 1986 *298*
Law of Distress Amendment Act 1888
  s. 7 *83*
Law of Property Act 1922
  s. 128 *27*
  s. 145 *64*
  Sch. 12 *27*
  Sch. 15 *65, 89*
Law of Property Act 1925 *7*
  s. 1 *16, 28, 29, 37, 236*
  s. 1(1) *30, 51, 54*
  s. 1(2)(a)–(e) *30, 83, 216*
  s. 1(3) *30, 159*
  s. 1(4) *16, 30*
  s. 1(5) *52*
  s. 1(6) *17, 31, 163, 167, 169, 271*

s. 2 *32, 154*
s. 2(1)(ii) *155*
s. 2(2) *155*
s. 3(3) *174*
s. 4(1) *17*
s. 5(1) *68*
s. 7(1) *38, 174*
s. 7(2) *38*
s. 10(1) *275*
s. 14 *155*
s. 15 *271*
s. 19 *272*
s. 19(1) *164*
s. 19(2) *272*
s. 19(6) *272*
s. 20 *271*
s. 23 *151*
s. 25 *149, 225*
s. 25(1) *152*
s. 25(2) *152*
s. 25(4) *149*
s. 26(1) *152*
s. 26(2) *152*
s. 26(3) *151*
s. 27(2) *154*
s. 28(1) *152, 169*
s. 28(2) *154*
s. 28(3) *165*
s. 29 *151*
s. 30 *152, 153, 165, 169*
s. 31(1) *150*
s. 34 *32, 169*
s. 34(2) *163*
s. 34(4) *164*
s. 35 *150, 164*
s. 36(1) *164, 170*
s. 36(2) *163, 166, 170*
s. 36(3) *164*
s. 37 *169*
s. 38 *171*
s. 40 *41, 42*
s. 40(1) *269*
s. 44 *32*
s. 44(1) *19*
s. 44(2) *275*
s. 45(1)(b) *276*
s. 45(6) *276, 279*
s. 46 *270*
s. 49(2) *275*
s. 51 *237*
s. 52 *67, 243*

s. 52(1)   *29, 56, 277*
s. 52(2)   *277*
s. 52(2)(d)   *56*
s. 53(1)   *67*
s. 53(1)(c)   *17, 192, 279*
s. 54(1)   *56*
s. 54(2)   *56, 67*
s. 56(1)   *87, 228*
s. 60(1)   *28, 41, 280*
s. 62   *59, 243, 245, 251, 293*
s. 62(1)   *20, 23, 243*
s. 62(2)   *280*
s. 65(1)   *243*
s. 70(1)   *232*
s. 72(4)   *165*
s. 78   *222*
s. 78(1)   *220, 222*
s. 79   *88, 222*
s. 83(3)   *196*
s. 84(1)   *229, 230*
s. 84(12)   *229*
s. 85   *28, 190*
s. 85(1)   *190, 211*
s. 86   *28*
s. 86(1)   *191*
s. 87   *191*
s. 87(1)   *191*
s. 88   *205, 206*
s. 89   *205, 206*
s. 91(2)   *205*
s. 91(7)   *212*
s. 93   *211*
s. 94   *199*
s. 94(1)   *199*
s. 94(3)   *199*
s. 94(4)   *199*
s. 95(1)   *200, 204*
s. 96(1)   *204*
s. 98   *203*
s. 99   *202, 203*
s. 100   *203*
s. 101   *212*
s. 101(1)   *206*
s. 101(1)(ii)   *211*
s. 101(1)(iii)   *209, 213*
s. 101(1)(iv)   *208*
s. 103(i)   *206*
s. 103(ii)   *206*
s. 103(iii)   *206*
s. 104   *206*
s. 104(1)   *212*

s. 104(2)   *207*
s. 105   *207*
s. 108(1)   *211*
s. 108(2)   *212*
s. 108(3)   *212*
s. 109(1)   *210*
s. 109(2)   *209*
s. 109(5)   *210*
s. 109(8)   *210*
s. 115(1)   *200, 201*
s. 121   *139*
s. 121(3)   *183*
s. 128   *27*
s. 130(1)   *28, 185*
s. 130(4)   *135*
s. 131   *26*
s. 134(1)   *135*
s. 135   *160*
s. 136   *220*
s. 136(1)   *223*
s. 137   *28*
s. 141   *87, 220*
s. 142(1)   *87, 89*
s. 144   *78*
s. 146   *81, 83, 86, 238*
s. 146(1)   *84*
s. 146(2)   *85*
s. 146(4)   *85*
s. 146(8)(ii)   *86*
s. 146(9)   *86*
s. 146(12)   *86*
s. 147(1)   *81*
s. 147(2)   *81*
s. 149   *26, 65*
s. 149(1)   *54*
s. 149(3)   *54*
s. 152   *144*
s. 153   *68, 196, 223*
s. 153(8)   *68*
s. 161   *26*
s. 162   *183*
s. 163   *181*
s. 163(1)   *181*
s. 164(1)   *176, 177*
s. 164(2)   *177*
s. 176   *14*
s. 183   *276*
s. 185   *67, 200*
s. 191   *232*
s. 196(3)   *166*
s. 198   *19, 20, 262*

s. 198(1) *262*
s. 199 *19*
s. 199(1)(ii)(b) *20*
s. 205(1)(ii) *244, 269*
s. 205(1)(vii) *189*
s. 205(1)(ix) *8, 20, 45*
s. 205(1)(x) *159*
s. 205(1)(xiv) *86, 139*
s. 205(1)(xvi) *189*
s. 205(1)(xviii) *149*
s. 205(1)(xix) *38, 56*
s. 205(1)(xx) *10*
s. 205(1)(xxiii) *50, 51*
s. 205(1)(xxvi) *159*
s. 205(1)(xxvii) *51, 54*
s. 205(1)(xxix) *149*
Sch. 1 *170, 171, 176*
Sch. 7 *25, 165*
Law of Property Act 1969 *229, 230*
s. 23 *19, 275*
s. 24 *20, 262*
s. 25 *20, 262*
Law of Property (Amendment) Act
  1926 *32, 132, 134, 149, 151, 165,
  269, 270*
s. 7 *130, 145, 152*
Sch. *38, 154*
Law of Property (Amendment) Act
  1929 *85*
Law of Property (Joint Tenants) Act
  1964
s. 1(1) *165*
Law of Property (Miscellaneous
  Provisions) Act 1989 *53*
s. 1(1)–(7) *57, 58, 279, 280*
s. 1(10) *58*
s. 2(1)–(3) *41, 42, 57, 192, 216, 243*
Leasehold Property (Repairs) Act
  1938 *81*
Leasehold Reform Act 1967 *90*
s. 1 *91*
s. 1(1)(b) *91*
s. 2(1)(a) *90*
s. 4 *91*
s. 5(5) *289*
s. 14(1) *91*
s. 17 *91*
s. 18 *91*
Leasehold Reform Act 1979 *91*
Legal Aid Act 1974
s. 9(6) *258*

Limitation Act 1939 *298*
Limitation Act 1963 *298*
Limitation Act 1975 *298*
Limitation Act 1980 *298, 302*
s. 15(1) *298, 303*
s. 15(2) *299*
s. 15(6) *305*
s. 15(7) *299*
s. 16 *196, 200, 201, 208, 299*
s. 17 *196, 302*
s. 18(1) *299*
s. 18(2) *299, 302*
s. 18(3) *302*
s. 19 *82, 299*
s. 20(1) *204, 300*
s. 20(2) *205*
s. 20(4) *300*
s. 20(5) *204, 300*
s. 20(6) *300*
s. 20(7) *300*
s. 28(1) *300*
s. 28(4) *301*
s. 29 *301*
s. 32 *301*
s. 32(1) *301*
s. 32(3) *301*
Sch. 1 *298, 301, 305*
Limitation (Amendment) Act 1980 *298*
Local Government Act 1972
s. 123(1) *225*
s. 131(1) *225*
Local Government and Housing Act
  1989
s. 174 *125, 126*
s. 186 *90*
Sch. 9 *77*
Sch. 10 *90*
Sch. 11 *90, 126*
Local Government (Misc. Provs.) Act
  1982
s. 34 *262*
Local Government, Planning and Land
  Act 1980
s. 101 *48*
s. 134 *49*
s. 172 *49*
Local Land Charges Act 1975
s. 3 *262*
s. 8 *262*
s. 9 *262*
s. 10 *263*

s. 17(1)(b) *259*

Married Women's Property Act 1882
169

Matrimonial Homes Act 1967 *260, 292*

Matrimonial Homes Act 1983 *260*

  s. 1 *260*

  s. 2(1) *260*

  s. 2(8)(b) *289*

  s. 2(9) *292*

  s. 5 *260*

  s. 8 *209*

Matrimonial Proceedings and Property
   Act 1970

  s. 37 *170*

Mental Health Act 1983 *191, 273*

  s. 96(1)(e) *273*

  s. 97 *273*

Minors' Contracts Act 1987

  s. 3 *272*

Mortmain and Charitable Uses Act 1888

  s. 1 *273*

Partition Act 1539 *165*

Partition Act 1540 *165*

Partition Act 1868 *165*

Perpetuities and Accumulations Act
   1964 *176, 178*

  s. 1(1) *179*

  s. 2(1) *180*

  s. 3 *180*

  s. 3(4)(a) *181*

  s. 3(4)(b) *181*

  s. 3(5) *180*

  s. 4 *181, 182*

  s. 9(1) *183*

  s. 12 *184*

  s. 13(1) *177*

Planning and Compensation Act 1991

  s. 10 *48*

  s. 55 *48*

Planning (Hazardous Substances) Act
   1990 *49*

Prescription Act 1832 *242, 246, 248,
   252*

  s. 1 *248*

  s. 2 *248, 249*

  s. 3 *249*

  s. 4 *249*

  s. 7 *249*

  s. 8 *249*

Protection from Eviction Act 1977

  s. 1 *75*

s. 1(2) *107*

s. 1(3) *106*

s. 3 *64*

s. 5 *61, 62, 66*

s. 5(1) *62*

Public Health Act 1936

  s. 92 *77*

Public Order Act 1986

  s. 39 *305*

Quia Emptores 1290 *26*

Race Relations Act 1976

  s. 24(1) *78*

Rent Act 1977 *48, 49, 93, 97*

  s. 1 *97, 107*

  s. 2(1)(a) *112*

  s. 4 *108*

  s. 5(1) *108*

  s. 6 *108*

  s. 7(1) *108*

  s. 9 *108*

  s. 12 *108*

  s. 13(1) *108*

  s. 19(2) *109*

  s. 67(1) *108*

  s. 70 *108*

  s. 98 *83, 112*

  ss. 103–6 *67*

  s. 119(1) *107*

  s. 137 *113*

  s. 147(1) *107*

  Sch. 1 *113*

  Sch. 11 *108*

  Sch. 15 *112*

  Sch. 16 *108*

Rent (Agriculture) Act 1976 *110, 115*

Rent (Amendment) Act 1985 *112*

Rentcharges Act 1977

  s. 1 *232*

  s. 2(1) *232*

  s. 4 *232*

  s. 5 *232*

  ss. 8–10 *232*

Reverter of Sites Act 1987 *38*

  s. 1 *174*

  s. 2 *174*

  s. 2(4) *174*

  s. 3 *174*

Rights of Light Act 1959 *249*

  s. 2 *250*

  s. 3(1) *250*

Sale of Goods Act 1979
 s. 61(1) *72*
Settled Land Act 1925 *129*
 s. 1 *183*
 s. 1(1) *133*
 s. 1(1)(ii) *133, 169*
 s. 1(1)(v) *133*
 s. 1(7) *130, 133*
 s. 2 *133*
 s. 3 *145*
 s. 4(1) *130*
 s. 4(3) *131*
 s. 5(1) *131*
 s. 6(a) *131*
 s. 7 *143, 144*
 s. 7(1) *143*
 s. 8 *144*
 s. 8(1) *144*
 s. 8(4) *144*
 s. 8(4)(b) *132*
 s. 10 *132*
 s. 13 *132, 144*
 s. 17 *137*
 s. 17(1) *145*
 s. 17(2) *145*
 s. 18 *131*
 s. 18(1) *142*
 s. 18(1)(b) *137*
 s. 19(1) 134
 s. 19(2) *134*
 s. 20(1) *135*
 s. 21(1) *134*
 s. 23 *130*
 s. 23(1) *136*
 s. 27 272
 s. 30(1) *136*
 s. 30(1)(iv) *150*
 s. 30(3) *136*
 s. 31(1) *134*
 s. 32 *134*
 s. 34(1) *137*
 s. 36 *169*
 s. 36(4) *167*
 s. 38(i) *138*
 s. 38(iii) *138*
 s. 39(1) *138*
 s. 39(2) *138*
 s. 39(3) *138*
 s. 39(4)(i) *139*
 s. 39(4)(iii) *144*
 s. 39(5) *139*

s. 39(6) *139*
s. 41 *139*
s. 42(1) *139*
s. 42(5) *139*
s. 44(2) *139*
s. 45(1)(i) *139*
s. 46 *141*
s. 47 *139*
s. 48(1)(i) *139*
s. 51 *140*
s. 51(2) *140*
s. 53(1) *140*
s. 55(1) *141*
s. 58(1) *137, 141*
s. 64(1) *141*
s. 64(2) *141*
s. 65 *138*
s. 67 *141*
s. 68 *137*
s. 68(1) *142*
s. 69 *140*
s. 71(1) *140*
s. 72 *32*
s. 72(2) *142*
s. 72(2)(i) *143*
s. 73(1)(i) *140*
s. 73(1)(iii) *141*
s. 73(1)(xi) *140*
s. 73(1)(xii) *140*
s. 75 *143*
s. 75(5) *143*
s. 79 *143*
s. 80 *143*
s. 80(1) *140*
s. 84(3) *141*
s. 90(1)(i) *140*
s. 96 *138*
s. 97(a) *137*
s. 97(b) *137*
s. 97(c) *137*
s. 98(1) *138*
s. 98(2) *138*
s. 101(4) *139*
s. 102(2) *137*
s. 104 *142*
s. 106(1) *141*
s. 107(1) *142*
s. 109(1) *141*
s. 110 *144*
s. 110(1) *144*
s. 110(2) *131, 144*

s. 110(3)(i)   *145*
s. 110(5)   *145*
s. 112(2)   *144*
s. 117   *130*
s. 117(1)(xv)   *139*
s. 117(1)(xxviii)   *134*
Sch. 1   *144*
Sch. 3   *141*
Sex Discrimination Act 1975
s. 31   *78*
Statute of Uses 1535   *7, 26*
Statute of Westminster 1275   *247*
Supreme Court Act 1981
s. 37(1)   *213*
s. 37(2)   *213*
s. 38   *83*
s. 49   *17*
Tenures Abolition Act 1660   *12, 27*
Theft Act 1968
s. 4(1)   *9*

s. 4(2)(b)   *23*
Tithe Act 1936   *31*
Town and Country Planning Act 1990
7, 9, 48
s. 236   *251*
s. 237   *231, 251*
s. 336(8)   *231*
Trustee Investments Act 1961   *140*
Universities and College Estates Act
1925   *25*
Variation of Trusts Act 1958   *141*
Vendor and Purchaser Act 1874   *32*
Water Acts 1973–89   *47*
Water Resources Acts 1963–91   *47*
Wills Act 1837   *42*
s. 3   *17*
s. 11   *272*
s. 28   *43*

Part one

Preliminary matters

1
Introduction to land law

General considerations

1. The province of land law
Land law, known also as the 'law of real property', is a branch of *private law*, i.e. that part of English law which is concerned with the *relationships* of members of the community *inter se*. It can be considered as a division of the wider law of property (which has itself been described as dealing with 'rights conferring a direct and immediate authority over things'), deriving its special nature from the unique characteristics of its subject matter, land. 'The solid portion of the earth's surface' (a typical, general, dictionary definition of 'land') is permanent, indestructible and immovable; hence the larger problems of land law — possession, ownership ('a complex bundle of rights') and the creation, transfer and termination of rights, interests and duties related to land — are unique in their nature. Land law seeks to provide a framework within which it will be possible to delineate and resolve those problems, some few typical examples of which are given below (and which may be used by revision students as a preliminary test):

(a) Where an article merely rests on the land, does it become, as a result, a fixture? (*See Hulme* v. *Brigham* (1943) at **22(a)** below.)
(b) Are there any limitations on a land owner's rights in the air space above his land? (*See Bernstein* v. *Skyviews* (1978) at 3:**28**.)
(c) Has the doctrine of frustration any application to a lease of land? (*See National Carriers Ltd* v. *Panalpina (Northern) Ltd* (1981) at 4:**41**.)
(d) What is the concept of 'the usual covenants' in a lease? (*See* 5:**3**.)
(e) Where there is a trust for sale, has the beneficiary the powers of a tenant for life? (*See* 11:**12**.)
(f) Conditions in partial restraint of marriage were attached to a gift of land. Are such conditions valid? (*See Re Bathe* (1925) at 13:**33(c)**.)
(g) Does a legal mortgage entitle the mortgagee to take possession

immediately it is made? (*See Four-Maids Ltd* v. *Dudley Marshall (Properties) Ltd* (1957) at 15:**11**.)

(h) Can a right to support of buildings exist as an easement? (*See Dalton* v. *Angus & Co.* (1881) at 17:**9(e)**.)

> NOTE: The question of the 'unique characteristics' of land arose during discussion by the House of Lords in *National Carriers Ltd* v. *Panalpina* (1981) (*see* 4:**41**.) 'Land was of its nature different from a chattel. It had in general a quality of indestructibility lacking in any chattel': *per* Lord Russell. Lord Hailsham, LC, accepted that systems of developed land law drew a vital distinction between land, which was relatively permanent, and other types of property, which were relatively perishable. But one could overdo the contrast. Coastal erosion, as well as the 'vast convulsion of nature' postulated by Viscount Simon in *Cricklewood Property & Investment Trust Ltd* v. *Leighton's Investment Trust Ltd* (1945) 'could cause houses, gardens, even villages and their churches to fall into the North Sea. . . There is no real difference between chattels and real property except in degree.' (For the meaning of 'chattels', *see* the diagram on p.11 below.)

2. The plan of this *Handbook*

The text is divided as follows:

(a) *Part one: preliminary matters.* Topics include: the concept of land, estates, tenures, equitable interests and the property legislation of the 1920s.

(b) *Part two: the fee simple and the term of years.* Topics include: the essential features of the fee simple, the leasehold and the licence. Recent legislation concerning protection of the residential tenant, such as the Rent Acts and the Housing Acts, is noted and analysed.

(c) *Part three: strict settlements and trusts for sale.* Topics include: the basis of the trust, the nature of settlements under the Settled Land Act 1925, and related problems, the creation of a trust for sale and the rights of trustees.

(d) *Part four: entailed and other interests.* Topics include: the nature of life and concurrent interests and an examination of the essential features of future, determinable and conditional interests.

(e) *Part five: incumbrances on land.* Mortgages are examined in some detail and the problems arising from easements and restrictive covenants are considered.

(f) *Part six: the transfer of land and limitation of actions.* Topics include: the transfer of unregistered and registered land and an outline of the procedures involved in conveyancing. Periods of limitation of action in relation to land are outlined, and adverse possession is discussed.

3. The vocabulary of land law: a caution

The abstruse vocabulary of land law may present problems to students. Some commonly-used words are endowed with uncommon, highly technical meanings (*land, interest, trust*); some phrases have virtually no signification outside this branch of the law (*fee simple, strict settlement, term of years*); many terms are estranged from their original meaning (*mortgage, licence, property*); feudal terminology persists (*seisin, chattels real, tenant pur autre vie*); Norman-French and Latin expressions survive (*profits à prendre, cestui que vie, rights in personam*); archaisms abound (*base fee, estoppel, coparcenary*).

But problems of vocabulary are not insuperable and should not be exaggerated. Frequent use of a law dictionary and some knowledge of the general historical background of the common law and land law, so that the original context of the terminology in question can be understood, will be of much assistance. Aspects of this background may be traced in e.g. *Historical Foundations of the Common Law* by S.F. Milsom (Butterworths), *The Background of the Common Law* by D. Roebuck (OUP), and *An Introduction to the History of Land Law* by A.W. Simpson (OUP).

Land and land law in legal history

4. The significance of land in legal history

Land is, in most forms of society, the most important of the finite natural resources required for the creation of wealth. As a direct result, control of the land brings economic power which, in turn, is often the basis of social and political power. To protect such power, to resolve the conflicts which arose from the possession, ownership and transfer of such a scarce resource as land, appropriate legal doctrines and institutions emerged, based on an implicit recognition of the unique nature of land and an awareness of the damage that could be inflicted on the social fabric by disputes turning on its possession and control. The significance of land was linked to changes within that fabric; hence, in English legal history *the development of land law mirrors to a considerable extent the economic and political development of society.*

5. The importance of land law

Land law did not develop in isolation. It affected, and in turn was affected by, developments in other areas of English law. From the development of concepts of equity emerged the *use* and the *trust*. Two vital questions in constitutional law — the right to sit as a member of a jury and the right to vote at Parliamentary elections — were directly related for centuries to the ownership of land. The doctrines of the law of succession owe much to the resolution of problems concerning the transfer of real property. There are few branches of our law which have not been touched at some points by the doctrines and procedures associated with land law.

6. The lasting influence of feudal concepts

Many principles found in today's land law can be traced directly to practices which were common in the feudal era (i.e. tenth–thirteenth centuries). Feudalism was characterised by the holding of land, directly or indirectly, of the king. 'Land, in fact, was not "owned" by anyone; it was "held" by superiors in a ladder of tenures leading to the king . . . "Tenure", derived from the Latin word *tenere*, "to hold", itself means "a holding" ' (Berman).

(a) Those who 'owned' the land during the feudal era were really no more than 'tenants' whose land holdings had been granted by superiors. The king's powerful tenants-in-chief held by direct grant from him — 'the sovereign lord, or lord paramount, either mediate or intermediate of all and every parcel of land within the realm' (Coke). *The 'true owner' (in the general sense of that term) of all the land in the kingdom was the Crown.*

(b) In return for being permitted to hold land, the tenant provided services or rent to his superior. The holding of land was the basis of rights which, in sum, became known as the 'estate' (*see* **14** below).

(c) The doctrines of estate and tenure, rooted in feudal thought and practice, may be discerned in our contemporary land law. *See also,* e.g. the 'freehold' and the 'leasehold'. *Note, too,* the 'trust' and 'future interests' — both powerful reminders of feudal notions.

(d) Note the vital feudal idea of *seisin* ('the right to occupy and control') according to which the *actual physical possession of land* was the basis of a freeholder's proprietary rights; vestiges remain in the modern concept of adverse possession (*see* 21:**13**).

Principal sources of land law

7. The sources enumerated

Our modern, developed land law stems from the common law, equity and statute.

(a) *Common law.* By 'common law' is meant here that part of English law which, prior to the Judicature Acts 1873–75 (*see* **17(d)** below) was associated with the common law courts and which grew from the ancient common customs of the country. It was applied to the country as a whole, as compared with the purely local law. *Much of the early common law was concerned with questions arising from ownership and possession of land.* Kiralfy states succinctly: 'At the critical formative period of common law, the English economy depended largely on agriculture and grazing.' From common law stem fundamental doctrines such as: all land is held of the Crown; the leasehold is considered as a species of personal (and not real) property (*see* **12** below). *The superstructure of modern land law rests firmly on the stratum of the common law.*

(b) *Equity.* Equity was based on the doctrines and procedures of the old Court of Chancery; it provided a supplement to the doctrines and procedures of the common law courts. From equity came, for example, the doctrine of the trust (*see* **16** below) and the discretionary remedies, such as specific performance and the injunction.

(c) *Statute.* Because of the social, political and economic significance of land, the community's rulers and representatives have legislated over the centuries on matters affecting its possession, ownership and utilisation. Outstanding examples are the Statute of Uses 1535, the comprehensive Law of Property Act 1925 (*see* Ch. 2) and the far-reaching contemporary measures such as the Town and Country Planning Act 1990, designed to extend social control over the land.

8. The modern land law

Our modern land law is the result of a long, often tortuous, development of earlier patterns of legal thought. It rarely breaks decisively with the past; rather does it exemplify the evolution and continuity which characterise much English law. The important statutes of the 1920s (*see* Ch. 2), and, in particular, the Law of Property Act 1925, form much of the basis of the modern land law. Political doctrines relating to the responsibility of the land owner to the community in general may be discerned in more recent legislation: *see*, e.g. the Environmental Protection Act 1990.

The legal concept of land

9. Definition

The law gives to the word 'land' a highly specialised meaning.

(a) Coke (1552–1634) stated: 'Land in the legal signification comprehendeth any ground, soil or earth whatsoever, as meadows, pastures, woods, moors, waters, marshes, furzes and heath . . . It legally includeth also all castles, houses, and other buildings.'

(b) The modern legal concept of land embraces not only the physical surface of the earth, but also buildings, minerals, etc. In *Rogers* v. *Longsdon* (1967) it was held that an artificial heap of waste could become part of the land when grass and trees grow on it. (Note the maxim embodying the general rule: *superficies solo cedit* — whatsoever is attached to the land forms part of it.)

(c) The statutory definition of land is given in LPA 1925, s. 205(1)(ix):

> '"Land" includes land of any tenure, and mines and minerals, whether or not held apart from the surface, buildings or parts of buildings (whether the division is horizontal, vertical, or made in any other way) and other corporeal hereditaments; also a manor, an advowson, and a rent and other incorporeal hereditaments, and an easement, right, privilege, or benefit in, over, or derived from land; but not an undivided share in land; and "mines and minerals" include any strata or seam of minerals or substances in or under any land, and powers of working and getting the same, but not an undivided share thereof . . .'

(d) Under the Interpretation Act 1978, Sch. 1, '"Land" includes buildings and other structures, land covered with water, and any estate, interest, easement, servitude or right in or over land.'

10. *Cujus est solum ejus est usque ad coelum et ad inferos*

'Whose is the soil, his is also that which is up to the sky and down to the depths of the earth.' This maxim has been dismissed by some legal writers as little more than a colourful, imprecise brocard, which should be considered as a very general statement only. It may be viewed as a presumption which can be maintained only in the absence of evidence to the contrary. *See Bernstein* v. *Skyviews* (1978) at 3:28. There is a number of exceptions to this general rule, as a result of which the owner of the soil has a less than absolute freedom relating to its use and exploitation. For example:

(a) the owner of land is not necessarily entitled to treasure trove discovered on his land (*see* 3:**26**);

(b) he may have no property in water which flows in a defined channel through his land (*see* 3:**29**);
(c) others may have rights over his land, e.g. a right of way (*see* 17:**9**);
(d) where chattels are found on the surface of the land, a finder may have claims superior to those of the land owner : *see Parker* v. *BA Board* (1982);
(e) statutory restrictions are numerous, e.g. Town and Country Planning Act 1990.
See 3:**22–31**.

The concept of property

11. What is property? (*Proprius* = one's own.)
The meaning of 'property' has been, and continues to be, the subject of debate among jurists. No single, generally-acceptable definition has emerged. 'In truth, the word "property" is not a term of art, but takes its meaning from its context and from its collocation in the document or Act of Parliament in which it is found and from the mischief with which that Act or document is intended to deal' : *per* Lord Porter in *Nokes* v. *Doncaster Amalgamated Collieries* (1940). (For an example of a statutory definition of property, *see* the Theft Act 1968, s. 4(1).)

(a) The following are examples of the many definitions of 'property': 'the highest right a man can have to any thing'; 'a right over a determinate thing, either a tract of land or a chattel'; 'an exclusive right to control an economic good'; 'an aggregate of rights guaranteed and protected by the government'; 'everything which is the subject of ownership'; 'a social institution whereby people regulate the acquisition and use of the resources of our environment according to a system of rules.'
(b) The following observations, dating from the early days of the development of property law are of interest; they indicate the significance of property in society and the 'rights' which constitute property.
   (*i*) 'The great end for which men entered society was to secure their property. That right is preserved sacred and incommunicable in all instances, where it has not been taken away or abridged by some public law for the good of the whole' : *per* Lord Camden in *Entick* v. *Carrington* (1765).
   (*ii*) 'By this [the full right of property] a man has the sole claim

to a subject, exclusive of all others, but can use it himself as
he thinks fit, and if he pleases, abuse or destroy it ... Property
is to be considered an exclusive right by which we can hinder
any other person from using in any shape what we possess
in this manner' : Adam Smith, *Lectures in Jurisprudence* (1762).

(*iii*) 'Property is only a foundation of expectation — the
expectation of deriving certain advantages from the thing
said to be possessed, in consequence of the relations in which
one already stands to it... Property and law are born and must
die together': Bentham, on *Principles of the Civil Code* (1830).

(c) Some contemporary jurists, building on Bentham's analysis, view
property as a 'dynamic relationship' between persons, things and the
rights to things. They perceive land law as arising from the structures
and problems inherent in these relationships — 'the rights and
obligations, privileges and restrictions governing the relations of
men with respect to things of value'.

(d) *See* Gray, 1 (*see* Appendix 1) for a discussion of recent attempts
to redefine property in terms of public rights from which may be
derived access to the resources on which society places a value.

(e) For the purposes of this text, 'property' is understood in a
deliberately narrow sense as *that which is the subject of ownership, tangible
or intangible, corporeal or incorporeal, real or personal. (See* LPA 1925,
s. 205(1)(xx) : ' "Property" includes any thing in action, and any
interest in real or personal property.') Note the classification of
property illustrated in the diagram on p.11.

12. Real and personal property: importance of the distinction

Assume that, in the medieval era, X took away, without good
reason, Y's cattle and turned Y out of his (Y's) freehold land. Y could
bring a *personal action* against X for the return of his cattle and, if Y
were successful in the action, X would hand back the cattle or pay Y
for their value. Y could bring a *real action* (*res* = a thing) against X for
the recovery of the land.

(a) *Real property (or realty)* was the phrase applied to property which
could be made the subject of a *real action. Personal property (or
personalty)* was the phrase applied to property which could be made
the subject of a *personal action.*

(b) *Real actions* were available in the case of *freehold interests.* They
were not available in the case of a term of years (i.e. leaseholds). As
a result, the *leasehold* (which was based on the existence of contractual,

personal rights) became classified as a species of *personal property* and the actions available in cases affecting a leasehold were the *personal actions*.

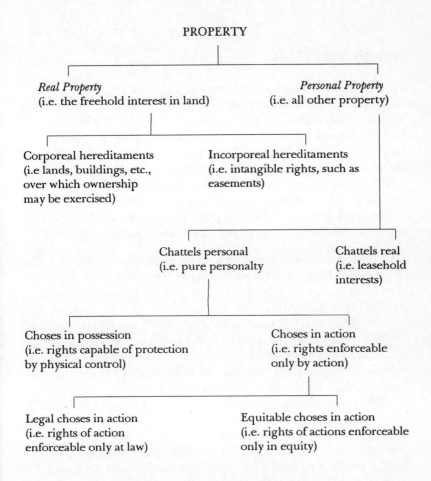

(c) The phrase *chattels real* was applied to *leaseholds* (*see* Ch. 4). Coke stated: 'Chattels real are such as concern or savour of the realty; as terms for years of land. . . these are called real chattels, as being interests issuing out of or annexed to real estates; of which they have one quality, *viz* immobility, which denominates them real, but want the other, *viz* a sufficient legal indeterminate duration, and this want it is that constitutes them chattels.'

(d) The 1925 legislation abolished many distinctions in the law affecting realty and personalty, but the fundamental distinction remains: *freehold land is real property*, whereas *the leasehold is personal property*.

Tenures and estates

13. The medieval notions of tenure and its forms

The doctrine of tenures reflected the *quality* of a person's holding and was concerned with the problem: '*Upon what conditions is land held?*' Tenure involved *holding of a superior*, so that the possessor of land was merely a tenant. (The Crown alone 'owned' land: *see* **6** above.) Tenure existed only as long as the tenant fulfilled his duties (often of an onerous nature) to his superior lord. (It should be observed that, *originally*, 'tenure' was not a legal concept, but an indicator of factual, social relationship between a tenant and his superior; effectively, it conferred and denoted *status*.)

(a)   Tenure depended for its *form* on the particular services owed by the tenant. Thus, in the time of Edward I (i.e. towards the end of the thirteenth and at the beginning of the fourteenth centuries) tenure existed in the following forms.

    (*i*) *Free tenures* (consisting of knight service, serjeanty, spiritual tenure and free socage — all involving services considered to be rendered *freely*).

    (*ii*) *Unfree tenures or copyholds* (comprising types of villein tenure which involved services of a *servile nature*).

    (*iii*) *Customary tenures* (such as *gavelkind*, abolished by AEA 1925, s. 45(1)(*a*)).

(b)   Under the Tenures Abolition Act 1660, most of the burdensome incidents affecting land held under free tenure were abolished, but escheat and forfeiture of land survived, free tenures were converted into free and common socage and it became impossible to create any further types of tenure. Copyhold, frankalmoign, some of the incidents of serjeanty and socage survived.

(c) The main forms of tenure may be illustrated as follows:

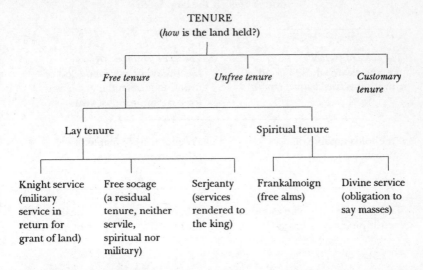

14. Forms of estate

The doctrine of estates was concerned with the problem: '*For how long is land held?*' Whereas *tenure* (*see* **13** above) applies to the *conditions* under which land is held, *estate* (derived from the Latin word *status*) applies to the *length of time* for which a tenant was entitled to hold the land. ('All estates are but times of their continuances' (Bacon). 'The land itself is one thing, and the estate in the land is another thing, for an estate in the land is a time in the land, or land for a time, and there are diversities of estates, which are no more than diversities of time': *Walsingham's Case* (1573).) (Note carefully that the word 'estate' is used here in a restricted sense and must not be confused with the word as used in phrases such as 'the estate of the deceased', or 'the vast estates of the Duke of Blankshire'.) Essentially, one owns an estate in land, rather than the land itself.

(a) Medieval land law held that estates varied according to their duration, that they might be freehold or less than freehold and that several persons might own estates *simultaneously* in the same parcel of land.

(b) The common law recognised the following estates: *freehold* (i.e. estates whose duration is not known) — estate in fee simple, fee tail, for life and *pur autre vie*; *less than freehold* (i.e. estates whose duration is *certain*) — leaseholds for a fixed term of years, tenancies from year to year. A classification is given in the diagram overleaf.

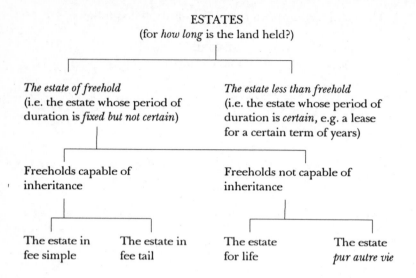

ESTATES
(for *how long* is the land held?)

The estate of freehold
(i.e. the estate whose period of
duration is *fixed but not certain*)

The estate less than freehold
(i.e. the estate whose period of
duration is *certain*, e.g. a lease
for a certain term of years)

Freeholds capable of
inheritance

Freeholds not capable of
inheritance

The estate in
fee simple

The estate in
fee tail

The estate
for life

The estate
pur autre vie

15. Freehold, leasehold and future estates in land

A general outline is given below. The estates are considered
further at appropriate places in the text.

(a) *Freehold estates* might take the following forms:

(i) *Estate in fee simple* (*see* 3:2). The fee simple is the largest estate
in terms of its duration. *Fee* (*feudum* = a fief, a sphere of
operation) indicates that the estate can be inherited. *Simple*
indicates that there are no restrictions as to tail (*see* (*ii*) below).
Hence a grant of land in fee simple 'to X and his heirs' meant
that the estate would endure for as long as the person entitled
at any time left an heir. 'He who has a fee simple in land has
a time in the land without end, or the land for time without
end.': *Walsingham's Case* (1573).

(ii) *Estate in fee tail* (*see further* 13:34). The estate tail (*taille* = cut)
can be inherited only by specified descendants of the original
grantee. Thus, where an estate was granted 'to X and the
heirs of his body', the rule was that X received a fee simple
conditional on children being born to him. This rule was
abrogated under the statute *De Donis Conditionalibus* 1285.
From the turn of the sixteenth century, the process of
'barring the entail' by the tenant in possession became
popular, resulting in conversion of the entail into a type of
fee simple. *See now* LPA 1925, s. 176.

   (*iii*)   *Life estate* (*see further* 12:1). This was an estate held by the grantee for his life. In the twelfth century this was the largest interest in land, but the inheritable fee (i.e. the fee simple) came to be an even greater estate. Under modern law, a life interest is an equitable interest (*see* **16** below).

   (*iv*)   *Life estate pur autre vie.* Such an estate was created where there was a limitation 'to X for the life of Y'. In such a case X was the tenant *pur autre vie* (=for another's life) and Y was known as *cestui que vie*. X could alienate during his lifetime and, upon his death, an alienee could hold for the life of Y. The estate determines on the death of Y, not X.

(b) *Leaseholds* (which can be considered today as estate *and* tenure) originated in agreement between an owner of land and a *termor* (= a tenant holding land for a term of years). The term and conditions of holding were definite (*see further* Chs 4, 5).

   (*i*)   A lease created for 'a term of years absolute' is one which is intended to last for a stated, fixed period, although it may be determined before the stated end of the period.

   (*ii*) 'Term of years' also refers to a term for less than a year, or from year to year, or for one year. Note that leases were classified as *chattels real: see* **12** above.

(c) *Future estates* are estates limited so that they are to come into existence at some future time: *see* **13**. A grant 'to X for life and then to the first of his sons who shall attain the age of 21' created an interest which takes effect, for the son, at some time in the future. Of particular importance were reversions and remainders (both known today as 'reversionary interests').

   (*i*)   *Reversions.* Where X, owner of the fee simple in Blackacre, grants Blackacre to Y for life, X has a *reversion*, since the land will revert to him on the death of Y. *See* **13:4**.

   (*ii*) *Remainders.* 'A remnant of an estate in lands or tenements, expectant upon a particular estate created together with the same at one time' (Coke). In a grant 'to X for life, then to Y in fee simple', X is entitled to actual possession, and his estate is known as the *particular estate*, Y's estate is known as a *remainder*, and Y is known as the *remainderman*. A *vested remainder* was one ready to come into possession as soon as the particular estate was determined. This type of remainder was recognised at common law only at the end of the fourteenth century. A *contingent remainder* was limited so that it depended on an event which might never happen until after the determination of the particular estate. (*See* **13:5**.)

The significance of equitable interests in land

16. Essence of the equitable interest

An equitable interest was originally an interest in property created and enforced by the Court of Chancery. Enforcement involved obedience to decrees issued by the Court and the Chancellors, and imprisonment for contempt. Equitable remedies came to include the injunction and specific performance. A typical example is seen in the origin and development of *the trust*.

17. Rights, estates and interests

A *legal right* is a right *in rem*, i.e. in the land itself; it is available 'against the world at large' and binds irrespective of any notice. An *equitable right* is essentially a right *in personam*, i.e. it can be enforced against certain persons only and not 'against the world at large'. Assume that X owns Blackacre in fee simple and that he conveys it to Y, instructing Y to hold it upon trust for Z. Y is now the legal owner and he possesses a *legal estate* in Blackacre. Z is the beneficial, or equitable, owner, i.e. the person entitled in equity to the benefit. Y's legal rights may be enforced against any person; Z's equitable rights may be enforced only against certain persons, such as Y's heirs who acquire an interest in Blackacre. (The owner of a legal estate is referred to as 'an estate owner' and his legal estate is referred to as his 'estate' : LPA 1925, s. 1(4).)

(a) Under LPA 1925, s. 1, a legal estate (i.e. an estate in land capable of subsisting or being conveyed or created at law) is *either* an estate in fee simple absolute in possession (*see* Ch. 3) *or* a term of years absolute. A legal interest is an interest or charge in or over land capable of subsisting or of being created or conveyed at law, e.g. an easement (*see* 17:2). All other estates, interests, and charges in or over land take effect as equitable interests. (This is explained at 2:14.)

(b) Other examples of equitable interests are: *the equitable lien*, in which a vendor of land, V, conveys it to the purchaser, P, before P has paid the purchase price, with the result that V acquires an equitable lien, i.e. a right to retain the property until P pays the purchase price, which may be enforced by a court order for the sale of the land (*see Re Birmingham* (1959)); *the equitable charge*, created where land becomes security for a debt, but where no legal charge has been created, so that the chargee has an equitable interest giving him a right to apply to the court for a receiver, or for the sale of the land (*see Matthews* v. *Goodday* (1861)); where land is granted to a minor (*see* LPA 1925, s. 1(6)); where land is conveyed to trustees in express terms for a beneficiary; where equity imposes a trust.

(c) Essentially, legal remedies are available to plaintiff *as of right*: equitable remedies are given *at the court's discretion*.

(d) The Judicature Acts 1873–75 had the effect of *fusing* matters of administration of law and equity. However, equity's rules prevail in matters affecting principle. '*In all matters . . . in which there is any conflict or variance between the rules of Equity and the rules of the Common Law with reference to the same matter, the rules of Equity shall prevail*' (JA 1873, s. 25(11), replaced by Supreme Court Act 1981, s. 49). The distinctions between legal and equitable rights and interests remain. *See Walsh* v. *Lonsdale* (1882) at 4:**20.**

18. Creation and disposition of equitable interests

It is doubtful whether new rights in equity can now be created. In *Re Diplock* (1948) the Court of Appeal stated that if a claim in equity were to be made, 'it must be shown to have an ancestry founded in history, and in the practice and precedents of the courts administering equity jurisdiction. It is not sufficient that because we think that the "justice" of the present case requires it, we should invent such a jurisdiction for the first time.' Under LPA 1925, s. 4(1), after the commencement of the Act, an equitable interest in land may be validly created only in any case in which an equivalent interest in property, real or personal, could have been validly created before the Act.

(a) 'A disposition of an equitable interest or trust subsisting at the time of the disposition must be in writing signed by the person disposing of the same, or by his agent thereunto lawfully authorised in writing or by will': LPA 1925, s. 53(1)(c).

(b) For the disposition of an equitable interest by will, *see* Wills Act 1837, s. 3, allowing a person to devise, bequeath or dispose of by will, all real and personal estate which he is entitled to, 'either at law or in equity', at the time of his death.

Equitable interests and the doctrine of notice

19. The doctrine of purchaser without notice

An equitable interest may be enforced, in general, against all except *a bona fide purchaser for value of the legal estate who has taken without notice of the existence of that interest, and against one who claims through him: Pilcher* v. *Rawlins* (1872); *Cave* v. *Cave* (1880). The plea of such a purchaser is 'an absolute, unqualified, unanswerable defence': *Pilcher* v. *Rawlins* (1872). It is important to note the implications of the phrase 'bona fide purchaser for value of a legal estate without notice', referred to by Maitland as 'Equity's darling'.

> NOTE: The protection given to a purchaser without notice is generally afforded to any person who claims through him, even though that person had notice: *Harrison* v. *Forth* (1695). *See also Gordon* v. *Holland* (1913).

(a) *Bona fide*. It is generally essential that the purchaser shall have acted in good faith and without fraud. *See*, however, *Midland Bank Trust Co. Ltd* v. *Green* (1981) at **(f)** below, and 18:**31**.

(b) *Purchaser*. The word is used in its technical sense in land law to indicate *one who takes property by sale or gift, for example, and not merely by operation of law (as on intestacy)*. The term includes a mortgagee and a lessee: *Re King's Leasehold Estate* (1873); LCA 1972, s. 17(1). Thus, X sells land to Y, or gives it to Y: Y is a 'purchaser'; X dies intestate and Y obtains X's property because he is his next of kin: Y is *not* a 'purchaser'.

(c) *Value*. Value must have been given. The word refers to any consideration in money, money's worth (e.g. shares in a company) or marriage (i.e. the consideration of a future marriage): *Salih* v. *Atchi* (1961). ('Money's worth' includes the satisfaction of a debt: *Thorndike* v. *Hunt* (1859).) The adequacy of the consideration need not be established: *Basset* v. *Nosworthy* (1673). See also *Midland Bank Trust Co. Ltd* v. *Green* (1981) below. Where a purchaser acquires a legal estate and does *not* give value, he takes subject to all existing equitable rights.

(d) *Legal estate*. The purchaser must obtain a legal estate (i.e. a legal fee simple absolute or a legal term of years): *Wigg* v. *Wigg* (1739). The estate must be vested in him before he can seek the protection of the doctrine. There is, however, an *exception* in the case of a purchaser who does not obtain a legal estate initially, but who acquires it *subsequently*, even if, at the time of such acquisition, he has received notice of the prior equity: *Taylor* v. *Russell* (1892); *Perham* v. *Kempster* (1907).

(e) *Without notice*. Unless the purchaser had no notice of the equitable interest, the equities are not considered to have equal weight and, in such a case, the doctrine will not apply. *See* 20 below.

(f) Note *Midland Bank Trust Co. Ltd* v. *Green* (1981) (at 18:**31**). In this case, the House of Lords referred to the doctrine of *bona fide purchaser for value without notice.* The following comments by Lord Wilberforce are of interest: 'The character in the law known as the bona fide (good faith) purchaser for value without notice was the creation of equity. In order to affect a purchaser for value of a legal estate with some equity or equitable interest, equity fastened upon his conscience and the composite expression was used to epitomise the circumstances in which equity would or rather would not do so. I think that it would generally be true to say that the words "in good faith" related to the existence of notice. Equity, in other words, required not only absence of notice, but genuine and honest absence of notice.'

20. The problem of notice

Notice involves *awareness of an event or a state of affairs*. (It does not include attention to 'vague rumours' : *Barnhart* v. *Greenshields* (1853).) The following types of notice are important.

(a) *Actual notice*. This exists where a purchaser is made expressly aware during negotiations of the existence of a prior equitable interest: *Reeves* v. *Pope* (1914). *See* LPA 1925, s. 198, at 18:**27**.

(b) *Constructive notice*. See LPA 1925, s. 199. A purchaser should take reasonable care to obtain relevant information relating to the property. Enquiries ought to be made of *all* occupiers of the property: *see Hunt* v. *Luck* (1902). Where he fails to make *a reasonable investigation*, he will be deemed to have had notice of what would have been discovered had he made normal and customary enquiries. See *Jones* v. *Smith* (1841); *Kingsnorth Trust* v. *Tizard* (1986) (a purchaser or mortgagee has to carry out a full inspection of property so as to discover who, other than a husband, is in occupation; he must look behind the husband's attempted concealment of his wife's occupation of the property, as where the husband arranged a mortgagee's inspection of property to coincide with the wife's absence).

   (*i*) In the case of title deeds (*see* Ch. 19), title for the last 15 years may be required to be shown: LPA 1925, s. 44(1), as amended by LPA 1969, s. 23. The purchaser is deemed to have notice of any equitable right recorded on the title during that period of time. Where he fails to examine title deeds, either because he negligently omitted to request their production, or imprudently accepted an excuse for their non-production, he is considered as having constructive notice of any equitable claims recorded therein: *Peto* v. *Hammond* (1861); *Walker* v. *Linom* (1907).

   (*ii*) Constructive notice is presumed where there has been express notice of one fact which should have led to notice of further facts: *Bisco* v. *Banbury* (1676), in which a purchaser had express notice of a mortgage but failed to examine a relevant deed which would have revealed other incumbrances. (For a review of the effect of constructive notice, *see Midland Bank* v. *Farmpride Hatcheries* (1981).)

(c) *Imputed notice.* Where, for example, a purchaser employs a solicitor or other agent, and the solicitor or other agent obtains actual or constructive notice of claims, such notice will be imputed *to the purchaser. See* LPA 1925, s. 199(1)(ii)(b). But no such notice will be imputed where an agent is acting so as to defraud his principal: *Kennedy* v. *Green* (1834). It is essential that the agent receive the notice in his capacity as agent: *Re Cousins* (1886). *See also Rock Permanent BS* v. *Kettlewell* (1956).

(d) *Statutory notice.* Registration of an interest (*see* Ch. 18) is considered as providing statutory notice of the existence of that interest to any person acquiring a subsequent interest in the property affected: LPA 1925, s. 198.

(*i*) Under LPA 1969, s. 24, where, under a contract for the sale of unregistered land (*see* Ch. 19), a question arises as to whether, at the time of entering such contract, the purchaser had notice of a registered land charge, the question will be determined by reference to his actual knowledge, and without reference to LPA 1925, s. 198.

(*ii*) Under LPA 1969, s. 25, where a purchaser completes the purchase without knowledge of a registered land charge which he has been unable to discover because it has been registered against a name which does not appear in the title to the property, he may receive compensation; but this has no application in the case of local land charges.

Fixtures

21. The problem

The general doctrine is *quicquid plantatur solo, solo cedit* — 'whatever is annexed to the soil becomes part of the soil'. (*See* LPA 1925, s. 62(1) at **17:19(b)**.) The resulting problem is: does a chattel which is affixed to land or to a building become a part thereof? (Note LPA 1925, s. 205(1)(ix): land includes buildings or parts of buildings.)

Examples: _____

(1) Seats are secured to the floor of a cinema. Are they then fixtures? (2) A heavy machine rests by its own weight on land. Is it then a fixture?

(Note the comments of Buckley J, cited in *Royco Homes* v. *Eatonwill Construction* (1978): 'The doctrine may be said to enshrine or express a rule of law regulating the ownership in appropriate cases of things which were previously chattels but had become physically attached to realty. It does not, I think, amount to a presumption, and it is certainly not a rule of construction, where the interpretation of any written document is involved. Where a chattel is physically attached to realty, one of three possible results may follow. The chattel may lose its character as a chattel and adhere to the realty so as to become part of it for all purposes; or the chattel may become part of the realty while it remains a chattel, without the person who owned it losing the right subsequently to detach it from the realty and repossess it as a chattel; or it may never lose its character as a chattel.')

22. The degree of annexation

In general, a chattel is not considered as a fixture *unless it is connected to the land or to a building upon that land in some substantial way.* See *Jordan* v. *May* (1947).

(a) Where an article *merely rests on the land* it does not become, as a result, a fixture: *Hulme* v. *Brigham* (1943) — very heavy printing machine secured to the floor by its own weight, held *not* to be a fixture; *Culling* v. *Tufnal* (1694) — Dutch barn resting on sockets let into the ground, held *not* to be a fixture; *Deen* v. *Andrews* (1986) — prefabricated greenhouse bolted to concrete plinth which was not fixed to the ground, but merely lay on it under its own weight, held *not* to be a fixture.

(b) Where a chattel is *attached to the land in a substantial way,* even though it could be removed with relative ease, it is held to be a fixture: *Buckland* v. *Butterfield* (1820) — verandah on brick foundation connected with a house, held to be a fixture.

23. The purpose of the annexation

'Perhaps the true rule is, that articles not attached to the land otherwise than by their own weight are not to be considered as part of the land, unless the circumstances are such as to show that they were intended to be part of the land . . . ; and that, on the contrary, an article which is affixed to the land even slightly is to be considered as part of the land, unless the circumstances are such as to show that it was intended all along to continue as a chattel, the onus lying on those who contend that it is a chattel': *per* Blackburn J, in *Holland* v. *Hodgson (1872)*.

The test is: what is the object of the annexation, and has the chattel been fixed with the purpose of permanently improving the land? See Simmons v. *Midford* (1969). Object *and* purpose must be considered.

(a)   Where a chattel has been affixed in a *seemingly durable manner* it is *not* held to be a fixture if the method of fixing was necessary for its proper enjoyment: *Leigh* v. *Taylor* (1902) — tapestries were affixed to a wall by nails and canvas-covered strips tacked to the tapestry; it was held that the tapestries were *not* fixtures. *See* also *Spyer* v. *Phillipson* (1931); *Lyon & Co.* v. *London City & Midland Bank* (1903) — chairs, hired temporarily, screwed to the floor of the theatre, held *not* to be fixtures.

(b)   'Blocks of stone placed on top of one another without any mortar or cement for the purpose of forming a dry stone wall would become part of the land, though the same stones, if deposited in a builder's yard and for convenience stacked on top of each other in the form of a wall, would remain chattels': *per* Blackburn J, in *Holland* v. *Hodgson* (1872).

(c)   Where a chattel is placed on land or affixed to it in a manner which manifests *an intention to improve the use of the land* it may be held to be a fixture: *Vaudeville Electric Co.* v. *Muriset* (1923) — seats secured to a cinema floor held to be fixtures: *D'Eyncourt* v. *Gregory* (1866) — stone garden seats secured by their own weight, but considered as a part of the design of a house's grounds, held to be fixtures.

24. The removal of fixtures

The problem is: *what are the circumstances in which fixtures may be removed lawfully from the land?*

(a)   *Mortgagor and mortgagee.* Where land has been mortgaged (*see* p. 189), fixtures are included in the mortgage, and a mortgagor may not remove any fixture which has been affixed to the land on a date *after* the making of the mortgage: *Reynolds* v. *Ashby & Son* (1904).

(b)   *Landlord and tenant.* The general rule is that the landlord *is* entitled to fixtures which have been attached by his tenant. The group of so-called 'tenants' fixtures' forms an exception to this rule, and fixtures of the type enumerated below may be removed by tenants. (*See New Zealand Government Property Corporation* v. *H M & S Ltd* (1982) — where a tenant remains in possession after the expiry of a lease by effluxion of time or surrender, he retains his rights as to tenants' fixtures.) *See Young* v. *Dalgely* (1987).

(*i*)   *Agricultural fixtures.* Under the Agricultural Holdings Act 1986, s. 10, a tenant of an agricultural holding who has attached to that holding any fixture may remove it during the tenancy, or within two months of its determination, provided that he has given one month's notice of its removal to the landlord, who is then given an option to purchase it, and provided that he has paid all rents, and that no avoidable damage is caused during its removal.

(*ii*)   *Trade fixtures.* A fixture attached by a tenant for the purposes of his trade or business may be removed before, but not after, the end of the tenancy: *Poole's Case* (1703); *Elliot* v. *Bishop* (1854); *Smith* v. *City Petroleum Ltd* (1940) — petrol pumps on a station forecourt.

(*iii*)   *Ornamental and domestic fixtures.* The fixture must be capable of being removed without causing any substantial injury. It may not be removed if it forms a permanent improvement to the property: *Leach* v. *Thomas* (1835) — ornamental chimney piece, held removable; *Darby* v. *Harris* (1841) — kitchen range, held removable.

(c)   *Vendor and purchaser.* Under a conveyance fixtures pass to the purchaser without express mention unless a contrary indication is given: LPA 1925, s. 62(1). A fixture attached at the time of the contract of sale is to be left for the purchaser: *Phillips* v. *Lamdin* (1949). *See also Moffatt* v. *Kazana* (1969); *Berkley* v. *Poulett* (1976), in which the court considered pictures screwed to panelling, and a marble statue, taken by a vendor of land who was sued by the purchaser, claiming that these were part of the land. The Court of Appeal held that the application of two tests (degree of attachment of items to the land and the reason for the attachment) showed that the items were *not* fixtures.

(d)   *Personal representative and devisee.* A devisee (i.e. the recipient of a gift of land by will) is entitled to fixtures. Personal representatives may not remove trade, ornamental or other fixtures: *Re Whaley* (1908).

NOTE: (1)   There is a duty at common law to make good any damage to premises caused by the removal of tenants' fixtures. The liability at common law is that of the person who removes the fixtures and not of the person, if different, who installed the fixtures originally: *Mancetter Developments Ltd* v. *Garmanson Ltd* (1986).

(2)   Fixtures may be 'stolen', within the terms of the Theft Act 1968, *only* if severed from the land: s. 4(2)(b).

Progress test 1

1.   Why has land law been of unusual significance in English legal history?   **(4, 5)**

2.   Outline the principal sources of English land law.   **(7, 8)**

3.   Comment on the definition of land in the Law of Property Act 1925.   **(9)**

4.   Is the maxim *cujus est solum* of any importance today?   **(10)**

5.   What is the significance today of the medieval concepts of tenure and estates?   **(13, 14)**

6.   'The doctrine of purchaser without notice is fundamental to land law.' Explain.   **(19)**

7.   What is meant by 'constructive notice'?   **(20)**

8.   What are the circumstances in which fixtures may be removed lawfully from land?   **(24)**

2
The property legislation of the 1920s

The legislation of 1925

1. Dissatisfaction with the land law

At the beginning of the twentieth century, English land law remained rooted in the doctrines and rules of the feudal system. Based on medieval concepts of *seisin* (i.e. physical possession enjoyed by the person 'seated' on the land), estates and tenures, and replete with anachronistic notions, it was failing to meet the novel needs of the industrial, urban society which had grown from a feudal, agricultural community. The principal causes of dissatisfaction with the land law as it then stood were:

(a) the cumbersome, awkward modes of conveyancing;
(b) the survival and continuing influence of medieval, complex principles and practices relating to land;
(c) the difficulties which arose from the separate rules for real and personal property.

2. General nature

The legislation of 1925 was radical and comprehensive although it did not result in codification of the land law. It consisted of the following Acts:

(a) the Law of Property Act ('An Act to consolidate the enactments relating to conveyancing and the law of property in England and Wales');
(b) the Settled Land Act;
(c) the Trustee Act;
(d) the Administration of Estates Act;
(e) the Land Registration Act;
(f) the Land Charges Act;
(g) the Universities and College Estates Act.

3. **Results of the legislation of 1925**
   Four important objectives were attained:

(a) many anachronistic rules and doctrines in the law of real property were abolished;
(b) tenures were reduced;
(c) the rules concerning real and personal property were brought closer together;
(d) conveyancing was simplified by the reduction in the number of estates.

The abolition of anachronisms

4. **General**
   By the twentieth century, many rules which had been of significance in earlier eras had become mere obstructions to the process of the creation and transfer of interests in land. Their abolition reflected the general intent of the legislature that the law of real property should be simplified and made appropriate to the conditions of the twentieth century.

5. **The clearing away of old forms, rules and doctrines**
   The following are examples of this process:

(a) The rules in *Shelley's Case* (1581) (concerning words of limitation) and in *Whitby* v. *Mitchell* (1890) (concerning remainders) were *abolished*: LPA 1925, ss. 131, 161.
(b) Most of the ancient canons of descent were *abolished*: AEA 1925.
(c) The doctrines of special occupancy and *interesse termini (concerning a lessee's entering into possession) were abolished*: AEA 1925, s. 45; LPA 1925, s. 149.
(d) The Statute of Uses 1535 was *repealed*: LPA 1925, Sch. 7.

The reduction in tenures

6. **Prior to the 1925 legislation**
   In the thirteenth century there had existed tenures of the following types: free, lay, spiritual, unfree (*see* 1:**13**).

(a) *Quia Emptores* 1290 prohibited any increase in the types of tenure. (The object of the statute has been described as 'the prevention of further growth of the festoons and thickets of tenure already created by subinfeudation'.) Henceforth, only the Crown was able to grant new tenures.

(b) The Tenures Abolition Act 1660 (*see* 1:**13(b)**) resulted in tenures being reduced to copyhold and socage.

7. Results of the legislation of the 1920s
The general results were as follows:

(a) Frankalmoign was *abolished*: AEA 1925, Sch. 2, Part I.

(b) Copyhold tenure was *abolished* and converted into socage tenure as from 1st January 1926: LPA 1922, s. 128.

(c) Customs of descent, such as gavelkind, were abrogated: AEA 1925, s. 45.

(d) Many manorial incidents (i.e. tenants' services) were *extinguished*.

  (*i*) Those which were, in essence, obsolete, were *extinguished*, and no compensation was paid: LPA 1922, Sch. 12.

 (*ii*) Certain incidents which could be valued in monetary terms, e.g. fines, reliefs, rents, the right of a lord to fell certain timber trees, were to be *extinguished*, after compensation, by 31st December 1935 (later extended to 1st November 1950). Where no agreement could be reached concerning the amount of compensation, either party could apply to the Ministry of Agriculture to fix the amount: LPA 1922, s. 128.

(*iii*) Certain incidents were *preserved permanently*, unless the lord and tenant agreed in writing to their abolition. These incidents included: tenant's rights of common; landlord's or tenant's rights to mines and minerals; liabilities of lord or tenant for the construction and maintenance of dykes, bridges, etc.; lord's rights concerning fairs, markets and sport: LPA 1922, Sch. 12.

8. Tenure today
As a result of the legislation of the 1920s there survives now only *one common law tenure* (as distinct from the leasehold), i.e. *freehold*. Feudal incidents, with the exception of those which have been preserved permanently (*see* **7(d)**(*iii*) above), have disappeared.

The converging of rules concerning real and personal property

9. The general problem
Differences between the rules affecting real and personal

property in the early twentieth century were of ancient origin. Some attempts at assimilation had been made prior to the twentieth century, but these were inadequate.

10. Ways in which the rules were further assimilated by the twentieth-century legislation
Five matters are of particular importance.

(a) *Interests in property.* At common law it was not possible to create limited interests, such as an interest for life, in personal property. But such interests *could* be created in *real property*. (Note that in equity, however, where a grant of personal property was made to trustees it was possible to create successive interests.)

(*i*)   LPA 1925, s. 130(1), allows the creation of entailed interests in real and personal property.

(*ii*) Entailed and life interests in real and personal property take effect as equitable interests: LPA 1925, s. 1 (*see* **15** below).

(b) *Words of limitation.* Prior to 1926, a conveyance for the transfer of a fee simple had to contain certain phrases, known as *words of limitation.* Failure to use the appropriate words resulted in failure to pass the fee simple.

(*i*)   Thus, before 1926, it was necessary, where one intended to pass a fee simple, to use phrases such as 'to A in fee simple'. Failure to employ such a phrase resulted in the transfer of a mere life interest. But this restrictive rule had no application in the case of leaseholds.

(*ii*) 'A conveyance of freehold land to any person without words of limitation, or any equivalent expression, shall pass to the grantee the fee simple or other the whole interest which the grantor had power to convey in such land, unless a contrary intention appears in the conveyance': LPA 1925, s. 60(1).

(c) *Mortgages.* Prior to 1926 the legal mortgage of a fee simple differed in method from the legal mortgage of leasehold land.

(*i*)   Under LPA 1925, ss. 85, 86, both freeholds and leaseholds may be mortgaged by the grant of terms of years.

(*ii*) The rule in *Dearle* v. *Hall* (1828) which governed the priority of mortgages of equitable interests in personal property prior to 1926 (*see* 14:**20**), now applies *also* to equitable interests in land: LPA 1925, s. 137.

(d) *Payment of debts.* Prior to 1926, the rules concerning the order in which the assets of a deceased debtor were used for the payment of debts allowed the personal estate to be made available first. Under AEA 1925, s. 34(3), where 'the estate of a deceased person is solvent his real and personal estate shall. . . be applicable towards the discharge of the funeral, testamentary and administration expenses, debts and liabilities payable thereout.'

(e) *Descent of realty and personalty on an intestacy.* Prior to 1926, the rules concerning the descent of personal property on intestacy differed from those concerning the descent of real property. Thus, in general, real property passed to the heir, personal property passed to certain of the next of kin. Under AEA 1925, ss. 45, 46, amended by Intestates' Estates Act 1952, the old rules were abolished and the new rules apply to real and personal property.

The simplifying of conveyancing

11. The complex nature of conveyancing

The difficulties of effecting a conveyance of real property prior to the twentieth century were often formidable. The process was usually complex and lengthy. The purchaser of land had to make sure that the vendor had good title to the land, and that existing incumbrances in favour of a third party were known. Failure by the purchaser to investigate these matters could affect him adversely.

12. The problem exemplified

Assume that P wished to purchase Blackacre. A might have a life estate in Blackacre; B might have the fee simple in remainder (*see* 13:5); C, D and E might have equitable interests, the existence and nature of which would have to be discovered and investigated by P. The problem demanded a radical solution, involving a reduction in the number of legal estates and interests and the creation of systems of registration for equitable interests and for title.

13. Reduction in the number of legal estates and interests

This was a very important result of LPA 1925, s. 1; *see* **15** below.

14. Essence of LPA 1925, s.1

This section is fundamental to the structure of modern English land law. It distinguishes those rights capable of subsisting or of being conveyed or created *at law,* and those which are capable of existing *in equity* only. It gives an indication of whether a particular property right is *capable* of subsisting at law; it does not say that the particular right *must* be legal. Thus, the right in question must satisfy the conditions of LPA 1925, s. 52(1) (*see* 4:**16**) before being considered as a legal estate.

15. LPA 1925, s. 1(1)–(4)

' **1.**—(1) The only estates in land which are capable of subsisting or of being conveyed or created at law are —

(*a*)   An estate in fee simple absolute in possession;

(*b*)   A term of years absolute.

(2)   The only interests or charges in or over land which are capable of subsisting or of being conveyed or created at law are —

(*a*)   An easement, right, or privilege in or over land for an interest equivalent to an estate in fee simple absolute in possession or a term of years absolute;

(*b*)   A rentcharge in possession issuing out of or charged on land being either perpetual or for a term of years absolute;

(*c*)   A charge by way of legal mortgage;

(*d*)   [. . .] and any other similar charge on land which is not created by an instrument;

(*e*)   Rights of entry exercisable over or in respect of a legal term of years absolute, or annexed, for any purpose, to a legal rentcharge.

(3)   All other estates, interests, and charges in or over land take effect as equitable interests.

(4)   The estates, interests, and charges which under this section are authorised to subsist or to be conveyed or created at law are (when subsisting or conveyed or created at law) in this Act referred to as "legal estates," and have the same incidents as legal estates subsisting at the commencement of this Act; and the owner of a legal estate is referred to as "an estate owner" and his legal estate is referred to as his estate.'

16. Preliminary comment on the rights mentioned in s. 1

Each of these rights is considered at its appropriate place in the text. Their meanings are noted briefly as follows:

(a) s. 1(1): an *estate in fee simple* is, in effect, the absolute ownership of land: *see* **3:2**. A *term of years absolute* is a lease, i.e. an estate limited to a certain fixed period: *see* **4:4**.

(b) s. 1(2)(a): an *easement* is a right attached to a piece of land entitling the owner to exercise it over the land of another: *see* **17:2**.

(c) s. 1(2)(b): a *rentcharge* is an arrangement whereby land is charged with payment to some person of an annual or other periodic sum: *see* **16:27**.

(d) s. 1(2)(c): a *charge by way of legal mortgage* is an arrangement whereby an estate in land is charged with the repayment of a debt or the carrying out of some other obligation: *see* 14:**4**.

(e) s. 1(2)(d): the missing terms are '*land tax, tithe rentcharge*'; they were repealed by the Tithe Act 1936 and the Finance Act 1963.

(f) s. 1(2)(e): a *right of entry* allows the landlord to recover his rights in property where a tenant fails to observe his obligations under a lease: *see* 5:**29**.

17. General effect of s. 1

As a result of this section:

(a) there exist now only *two* legal estates: the fee simple absolute in possession, and the term of years absolute;

(b) there exist now only *five* legal interests or charges in or over land capable of subsisting or of being conveyed or created at law;

(c) other rights may exist only as equitable interests behind a trust, e.g. under a trust for sale (*see* Ch. 11).

NOTE: A minor may not hold a *legal estate* in land: LPA 1925, s. 1(6).

18. The registration of equitable interests

Under the Land Charges Act 1925 (repealed, but re-enacted in large measure by the Land Charges Act 1972) (*see* Ch. 18), almost all equitable interests can be recorded in the registers of the Land Registry.

(a) The registration of a registrable interest acts as statutory notice of that right to anyone who acquires the land.

(b) A failure to register a registrable interest renders that interest void against a purchaser of the legal estate (even if he has actual notice of its existence).

19. The principle of overreaching

Some equitable interests (e.g. a charge on the rents of Blackacre) could be satisfied out of the purchase money. Thus, by 'overreaching' is meant *the transferring of rights from land to the purchase money paid for it. See* 18:**26**.

(a) *Not all equitable interests can be overreached* (e.g. restrictive covenants, equitable easements), since they cannot be represented in monetary terms: *See* Land Charges Act 1972, at 18:**26**.

(b) *The process is as follows*: assume that P is buying a legal estate from trustees. When the legal estate is sold the trustees are able to pass to P *an estate which is free from incumbrances*. The incumbrances do not 'disappear'; they will be attached automatically to *the money* which P has paid to the trustees. The trustees are obliged to invest this purchase money, and the owners of the equitable interests will be *compensated* out of the interest which arises from this investment. *See* LPA 1925, s. 2; SLA 1925, s. 72; LP(Amendment)A 1926.

> NOTE: (1) Overreaching was considered recently by the House of Lords in *City of London BS* v. *Flegg* (1988). *See* 11:**22**.
> (2) See the Report in the Law Commission Working Paper No. 106 (1988), entitled 'Overreaching'. The Report favoured a scheme whereby a beneficiary should be able to protect his interest by registration; and no overreaching should be possible without the consent of every occupying beneficiary concerned, irrespective of whether or not a beneficiary had registered. The requirement of consent might be restricted to occupying beneficiaries of full age.

20. Other reforms in conveyancing

The following reforms also had the effect of simplifying the process of conveyancing. *See* Chs 19, 20.

(a) *Investigation of title.* All documents concerning transactions in the land to be transferred had to be investigated. Transactions which had taken place during a period of at least sixty years before the intended transfer had to be investigated. This period was reduced to forty years by Vendor and Purchaser Act 1874. By LPA 1925, s. 44, the period became thirty years (and is now *15 years*).

(b) *Tenancies in common.* Legal tenancies in common (i.e. where two or more persons are entitled to land so that they have several freeholds but undivided possession) were *abolished* by LPA 1925. (Tenancies in common can exist, however, as equitable interests under a settlement: LPA 1925, s. 34.)

(c) *Registration of title.* Registration of title was encouraged under the Land Registration Act 1925. 'The system of land registration was introduced into our law in response to the lay demand that dealings with land should be assimilated to dealings with chattels and should cease to be a mystery understood only by conveyancers': *per* Harman LJ in *Re White Rose Cottage* (1965). (It is important to keep separate in one's mind the *two systems* of 'registration'. The registration of *charges*, which applies in the case of the old system of conveyancing land where title deeds for the last 15 years are investigated, is covered by the Land Charges Act 1972 (*see* **18** above and 18:3). The system of registration of *title* is contained in the Land Registration Acts 1925–88 and the Land Registration Rules (*see* 20:**3**).)

Progress test 2

1. Account for the general dissatisfaction with the land law during the early part of the twentieth century. **(1)**

2. In what ways did the legislation of the 1920s succeed in bringing about a convergence of rules concerning real and personal property? **(9, 10)**

3. 'The main achievement of the legislation of the 1920s was its reduction in the number of legal estates and interests.' Comment. **(15, 16, 17)**

4. What is the significance of the principle of overreaching? **(19)**

Part two

The fee simple and the term of years

3
The fee simple absolute in possession

Meaning of the phrase

1. LPA 1925, s. 1
Under this section of the Act (*see* 1:**17(a)**), the fee simple absolute in possession is one of the two estates in land which, after 1925, are capable of subsisting or being conveyed or created at law, i.e. which are *legal estates* (*see* 2:**15**).

2. Essence of the fee simple
See 1:**15(a)**. The rights over land possessed by a person are determined, in large part, by the nature of his estate (*see* 1:**14**). *The largest estate known to English law is the fee simple — its duration in time is unlimited, and it allows its owner extensive powers over the land.*

(a) The fee simple is known also as the *freehold estate*; the fee simple owner is often referred to as the *freeholder*.
(b) Note the use of the phrase *'tenant* in fee simple', often utilised synonymously for *'owner* in fee simple' — a reminder of the doctrine that the fee simple refers to the period during which land in England is held of the Crown. Although, *in theory*, the fee simple does not amount to absolute ownership, *in practice*, the owner of the fee simple absolute in possession is virtually the absolute owner.

3. 'Fee' (feudum = a fief)
'Fee' denotes an *estate of inheritance* in land, i.e. the estate does not necessarily end on the death of the tenant.

4. 'Simple'
'Simple' denotes an ordinary fee which can pass to the general heirs of the tenant and which *carries no conditions* as to its passing to one particular class of heir. Compare the entailed interest: *see* 13:**34**.

5. 'Absolute'

'Absolute' means that the estate is not subject to determination by an event other than that which is implied in the words of limitation: *see* **13** below. Thus, the fee simple absolute is *determined only on the failure of an appropriate successor in title*. It continues, therefore, indefinitely for as long as there is some person entitled to take under the will of the previous owner or in the event of his intestacy. A determinable fee simple and a conditional fee simple are not classified under the heading of 'fee simple absolute'. Thus a grant 'to X in fee simple until Y shall marry' will not create a fee simple absolute. ('Absolute' does not necessarily imply that the land is not subject to the rights of others; it may be subject to a mortgage, for example.)

(a) LPA 1925, s. 7(1): 'A fee simple which, by virtue of the Lands Clauses Acts, the School Sites Acts, or any similar statute, is liable to be divested, is for the purposes of this Act a fee simple absolute, and remains liable to be divested as if this Act had not been passed.' This type of Act, under which land might be acquired for certain public purposes, provided that such land would revert to its original owner or vest in some other person if the purpose was not carried out, or if it ceased to be used for that purpose in the future: *Tithe Redemption Commissioner* v. *Runcorn UDC* (1954). *See* the Reverter of Sites Act 1987, at **13:4**.

(b) LPA 1925, s. 7(2): 'A fee simple vested in a corporation which is liable to determine by reason of the dissolution of the corporation is, for the purposes of this Act, a fee simple absolute.'

(c) LP (Amendment)A 1926, Schedule. The concept of the fee simple absolute excluded a fee simple to which conditions were annexed. The Schedule to LP (Amendment)A 1926, stated that 'a fee simple subject to a legal or equitable right of entry or re-entry is for the purposes of this Act a fee simple absolute'.

6. 'In possession'

'In possession' denotes an estate which is *immediate* and hence neither in reversion nor in remainder. *See Pearson* v. *IRC* (1981) — the phrase has the effect of giving 'a present right of present enjoyment'.

(a) LPA 1925, s. 205(1)(xix), states: '"Possession" includes receipt of rents and profits or the right to receive the same . . . '

(b) Thus, if X, tenant in fee simple, leases Blackacre to Y, X remains the owner of a fee simple in possession (i.e. a legal estate), since he is entitled to the rent from the lease, even though he is not physically in possession of Blackacre.

(c) A grant 'to X for life, remainder to Y in fee simple' does not confer a fee simple upon Y at once. His estate is *in futuro,* and his interest, is, therefore, *equitable* (i.e. he has an *equitable fee simple*).

Types of fee simple

7. General

Several types of fee simple are enumerated here:

(a) fee simple absolute in possession (*see* 1–6 above);
(b) determinable fee simple (*see* 8 below); *
(c) conditional fee simple (*see* 9 below); *
(d) base fee (*see* 12 below). *

(* Modified fee simple)

8. Determinable fee simple

This is a fee simple which determines *automatically* on the occurrence of an event which is specified, *but which may never occur.* Example: 'Blackacre to X in fee simple until he shall qualify as a solicitor'. Essentially, in this example, there is uncertainty at the time of the grant of Blackacre as to whether X will ever qualify. Phrases creating the determinable fee simple include time references, e.g. 'until', 'so long as', 'during', 'while', and mark out the limit of the estate granted. *See Re Rowhook Mission Hall* (1985).

9. Conditional fee simple

This is a fee simple created in the ordinary way, but cut short by a later, independent, clause (introduced by, e.g. 'on condition that', 'but if', 'provided that').

(a) *Fee simple on condition subsequent.* Such a condition, when activated, *defeats an existing interest.* Example: 'to X in fee simple on the condition that he shall never sell it to persons outside the family'. *See Re Macleay* (1875). Note that, should a condition subsequent be void, the grantee will take the fee simple absolute free from all conditions. *See Re Greenwood* (1903).

(b) *Fee simple on condition precedent.* Such a condition, when added to a grant, provides that the fee simple shall not commence *until an event, which is specified, occurs.* Example : 'Blackacre to X and his heirs in fee simple if he reaches the age of 25'.

NOTE: Where X grants Y a conditional fee simple, X retains an interest known as a 'right of re-entry' (i.e. the right to recover the land); if X grants Y a determinable fee simple, X retains an interest known as a 'right of reverter'.

10. Limitations and public policy

Where an estate owner grants an interest subject to limitations (e.g. 'to X on the condition that he shall *never* marry') the courts may intervene should the limitations be interpreted as *contrary to public policy*. Thus, a limitation attempting to prevent marriage *may* be considered to be contrary to public policy; in such a case the grant takes effect absolutely and is freed from the attempted limitation (*see Kelly* v. *Monck* (1795)). A limitation in partial restraint of marriage may be valid: *Re Bathe* (1925); in *Morley* v. *Rennoldson* (1843) a grant 'to X in fee simple until he marries' was held valid. *See further:* **13:33.**

11. Conditional and determinable fee simple: essential differences summarised

The following points should be noted:

(a) The conditional fee simple is a 'complete' fee simple with a condition *attached to it,* e.g. 'to X in fee simple on condition that he shall not take a degree in philosophy'. The determinable fee simple contains *within it the expression* which creates its own limiting circumstance, e.g. 'to Y in fee simple until he shall qualify as a chartered accountant'.

(b) The conditional fee simple takes effect as a *legal estate.* The determinable fee exists only as *an equitable interest.*

(c) The conditional fee continues unless and until the grantor exercises his *right of re-entry.* The determinable fee ends *automatically* as soon as the specified event occurs.

(d) Where a conditional fee contains a condition which is contrary to public policy, that condition may be *struck out,* leaving the grant to operate as a fee simple absolute. In the case of a determinable fee, the grant containing such a limiting circumstance held as contrary to public policy would be *totally destroyed.*

12. Base fee

A base fee is a fee simple which is created by *the partial barring of an entail.* (*See* **13:36.**) Example: 'To X for life, remainder to Y in tail, remainder to Z in fee simple.' If, during the life of X, Y barred the entail without X's co-operation, a base fee would be created which would continue only for as long as Y's entail would have continued, but after that Z would be entitled.

Note that after 1925 the base fee cannot exist as a legal estate; it exists as *an equitable interest*.

Creation of the fee simple absolute in possession

13. The importance of words of limitation
Assume that a grant has been made 'to X and his heirs'.

(a) The words 'to X' are known as *words of purchase*, i.e. they 'mark out' X as a *'purchaser'*, that is, *one who takes by grant and not merely by operation of law. See* 1:**19(b)**.

(b) The words 'and his heirs' are *words of limitation*, i.e. they limit the estate granted to X; they 'mark out' the estate X is to take; they confer no estate on the heirs.

(c) In order to create an estate of a particular size, appropriate words of limitation had to be used.

(d) The rules varied according to whether the grant was made by deed or by will. This has now changed: *see* **14** below.

14. Grant of a fee simple by deed
Note the following:

(a) Under LPA 1925, s. 60(1): 'A conveyance of freehold land to any person without words of limitation, or any equivalent expression, shall pass to the grantee the fee simple or other the whole interest which the grantor had power to convey in such land, unless a contrary intention appears in the conveyance.'

(b) The position today is that, in the case of a grant by deed, phrases such as 'to X in fee simple', or 'to X for ever', will suffice to pass the entire fee simple to the purchaser *unless* the conveyance shows the existence of a contrary intention.

(c) In the case of *registered land* (*see* Ch. 20) a transfer *inter vivos* by the registered proprietor requires no words of limitation in the transfer, but the transferee does not obtain the legal estate until completion of the transfer by appropriate registration. *See Dunning Ltd* v. *Sykes & Son Ltd* (1987).

15. LP (Misc. Provs.) A 1989, s. 2
Under this Act, which repealed LPA 1925, s. 40 (*see* 1989 Act,

s. 2(8)), contracts for the sale or other disposition of an interest in land can now be made *only in writing*. Section 2(1)–(3) reads as follows:

> ' 2. (1) A contract for the sale of land or other disposition of an interest in land can only be made in writing and only by incorporating all the terms which the parties have expressly agreed in one document or, where contracts are exchanged, in each.
>
> (2) The terms may be incorporated in a document either by being set out in it or by reference to some other document.
>
> (3) The document incorporating the terms or, where contracts are exchanged, one of the documents incorporating them (but not necessarily the same one) must be signed by or on behalf of each party to the contract.'

NOTE: (1) 'Interest in land' means any estate, interest or charge in or over land or in or over the proceeds of sale of land: s. 2(6). (2) Section 2 does *not* apply in relation to short leases (i.e. for terms of no more than three years), to contracts made during a public auction, to contracts regulated under the Financial Services Act 1986, and to the creation or operation of resulting, implied or constructive trusts: s. 2(5).

16. Comments on s. 2

The following points should be noted:

(a) Under the (repealed) LPA 1925, s. 40, the contract *or some memorandum or note thereof* had to be in writing. An oral contract might be evidenced in writing. *This is no longer the case.* A contract for the sale or disposition of an interest in land can be made now *only* in writing, with all expressly agreed terms contained in one document; all parties must sign.

(b) 'Expressly' suggests that implied terms (such as vacant possession) need not necessarily be included in the document.

(c) LPA 1925, s. 40, was, essentially, a rule of evidence; non-compliance rendered the contract unenforceable by action. The provision in s. 2(1) above means clearly that failure to comply will produce *no contract*. Equitable rules relating to part performance will *not* apply.

For other details concerning the 1989 Act, *see* 4:**18**. *See Tootal Clothing Ltd* v. *Guinea Properties Management Ltd* (1992).

17. Fee simple by will

The position is governed by the Wills Act 1837.

(a) *Under the Wills Act 1837*, s. 28: 'Where any real estate shall be devised to any person without any words of limitation, such devise shall be construed to pass the fee simple, or other the whole estate or interest which the testator had power to dispose of by will in such real estate, unless a contrary intention shall appear by the will.'

(b) *The position today is that* the testator's whole estate will pass to the devisee *unless a contrary intention is apparent in the will*. There is now no difference in the rules as applied to deeds and wills.

> NOTE: A *devise* is a gift of *real property* made by will to a donee, who is known as the *devisee*. (A gift of *personal property* by will is a *legacy* or *bequest* made to a *legatee*.)

Rights of the fee simple owner

18. The general rights attaching to the fee simple
The fee simple is the largest estate known to our law ('the most extensive in quantum'), and the fee simple owner has correspondingly, extensive rights:

(a) certain so-called natural rights (*see* **19** below);

(b) rights of alienation (*see* **20** below);

(c) rights of enjoyment of the land (*see* **21** below).

19. Natural rights
The term 'natural rights' is used to differentiate these rights, which exist automatically, from rights of a somewhat similar nature, such as easements (*see* Ch. 17) which can be acquired by a tenant. Among such natural rights are:

(a) *The right to support.* A landowner, X, is entitled to such support from the land of his neighbour, Y, as is necessary to keep his (X's) soil at its natural level.

    (i) Thus, Y must not, for example, excavate so near to X's boundary as to cause the subsidence of X's land.

    (ii) An action will not succeed where the removal of such support results from natural causes: *Rouse* v. *Gravelworks Ltd* (1940) — support removed as the result of the movement of water in a gravel pit.

    (iii) The right also exists where different persons own the surface of the land and the soil which is underneath: *L & N W Railway* v. *Evans* (1893).

    (iv) The right does *not* apply in the case of support for buildings:

> *Wyatt* v. *Harrison* (1832); *Smith* v. *Thackerah* (1866); *Redland Bricks Ltd* v. *Morris* (1970).

(b)   *The right to air.* Where the landowner receives a flow of air to premises he is entitled to receive that air unpolluted.

20. Rights of alienation

By 'alienation' is meant the power vested in one person to dispose of property to another person. In general, the fee simple owner may alienate his estate as he wishes, by deed or by will. He may alienate his whole interest or any part of it.

21. Rights of enjoyment of the land

See **1:10**. In general, the rights of enjoyment possessed by a fee simple owner are very wide.

(a)   He has the right to act as he wishes on his land, provided that he does not interfere with the legal rights of others. *Sic utere tuo ut alienum non laedas* — 'so use your own property as not to injure that of others'. Note the Access to Neighbouring Land Act 1992, enabling persons who desire to carry out works to any land which are reasonably necessary for the preservation of that land to obtain access to neighbouring land in order to do so.

(b)   He has the right to enjoy everything on, beneath and above the land. *Cujus est solum ejus est usque ad coelum et ad inferos* — 'whose is the soil, his is also that which is up to the sky and down to the depths of the earth'. (*See* **1:10**.)

(c)   He may use his property as he thinks fit, and may 'waste' the land if he so desires: *Wilson* v. *Waddell* (1876); *Brady* v. *Warren* (1900). (*See* **5:7**.)

Limitations of the rights of a fee simple owner

22. Limited nature of the owner's rights

The rights of the fee simple owner are not absolute; restrictions of those rights are varied, and will be considered under the following headings:

(a)   limitations of the right of alienation (*see* **23** below);
(b)   rights of others over his land (*see* **24** below);
(c)   liability in tort (*see* **25** below);
(d)   limitations of the right to minerals (*see* **26** below);
(e)   limitations of the right to property in wild animals (*see* **27** below);

(f) limitations of the right to air space (*see* **28** below);
(g) limitations of rights over water and fish (*see* **29–30** below);
(h) limitations by statute of the right to full enjoyment of land (*see* **31** below).

23. Limitations of the right to alienation

Although the owner of a fee simple estate may generally dispose of it as he wishes, a disposition by will is subject to his making reasonable provision in certain cases for his family and dependants: Inheritance (Provision for Family and Dependants) Act 1975, as amended.

24. Rights of others over his land

A right of the fee simple owner to the unfettered use of his land may be limited by the rights possessed by others over his land, e.g.:

(a) rights of way;
(b) rights of tenants holding under leases;
(c) restrictive covenants (*see* 16:1).

25. Liability in tort

The maxim *sic utere tuo* (*see* **21(a)** above) implies a limitation of the right to do as one wishes on one's land. Thus, liability in tort may arise, for example, in the following cases:

(a) where the tenant causes a nuisance: *Bland* v. *Yates* (1914) — excessive heaping of manure which caused a smell and attracted flies;
(b) where the tenant collects water on his land and its escape damages his neighbour's land: *Rylands* v. *Fletcher* (1868). *See,* however, *Smith* v. *Scott* (1973) — liability of landlord for tenants who cause nuisance to neighbours.

26. Limitations of the right to ownership of minerals, treasure trove, chattels found on the ground

The maxim generally applicable is *cujus est solum* (*see* 1:**10**; and **21(b)** above). The right to all *minerals* is restricted. (For 'mines and minerals', *see* LPA 1925, s. 205(1)(ix) at 1:**9(c)**, and *Lonsdale (Earl)* v. *A.-G.* (1982).) Thus: gold and silver in mines generally belong to the Crown (*see The Case of Mines* (1568); *A.-G.* v. *Morgan* (1891)); and interests in coal are vested in the British Coal Corporation (*see* the Coal Industry Nationalisation Act 1946, as amended by the Coal Industry Act 1987, s. 1(1)). For further limitations of the rights implied in *cujus est solum*, *see*, e.g. the case of *fixtures*, at 1:**21**.

(a) Note the limitations imposed in the case of *treasure trove*. This is gold or silver, the true owner of which is unknown, and which has been hidden deliberately and not merely abandoned or lost: *see A.–G. v. Moore* (1893). A coroner's jury determines whether or not a find is treasure trove; if it is, it goes to the Crown. The Crown may make an *ex gratia* payment to a finder who reports immediately to the local authority. Note that goods will not be considered as treasure trove if found *upon* the earth or in the sea. The Crown has no prerogative right to treasure trove beyond gold and silver: *A.–G. of the Duchy of Lancaster* v. *Overton Farms Ltd* (1980). *See* Law Commission Report (1987) — 'Treasure Trove: Law Reform Issues'.

(b) For the case of *chattels found on the ground, see Parker* v. *B A Board* (1982) — an occupier of a building has rights superior to those of a person who finds chattels in it, *provided that* he has manifested an intention (expressly or impliedly) to exercise control over the building and the things which may be upon it or in it. ('The chattel is to be treated as an integral part of the realty as against all but the true owner.')

27. Limitations of the right to property in wild animals

In general, a wild animal is not within the absolute ownership of any person: *The Case of Swans* (1592). There are limited exceptions to this rule.

(a) A landowner, or a person to whom he has granted sporting rights, has a right to kill and to appropriate wild animals on the property: *Blades* v. *Higgs* (1865).

(b) Where game is killed by a trespasser the absolute property vests in the landowner: *Sutton* v. *Moody* (1697); *R* v. *Townley* (1871).

28. Limitations of the right to air space

See **1:10**. The scope of the maxim *cujus est solum* is limited, e.g. by the Civil Aviation Act 1982, s. 76, which provides: 'No action shall lie in respect of trespass or in respect of nuisance, by reason only of the flight of an aircraft over any property at a height above the ground, which having regard to wind, weather and all the circumstances of the case is reasonable, or the ordinary incidents of such flight so long as the provisions of any Air Navigation Order (*see* s. 61) and of any orders under s. 62 (control of aviation in emergencies and war) have been duly complied with and there has been no breach of s. 81 (dangerous flying).' A landowner has rights in the air space above his land only to the height necessary for the ordinary use and enjoyment of that land and the structures upon it: *Bernstein* v. *Skyviews* (1978).

See *Anchor Developments* v. *Berkley House* (1987) — oversailing booms of a crane invaded plaintiff's airspace and constituted a trespass, sufficient to justify an injunction; *Uniting Church in Australia* v. *Immer* (1992).

29. Limitation of rights over water

See Water Resources Acts 1963–91 and Water Acts 1973–89. In general, a landowner has no rights over water which flows through his land in a defined channel, or which percolates through that land, but such water may become the property of a landowner who appropriates it: *Mason* v. *Hill* (1833); *Ballard* v. *Tomlinson* (1885). (Note *Stephens* v. *Anglian Water Authority* (1988) in which the Court of Appeal held that a landowner who abstracts subterranean water from his land does *not* owe any duty to his neighbour when doing so and cannot be liable for resulting damage.)

(a) Where water percolated, a landowner had *common law rights* whereby he could draw it off without taking into account the neighbouring owner. See *Langbrook Properties* v. *Surrey CC* (1970). This right is now restricted *by statute*, under which the water may be taken for domestic purposes only, unless a licence has been granted by an appropriate authority: Water Resources Act 1991, ss. 24, 27. *See also* Water Acts 1973–89.

(b) A landowner is entitled to a flow of water through his land without any alteration in its quality or quantity, but this right is subject to reasonable use by the other persons through whose land the water flows: *John Young & Co.* v. *Bankier Distillery Co.* (1893). See *Scott-Whitehead* v. *NCB* (1987).

(c) A riparian owner (i.e. one who owns land adjoining a watercourse) may use the water for ordinary and extraordinary purposes if the use is connected with his tenement, if the use is reasonable and if he restores the water substantially unchanged in character and volume: *Embrey* v. *Owen* (1851); *Rugby Joint Water Board* v. *Walters* (1966).

(d) A riparian owner may not use water for a purpose which has no connection with his tenement: *Swindon Waterworks Co* v. *Wilts & Berks Canal Navigation Co.* (1875) — a company owning a mill on the banks of a stream was not entitled to collect the water for the use of a nearby town.

(e) The bed of a non-tidal river belongs to the riparian owner; the bed of a tidal river belongs to the Crown unless rights have been granted to a subject: *A.–G.* v. *Lonsdale* (1868).

(f) Where public rights to navigation in a tidal river have been established, those rights override the riparian owner's rights: *A.–G.* v. *Terry* (1874).

(g) For an occupier's preventative action in a case of flooding, *see* *Home Brewery Co* v. *Davis & Co.* (1987).

30. Limitations of the right to fish

The right of fishing in a non-tidal river accrues to the owner of the bed of the river or to persons who have been granted a right by the owner: *Eckroyd* v. *Coulthard* (1898). (In the case of a tidal river the public have a right to fish up to the point of ebb and flow of the tide.) Where there are different riparian owners of the two banks, each owns the right to fish to the 'middle line' of the stream: *Hanbury* v. *Jenkins* (1901).

31. Limitations by statute of the owner's right to unrestricted enjoyment of land

As governments have come to consider the ownership and use of land to be a matter of social importance, so legislation has restricted the unfettered enjoyment of land by the owner.

(a) The Town and Country Planning Acts seriously limit the rights of a landowner to use his land as he wishes. As a result of these Acts a landowner must obtain permission from his local planning authority if he wishes to develop his land. 'Development' was defined as 'the carrying out of building, engineering, mining and other operations, on, over or under land or the making of any material change in the use of any buildings or other land': Town and Country Planning Act 1990, s. 55. Thus, a change in the use of a house, so that it becomes a shop, for example, requires permission. *See also* Town and Country Planning (Use Classes) Order 1987 (SI 1987/764). For *permitted development rights, see* General Development Order 1988; SI 1991/2805. *See* the Planning and Compensation Act 1991, s. 10, for certificates of 'lawful use or development'. *See Secretary of State for the Environment* v. *Cambridge CC* (1992).

(b) The Rent Act 1977, gave a measure of protection to a tenant against his landlord.

(c) The Agricultural Holdings Act 1986, protected security of tenure in the case of an agricultural holding.

(d) The Planning and Compensation Act 1991 allows, *inter alia*, the compulsory purchase of land.

(e) The Community Land Act 1975 (repealed by the Local Government, Planning and Land Act 1980, s. 101), empowered an authority to acquire compulsorily any land which, in its opinion, was suitable for development.

(f) The Housing Act 1980, which substantially amended the Rent Act 1977, gave a measure of security to public, private sector and 'secure' tenants. *See* now the Housing Acts 1985, 1988.

(g) The Local Government, Planning and Land Act 1980, ss. 134–72, created urban development areas and urban development corporations. *See* now the Local Government and Housing Act 1989.

(h) The Housing and Planning Act 1986 created 'simplified planning zones' and extended control over hazardous substances on land. *See* now the Planning (Hazardous Substances) Act 1990 and the Environmental Protection Act 1990, Sch. 13.

Progress test 3

1. What is the essence of the fee simple absolute in possession, and what is the meaning of the word 'absolute' in this context? **(2, 5)**

2. Comment on the following dispositions of land made today:
(a) 'Blackacre to John in fee simple on the condition that he shall never alienate to a person beyond the immediate family circle':
(b) 'Whiteacre to James and his heirs in fee simple if he reaches the age of 27'. **(9)**

3. What is the importance for land law of the Law of Property (Miscellaneous Provisions) Act 1989, s. 2? **(15)**

4. Discuss the rights of the fee simple owner in relation to the ownership of minerals and to property in wild animals. **(26, 27)**

5. What are the general rights of the landowner in relation to water? **(29)**

4
The term of years (1)

General terminology

1. General

The terminology of the modern land law is highly technical; that section of land law which deals with the estate known as the *term of years* illustrates this point well. Phrases such as *tenancy at sufferance, tenancy at will, leasehold,* take on highly specialised meanings. Some important words, phrases and their meanings are listed at **2** below.

2. Terminology

In this chapter, 'L' will be used to signify the landlord (lessor) and 'T' the tenant (lessee).

(a) *Term of years:* an estate or interest in land which is limited to a certain fixed period. (*Terminus* = limit or boundary.) The phrase *term for years* has the same meaning.

(b) *Lease:* the document normally used to bring into existence a term of years. 'Lease' is also used in the sense of term of years, leasehold, demise, tenancy: *see*, e.g. Landlord and Tenant Act 1987, s. 59(1). *See* the HA 1985, s. 621. ('Tenancy' tends to be used in relation to short periods; 'lease' in relation to longer periods.)

(c) *Leasehold:* the interest (i.e. the term of years) created by a lease.

(d) *Lessor and lessee:* where L grants a lease to T, L is known as the lessor and T is known as the *lessee.*

(e) *Reversion:* where L grants a lease to T, L retains a *reversion,* i.e. an interest which remains in him. *See* 13:4.

(f) *Assignment:* T may assign the lease, i.e. he may transfer the entire interest to X. T is the assignor, X is the *assignee.*

(g) *Sub-lease:* T may grant a lease, known as a *sub-lease, or subterm* to Y. T is then the *sub-lessor;* Y is the *sub-lessee.* (Where T has any reversion, there is a sub-lease.)

(h) *Fine:* a lump sum payment, a premium, for the grant or renewal of a lease. *See* LPA 1925, s. 205(1)(xxiii).

(i) *Rent:* a periodic payment made by T to L for the possession and use of land. *See* LPA 1925, s. 205(1)(xxiii).

The term of years absolute under LPA 1925

3.   A legal estate
Under LPA 1925, s. 1(1), a term of years absolute and the fee simple absolute in possession are the only estates in land capable of subsisting or of being conveyed or created *at law*. *See* **1:17(a)**.

4.   Definition of the term of years absolute
Under LPA 1925, s. 205(1)(xxvii), 'term of years absolute' means:

'a term of years (taking effect either in possession or in reversion whether or not at a rent) with or without impeachment for waste, subject or not to another legal estate, and either certain or liable to determination by notice, re-entry, operation of law, or by provision for cesser on redemption, or in any other event (other than the dropping of a life, or the determination of a determinable life interest); but does not include any term of years determinable with life or lives or with the cesser of a determinable life interest, nor, if created after the commencement of this Act, a term of years which is not expressed to take effect in possession within twenty-one years after the creation thereof where required by this Act to take effect within that period; and in this definition the expression "term of years" includes a term for less than a year, or for a year or years and a fraction of a year or from year to year.'

5.   Term of years under s. 205
The following points arise:

(a) The definition under the Act includes not only a term for a year or for years, but a term for less than a year, and a fraction of a year. Hence, the phrase 'term of years' includes *a lease for any period of time which has a fixed and ascertainable maximum duration: see Harvey* v. *Pratt* (1965).
(b) The word 'absolute' is *not* used in the sense in which it appears in the phrase 'fee simple absolute' (*see* **3:5**). Thus, where L grants a lease to T, and where it may be determined before the end of the stated period, e.g. by L's serving on T a notice to quit, that term of

years may, nevertheless, be considered 'absolute'. (In effect, therefore, the word has little meaning in this context.)

(c) It is *not* required that the term of years should be 'in possession'. Thus, L may grant a lease to T in 1990, to commence in 1993, and such a lease would be a legal interest although limited to commence at a date in the future (*see* **11(b)** and **31** below).

6.   Legal estates may subsist concurrently

'A legal estate may subsist concurrently with or subject to any other legal estate in the same land in like manner as it could have done before the commencement of this Act': LPA 1925, s. 1(5). Thus:

(a) L who owns the fee simple in Blackacre may grant a lease to T;
(b) T may grant a sub-lease to X; and
(c) in this event *three legal estates in Blackacre exist concurrently*.

General background

7.   Historical origins

The lease may have originated in the necessity for the provision of security for a loan. This type of lease may have been granted by L to T following on T's loan of money to L; it would have ended when L repaid the loan. The leaseholder was never considered to be seised of the land and his interest in the land was *not* considered as real property. Originally the real actions were *not available* for the protection of the leaseholder.

8.   Term of years and fee simple

Although these two estates are classified together as the only legal estates known to the law, they are essentially different.

(a) The term of years is, in theory, held of a freeholder by leasehold tenure; the fee simple is, in theory, held of a 'superior lord', by freehold tenure.
(b) The leasehold is a species of personal property (*see* **1:12**); the fee simple is considered as *real property*.
(c) The freehold estate is, in essence, uncertain in duration; the leasehold has defined limits (*see* **1:14**).
(d) The estate less than freehold, i.e. the leasehold, has been considered as, in some ways, 'inferior' to the freehold. 'A freehold interest of the smallest duration is greater in the contemplation of law than the longest term': *per* Malins VC in *Re Russell Road Purchase Moneys* (1871).

The essence of the lease

9.   General
A lease must:

(a) be created by legally competent parties and with the required *formalities*;
(b) be created for a *fixed and definite period*;
(c) confer upon the lessee the right to *exclusive possession* of the land leased to him, which must be identified with certainty.

10. The required formalities
In general, a lease for *more than three years* must be created *by deed*. A lease for *not more than three years* may be created *by word of mouth, or by writing without formalities*. The lessor must retain a reversionary interest. *See* **15–19** below. *See* LP (Misc. Provs.) A 1989.

11. Definite period
A term of years is based upon a period *of any length*, the beginning and ending of which must be capable of being ascertained. 'Every estate which must expire at a period certain and prefixed, by whatever words created, is an estate for years. And therefore this estate is frequently called a *term*, *"terminus"*, because its duration or continuance is bounded, limited and determined: for every such estate must have a certain beginning, and certain end': Blackstone (*Commentaries, Book II*).

(a) *The date of commencement of the term.* In general *this must be fixed, or must be capable of ascertainment before the lease takes effect.* 'It is settled beyond question that, in order for there to be a valid agreement for a lease, the essentials are that there shall be determined not only the parties, the property, the length of term and the rent, but also the date of its commencement': *per* Lord Denning in *Harvey* v. *Pratt* (1965).

    (i) L and T may create a lease which is to begin on the date of occurrence of some event which is not certain: *Swift* v. *Macbean* (1942) — lease to commence on the declaration of war.

    (ii) Immediately the event occurs the agreement is enforceable.

    (iii) Where a date for commencement is not stated, the grant may be effective immediately on the taking of possession: *Furness* v. *Bond* (1888).

(b) *The reversionary lease.* A reversionary lease is one which is to commence at a future date, e.g. as in the example at **5(c)** above. But note LPA 1925, s. 149(3): *see* **31** below.

(c) *Date of termination.* In general this should be fixed, so that the lease is created for a fixed, and not an indefinite, period.

> (*i*) *Id certum est quod certum reddi potest* (that is certain which can be made certain). This maxim is applied so that, for example where Blackacre is leased 'to T for a period of years to be fixed by L', the lease will not be void if the period has been decided prior to the lease coming into effect.

> (*ii*) Where the date of termination of a lease remains uncertain after the lease is supposed to have taken effect, the lease is invalid. *See* **12** below.

(d) *The doctrine of interesse termini.* Until 1926, a lessee had to enter into possession before he was considered to have acquired an estate. The doctrine was abolished by LPA 1925, s. 149(1). *See Lewis* v. *Baker* (1905).

(e) Although a term of years under a lease runs from the date of execution of the lease, obligations under that lease can be made to run from some date *prior* to its execution: *Bradshaw* v. *Pawley* (1979).

12. Leases must be of certain duration: a recent House of Lords decision

In *Prudential Assurance Co. Ltd* v. *London Residuary Body and Others* (1992), the House of Lords held that *it was a requirement of all leases and tenancy agreements that the term created was of certain duration.* Therefore, an agreement purporting to 'continue until the . . . land is required by the council for road widening' did *not* create a lease.

(a) Lord Templeman, reviewing the background to the law relating to the duration of leases stated that 'a demise for years is a contract for the exclusive possession and profit of land for some determinate period'. In *Say* v. *Smith* (1530) a lease for a certain term purported to add a term which was uncertain; the lease was held valid only as to the certain term. This theme had been taken up in LPA 1925, s. 1(1) (*see* 2:**15**) and s. 205(1)(xxvii).

(b) Ancient authority, recognised by the 1925 Act, was applied in *Lace* v. *Chantler* (1944). Lord Templeman cited the words of Lord Greene in that case, in which it was held that a tenancy 'for the duration of the war' did *not* create a good leasehold interest: 'A term created by a leasehold tenancy agreement must be expressed either with certainty and specifically or by reference to something which can, at the time when the lease takes effect, be looked to as a certain ascertainment of what the term is meant to be . . . the duration, as well as the commencement of the term, must be stated.'

(c) The agreement in the present case lacked a fixed and certain term and failed to grant an estate in land.

(d) *See, further,* **25** below.

13. A criticism of the law

Lord Browne-Wilkinson, agreeing with Lord Templeman's reasoning, added that the 'bizarre outcome' of the case resulted 'from the application of an ancient and technical rule of law which required the maximum duration of a term of years to be ascertained from the outset'. No one had produced any satisfactory rationale for the genesis of the rule; no one had been able to point to any useful purpose that it served at the present day. He expressed the hope that the Law Commission might look at the subject to see whether there was in fact any good reason now for maintaining the rule.

14. The right to exclusive possession

The creation of a term of years involves L's conferring upon T a right to exclusive possession of the land (*not* exclusive occupation). The right to exclusive possession usually implies the right to exclude everyone, including L, from the land, except in some circumstances. (L retains a reversion, however.) The concept of exclusive possession is of particular importance in relation to licences. (*See Street* v. *Mountford* (1985) at 6:**13, 14**.)

(a) 'The tenant possessing exclusive possession is able to exercise the rights of an owner of land, which is in the real sense his land albeit temporarily and subject to certain restrictions. A tenant armed with exclusive possession can keep out strangers and keep out the landlord': *per* Lord Templeman in *Street* v. *Mountford* (1985).

(b) A lease may reserve a right for L to enter the premises so as to view the state of repair, etc., but this must be exercised in a reasonable manner. *See Appah* v. *Parncliffe Investments Ltd* (1964).

Modes of creation of a leasehold

15. General

It is possible to create *at law* a leasehold by a conveyance known as a lease, or *in equity* by an agreement for a lease.

(a) *By lease.* A lease which is made in accordance with the necessary rules creates a legal leasehold estate.

(b) *By agreement for a lease.* An agreement for a lease does not create a legal estate. But, on the basis of the maxim 'equity looks on that as done which ought to be done', equity considers that a leasehold interest, which is enforceable as an *equitable interest (see* 1:**16**), arises immediately such an agreement is made.

16. The formalities of a lease

Under *common law rules* leases could be created *orally.*

(a) LPA 1925, s. 52(1): 'All conveyances of land or of any interest therein are void for the purpose of conveying or creating a legal estate *unless made by deed*.' But this section does not apply to those leases or tenancies or other assurances not required by law to be made in writing: s. 52(2)(d). *See* s. 54(2) at **(b)** below. *See Crago* v. *Julian* (1992) (the assignment of *all* leases, however created, must be by deed).

(b) LPA 1925, s. 54(1): 'All interests in land created by parol and not put in writing and signed by the persons so creating the same, or by their agents thereunto lawfully authorised in writing, have, notwithstanding any consideration having been given for the same, the force and effect of interests at will only.' But under s. 54(2): 'Nothing in the foregoing provisions of this Part of the Act shall affect the creation by parol of leases taking effect in possession *for a term not exceeding three years* (whether or not the lessee is given power to extend the term) at the best rent which can be reasonably obtained without taking a fine.'

(c) *The position is, therefore, that a lease which purports to create a legal estate must be made by deed, but that no such formalities are required in the case of a lease which is to take effect in possession for a term not exceeding three years at the best rent which can be reasonably obtained without taking a fine.*

   (*i*)   *'Take effect in possession'*. The term 'possession' includes the receipt of rents and profits: LPA 1925, s. 205(1)(xix).
   (*ii*) *'Not exceeding three years'*. The term of three years is calculated as from the date of the grant of the lease: *Rawlins* v. *Turner* (1699). Included within the meaning of the phrase are fixed terms for a period of up to three years which may be extended by an exercise of the tenant's option.
   (*iii*) *'Without taking a fine'*. This refers to the taking of a lump sum (or premium) in consideration of a reduced rent.

17. The equitable lease (made without some formalities)

A lease for more than three years which would be void because of its lack of the requisite formalities may be held in equity to be equivalent to an agreement for a lease (*see* **20, 21** below), *if* granted for value *and* made in writing (*see* LP(Misc. Provs.)A 1989, s. 2(1) (at **3:15**)).

18. LP(Misc. Provs.)A 1989, s. 1

This section makes new provision with respect to deeds and their execution. It is of particular relevance for *leases made by deed*.

' 1. — (1) Any rule of law which —
  (a) restricts the substances on which a deed may be written;
  (b) requires a seal for the valid execution of an instrument as a deed by an individual; or
  (c) requires authority by one person to another to deliver an instrument as a deed on his behalf to be given by deed, is abolished.

(2) An instrument shall not be a deed unless —
  (a) it makes it clear on its face that it is intended to be a deed by the person making it or, as the case may be, by the parties to it (whether by describing itself as a deed or expressing itself to be executed or signed as a deed or otherwise); and
  (b) it is validly executed as a deed by that person or, as the case may be, one or more of those parties.

(3) An instrument is validly executed as a deed by an individual if, and only if —
  (a) it is signed —
    (*i*) by him in the presence of a witness who attests the signature; or
    (*ii*) at his direction and in his presence and the presence of two witnesses who each attest the signature; and
  (b) it is delivered as a deed by him or a person authorised to do so on his behalf.

(4) In subsections (2) and (3) above "sign", in relation to an instrument, includes making one's mark on the instrument and "signature" is to be construed accordingly.

(5) Where a solicitor or licensed conveyancer, or an agent or employee of a solicitor or licensed conveyancer, in the course of or in connection with a transaction involving the disposition or creation of an interest in land, purports to deliver an instrument as a deed on behalf of a party to the instrument, it shall be conclusively presumed in favour of a purchaser that he is authorised so to deliver the instrument.

(6) In subsection (5) above —

"disposition" and "purchaser" have the same meanings as in the Law of Property Act 1925; and

"interest in land" means any estate, interest or charge in or over land or in or over the proceeds of sale of land.

(7) Where an instrument under seal that constitutes a deed is required for the purposes of an Act passed before this section comes into force, this section shall have effect as to signing, sealing or delivery of an instrument by an individual in place of any provision of that Act as to signing, sealing or delivery . . .'

19. Comments on s. 1
The following matters should be noted:

(a) The old rules concerning the sealing of a deed are abolished.

(b) The instrument must make clear *on its face* that it is intended to be a deed, and it requires valid execution, signature and delivery.

(c) The signature must be attested by a witness present at the time of signature. Two witnesses are necessary in certain circumstances.

(d) Section 1 applies to *all* deeds, not merely those relating to land.

(e) Section 1 as it concerns the execution of a deed by an individual, does not include execution by a corporation sole: s. 1(10).

The doctrine of *Walsh* v. *Lonsdale*: leases in equity

20. *Walsh* v. *Lonsdale* (1882)
L made a written contract with W to grant W a seven years' lease of property, rent to be payable on L's demand a year in advance. Before the lease was granted W entered into possession, paying his rent quarterly and not in advance. L asked, six months later, for a year's rent and W refused to pay. L distrained. W asked for an injunction, arguing that at law he was a tenant from year to year at a rent which was not payable in advance.

(a) It was held by the Court of Appeal that, since equity regarded that as done which ought to have been done, *W held on the conditions which would have applied had a lease been granted.*

(b) 'The question is one of some nicety. There is an agreement for a lease under which possession has been given. Now since the Judicature Act [1873] the possession is held under the agreement. There are not two estates as there were formerly, one estate at common law by reason of the payment of the rent from year to year, and an estate in equity under the agreement. There is only one court, and the equity rules prevail in it. The tenant holds under an agreement for a lease. He holds, therefore under the same terms in equity as if a lease had been granted': *per* Jessel MR.

21. Effect of the doctrine

It was suggested, as a result of *Walsh* v. *Lonsdale*, that an agreement for a lease was as good as a lease. Thus, in *Re Maugham* (1885), Field J stated: 'Since the Judicature Acts there is now no distinction that I can see between a lease and an agreement for a lease.' But in *Manchester Brewery Co.* v. *Coombs* (1901), Farwell J stated: 'Although it has been suggested that the decision in *Walsh* v. *Lonsdale* takes away all differences between the legal and the equitable estate, it, of course, does nothing of the sort and the limits of its applicability are really somewhat narrow.' There are several ways in which an agreement for a lease differs from a lease.

(a) An agreement for a lease is not a conveyance under LPA 1925, s. 62. An equitable tenant cannot claim the benefit of s. 62 (*see* **17:19(b)**).

(b) A lease may confer a legal estate upon the lessee, and his assignment of the lease may pass to the assignee the lessee's rights and obligations. But an agreement for a lease does not confer a legal estate, and the benefits, but not the burdens, of any covenant (*see* **16:8**) are assignable.

(c) The granting of the remedy of specific performance in the case of an agreement for a lease is at the discretion of the court: *Cornish* v. *Brook Green Laundry Ltd* (1959).

(d) An agreement for a lease is void against a *bona fide* purchaser for value of the legal estate without notice (*see* **1:19**). Hence an agreement for the creation of a lease should be registered as an *estate contract* under the Land Charges Act 1972, s. 2(4): *see* **18:20(d)**.

Types of leases and tenancies

22. Enumeration of leases and tenancies

The following are considered here:

(a) leases for a fixed period (*see* **23** below);
(b) tenancies from year to year (*see* **24** below);
(c) tenancies from week to week (*see* **26** below);
(d) tenancies at will (*see* **27** below);

(e) tenancies at sufferance (*see* **28 below**);
(f) perpetually renewable leases (*see* **29** below);
(g) leases for lives (*see* **30** below);
(h) future leases (*see* **31** below).
(i) tenancies by estoppel (*see* **32** below).

23. Leases for a fixed period

A lease for a fixed period (or 'term certain') may be created for *any duration*, such as a month or 500 years. The rules concerning the ascertainment of commencement and termination are stated at **11** above. In general, where a lease has been created for a fixed period it will be determined *automatically* at the end of that period (*see* **38** below).

24. Tenancies from year to year

A tenancy from year to year (known also as a yearly tenancy) continues until it is ended by proper notice from either party.

(a) *Creation.* A yearly tenancy may be created expressly or by implication.

    (*i*) *Express creation.* 'To T from year to year' will create a yearly tenancy. But 'to T for a year and thereafter from year to year' confers a minimum tenancy of two years upon T, i.e. an express term of one year *plus* a yearly tenancy which may be terminated not earlier than the end of the second year: *Re Searle* (1912).

    (*ii*) *By implication.* Assume that T occupies L's land with L's permission and that T is not a licensee. Then, if T pays a rent which is computed and accepted by L with reference to a year, T will, by implication of law, be considered as a yearly tenant. There will be no such implication where L accepts such rent in ignorance of all the circumstances: *Tickner* v. *Buzzacott* (1965). The implication of a yearly tenancy may arise although the rent is paid, for example, at monthly intervals, as in an agreement between L and T for '£12,000 per annum to be paid monthly'. Here the relevant question is, 'What is the period on the basis of which the rent was calculated?': *Shirley* v. *Newman* (1795). (Note that, under the Agricultural Holdings Act 1986, s. 2(1), any periodical tenancy of an agricultural holding, based on a term of less than one year, is, in general, converted into a yearly tenancy.) *See E.W.P.* v. *Moore* (1992); *Gold* v. *Amand* (1992).

(b) *Continuation.* The yearly tenancy will continue until ended by proper notice, and this is not affected by the death of L or T.

(c) *Ending a yearly tenancy.* Notice may be given in accordance with any agreement between L and T. Where there is no such agreement, notice of at least half a year must be given, so that it expires at the end of a period of the tenancy. Note, e.g. the Protection from Eviction Act 1977, s. 5, at **26(b)** below.

  (*i*) 'Half a year' is construed in a special way. Should the tenancy commence on a quarter-day, notice must be given at least two quarter-days before it is intended that it shall expire. (Note: the quarter-days are: Lady Day — 25 March; Midsummer Day — 24 June; Michaelmas — 29 September; Christmas — 25 December.) Where the tenancy commences on a day which is not a quarter-day, 'half a year' means at least 182 days: *Anon* (1575); but six calendar months' notice may be agreed between the parties to be sufficient.

  (*ii*) There are exceptions to the rule under which six months' notice may be required: first, where L and T have agreed as to a different period of notice: *Allison* v. *Scargall* (1920); secondly, in the case of an agricultural holding, in which case one year's notice is required: Agricultural Holdings Act 1986, s. 25(1). Note that an agricultural tenancy ceases to be agricultural if, during the tenancy, before service of notice to quit, agricultural activity is wholly or substantially abandoned, regardless of L's consent: *Wetherall* v. *Smith* (1980).

25. Yearly tenancies reconsidered: a recent decision of the House of Lords

In *Prudential Assurance Co. Ltd* v. *London Residuary Body and Others* (1992) (*see* **12** above), the House of Lords examined the yearly tenancy. Lord Templeman considered that the principle in *Lace* v. *Chantler* (1944) (*see* **12(b)** above) reaffirming 500 years of judicial acceptance of the requirement that a term must be certain applied to *all* leases *and* tenancy agreements.

(a) A tenancy from year to year was saved from being uncertain because each party had power by notice to determine at the end of any year. The term continued until determined as if both parties made a new agreement at the end of each year for a new term for the ensuing year.

(b) A power for nobody to determine or for one party only to be able to determine was *inconsistent* with the concept of a term from year to year. A grant for an uncertain term which took the form of a yearly tenancy which could not be determined by the landlord did *not* create a lease.

(c) *Re Midland Railway Co.'s Agreement* (1971), in which the Court of Appeal held that *Lace* v. *Chantler* did not apply to a tenancy from year to year, was wrongly decided (as was *Ashburn Anstalt* v. *Arnold* (1989)).

26. Tenancies from week to week, etc.

Tenancies from week to week, or from month to month, or similar periodic tenancies, may arise expressly or by implication.

(a) *Creation.* Express agreement may create such tenancies, or an implication may emerge from the payment by T, and the acceptance by L, of a rent which has been computed by reference to a week, or some other period: *Cole* v. *Kelly* (1920). (See, however, **27(e)** below.)

(b) *Ending a periodic tenancy.* Where notice is given, it must be for the complete period, i.e. it must not be less than the period of a tenancy. Thus, a weekly tenancy may be terminated by notice of at least one week: *Lemon* v. *Lardeur* (1946); *Precious* v. *Reedie* (1924). *See also Centaploy* v. *Matlodge* (1974).

    (*i*) The notice should end the tenancy at the end of the current period.

   (*ii*) L and T may agree to another period of time: *Re Threlfall* (1880).

  (*iii*) In *Hammersmith and Fulham LBC* v. *Monk* (1991), the House of Lords upheld a decision by the Court of Appeal that a periodic tenancy can be continued only with the consent of *all* the parties; hence a valid notice to quit can be given by one of two or more joint tenants (*see* **12:10**) without the agreement of the other(s).

  (*iv*) The Protection from Eviction Act 1977, s. 5(1), provides that, in the case of a dwelling, notice to quit will not be valid unless it is in writing *and* contains the required particulars, *and* is given at least four weeks before the date on which it is to take effect. A proper quitting day at common law must be selected for the operation of the notice. *See Elsden* v. *Pick* (1980). Note also HA 1988, s. 32(1) (bringing non-excluded licences within the 1977 Act, s. 5).

27. Tenancies at will

A tenancy at will exists if T occupies the land of L, with L's consent, on terms under which T or L may determine the tenancy *at any time*. 'In this case the lessee is called tenant at will because he hath no certain or sure estate, for the lessor may put him out at what time it pleaseth him': Littleton.

(a) *Creation.* A tenancy at will may be created by express agreement, or, more usually, by implication. Thus, where T holds over (continues in possession although his term has ended) with L's permission and has not paid any rent computed with reference to a period, a tenancy at will is created; or where T is allowed rent-free and indefinite occupation of L's house. In these cases T's possession does not arise by virtue of his being L's agent or servant. *See Braythwayte* v. *Hitchcock* (1842); *Hagee Ltd* v. *Erikson & Larson* (1976) — creation of tenancy by will by express agreement.

(b) *Ending a tenancy at will.* The tenancy may be ended by L or T, even though at its creation it is stated to be determinable at L's will only. It ends if either L or T should assign the land, or die: *James* v. *Dean* (1805); or if one party should perform an act which, by its nature, is not consistent with the continuance of the tenancy, e.g. where T commits voluntary waste: *Countess of Shrewsbury's Case* (1600).

(c) *Under the tenancy.* L is entitled to *compensation* for T's use of the land, unless there is an agreement for rent-free occupation: *Howard* v. *Shaw* (1841). T has the right to emblements (the right to take away crops he has sown — *see* 5:5).

(d) *Payment of a yearly rent by a tenant at will.* Where a tenant at will begins to pay a rent which is paid and accepted with reference to a year, he will become a tenant from year to year: *Richardson* v. *Langridge* (1811). *See also British Railways Board* v. *Bodywright* (1971) (the defendant went into possession during the negotiations for a lease and paid certain sums towards the rent; that rent was *not* calculated by reference to a year and no lease was entered into. It was held that the defendant was a tenant at will).

(e) In *Longrigg Burrough and Trounson* v. *Smith* (1979), the Court of Appeal considered an 'implied tenancy' which, it was argued, had been created by the payment and acceptance of rent following the expiry of a lease of business premises with a flat above. 'The old common law presumption of a tenancy from the payment and acceptance of a sum in the nature of rent dies very hard': *per* Ormrod LJ. *The presumption no longer holds.* 'The question now is a purely open question: it is simply: is it right and proper to infer from all the circumstances of the case, including the payments, that the parties had reached an agreement for a tenancy? I think it does not now go any further than that.' (*See also Marcroft Wagons Ltd* v. *Smith* (1951).)

(f) In *Javad* v. *Aqil* (1991), the Court of Appeal noted that entry into possession while negotiations were proceeding constituted one of the classic circumstances in which a tenancy at will may exist. ('When and so long as parties are in the throes of negotiating larger terms, caution must be exercised before inferring or imputing to the parties an intention to give to the occupant more than a very limited interest, be it licence or tenancy': *per* Nicholls LJ.) *See also Brent LBC* v. *O'Bryan* (1992).

28. Tenancies at sufferance
('Suffer' = 'to allow'.) A tenancy at sufferance is created where T is in occupation 'by lawful demise and after his estate endeth continueth in possession and wrongfully holdeth over': Coke. The tenant at sufferance differs from the tenant at will in that the latter's tenancy is in existence with L's consent.

(a) *Creation.* The tenancy at sufferance arises only by implication of law, since its very nature implies no agreement between L and T. *See Wheeler* v. *Mercer* (1957).

(b) *Ending a tenancy at sufferance.* Notice by either L or T is not required. But where L gives T written notice and T, who is a tenant for years or life, fails to quit, T is liable to L for twice the annual value of the property, as computed by reference to the period of his holding over. (*See also* Distress for Rent Act 1737.)

(c) *Under the tenancy.* T is not entitled to emblements. T may leave at any time, and L may enter at any time. L may sue for use and occupation, and T may bring an action for trespass against a third party.

(d) *Payment of a yearly rent by a tenant at sufferance.* Where rent is paid and accepted on a yearly basis, a yearly tenancy is created: *Dougal* v. *McCarthy* (1893). *See Adler* v. *Blackman* (1953).

(e) *See* Protection from Eviction Act 1977, s. 3; Criminal Law Act 1977, s. 6.

29. Perpetually renewable leases
Such leases gave T a perpetual right of renewal, as where a lease for *x* years gave T the right to require L to grant a new lease for *x* years, and the right to demand a further renewal for *x* years. This type of lease was *abolished* as from 1 January 1926: LPA 1922, s. 145. *See Re Hopkins' Lease* (1972); *Marjorie Burnett* v. *Barclay* (1981). (In this case a seven-year lease included a clause allowing T to renew 'for a further seven years at a rent to be agreed', such lease to contain 'a like covenant for a further term of seven years on the expiration of the term thereby granted'. It was held that this did *not* create a

perpetually renewable lease; it was clear that the parties intended no more than the creation of a maximum of three terms. In particular, a provision for rent review every seven years was considered inimical to a 2,000 year lease.)

(a) Leases of this type were converted under the Act into terms of *2,000* years, as calculated from the date of commencement of the existing term.

(b) A lessee (but *not* a lessor) may terminate such a lease by *ten days' written notice* before a date on which, but for the Act, the lease would have expired if not renewed.

(c) A lessee must register with the lessor any assignment of the lease within *six months* of such an event.

(d) Where T assigns the lease he will not be liable for any breach of covenant which occurs *after* the date of assignment.

(e) After 1925, any contract to renew a lease for *more than sixty years* from the end of the lease is void: LPA 1922, Sch. 15. *See Parkus* v. *Greenwood* (1950).

30. Leases for lives, etc.

Any lease for life or lives, or for any term of years determinable with a life or lives or on the lessee's marriage was converted by LPA 1925, s. 149, into a lease for *ninety years*. On the end of the life or lives, or on the lessee's marriage, the lease can be determined (where it is a lease at a rent or in consideration of a fine) by the lessee or lessor giving at least a month's notice expiring on a quarter day which has application to the tenancy, or any usual quarter day.

31. Future leases

Under LPA 1925, s. 149, the grant, after 1925, of a lease which will become effective *more than twenty-one years* after the date of such grant is *void*. A contract to grant such a lease is invalid. But a contract to grant a lease which is to commence more than twenty-one years from the date of the contract is not thereby invalidated: *Re Strand & Savoy Properties Ltd* (1960). *See Weg Motors Ltd* v. *Hales* (1961).

32. Tenancies by estoppel

Where X, who has no title to land, leases it to T, and later acquires title to it, that later title is said to 'feed the estoppel' so as to make good T's title. *See Church of England Building Society* v. *Piskor* (1954).

Modes of determination of tenancies and leases

33. General
Tenancies and leaseholds may be determined (i.e. brought to an end) in the following ways:

(a) by forfeiture (*see* **34** below);
(b) by notice to quit (*see* **35** below);
(c) by surrender (*see* **36** below);
(d) by merger (*see* **37** below);
(e) by expiry of agreed period (*see* **38** below);
(f) by enlargement (*see* **39** below);
(g) by becoming a satisfied term (*see* **40** below);
(h) by frustration (*see* **41** below);
(i) by disclaimer (*see* **42** below).

34. Forfeiture
Forfeiture may arise where, as the result of the breach of certain covenants, the lease is considered to be at an end, and where the lessor exercises his rights of re-entry. This is considered at 5:**33.** (Note the Law Commission Report No.142 (1985) on 'Forfeiture of Tenancies', recommending the abolition of the existing law and its replacement by a 'termination order scheme' in which the landlord would base his application for a termination order on a 'termination order event', covering breaches of leasehold covenant or the tenant's bankruptcy.)

35. Notice to quit
Notice must be given in the case of yearly and other periodic tenancies.

(a) The notice must be in accordance with the terms of the lease.
(b) The notice must be unconditional: *Gardner* v. *Ingram* (1889).
(c) Where notice is given by L to T it must relate to the entire premises which are the subject of the lease.
(d) The notice must indicate the correct day on which the tenancy is to end: *Addis* v. *Burrows* (1948). *See Dodds* v. *Walker* (1981).
(e) In some cases covered by the Agricultural Holdings Act 1986, special notice may be required (*see* **24(c)**(*ii*) above).
(f) No notice to quit premises let as a dwelling is valid unless it is *in writing and* contains information prescribed by the Secretary of State by statutory instrument *and* unless it is given not less than *four weeks* before the date on which it is to take effect: Protection from Eviction

Act 1977, s. 5. *See Meretune Investments* v. *Martin* (1984); *Norris* v. *Checksfield* (1991).

(g) *See also* RA 1977, ss. 103–6, as amended; HA 1985, Sch. 2; HA 1988, Part I (requirement of court order); Landlord and Tenant Act 1954.

(h) A notice to quit is invalid if it contains a false statement made fraudulently by L, irrespective of whether T was deceived: *Rous* v. *Mitchell* (1991).

36. Surrender by agreement of both parties

Where T surrenders his lease to L, and L accepts that surrender, the lease is merged in L's reversion and comes to an end. *See Short Bros* v. *Edwards* (1978); *Deanplan* v. *Mahmoud* (1992).

(a) Surrender may be *express*. Where the lease does not exceed a period of three years surrender may be made by written instrument: LPA 1925, ss. 53(1), 54(2). In the case of a lease for a longer period it must be made by deed: LPA 1925, s. 52.

(b) Surrender may arise *from operation of law*, e.g. where a new lease is granted by L to T so that it begins during the currency of an existing lease, or where T delivers possession to L, who accepts it: *Dodd* v. *Acklom* (1843). Such a surrender need not be in written form: LPA 1925, s. 52. *See also Hulme* v. *Langford* (1985).

37. Merger

A right may be determined when it coincides with a greater right in one and the same person. Thus, where T obtains the reversion and keeps the lease, the lease then merges with the reversion and is extinguished (or where L conveys the fee simple to T). *See* LPA 1925, s. 185; *Hoggett* v. *Hoggett* (1979).

38. Expiry of agreed period

In the case of a lease for a fixed period, the tenancy will be determined *automatically* when that period comes to an end. This general rule has no application in the case of a tenancy determining on death, or one which is covered by the Rent Acts, or in the case of a business lease, an agricultural holding, or a dwelling house held on a long lease at a low rent. *See* the Landlord and Tenant Act 1954, Part II. (Note the 'break clause', which is an option to terminate a clause in a lease after a certain period, e.g. at the end of the tenth or fifteenth year of a thirty-year lease.)

39. Enlargement
A lease may be enlarged under LPA 1925, s. 153, into a fee simple. This applies under the following conditions:

(a) the term must have been originally created for not less than 300 years;
(b) there must be an unexpired residue of at least 200 years;
(c) there must be no trust or right of redemption affecting the term in favour of the freeholder or other person entitled in reversion expectant on the term;
(d) there must be no rent of any money value payable;
(e) the lease must not be liable to be determined by re-entry for condition broken.

> NOTE: Where a fee simple is created by enlargement it is subject to the trusts, powers, equities, covenants and obligations the term would have been subject to if it had not been so enlarged: LPA 1925, s. 153(8).

40. Satisfied term
Where a term of years has been created for a certain purpose and that purpose has become satisfied, the term merges in the reversion expectant upon it and ceases accordingly: LPA 1925, s. 5(1).

41. Frustration
In *National Carriers* v. *Panalpina Ltd* (1981), lessees of a warehouse leased for a term of ten years, were deprived of its use, after 5 years, for a period of 20 months, when the local authority closed the only street allowing access by lorries. They claimed that the lease had been frustrated.

(a) The claim was *rejected* by the House of Lords, on the ground that there would still be three years of the lease to run after the disruption had ended.
(b) The House held, however, that *the doctrine of frustration could apply, but only in very rare cases, to leases of land*, and most probably in the case of a short-term lease. (An example might be found where a holiday bungalow, rented for a month, is burned down.)
(c) Lord Hailsham LC stated that he found it difficult to accept the 'strongly-urged difference in principle' between real and chattel

property, once it had been decided, as had long been the case, that time and demise charters even of the largest ships, and of consideration, could in principle be frustrated. He approved of the argument of Lord Justice Atkin, in a dissenting judgment in *Matthey* v. *Curling* (1922), quoted with approval by Viscount Simon in *Cricklewood Property Ltd* v. *Leighton's Investment Trust* (1945) :

> 'It does not appear to me conclusive against the application to a lease of the doctrine of frustration that the lease, in addition to containing contractual terms, grants a term of years. Seeing that the instrument as a rule expressly provides for the lease being determined at the option of the lessor upon the happening of certain specified events, I see no logical absurdity in implying a term that it shall be determined absolutely on the happening of other events, namely, those which, in the ordinary contract work a frustration.'

42. Disclaimer

Where the tenant denies the landlord's title, the lease is automatically liable to forfeiture: *see* e.g. *Warner* v. *Sampson* (1959). For disclaimer by a trustee in bankruptcy of a lease owned by the bankrupt, see the Insolvency Act 1986, s. 315. *See W.G. Clark Ltd* v. *Dupre Properties* (1991) (L's title denied in part by T); *Re Yarmarine* (1992).

Progress test 4

1. What is the meaning of 'term of years absolute'? **(4)**

2. 'Leases must be of a certain duration.' Discuss. **(12)**

3. Consider the formalities of a lease. **(16)**

4. How has recent legislation affected leases made by deed? **(18)**

5. Outline the essence of the tenancy from year to year. **(24, 25)**

6. What is the situation concerning perpetually renewable leases? **(29)**

7.   Explain the principles of 'notice to quit' in relation to yearly and other periodic tenancies.   **(35)**

8.   Comment on *National Carriers* v. *Panalpina Ltd.* (1981).   **(41)**

5
The term of years (2)

Rights and obligations of lessor and lessee

1. Rights and obligations

When a lease is created, certain rights vest in the lessor, such as the right to receive rent, and in the lessee, such as the right to quiet enjoyment of the premises leased. Correlative duties or obligations also come into existence, e.g. the obligation of the lessor to allow quiet enjoyment, and the obligation of the lessee to pay the agreed rent. Among the lessor's *express statutory obligations* are: duties concerning fitness and repair of premises (*see* **13** below); disclosure of specified information, e.g. landlord's identity (*see* Landlord and Tenant Act 1985, s. 1(1)); provision of rent book (1985 Act, s. 4(1)).

2. Covenants

A covenant is an agreement which creates an obligation, and which is contained in a deed. A *positive covenant* stipulates the performance of a certain act; a *negative or restrictive covenant* prohibits the commission of a certain act.

(a) Rights and obligations, in the case of lessor and lessee, are stated in *express covenants* which form part of the lease.
(b) Certain covenants, while they may not be stated expressly in the lease are, nevertheless, *implied*.
(c) The so-called *usual covenants* are considered at **3** below.

3. The 'usual covenants'

Where a lease does not specify covenants, but merely makes reference to the 'usual covenants', these are generally held to refer to: covenant by the lessee to pay rent and taxes; covenant to keep the premises in repair and to deliver them up in repair; condition for re-entry on the lessee's non-payment of rent; covenant to allow the lessor to view the state of repairs; covenant on the lessor's part to allow quiet enjoyment: *Hampshire* v. *Wickens* (1878).

(a) Covenants other than those mentioned above might be held to be 'usual'. 'If it is established that... in nine cases out of ten the covenant would be found in a lease of premises of that nature for that purpose and in that district, I think the court is bound to hold that the covenant is usual': *per* Maugham J in *Flexman* v. *Corbett* (1930).

(b) The court will consider all the circumstances of the case in deciding whether a certain covenant may be classified as 'usual'. *See* comments of Foster J in *Chester* v. *Buckingham Travel Ltd* (1981) — where parties are unable to agree terms of a lease, the covenants to be inserted therein are those usually to be found in leases of similar premises at the date of agreement. (A covenant that the premises are 'fit for habitation' is *not* a 'usual covenant'.)

Implied rights of the lessee

4.   The right to certain fixtures

In some cases a lessee is entitled to remove so-called 'tenants' fixtures' on the determination of the lease. This is considered at **1:24(b)**.

5.   The right to emblements and estovers

Emblements are the vegetable products resulting annually from agricultural labour. (Note the Sale of Goods Act 1979, s. 61(1).) *Estovers* are the rights to wood and timber for certain repairs.

(a) *The right to emblements.* A lessee, or his personal representatives, may enter after the determination of the lease so as to reap certain crops which the lessee has sown: *Graves* v. *Weld* (1833): see **12:5.**
  - (*i*)   The right arises in the case of *cultivated crops*, e.g. corn. It does not arise in the case of timber.
  - (*ii*)   The right arises in the case of crops sown by the lessee which are growing at the time at which the lease comes to an end.

(b) *Estovers* (*estovoir* = to be necessary). A lessee may take wood or timber (*see* **7(a)(i)** below) for certain necessary and immediate repairs:
  - (*i*)   hay-bote (for the repair of fences and hedges);
  - (*ii*)   house-bote (for the repair of a house, or for fuel);
  - (*iii*)   plough-bote (for the making and repairing of agricultural implements).

6.   Other implied rights

A lessee may be given rights by statute in some cases, for example under the Agricultural Holdings Act 1986, s. 60. Where a lessee of an agricultural holding quits as the result of notice given by the lessor, he is entitled to compensation for disturbance, unless the notice has been given for certain reasons specified in the Act.

Implied obligations of the lessee

7. The obligation to repair and not to commit waste

A tenant for *yearly and other periodic tenancies* is expected generally to keep the leased premises in 'a tenant-like manner': *Marsden* v. *Edward Heyes Ltd* (1927). (*Per* Denning LJ in *Warren* v. *Keen* (1954): 'The tenant must take proper care of the place... he must do the little jobs about the place which a reasonable tenant must do. In addition, he must not damage the house, wilfully or negligently; and he must see that his family and guests do not damage it; and if they do he must repair it. But apart from such things, if the house falls into disrepair through fair wear and tear or lapse of time or for any reason not caused by him, then the tenant is not liable to repair it.') *See Barrett* v. *Lounova Ltd* (1989). The tenant may have an obligation, also, in relation to *waste*.

(a) *Waste* consists of acts which alter the nature of the land. ('Waste is a familiar term of art in the law of real property and carries the meaning of damage or prejudice to the reversion': *per* Cumming-Bruce LJ in *Somma* v. *Hazelhurst* (1978).)

   (i) *Voluntary waste* arises from an injury to the land actively caused by the tenant, e.g. cutting timber: *Honywood* v. *Honywood* (1874).

   (ii) *Permissive waste* arises from an omission by the tenant to do that which should be done, e.g. failing to repair buildings: *Powys* v. *Blagrave* (1854).

   (iii) *Ameliorating waste* consists of alterations which, in fact, improve the land: *Doherty* v. *Allman* (1878) — injunction refused in the case of a tenant who was converting old and dilapidated store houses into dwellings.

   (iv) *Equitable waste* consists of malicious or wanton destruction of property, e.g. destruction of trees planted for shelter or ornament, or stripping a house of its glass and doors, etc.: *Vane* v. *Lord Barnard* (1716); *Weld-Blundell* v. *Wolseley* (1903). It was described by Lord Campbell in *Turner* v. *Wright* (1860) as 'that which a prudent man would not do in the management of his own property.' (*See* 12:**6**.)

(b) *A tenant for years* is liable for permissive and voluntary waste, unless excluded by agreement: *Davies* v. *Davies* (1888).

(c) *A yearly tenant* is liable for voluntary waste.

(d) *A weekly tenant* is not liable for permissive waste: *Warren* v. *Keen* (1954).

(e) *A tenant at will* who commits voluntary waste is liable in damages, and his tenancy may be terminated as a result: *Countess of Shrewsbury's Case* (1600).

(f) *A tenant at sufferance* is liable for voluntary waste.

NOTE: The liability of the tenant for life for waste is discussed at 12:**6**.

8.   The obligation to allow the lessor to view the state of repair of the premises
A lessee must allow the lessor to enter for this purpose: *Mint* v. *Good* (1951). The lessor may have a statutory right to enter: Agricultural Holdings Act 1986, s. 23.

9.   The obligation to pay rent, rates and taxes
Note, concerning rent, the comments of Lord Denning in *C. H. Bailey Ltd* v. *Memorial Enterprises Ltd* (1974): 'The time and manner of the payment is to be ascertained according to the true construction of the contract, and not by reference to outdated relics of medieval law.' (It was held in this case that rent may be payable from a date which has passed notwithstanding that the sum due was not ascertained at that date.) Note, further, the comments of Lord Diplock in *United Scientific Holdings* v. *Burnley BC* (1977): 'The medieval concept of rent as a service rendered by the tenant to the landlord has been displaced by the modern concept of a payment which a tenant is bound by his contract to pay to the landlord for the use of his land.' There is an implied obligation that the lessee will pay rates and taxes, other than those for which the lessor is directly liable.

Implied obligations of the lessor

10. The obligation to allow the lessee quiet enjoyment
There is in a lease an implied covenant that the lessee's peaceful enjoyment of the premises shall not be interfered with by the lessor or by any person who claims under him. The covenant covers all conduct which interferes with the tenant's freedom of action in

exercising his rights as tenant: *per* Lord Denning in *McCall* v. *Abelesz* (1976). This applies to all types of tenancy, whether created by deed or orally: *Markham* v. *Paget* (1908). (For unlawful eviction or harassment of a tenant, *see* Protection from Eviction Act 1977, s. 1, at 7:**4, 5**.) *See*, e.g. *Queensway Marketing* v. *Associated Restaurants* (1984).

(a) 'Quiet' is not restricted to absence of noise. It involves freedom to enjoy the property without disturbance: *Jenkins* v. *Jackson* (1888). *See Browne* v. *Flower* (1911). (L built a staircase outside T's bedroom window; T claimed that this interfered with his privacy. It was held that L's action did not amount to a breach of covenant. 'There must be some physical interference with the enjoyment of the demised premises . . . A mere interference with the comfort of persons using the demised premises by the creation of a personal annoyance such as might arise from . . . invasion of privacy is not enough': *per* Parker J.)

(b) Examples of the breaking of such an implied covenant: *Kenny* v. *Preen* (1963) — L attempted to drive out T by threatening him; *Markham* v. *Paget* (1908) — L's mining caused a subsidence of premises leased to T; *Lavender* v. *Betts* (1942) — removal of doors and windows; *Owen* v. *Gadd* (1956) — erecting scaffolding in front of access to a shop.

(c) The lessee may recover damages if his quiet enjoyment is disturbed in *a substantial way*. *See Sampson* v. *Hodson-Pressinger* (1981).

(d) The lessee has no remedy under the covenant if the disturbance results from the activities of some person who claims under a title paramount, i.e. as superior landlord: *Baynes & Co* v. *Lloyd & Sons* (1895). *See Celsteel* v. *Alton House Ltd* (No. 2) (1987).

11. The obligation not to derogate from his grant

The general principle is that *a grantor may not derogate from his grant*, i.e. he may not act so as to make difficult the use of that which he has granted: *Aldin* v. *Latimer Clark, Muirhead & Co* (1894) — flow of air to timber drying sheds on land leased for timber merchant's business was interrupted by landlord's building operations on adjoining land. *See also Ward* v. *Kirkland* (1967).

(a) The obligation extends to persons claiming under the lessor.

(b) The essence of a derogation in this context is that the fitness of the property for the purposes for which it was let is reduced substantially, i.e. if property is 'rendered unfit or materially less fit to be used for the purpose for which it was demised': *per* Parker J in *Browne* v. *Flower* (1911).

12. Implied contractual duty of care

The House of Lords held, in *Liverpool CC* v. *Irwin* (1977), that some duties of care on the part of the landlord could be *implied* in a contract of tenancy. In this case it was held that the council had a contractual duty to take reasonable care to keep in reasonable repair and usability the common facilities in a highrise block. The duty could be excluded, however, by express contractual limitation. For a landlord's liability in negligence for defects arising after commencement of a tenancy, *see*, e.g. *Sharpe* v. *Manchester CC* (1977). For a landlord's liability for nuisance, *see*, e.g. *Guppys Ltd* v. *Brookling* (1984) (disconnection of water and electricity).

13. The obligation that the premises shall be reasonably fit for human habitation

There is no generally implied covenant of fitness for human habitation. But in some circumstances such an obligation may arise.

(a) In the case of *furnished lettings* there is (in the absence of any agreement to the contrary) an implied undertaking that they are fit for habitation at the time of the letting: *Smith* v. *Marrable* (1843).

(*i*) In *Smith* v. *Marrable* (1843), T, on taking possession, found the premises infested with bugs. It was held that this rendered the leased, furnished premises unfit for habitation so that T was entitled to quit without giving notice.

(*ii*) *Per* Parke B: 'If the demised premises are incumbered with a nuisance of so serious a nature that no person can reasonably be expected to live in them, the tenant is at liberty to throw them up.'

(*iii*) There is *no* obligation on the landlord to keep the premises fit for habitation *after* the lease has taken effect: *Sarson* v. *Roberts* (1895).

(*iv*) The implied obligation does *not* extend to unfurnished premises, or to non-residential tenancies.

(*v*) Matters of ordinary disrepair, making habitability merely unpleasant, are *not* covered by the obligation.

(b) *Landlord and Tenant Act 1985, s. 8(1)*. In the case of tenancies *at low rents*, there are implied terms that the dwelling house is fit for human habitation at the commencement of the tenancy and that it will be kept by the landlord fit for human habitation during the tenancy. Defects which might render the dwelling unfit refer, e.g. to condition of repair, sanitation, drainage: s. 10. (Note that s. 8 does *not* apply to a tenancy for three years or more: s. 8(5).)

(c) *Landlord and Tenant Act 1985, s. 11, amended by HA 1988, s. 116.*

This section applies generally to the lease of a dwelling-house (or part of a house) granted after October 1961, for a term of less than seven years. The landlord has an obligation to keep in repair 'the structure and exterior of the dwelling-house (including drains, gutters and external pipes) . . . to keep in repair and proper working order the installations in the dwelling house for the supply of water, gas and electricity and for sanitation (including basins, sinks . . .) . . . to keep in repair and proper working order the installations for space heating and heating water.' *See Irvine* v. *Moran* (1991) (the 'structure of the dwelling-house' consists of those elements which give the premises their essential appearance, stability and shape); *King* v. *S. Northants DC* (1992).

(d) *Defective Premises Act 1972, s. 4.* Where a landlord has an obligation to the tenant for maintenance or repair of premises, the landlord owes to all persons who might reasonably be expected to be affected by defects in the state of the premises, a duty to take such care as is reasonable in all the circumstances to see that they are reasonably safe from personal injury or from damage to their property caused by a relevant defect. *See Pirelli Cables* v. *Faber* (1983); *McAuley* v. *Bristol CC* (1991).

See Rimmer v. *Liverpool CC* (1985); *McNerny* v. *Lambeth LBC* (1988); *Andrews* v. *Schooling* (1991).

NOTE: A local authority is empowered to issue 'repair notices' in respect of unfit houses (*see* HA 1985, Part IV) and to make an annual review of housing conditions to determine what action to take: *see* Local Government and Housing Act 1989, Sch. 9. *See also* HA 1988, Sch. 15; Public Health Act 1936, s. 92; Building Act 1984, s. 76 (serving of landlord with nine-day notice in case of urgency); 1989 Act, Part VIII (grant-aid towards cost of repairs); *Law Commission Report (1992) No. 123* (responsibilities for state and repair of properties).

Express covenant not to assign or underlet, etc.

14. Absolute and qualified covenants

Where there is *no express prohibition* in the lease, a lessee may, at common law, freely assign the lease or underlet, etc., without the consent of the lessor. Note that *express covenants* against assigning, etc. have been construed strictly: *see Marks* v. *Warren* (1979); *Field* v. *Barkworth* (1986). Note also that 'the usual covenants' (*see* **3** above) will not include any covenant which purports to alter the position at common law.

(a) An *absolute covenant* involves an *unconditional prohibition* against assigning etc. although it may be waived by the landlord. *See*, e.g. *Chrisdell* v. *Johnson* (1987).

(b) *A qualified covenant* prohibits assignment, underletting, etc. *without the consent of the landlord.* Under the Landlord and Tenant Act 1927, s. 19(1), such consent shall not be unreasonably withheld. *See*, e.g. *Woolworth* v. *Charlwood Properties* (1987); *Fuller* v. *Judy Properties* (1991).

(c) The question of whether a refusal to consent is reasonable or not is considered in the context of all the circumstances.

(d) The problem of unreasonableness of consent was reviewed by the Court of Appeal in *International Drilling Fluids Ltd* v. *Louisville Investments Ltd* (1986). The Court of Appeal held that in every such case it is a question of fact whether the landlord's consent is being unreasonably withheld; that in every case the test is objective; and that while a landlord need usually only consider his own relevant interests, there may be cases where there is such a disproportion between the benefit to the landlord and the detriment to the tenant if the landlord withholds his consent, that it is unreasonable for the landlord to refuse consent.

15. Other relevant statutes

See LPA 1925, s. 144; Sex Discrimination Act 1975, s. 31; Race Relations Act 1976, s. 24(1); HA 1985, ss. 93, 94; Landlord and Tenant Act 1988 (*see* **16, 17** below).

16. Landlord and Tenant Act 1988

This Act has imposed *new provisions relating to covenants in tenancies against assigning, etc. without consent.*

(a) Section 1 imposes a *qualified duty to consent* to assigning, underletting, etc. of premises. It applies where a tenancy includes a covenant on the part of the tenant not to enter into one or more of the following transactions, that is, assigning, underletting, charging or parting with the possession of premises comprised in the tenancy or any part of the premises without the consent of the landlord, *but* the covenant is subject to the qualification that the consent is not to be unreasonably withheld (whether or not it is also subject to any other qualification): s. 1(a), (b).

(b) Where there is served on the person who may consent to a proposed transaction a *written application* by the tenant for consent to the transaction, he owes a duty to the tenant within a reasonable time, to give consent, *except* in a case where it is reasonable not to give consent, to serve on the tenant *written notice* of his decision whether or not to give consent, specifying in addition, if the consent is given subject to conditions, the conditions, or if the consent is withheld, the reasons for withholding it: s. 1(3). Note that giving consent subject to an unreasonable condition does not satisfy the duty under s. 1(3): s. 1(4); and that 'served' means served in any manner provided in the tenancy, and, in respect of any matter for which the tenancy makes no provision, served in any manner provided by the Landlord and Tenant Act 1927, s. 23: s. 5(2).

(c) For the purposes of the 1988 Act it is reasonable for a person not to give consent to a proposed transaction only in a case where, if he withheld consent and the tenant completed the transaction, the tenant would be in breach of covenant: s. 1(5).

(d) It is for the person who owed any duty under s. 1(3): if he gave consent, and the question arises whether he gave it within a reasonable time, to show that he did; if he gave consent subject to any condition and the question arises whether the condition was reasonable, to show that it was; if he did not give consent and the question arises whether it was reasonable for him not to do so, to show that it was reasonable; and, if the question arises whether he served notice under s. 1(3), within a reasonable time, to show that he did: s. 1(6).

(e) In *Midland Bank* v. *Chart Enterprises* (1990), it was held that where L had failed for nearly three months to respond to T's request for a licence to assign, and had delayed further, they had unreasonably delayed in communicating their decision to T within the 1988 Act, ss. 1, 6.

17. Other provisions of the 1988 Act

A claim that a person has broken any duty under the Act may be made the subject of civil proceedings in like manner as any other claim in tort for breach of statutory duty: s. 4. The Act does not apply to a secure tenancy (*see* 9:3): s. 5(3). The Act applies only to applications for consent or approval served after its coming into force: s. 5(4).

Express covenant to repair

18. The extent of liability

Where there is an express covenant to repair, the covenantor must maintain the premises in a condition in which they would be maintained by a reasonably minded owner, taking into account their age, locality and character: *Proudfoot* v. *Hart* (1890). In the case of a plain breach of L's covenant to repair, the court may order *specific performance* of the covenant: *Jeune* v. *Queen's Cross Properties* (1973). See *Stent* v. *Monmouth* (1987) — repair of defective front door; *Hammond* v. *Allen* (1992). For a review of 'repair' cases, *see Elite Investments* v. *Bainbridge Silencers* (1986).

19. 'Wear and tear'

Where a repairing covenant exempts the covenantor from liability for reasonable wear and tear, 'the tenant is bound to do such repairs as may be required to prevent the consequences flowing originally from wear and tear from producing others which wear and tear would not directly produce': *per* Talbot J in *Haskell* v. *Marlow* (1928). He is not liable, therefore, for the repair of damage resulting from the reasonable use of the property. *See Regis Property* v. *Dudley* (1959).

20. Notice and damages

Liability upon the covenant to repair does not arise until L has notice of the damage to the property: *Torrens* v. *Walker* (1906); *O'Brien* v. *Robinson* (1973).

(a) Under the Landlord and Tenant Act 1927, damages for the breach of a covenant to repair must not exceed the sum by which the value of the reversion has diminished: s. 18. *See Haviland* v. *Long* (1952).

(b) Damages are not recoverable if the premises are to be demolished or altered so as to render the repairs valueless, at, or soon after, the end of the tenancy: Landlord and Tenant Act 1927, s. 18: *Cunliffe* v. *Goodman* (1950). See *Family Management* v. *Gray* (1979); *Mather* v. *Barclays Bank* (1987).

(c) In *British Anzani Ltd* v. *International Marine Management* (1979), it was held that a tenant who does not pay his rent because of the landlord's breach of covenant to repair can set off damages for breach in a landlord's action for recovery of rent.

(d) The tenant is not entitled to treat the lease as being at an end merely because the landlord is in breach of covenant to repair: *Surplice* v. *Farnsworth* (1844).

(e) Notice of want of repair is required, even where the defect is latent: *see Morgan v. Liverpool Corp.* (1927); *O'Brien* v. *Robinson* (1973).

(f) *See* Consultation Paper — *Landlord and Tenant: Responsibility for State and Condition of Property* (Law Commission (1992), No. 123).

21. By statute
Relevant statutes are:

(a) LPA 1925, s. 147(1), which empowers the court to grant relief against notice to effect decorative repairs 'if the court is satisfied that the notice is unreasonable'. But this does not apply where liability arises under express covenant and it has never been performed: s. 147(2).

(b) Leasehold Property (Repairs) Act 1938, as amended. In the case of premises, except an agricultural holding, let for not less than seven years, should *three years* remain unexpired, L cannot recover damages for breach of a repairing covenant unless he has served on T, at least one month prior to the action, a notice stating the breach of the covenant, requiring it to be remedied, and demanding compensation. T may serve a counter-notice, under LPA 1925, s. 146, within twenty-eight days. *See also Land Securities* v. *Receiver for MPD* (1983); *Associated British Ports* v. *C.H. Bailey plc* (1990).

Express covenant to insure against fire

22. Covenant to insure
The lessee is expected to insure the premises for their *full value* during the entire period of the lease. If the premises are uninsured even for a short period, the covenant is broken: *Penniall* v. *Harborne* (1848).

23. Insurance with a named company
Where T covenants to insure the premises with a named company, L may refuse to approve an insurance with another company and he is not obliged to state his reasons for refusal: *Viscount Tredegar* v. *Harwood* (1929).

Express covenant to pay rent

24. General
Rent is usually payable in arrear, unless the lease expressly refers to payment in advance: *Coomber* v. *Howard* (1845). Liability for the payment of rent continues even after the occurrence of an event which renders the premises incapable of being used: *Matthey* v. *Curling* (1922) — destruction by fire; *Crown Land Commissioners* v. *Page* (1960) — requisition by the Crown.

(a) The rent must be certain. It will be sufficiently certain if it is possible to calculate it at the time payment is to be made: *Greater London Council* v. *Connolly* (1970).

(b) If the covenant does not state the exact dates on which payment of rent is due, it will be held to be due at the end of the periods by reference to which the rent has been assessed.

25. Enforcement of the covenant

Several remedies are available to the lessor. These are discussed below.

Remedies concerning a covenant for rent

26. General

A landlord may enforce the covenant for payment of rent in the following ways:

(a) by an action for recovery of arrears (*see* **27** below);

(b) by distress (*see* **28** below);

(c) by forfeiture (*see* **29** below).

27. Action for recovery of arrears

Under LA 1980, s. 19 (*see* Ch. 21), arrears of rent recoverable by action are limited to *six years*. An action for recovery may not be brought if the lessor has levied distress, until the property so distrained has been sold and found to be of an inadequate value: *Archbold* v. *Scully* (1861).

28. Right of distress

The right to levy distress is the right of the landlord to remove certain property from the possession of a person in order to compel that person to perform an obligation.

(a) *At common law.* The landlord was allowed only to retain goods taken, until the Distress for Rent Act 1689, which permitted him to sell them. Distress could be levied not earlier than the day after rent was due, but could not be levied between sunset and sunrise, or on Sundays.

    (*i*) *What may be seized.* In general, any personal chattels found on the leased premises may be taken.

    (*ii*) *What may not be seized.* Animals *ferae naturae*; live-stock and machinery belonging to a third person; clothes, bedding and tools up to a value fixed by order; things in actual use; perishables.

(iii) *What may be seized only if there are not sufficient distrainable goods on the premises.* Sheep; beasts of the plough; instruments used in a man's trade or profession.

(b) *Levying a distress.* A certificated bailiff (one who has a certificate granted by the County Court) must be employed: Law of Distress Amendment Act 1888, s. 7. After the goods are seized and impounded the lessee must be given notice of the place to which the goods have been removed. After five days, during which the lessee may pay arrears of rent (or fifteen days, if security is given) a sale, usually by auction, is held. *See* **7:6**.

(c) *Arrears recoverable.* Six years' arrears of rent are recoverable by distress. In the case of an agricultural holding, one year's arrears only may be recovered by distress: Agricultural Holdings Act 1986, s. 16.

29. Forfeiture

The lease may give the landlord a right (i.e. a proprietary interest) to re-enter the land on non-payment of rent. *See* LPA 1925, ss. 1(2)(e), 146. (Note that a landlord who uses force to re-enter may be guilty of an offence under the Criminal Law Act 1977, ss. 6, 7.) *See also* Supreme Court Act 1981, s. 38; *Di Palma* v. *Victoria Square Property Co.* (1986); *United Dominions Trust* v. *Shellpoint Trustees* (1992).

(a) A demand for the rent must be made formally, *unless* the landlord is exempted from making a demand (*see* **(b)** below). The exact sum must be demanded on the day payment falls due, and the demand must be made on the leased premises: *Duppa* v. *Mayo* (1669).

(b) If the lease refers to rent 'whether formally demanded or not', the landlord need not make a demand in formal fashion. Additionally, the Common Law Procedure Act 1852, enacted that a formal demand in an action for forfeiture need not be made if half a year's rent is in arrear, and if distrainable goods are insufficient to satisfy all arrears: s. 210.

(c) A tenant may stay proceedings by paying arrears and costs before the trial: Common Law Procedure Act 1852, s. 212. (*See also* County Courts Act 1984, s. 138(2) and Administration of Justice Act 1985, s. 55(2).)

(d) Forfeiture usually involves an action for possession. *See*, e.g. Rent Act 1977, s. 98.

30. Relief in equity

Where a tenant has paid the rent due under the lease and any expenses incurred by his landlord, and where the court considers that, in all the circumstances, *it is just and equitable to grant relief,* the court's discretion can be exercised so that, in spite of the lease's having been forfeited, the tenant will be restored to his former position: *Belgravia Insurance Co.* v. *Meah* (1963). Application must be made within six months from the landlord's re-entry: Common Law Procedure Act 1852. Where the court grants relief, the tenant will hold under the existing lease.

31. Waiver

Following the commission of an act of forfeiture, the landlord may continue to consider the lease as in existence, e.g. by claiming rent accruing after the breach: *Central Estates (Belgravia) Ltd* v. *Woolgar (No. 2)* (1972). *See Official Custodian of Charities* v. *Parway Estates* (1984); *Chrisdell Ltd* v. *Johnson* (1987).

(a) Waiver arises only where L is aware that T has committed an act of forfeiture.

(b) Waiver may be express or implied. It involves, essentially, an act by L which assumes the continuation of the lease, e.g. granting a new lease to run from the original date of expiration of the forfeited lease: *Ward* v. *Day* (1864).

(c) Waiver is implied only if L knows the facts and 'does some unequivocal act recognising the continued existence of the lease. . . Therefore, though an act of waiver operates with regard to all known breaches, it does not operate with regard to breaches which were unknown to the lessor at the time when the act took place': *per* Parker J in *Matthews* v. *Smallwood* (1910).

(d) A statement or act by L which is not communicated to T will not constitute an act of waiver: *London & County Ltd* v. *Wilfred Sportsman Ltd* (1971).

Remedies concerning other covenants

32. Failure to observe non-rent covenants

L may sue T and may claim damages, or he may seek an injunction in the case of T's failing to observe non-rent covenants. *See,* e.g. *Expert Clothing Ltd* v. *Hillgate House Ltd* (1986) (*see* **37** below); *Darlington BC* v. *Denmark Chemists Ltd* (1992).

33. Forfeiture and LPA 1925, s. 146(1)

'A right of re-entry or forfeiture under any proviso or stipulation in a lease for a breach of any covenant or condition in the lease shall not be enforceable, by action or otherwise, *unless and until the lessor serves on the lessee a notice*:

(a) specifying the particular breach complained of; and
(b) if the breach is capable of remedy, requiring the lessee to remedy the breach; and
(c) in any case, requiring the lessee to make compensation in money for the breach;

and the lessee fails, within a reasonable time thereafter, to remedy the breach, if it is capable of remedy, and to make reasonable compensation in money, to the satisfaction of the lessor, for the breach.'

See Hagee v. *Co-operative Insurance Society* (1992).

34. LPA 1925, s. 146(2)

'Where a lessor is proceeding, by action or otherwise, to enforce such a right of re-entry or forfeiture, the lessee may, in the lessor's action, if any, or in any action brought by himself, apply to the court for relief; and the court may grant or refuse relief, as the court, having regard to the proceedings and conduct of the parties under the foregoing provisions of this section, and to all the other circumstances, thinks fit; and in case of relief may grant it on such terms, if any, as to costs, expenses, damages, compensation, penalty, or otherwise, including the granting of an injunction to restrain any like breach in the future, as the court, in the circumstances of each case, thinks fit.'

See Shiloh Spinners v. *Harding* (1973); *St Marylebone Property Co.* v. *Tesco* (1988).

35. LPA 1925, s. 146(4)

Where a head lease (i.e. one from which lesser interests have been created) is forfeited, a sub-lease created from it is destroyed *automatically*. An underlessee may apply for relief against forfeiture of the head lease. *See* LP (Am.)A 1929; *Abbey National BS* v. *Maybeech* (1985).

36. Covenants, for the breach of which statutory notice need not be served

Such covenants include, for example, the following.

(a) A covenant for inspection in a mining lease, where a mining tenant fails to provide access to books and accounts: LPA 1925, s. 146(8)(ii). (For 'mining lease', *see* LPA 1925, s. 205(1)(xiv).)

(b) A covenant concerning forfeiture on the tenant's bankruptcy: LPA 1925, s. 146(9). Statutory provisions concerning notice are excluded in the case of leases involving: a furnished house; a public house; mines; agricultural land; property the value or character of which will be affected by the tenant's personal qualifications. Forfeiture, without possibility of relief, may follow bankruptcy of the tenant in these cases.

    (*i*) Where the land leased is not in these categories and where the lessee's interest is sold within one year of his bankruptcy, the statutory provisions will apply without any time limit and the lessee may apply for relief.

    (*ii*) Where the lessee's interest is not sold within one year of his bankruptcy, the statutory provisions will have application during that year only.

37. Further points concerning s. 146

The following should be noted:

(a) The section has effect notwithstanding any stipulation to the contrary: s. 146(12).

(b) For non-application of the section (e.g. as in the case of a covenant to pay rent), *see* s. 146(8), (9).

(c) In *Expert Clothing Service* v. *Hillgate House Ltd* (1986), T agreed with L to convert the premises but failed to do so, because of a shortage of funds, and L issued a notice under s. 146, claiming that the breach of covenant was irremediable. The Court of Appeal held that a breach of a positive covenant, whether a continuing or a once and for all breach, is ordinarily capable of remedy by performance of the covenant and the payment of compensation. The landlords had suffered no irremediable loss, the breach could be remedied and the issue of a s. 146 notice was invalid.

(d) In *Billson* v. *Residential Apartments* (1992), the House of Lords held that where L peaceably re-entered without the benefit of a court order, T could still apply for relief against forfeiture. (*See also Fuller* v. *Judy Properties* (1992).)

> NOTE: For breach of a covenant 'not to do or permit to be done on the premises anything which may be or become a nuisance or annoyance or be injurious or detrimental to the reputation of the premises', *see Commercial General Administration* v. *Thomsett* (1979). *See also GMS Syndicate Ltd* v. *Gary Elliot Ltd* (1982).

The problem of the running of covenants affecting land

38. The general problem

At *common law*, no person may sue, or may be sued, on a contract unless he is a party to that contract. At common law, also, the parties to a contract may assign the benefit, but not the burden of a contract. The problem is, therefore: 'In what circumstances, if any, may persons other than L and T be sued, or sue, upon covenants in a lease?'

39. The problem exemplified

L assigns his reversion to X. May X be sued upon a covenant in favour of T? T assigns his interest to Y. May Y be sued upon a covenant in favour of L?

40. The general rule

A covenant in a lease may be enforceable in circumstances such as those mentioned in **39** above:

(a) when the covenants 'touch and concern' the land;
(b) when privity of contract or privity of estate exists between the party suing, and the party sued. (By 'privity of estate' is meant a current legal relationship arising from successive interests in the same leasehold estate. A test of its existence is that one party pays rent to another.)

> NOTE: 'A person may take an immediate or other interest in land or other property, or the benefit of any condition, right of entry, covenant or agreement over or respecting land or other property, although he may not be named as a party to the conveyance or other instrument': LPA 1925, s. 56(1).

41. Covenants which 'touch and concern' the land

Such covenants are those which have *direct reference to the land*, i.e. which refer to the subject matter of the lease, and affect the landlord *qua* landlord and the tenant *qua* tenant. *See Congleton Corp.* v. *Patterson* (1808); LPA 1925, ss. 141, 142 (benefit and burden of covenants of this nature run with the reversion).

(a) *Covenants held to touch and concern the land.* To renew a lease, *Weg Motors Ltd* v. *Hales* (1961); to repair property or fixtures, *Williams* v. *Earle* (1868); not to build on part of the adjoining land, *Ricketts* v. *Enfield Churchwardens* (1909); to deal exclusively in one brand of oil in a leased filling station, *Regent Oil Co.* v. *Gregory Ltd* (1966).
(b) *Covenants held not to touch and concern the land.* To pay an annual

sum to a third party, *Mayho* v. *Buckhurst* (1617); not to open another public house within a stated distance, *Thomas* v. *Hayward* (1869); to repair houses in the neighbourhood, *Dewar* v. *Goodman* (1909).

42. 'Touch and concern the land': recent decisions

In *Kumar* v. *Dunning* (1987), the Court of Appeal held that a guarantee of obligations which touch and concern demised land is capable of constituting a covenant running with the land. The decision was affirmed by the House of Lords in *Swift Investments* v. *Combined English Stores Group* (1988): a covenant by a surety guaranteeing payment of rent under a lease is a covenant 'touching and concerning the land' *and runs with the land*: hence, if the reversion of the lease is assigned, the assignee can enforce payment of the rent by the surety if the tenant defaults in payment of the rent. Lord Oliver proposed the following test to ascertain whether a covenant did 'touch and concern' the land:

(a) the covenant should benefit only the reversioner for the time being;
(b) the covenant should affect the nature, quality and mode of user or value of the reversioner's land;
(c) the covenant should not be expressed as being personal;
(d) the fact that a covenant involved payment of a sum of money should not prevent its touching and concerning the land provided that the three conditions above were satisfied and the covenant was connected with something to be done, on, to, or in relation to the land.

43. Common law and statutory rules

The common law rules were enunciated in *Spencer's Case* (1583).

(a) Where T assigns his interest to X, X can be sued on covenants which touch and concern the land: *Spencer's Case* (1583); LPA 1925, s. 79. ('(1) A covenant relating to any land of a covenantor or capable of being bound by him shall, unless a contrary intention is expressed, be deemed to be made by the covenantor on behalf of himself, his successors in title, and the persons deriving title under him or them, and, subject as aforesaid, shall have effect as if such successors and other persons were expressed.')
(b) Where T assigns his interest to X, X can sue on the covenants which touch and concern the land, and which are included in the lease in T's favour: *Spencer's Case* (1583).

(c) Where L assigns his reversion to Y, Y can be sued on those covenants included in the lease in T's favour: LPA 1925, s. 142(1).

(d) Where L assigns his reversion to Y, Y can enforce those covenants included in the lease in L's favour.

44. Enforcement of the covenants
This is possible only:

(a) if the *entire interest* is transferred: *South of England Dairies Co.* v. *Baker* (1906);

(b) if *either* privity of contract *or* privity of estate exists between the parties.

    (*i*) Privity of contract exists for the whole term of the lease between L and T, and arises from the contract between them. It continues to exist *after assignment* of interests. Note LPA 1922, Sch. 15, para. 11(i).

    (*ii*) Privity of estate exists between parties A and B, who hold the estates which were created under the lease between L and T. (Even though A and B have not contracted with each other, there is, between them, a relationship of tenure.)

Example:

L leases land to T. T then assigns his interest to X. X then assigns to Y. Assume that Y is in breach of a covenant which is held to touch and concern the land. In such a case L may sue T, since there is privity of estate between them. L may sue Y, since there is privity of estate between them. L may not sue X, since neither privity of contract, nor privity of estate, exists between them.

Recent legislation affecting regulation of leases

45. Recent tendencies
In the twentieth century, particularly since the end of the First World War, tendencies towards state interference in the landlord-tenant relationship have been marked. In general, Parliament has been concerned with the protection of the tenant, and the resulting legislation, which has affected in considerable measure the rights of tenants and landlords, has been wide in scope and complex in nature. It is noted below merely as exemplifying the continuing tendency towards statutory regulation of leases. For further detail, *see* Chapters 7, 8.

46. The agricultural tenancy

Reference is made elsewhere in the text to some of the provisions of the Agricultural Holdings Act 1986. In general, at least 12 months' notice to quit must be given to tenants of agricultural holdings, but such notice will not be effective without the consent of the Agricultural Land Tribunal, provided that T serves a counter-notice on L within one month of receipt of notice. *See* ss. 26, 27. *See also* HA 1988, ss. 24, 25, ('assured agricultural occupancies'); Agricultural Holdings (Amendment) Act 1990; *Rous* v. *Mitchell* (1991).

(a) A counter-notice is ineffective in certain cases, e.g. where T has been certified by the Tribunal as having been farming in a manner not in accordance with the rules of good husbandry. *See* Agricultural Holdings Act 1986, s. 27.
(b) Where none of the cases applies, the Tribunal must decide whether to consent to a termination of the tenancy, or not. No such consent will be given unless L's application is based on special grounds, e.g. that the carrying out of L's purpose (for which he proposes to determine the tenancy) is desirable in the interests of good husbandry, or that greater hardship would be caused by withholding than by giving consent: *Purser* v. *Bailey* (1967).
(c) If the Tribunal is satisfied concerning one or more of the grounds indicated at **(a)** above, then it will give consent to the ending of the lease. But consent will not be given if, in all the circumstances, a 'fair and reasonable landlord' would not insist on possession: Agricultural Holdings Act 1986, s. 27(2).

47. Long leases of residential premises

Under the Local Government and Housing Act 1989, s. 186, Sch. 10, protection may be granted to a tenant who holds a long tenancy (one granted for a term of years exceeding twenty-one) at a low rent. The tenant must also show that if his tenancy had not been at a low rent he would have been able to retain possession under the Rent Act.

48. Enfranchisement and extension of long leaseholds

The Leasehold Reform Act 1967 as amended by the Local Government and Housing Act 1989, Sch. 11, enables tenants of houses held on long leases and at low rents to acquire an extended lease or the freehold. (Note that the Act applies to a *house only*, not a flat: s. 2(1)(a).) *See Gratton-Story* v. *Lewis* (1987); *Sharpe* v. *Duke Street Securities* (1987); *Malpas* v. *St Ermin's Properties* (1992) — a maisonette is a house for the purposes of the Act.

(a) The tenancy must be one which has been granted for a term of years certain *exceeding twenty-one years*, and must be at a *low rent,* i.e. less than two-thirds of the rateable value of the premises: s. 4. *See Hembry* v. *Henry Smith's Charity Trustees* (1987); *Dixon* v. *Allgood* (1987).

(b) The tenant must have occupied the house for the last three years, or for periods totalling three years during the last ten years: s. 1(1)(b), amended by HA 1980, Sch. 21. (In *Poland* v. *Earl Cadogan* (1980), the Court of Appeal held that a period during which mortgages of leasehold property have been in possession is not a 'period of residence' for purposes of qualification under s. 1.)

(c) Such a tenant may purchase the freehold, or may extend the lease by fifty years after the end of the current term: s. 14(1).

(d) The tenant must serve notice on the landlord of his wish to extend the lease, or to purchase the freehold, and the landlord must serve a counter-notice within two months stating whether or not he will admit the tenant's right.

(e) Section 17 allows a landlord to obtain possession, subject to payment of compensation to the tenant, if he intends, for the purpose of redevelopment, to demolish or to reconstruct the house.

(f) Section 18 allows a landlord to obtain possession, subject to payment for compensation to the tenant, if he establishes his need of the property for occupation as the main, or sole residence for himself or an adult member of his family.

(g) The Leasehold Reform Act 1979 protected a tenant in possession, claiming under the 1967 Act, against artificial inflation of the selling price.

Progress test 5

1. Explain the nature and significance of 'the usual covenants' in a lease. **(3)**

2. Outline the essential features of the lessee's implied obligation to repair. **(7)**

3. How does *Browne* v. *Flower* (1911) illustrate the essence of the lessor's obligation concerning 'quiet enjoyment'? **(10)**

4. 'Leased premises shall be reasonably fit for human habitation.' Comment. **(13)**

5.   How has the Landlord and Tenant Act 1988 affected the general requirements concerning assigning or underletting premises?   **(16)**

6.   Explain the extent of liability in relation to an express covenant to repair.   **(18)**

7.   In what ways may a landlord enforce a covenant for payment of rent?   **(26–31)**

8.   Outline the Law of Property Act 1925, s. 146(2). What is its importance?   **(34)**

9.   Comment on *Expert Clothing Service* v. *Hillgate House Ltd* (1988).   **(37)**

10. What are 'covenants which touch and concern the land'?   **(41, 42)**

11. Outline the principal features of the Leasehold Reform Act 1967.   **(48)**

6
The term of years (3)

Preliminaries

1. Licence or lease

It is one thing to define a 'lease' and a licence', but quite another to distinguish them *in practice*. Indicia may suggest with apparent clarity a relationship between A and B as that of landlord and tenant, whereas both A and B fully intended to create the relationship of licensor and licensee. The fact that the protection offered by the Rent Act 1977, as subsequently amended, is available to a tenant but not to a licensee, makes the distinction between licence and lease of considerable significance.

2. The problem exemplified

A agrees to lease a flat to B. An appropriate document, which declares that both intend the creation of a tenancy, is signed. The terms of the five-year lease are stated precisely and include, *inter alia*, duration of the lease, covenants, rent payment details, and a statement that A grants B exclusive possession of the flat, and that A undertakes to provide B with daily breakfast, involving unrestricted access by A (or his servants) to the flat every morning for that purpose. Has a lease been created? May B seek the protection of the Rent Act?

3. Competing criteria

Two determinants have emerged in attempted solutions of the 'lease or licence' problem: 'exclusive possession' and 'expressed intention'. Both have competed for recognition by the courts. Three landmark cases are considered below.

(a) *Facchini* v. *Bryson* (1952). 'Exclusive possession' was seen as essential to the creation of a tenancy. *See* 11 below.
(b) *Somma* v. *Hazelhurst* (1978). 'Expressed intention' of the parties became the governing test for the existence of a lease. *See* 12 below.

(c) *Street* v. *Mountford* (1985). The House of Lords reinstated the basic significance of 'exclusive possession' in determining the existence of a lease. *See* **14** below.

Licences

4.   Characteristics

A licence, in relation to land, is a mere *permission, usually of a temporary nature, granted by the licensor to the licensee to enter and remain on the licensor's land.* Assume that X allows Y to reside in his (X's) house as a lodger. Without permission to enter and remain (which constitutes a 'licence'), Y's acts involved in lodging might constitute a trespass. '[The licence] properly passeth no interest nor alters nor transfers property in any thing, but only makes an action lawful, which without it had been unlawful': *per* Vaughan CJ in *Thomas* v. *Sorrell* (1673). Types of licence and the problems arising from the 'licence or lease' question are discussed below.

5.   The bare licence

This is no more than *permission granted to enter on land.* ('No man can set his foot upon my ground without my licence': *per* Lord Camden, in *Entick* v. *Carrington* (1765).) It is given gratuitously; it is not coupled with any grant of interest; it may be created in express terms or by implication; it may be revoked by the licensor at will, provided reasonable notice is given and, on revocation, the licensee must vacate within a reasonable time — should he fail to do so, he becomes a trespasser automatically. *See*, e.g. *Booker* v. *Palmer* (1942); *Armstrong* v. *Sheppard & Short Ltd* (1959).

6.   The licence coupled with grant of an interest

This generally relates to a *permission to enter land, granted as an adjunct to some validly-created interest in that land,* as where X allows Y to enter on his (X's) land in order to cut the standing timber sold by X to Y. The licence cannot be revoked while the interest to which it is coupled endures: *see*, e.g. *Hounslow LBC* v. *Twickenham Garden Developments* (1971) — a building owner, who, under a building contract, granted a licence to a building contractor to enter on his land and work there, could not determine the licence save in accordance with the contract. A licence of this nature binds the licensor and his successors in title, and it can be assigned to third parties (unlike the bare licence). *See*, e.g. *Marshall* v. *Green* (1875).

7.   The contractual licence

In this case a licence is granted *under the terms of a contract (express or implied) and valuable consideration is given by the licensee to the licensor*, as in the case of admission to a cinema after purchase of a ticket. *See*, e.g. *Hurst* v. *Picture Theatres Ltd* (1915); *Ashby* v. *Tolhurst* (1937); *Horrocks* v. *Forray* (1976).

(a) *Revocation.* The common law rule allowed revocation at any time, with reasonable notice, giving the licensee the right to sue for damages in contract. *See*, e.g. *Wood* v. *Leadbitter* (1845). More recently, however, equitable remedies have been granted. *See Winter Garden Theatre Ltd* v. *Millenium Productions* (1948) — licensor may be restrained by *injunction*; *Verrall* v. *Great Yarmouth BC* (1981) — grant of *specific performance* to enforce hire of public hall.

(b) *Third parties.* The general rule was that a contractual licence did *not* confer on the licensee any proprietary interest in the land and did *not* bind third parties: *see*, e.g. *King* v. *David Allen Ltd* (1916). Note, however, more recent decisions, such as *Binions* v. *Evans* (1972) — widow of former employee allowed to live rent free in cottage which she agreed to maintain; she acquired a contractual licence binding a purchaser with express notice of her interest. (Contractual licences are *not* registrable under LCA 1972 — *see* Ch. 18.)

(c) *'The equitable licence'.* 'The infusion of equity means that contractual licences now have a force and validity of their own and cannot be revoked in breach of contract. Neither the licensor nor anyone who claims through him can disregard the contract except a purchaser for value without notice': *per* Denning LJ in *Errington* v. *Errington* (1952). It should be noted, however, that in *Bristol & WBS* v. *Henning* (1985), the existence of the protected equitable interest was not recognised. Note also *Maharaj* v. *Jai Chand* (1986).

8.   The licence based on proprietary estoppel

'If a man under a verbal agreement with a landlord for a certain interest in land, or, what amounts to the same thing, under an expectation, created or encouraged by the landlord, that he shall have a certain interest, takes possession of such land, with the consent of the landlord, and upon the faith of such promise or expectation, with the knowledge of the landlord, and without objection by him, lay out money upon the land, a Court of equity will compel the landlord to give effect to such promise or expectation': *per* Lord Kingsdown in *Ramsden* v. *Dyson* (1866).

(a)   *See Inwards* v. *Baker* (1965). X encouraged his son, Y, to build a bungalow on X's land; it was held that Y had a right (a licence coupled with an equity) to occupy that land for as long as he wished. In *Crabb* v. *Arun DC* (1976), X assured Y that he (Y) would have a right of access across X's land and Y sold land (relying on X's promise) which provided an alternative access. X was estopped from denying Y's right of access to the land.

(b) In *Shaw* v. *Applegate* (1977), it was held that the doctrine of acquiescence or estoppel would bind a landlord if it would be 'dishonest or unconscionable' for him to argue otherwise. *See Taylors Fashions* v. *Liverpool Victoria Friendly Soc.* (1982), in which it was stated by Oliver J that the important enquiry for the court is 'whether, in particular individual circumstances, it would be unconscionable for a party to be permitted to deny that which, knowingly or unknowingly, he has allowed or encouraged another to assume to his detriment.' *See Lim* v. *Ang* (1991).

(c) In *Re Basham* (1986), it was stressed that in cases of proprietary estoppel the factor which gives rise to the equitable obligation is the alteration of one's position on the faith of an understanding. The principle of proprietary estoppel *did* extend to acts done in a belief that future rights would be granted; it was not limited to acts done in reliance on a belief relating to an existing right. X established that she had acted to her detriment in relying on a belief, encouraged by the deceased, Y, that she would ultimately benefit by receiving Y's property on his death. X was absolutely and beneficially entitled to residuary estate, including the house she had helped to run.

(d) In *Brinnand* v. *Ewens* (1987), T1 and T2 had been tenants of a ground floor and back bedroom on the first floor of a house owned by L. When the rest of L's house became vacant they moved into all of it, and, from that time, expended £30,000 in repairs and improvement. The Court of Appeal held that T1 and T2 had not established that the expenditure they had incurred had taken place because they believed that they would obtain an interest in the property. Nor could it be shown that L had encouraged their belief, since he had no knowledge of it. T1 and T2 had failed to establish the existence of the necessary ingredients of proprietary estoppel. The Court stated that, in order to establish proprietary estoppel, it was necessary to show the following: the claimant must show that he had acted to his prejudice or detriment; the claimant's acts must have taken place because he thought that he had a sufficient interest in the property or that he was likely to obtain such an interest; the claimant's beliefs must have been encouraged by the landowner, or others who were acting for him; there should be no bar to the equity.

9. The licence and registered land

See Ch. 20. A licence coupled with a grant and constituting a *profit à prendre* (*see* 17:**13**) can be protected as a minor interest (*see* 20:**14**) by entry of a notice on the licensor's title recorded on the register. *See also* LRA 1925, s. 70(1)(a), at 20:**11**. If a contractual licence is in fact an interest in land it should be protected by entry of notice; it may fall, however, under s. 70(1)(g) (*see* 20:**12**). A licence by estoppel does require protection by entry of a notice; it may be covered by s. 70(1)(g).

Licences and leases

10. Importance of the distinction

The significance of the substantial difference between the licence and the lease does not arise from the mode of creation; it emerges from what is conferred on the occupier. Thus, the *lease* confers upon the occupier a proprietary estate and the right of exclusive possession which can be enforced against anyone, including the lessor. The *licence* confers upon the occupier no interest in land, and little more than mere personal permission to occupy. Essentially, the *lease* is a proprietary interest in land; the *licence* is merely in the nature of a contract between licensor and licensee. A tenant, but not a licensee, may sue a third party in nuisance or trespass. A tenant, but not a licensee, can be subjected to distress for rent arrears (*see* 5:**28**). A very important practical matter has emerged in recent years in the area of tenants' protective legislation, particularly under the Rent Act 1977. *The full protection of the 1977 Act is given, with limited exceptions, to a tenant, but not to a licensee: see* s. 1. Hence the distinction between lease and licence is of much importance for landlords and tenants.

11. The concept of 'exclusive possession'

Until the mid-1970s, the enjoyment of exclusive possession was a vital indicator of a tenancy. *See Facchini* v. *Bryson* (1952) — '[The relationship of the parties] *is determined by law and not by the label which they choose to put on it* ... it is simply a matter of finding the true relationship of the parties': *per* Denning LJ. *Exclusive possession, for a fixed period at a rent, suggested, almost certainly, the existence of a tenancy,* save where 'there has been something in the circumstances, such as a family arrangement, an act of friendship or generosity, or such like, to negative any intention to create a tenancy.'

12. The concept of 'expressed intention'
    Attempts to evade or avoid the controls imposed by the Rent Acts (e.g. right to remain in possession after expiry of original term, and maximum 'fair' rents) became widespread, culminating in the growth of 'occupation licences' (*see Heslop* v. *Burns* (1974).) In *Somma* v. *Hazelhurst* (1978), the Court of Appeal held that where an agreement between parties was, *truly*, that a landlord should license two persons each to occupy part of a room and each to be responsible for separate weekly occupation instalments, the letting was a *licence*, not a tenancy. If both parties *intended* to create a licence and framed a written agreement in such a way as to demonstrate that 'it was not really an agreement for a lease masquerading as a licence', they should be allowed to do so. '[We cannot see why the parties'] common intentions should be categorised as bogus or sham merely on the ground that the court disapproves of the bargain': *per* Cumming-Bruce LJ. Henceforth, it seemed, *the vital indicator of the distinction between licence and tenancy would rest on the expressed intention of the parties.*

An attempted resolution of the problem — *Street* v. *Mountford* (1985)

13. Lease or licence?
    In *Street* v. *Mountford* (1985), X, the occupier of a self-contained furnished flat, was allowed exclusive occupancy on payment of a 'weekly licence fee' to L. A signed agreement was described specifically as a 'licence agreement', in which X stated clearly that *she had no intention of taking a tenancy*. Under the agreement L could re-enter with an immediate termination of the 'licence' if the flat were left vacant and unoccupied.

(a) The Recorder held that a *tenancy had been created*.
(b) This was *rejected* by the Court of Appeal. The issue was one of *objective intentions*, so that X held the flat as a licensee. 'The true intentions [of the parties] are the decisive consideration in determining whether an agreement creates a tenancy or a licence': *per* Slade LJ. The rights to be granted by L were those of a personal right of use and *not* those of a tenant. *A licence only had been created.*

14. 'Exclusive possession' test reinstated

The House of Lords rejected the decision of the Court of Appeal (and also overruled *Somma* v. *Hazelhurst* : *see* **12** above). *X had been granted a tenancy*. The test relates to *substance, not form*; 'exclusive possession' as the test in deciding 'lease or tenancy' was reinstated. The sole 'intention' which is of relevance is that related to the intention to grant exclusive possession for a term at a rent.

(a) 'Where the only circumstances are that residential accommodation is offered and accepted with exclusive possession for a term at a rent, the result is a tenancy. . . *If the agreement satisfied all the requirements of a tenancy, then the agreement produced a tenancy and the parties cannot alter the effect of the agreement by insisting that they only created a licence*. The manufacture of a five-pronged implement for manual digging results in a fork even if the manufacturer, unfamiliar with the English language, insists that he intended to make and has made a spade': *per* Lord Templeman.

(b) Note, further, the comments of Lord Templeman on 'lodgers' and 'tenants'. 'An occupier of residential accommodation at a rent for a term is either a lodger or a tenant. The occupier is a *lodger* if the landlord provides attendance or services which require the landlord or his servants to exercise unrestricted access to and use of the premises . . . *If, on the other hand, residential accommodation is granted for a term at a rent with exclusive possession, the landlord providing neither attendance nor services, the grant is a tenancy*. Henceforth, the courts which deal with these problems will, save in exceptional circumstances, only be concerned to inquire whether as a result of an agreement relating to residential accommodation the occupier is a lodger or a tenant.'

15. Some 'exceptional circumstances'

Lord Templeman noted, in *Street* v. *Mountford* (1985), the existence of exceptional circumstances in which an occupier might be a mere licensee, although possessing a right to exclusive occupation. These circumstances included the following:

(a) Where the occupancy is under a contract for the sale of land (*see Bretherton* v. *Paton* (1986)), or is related to a contract of employment or the holding of an office.

(b) Where the circumstances indicate that the parties do not intend to create legal relationships (as stated by Denning LJ in *Facchini* v. *Bryson* (1952), at **11** above).

16. Decisions after *Street* v. *Mountford*: (1)

The following cases should be noted carefully. Each case turns on its facts; exact identification of the factual situation is essential.

(a) *Dellneed* v. *Chin* (1987). Under a so-called 'management agreement', X took over a restaurant, running it for himself, and paying a weekly fee to the owner for use of fixtures and fittings. It was held that *a tenancy had been created*. In reality, X had exclusive possession, for a term, at a rent; even though the agreement did not expressly confer a right to enter and use the premises, such a right was necessarily inferred.

(b) *Dresden Estates* v. *Collinson* (1987). L purported to grant to X a 'licence' to occupy a workshop and store, under a written agreement which provided *inter alia* that the licensor was entitled to require the licensee to transfer his occupation to other premises within the licensor's adjoining property. The Court of Appeal held that L's entitlement to require X to transfer to other premises was totally inconsistent with a right to exclusive possession during the continuation of the agreement. *Only a licence had been conferred.* The Court of Appeal suggested that the indicia making the existence of a tenancy apparent in the case of a residential occupier may be less applicable in the case of some business tenancies. Lloyd CJ stated that the decision of the Court to consider the intention of the parties, in the particular circumstances, was *not* to be regarded 'as providing a way round *Street* v. *Mountford*. It will be in only a limited class of case that it would be appropriate.'

(c) *AG Securities* v. *Vaughan* (1988). A four-roomed flat was occupied by four persons, each of whom had signed a separate agreement with L, at separate times, as purported licensees, giving them the right to use the flat, but without the right to exclusive possession of any part. Each time an occupant left, a replacement was selected from applicants, and the rooms were re-allocated by the occupants among themselves. L sought possession on the grounds that the occupants were mere licensees. They appealed.

> (*i*) *Court of Appeal*. The appeal was allowed. The appropriate test was *Street* v. *Mountford*, namely, whether there was a grant of exclusive possession for a term at a rent. A joint right to exclusive possession had been created. The different amounts payable by the occupants constituted a rent. The four unities of possession, time, title and interest, necessary for the creation of a joint tenancy, were satisfied, and the *occupants were joint tenants*.

(*ii*) *House of Lords. There was no joint tenancy.* It was impossible to say that the agreements created either individually or collectively a single tenancy either of the entire flat or any part of it. The fact that under each agreement an individual had the privilege of user and occupation for a term which overlapped the term of user and occupation of other persons in the premises did *not* create a single, indivisible term of occupation for all four consisting of an amalgam of the individual overlapping periods. Nor was there a single sum of money payable in respect of use and occupation; each person was individually liable for the amount he had agreed. The 'four unities' were absent (*see* 12:11).

(**d**) *Antoniades* v. *Villiers* (1988). X and his girl friend, Y, occupied a one-bedroom flat, each having signed separate, but identical, agreements with L, who knew that they would be living as husband and wife. The agreement provided that exclusive possession was not granted; it allowed L to permit others to occupy the flat from time to time in common with X and Y. X and Y claimed to be tenants, entitled to the protection of the Rent Acts. L contended that they were licensees. The judge held the agreements to be designed to avoid the Rent Acts. He found that *X and Y were tenants.* L appealed.

(*i*) *Court of Appeal. L's appeal was allowed.* The agreements did not grant a tenancy because they did not grant exclusive possession. L had *intended* that exclusive possession should *not* be given.

(*ii*) *House of Lords. There was a grant of a joint tenancy.* X and Y applied to rent the flat jointly and to enjoy exclusive possession. L had allowed them jointly to enjoy exclusive occupation and had accepted rent; a tenancy had been created. L's power to deprive X and Y of exclusive occupation was inconsistent with the Rent Acts; that power was a pretence only to deprive X and Y of the protection of the Rent Acts. Lord Templeman referred to his statement in *Street* v. *Mountford*: 'The court should ... be astute to detect and frustrate sham devices and artificial transactions whose only object is to disguise the grant of a tenancy and to evade the Rent Acts.' He commented that it would have been more accurate and less liable to give rise to misunderstanding if he had substituted the word 'pretence' for the reference to 'sham devices' and 'artificial transactions'.

(**e**) *Ogwr BC* v. *Dykes* (1989). The Ogwr Borough Council, carrying out its obligation to rehouse homeless persons (under HA 1985,

s. 65(3)), gave possession of a house to X for a period limited to 13 weeks, under the terms of a letter headed 'Licence to Occupy'. X remained in possession after the expiry of 13 weeks and the housing authority purported to determine the licence.

    (i) *The judge's decision.* The judge held that the agreement under which X went into possession was a *licence* for a limited period. The instant case was of the type referred to by Lord Templeman in *Street* v. *Mountford*, where he said: 'Sometimes it may appear from the surrounding circumstances that the right to exclusive possession is referable to a legal relationship other than a tenancy.' X appealed.

    (ii) *Court of Appeal. X's appeal was dismissed.* If the terms on which the right to exclusive possession was conferred negatived the grant of a tenancy, then some other interest would be created. The background to the case negatived the inference that a tenancy was created when X was allowed to occupy the premises. The right to exclusive possession was referable to the grant to occupy for a limited period, and, as such, *the case was an exception to the doctrine laid down by the House of Lords in Street* v. *Mountford.*

17. Decisions after *Street* v. *Mountford*: (2)
The following selection of cases should be noted:

(a) *Aslan* v. *Murphy* (1990). T occupied a single room under an agreement which stated that L, the licensor, was not willing to grant T exclusive possession, that L had a licence to use the room at almost any hour of the day, that L would retain the keys to the room and that L could permit persons other than L to use the room in common with T. L provided almost no services. L applied for an order for possession.

    (i) *The judge's decision.* The agreement created a licence, and possession was ordered. T appealed.

    (ii) *Court of Appeal.* The provisions for sharing the room, licensing occupation of the room for only a part of the day, were, on the facts, *mere pretence*, and could be ignored. The touchstone of whether an occupation agreement existed turned on exclusive possession, but the court had to look to the true nature of the bargain between the parties. In the event, *a tenancy had been created.*

(b) *Ward* v. *Warnke* (1990). Parents bought a cottage and allowed their daughter and son-in-law to live there. Weekly payments at a low rent were made. The parents kept a key and visited the cottage occasionally. The son-in-law claimed security of tenure following his divorce.

(i) *The judge's decision.* A tenancy had been created. The parents appealed.

(ii) *Court of Appeal.* There was no real basis for saying that there had been no intention to enter into legal relations. A transaction between family members did not prevent the creation of a legal relationship. There was an agreement for exclusive occupation at a weekly rent, and *a tenancy had been created.*

(c) *Westminster CC* v. *Basson* (1990). The defendant occupied premises with her friend, a tenant of the Council. He left after his tenancy was terminated. The Council told the defendant to leave. The Council's letter to her also requested payment by way of use and occupation charges of £30 per week, although it stated that the arrangement was not intended as the creation of a tenancy. Later, the defendant applied to a different department of the Council and was given a rent book. The Council applied for a possession order.

(i) *The judge's decision.* A possession order was granted. The defendant appealed, claiming she had been granted a tenancy, not a licence.

(ii) *Court of Appeal.* The Council had made it quite clear that it did not intend to grant a tenancy to the defendant. Further actions by a department of the Council *did not create a tenancy* in the defendant's favour.

(d) *Westminster CC* v. *Clarke* (1992). The defendant occupied a single room in a men's hostel run by the Council, pursuant to an agreement entitled 'licence to occupy'. The licence included a term stating that it was not intended to give the defendant any of the rights of a tenant and did not create the relationship of landlord and tenant. Following complaints concerning the defendant's misbehaviour, he was given notice terminating the licence. The Council asked for a possession order.

(i) *The judge's decision.* An order for possession in the Council's favour was made. The defendant appealed.

(ii) *Court of Appeal.* The defendant was a licensee entitled to security of tenure under HA 1985, Part IV. The Council appealed.

(iii) *House of Lords.* The House ruled that the defendant was a licensee and *not a secure tenant.* The provisions of the licence to occupy had been inserted to allow the Council to discharge its responsibilities to the vulnerable persons accommodated at the hostel. The Council had legitimately and effectively retained for themselves possession of the room occupied by the defendant, who was a licensee with rights corresponding to those of a lodger. The Council had not acted so as to avoid the creation of a secure tenancy. This was a special case. The decision would not allow a landlord to free himself from the Rent Acts or from the restrictions of a secure tenancy merely by adopting or adapting the language of the licence to occupy.

18. The current situation

It would seem that the decision of the House of Lords in *Street* v. *Mountford* (1985) has not brought certainty to the area of landlord-tenant relations which was in question. Problems remain and 'exceptions to the rule' appear to be set for proliferation. The distinction between the lease and the licence remains imprecise in practice, and difficulties resulting from the distinction have not disappeared.

Progress test 6

1. What is the importance in land law of the concept of the 'licence'?   **(1, 2)**

2. Explain the nature of the 'contractual licence'.   **(7)**

3. How did *Street* v. *Mountford* (1985) attempt to resolve the 'lease *v.* licence' problem?   **(13, 14)**

4. Consider *Antoniades* v. *Villiers* (1988) in relation to *Street* v. *Mountford* (1985).   **(16)**

5. Comment on the decision of the House of Lords in *Westminster CC* v. *Clarke* (1992).   **(17)**

Statutory protection of the residential tenant (1)

Preliminaries

1. Essence of the protective legislation

Legislative interference with the workings of the free market in housing accommodation, whereby rents were determined largely by the supply of, and the demand for, residential accommodation, and the eviction of tenants, because of rent-payment default and other reasons, was often unrestrained, has characterised the present century. Statutory protection in the private sector has taken the form of Rent Acts; statutory protection in the public sector has resulted in the Housing Acts. In these chapters, attention is drawn to the principal methods of protection of tenants offered by the legislation.

2. Rent Acts

This body of legislation may be traced to the Increase of Rent and Mortgage Interest (War Restriction) Act 1915, restricting rents and landlords' exercise of the right to possession. The Rent Acts of 1957, 1965, 1968 and 1974 enlarged the nature of the protection afforded to tenants.

(a) These measures arose from a policy which 'was and is to protect the tenant in his home, whether the threat be to extort a premium for the grant or renewal of his tenancy, to increase his rent or to evict him . . . The Rent Acts have throughout their history constituted an interference with contract and property rights for a specific purpose — the redress of the balance of advantage enjoyed in a world of housing shortage by the landlord over those who have to rent their homes': *per* Lord Scarman in *Horford Investments Ltd* v. *Lambert* (1976). Note the reference by Lord Simon in *Johnson* v. *Moreton* (1980) to the legislation which 'came to intervene repeatedly to modify freedom of contract between landlord and tenant.'

(b) RA 1977 was an important consolidating measure which, until recently, formed one of the pillars of housing law. It created 'protected tenancies' and 'statutory tenancies'; it protected tenure and allowed the exercise of a measure of statutory control over the level of rents.

(c) HA 1988 aims to phase out the protection of RA 1977 (*see*, in particular, HA 1988, Chapter V). Existing lettings continue under the protection of RA 1977, as before; new lettings, after HA 1988 becomes effective, fall under the new provisions of the 1988 Act.

3.   Housing Acts

These Acts were intended, in general, to give tenants in the public housing sector 'the same kind of protection from being evicted from their homes without good and sufficient cause as had been enjoyed by tenants in the private sector for many decades under the Rent Acts': *per* Brandon LJ in *Harrison* v. *Hammersmith & Fulham LBC* (1981).

(a) HA 1980 introduced the concept of the 'secure tenancy'. Its object was 'to give security of tenure, and the right to buy their houses, to tenants of local and other bodies, to make other provisions with respect to those and other tenants, to amend the law about housing in the public sector . . . to restrict the discretion of the court in making orders for the possession of land. . .'

(b) HA 1985, Part IV, consolidated previous Housing Acts and dealt specifically with the tenant's right to buy, repairs, improvements, overcrowding, etc.

(c) HA 1988 replaces the 'protected tenancy' by the new-style 'assured tenancy', creates Housing Action Trust Areas, and confers (in Part IV) on approved persons the right to acquire from public sector landlords certain dwelling-houses occupied by secure tenants.

Protection against harassment, eviction, etc.

4.   Harassment

It is an offence under the Protection from Eviction Act 1977, for a person, with intent to cause the residential occupier to give up his occupation or to refrain from exercising any right or remedy in respect of the premises, to do acts likely to interfere with the peace or comfort of the residential occupier or members of his household or persistently to withdraw or withhold services reasonably required for occupation of the premises as a residence: s. 1(3), as amended by HA 1988, s. 29(1). A person is not guilty of the offence if he proves that he had reasonable grounds for doing the acts or withholding the services in question: HA 1988, s. 29(2).

5. Unlawful eviction

Under the Protection from Eviction Act 1977, if any person unlawfully deprives a residential occupier of his occupation of the premises or any part thereof, or attempts to do so, he is guilty of an offence unless he proves that he believed reasonably that the residential occupier had ceased to reside in the premises: s. 1(2).

(a) HA 1988, s. 27(3), enables damages in tort to be awarded against a landlord responsible for unlawful eviction, or a person acting on his behalf.

(b) For the measure of damages, *see* HA 1988, s. 28; *Tagro* v. *Cafane* (1991).

6. Distress

See 5:28. L's right to distrain upon T's goods is restricted by RA 1977, s. 147(1), and HA 1988, s. 19 (in the case of an assured tenancy). Distress may not be levied save by leave of the court; the court has the power to adjourn, suspend or postpone proceedings.

7. Unlawful payments

It is a criminal offence to require a person, as a condition of the grant, renewal or continuance of a protected tenancy (*see* 8 below) to pay a premium or to make a loan, secured or unsecured: RA 1977, s. 119(1). *See Saleh* v. *Robinson* (1988).

Tenancies affording a measure of protection (1)

8. The 'protected' tenancy

'A tenancy under which a dwelling-house (which may be a house or part of a house) is let as a separate dwelling': RA 1977, s. 1.

(a) The following conditions had to be fulfilled under RA 1977: there had to be, in fact, a tenancy, but its type was irrelevant; the subject of the tenancy had to be a 'dwelling house', and it was a question of fact whether premises were within that term, so that it was open to the court to look at the circumstances of the letting; the dwelling-house had to be let as a 'separate dwelling', i.e. as a single unit: *Grosvenor Estates* v. *Amberton* (1983) — the rent had to be capable of being expressed in terms of money; the appropriate rateable limits (*see* RA 1977, s. 4) had to apply.

(b) A protected tenancy did *not* arise where, e.g.: the tenancy was classified as 'low rent' (*see* RA 1977, s. 5(1)); there was a 'resident landlord' who occupied as his residence another dwelling house which formed part of the flat or building let (*see* RA 1977, s. 12; *see Lewis-Graham* v. *Conacher* (1992); *Markou* v. *Da Silvaesa* (1986), and *see also* HA 1980, s. 65); the object of the tenancy was to confer on T the right to occupy the dwelling-house for a holiday (*see* RA 1977, s. 9: *Francke* v. *Hakmi* (1984)); the rent included payments in respect of board or attendance, for which *see below* (*see* RA 1977, s. 7(1); and SI 1988/1683; *Otter* v. *Norman* (1988)); the dwelling-house was let to students (*see* RA 1977, s. 6); L's interest belonged to the Crown or a government department (*see* RA 1977, s. 13(1); HA 1980, s. 73(1); *Crown Estate Commissioners* v. *Wordsworth* (1982)).

(c) In the case of a protected tenancy, L or T, or both jointly, had the right to apply to a local rent officer for registration of a 'fair rent': RA 1977, s. 67(1). Details of assessment and registration of the fair rent were set out in RA 1977, s. 70, Sch. 11. *See BTE* v. *Merseyside and Cheshire Rent Assessment Committee* (1992). Note the comments of Lord Kilbrandon in *Mason* v. *Skilling* (1974): '[The fixing of a fair rent] calls for a skilled estimate of a hypothetical figure, namely, the rent which a landlord would demand and a tenant would be prepared to pay if the market were roughly in a state of equilibrium, without serious shortage or surplus available for letting.' *See also* HA 1988, Sch. 17, para. 22; *Prudential Assurance Co. Ltd* v. *Salisbury's Handbags* (1992).

> NOTE: Under RA 1977, s. 7(1), a tenancy is not a protected tenancy if the dwelling-house 'is *bona fide* let at a rent which includes payments in respect of board or attendance'. *See Nelson Developments* v. *Taboada* (1992) — daily room cleaning, removal of refuse and window cleaning constituted 'attendance' for purposes of s. 7.

9.   The protected tenancy following HA 1988

Under s. 34, tenancies entered into after the commencement of the 1988 Act *cannot be protected tenancies* unless: entered into in pursuance of a contract made before commencement of the Act; or granted to a person who immediately before the tenancy was granted was a protected or statutory tenant, and is so granted by the person who was the landlord under the protected or statutory tenancy; or it is granted to a person in circumstances specified in HA 1988, s. 34(1)(c) (relating to availability of 'suitable alternative accommodation': *see* RA 1977, Sch. 16); or it relates to HA 1988,

s. 38(1),(3),(4) (concerning transfer of tenancies from the public to the private sector). Effectively, HA 1988 replaces the protected tenancy with the new-style 'assured tenancy'. A letting after the HA 1988 is in force, which would have created a protected tenancy under RA 1977, will now give rise to an assured tenancy (with an appropriate measure of security of tenure).

10. The restricted contract

This was, under RA 1977, s. 19(2) 'a contract . . . whereby one person grants to another person, in consideration of a rent *which includes payment for the use of furniture or for services*, the right to occupy a dwelling as a residence.' Deferment of repossession for a period of up to three months was allowed, and the owner or occupier could apply to a tribunal for the fixing and registration of a 'reasonable' rent.

11. The restricted contract following HA 1988

Under HA 1988, s. 36(1), a tenancy or other contract entered into after the commencement of the Act *cannot* be a restricted contract for purposes of RA 1977, unless it is entered into in pursuance of a contract made before the commencement of the 1988 Act. RA 1977, s. 19(2) (*see* **10** above), is repealed under HA 1988, Sch. 18. *See also* HA 1988, Sch. 17, para. 23.

12. The 'old-style' assured tenancy under HA 1980

Under HA 1980, s. 56, the assured tenancy applied to a dwelling-house let as a separate dwelling (and not a housing association tenancy), where the interest of L belonged to an approved body, the dwelling-house formed part of a building erected after 1980, and, before T first occupied the dwelling-house, no part of it had been occupied except under an assured tenancy agreement.

13. The 'new-style' assured tenancy following HA 1988

HA 1988, Sch. 18, *repeals* HA 1980, s. 56. *There are to be no further assured tenancies under HA 1980* after January 1989: HA 1988, s. 37(1). 'Old-style' assured tenancies under HA 1980, s. 56, are converted into 'new-style' assured tenancies for purposes of the 1988 Act: HA 1988, s. 1(3).

14. The housing association tenancy

See 9:**1**. Security was afforded under RA 1977, Part VI, to certain persons holding tenancies of housing associations which were registered.

15. The housing association tenancy following HA 1988

A tenancy entered into after the commencement of the 1988 Act cannot be a housing association tenancy unless, e.g. entered into in pursuance of a contract made before the commencement of the 1988 Act; or granted to a person who immediately before the tenancy was granted was a tenant under a housing association tenancy and is so granted by the person who at the time was the landlord under that tenancy: HA 1988, s. 35(2).

> NOTE: For amendments to the Rent (Agriculture) Act 1976 and the creation of assured agricultural occupancies, carrying security of tenure, *see* HA 1988, ss. 24–26. Sch. 3 deals with necessary conditions for the creation of the assured occupancy in relation to a dwelling-house.

Tenancies affording a measure of protection (2)

16. The secure tenancy

A secure tenancy involves a *public sector letting* by a body specified in HA 1985, s. 80, e.g. a local authority, new town corporation. It requires the fulfilment of a 'landlord condition' and a 'tenant condition'.

(a) The 'landlord condition' involves a tenancy under which a dwelling-house is let as a separate dwelling by a landlord whose interest belongs to one of the bodies specified under HA 1985, s. 80(1). *See* HA 1988, s. 83; *R* v. *Plymouth CC ex p. Freeman* (1987). *See also Tower Hamlets LBC* v. *Miah* (1992).

(b) The 'tenant condition' involves a tenant who is an individual and occupies the dwelling-house as his only or principal home; or, where the tenancy is a joint tenancy, each of the joint tenants is an individual and at least one of them recognises the dwelling-house as his only or principal home: HA 1988, s. 81.

17. Security of tenure

The following principles of security are available under the HA 1985.

(a) *Grounds for possession.* These are set out in HA 1985, Sch. 2.
    (i) Part I of the Schedule lists *eight grounds* on which the court *may* order possession if it considers it reasonable, e.g. where

rent has not been paid, or where T has caused annoyance to neighbours.

(*ii*) Part II contains *three grounds* on which the court *may* order possession if suitable alternative accommodation is available, e.g. where L is a charity and T's continued occupation would conflict with the charity's objects.

(*iii*) Part III contains *five grounds* on which the court *may* order possession if it considers it reasonable and suitable accommodation is available, as where the dwelling-house is designed for occupation by a physically-disabled person and there is no longer such a person residing there, and L requires it for occupation by such a person.

(b) *Succession on death of a tenant under a secure tenancy.* A person is qualified to succeed T under a secure tenancy if he occupies the dwelling-house as his own or principal home at the time of T's death and he is T's spouse, or another member of T's family, and has resided with T throughout the twelve months ending with T's death: HA 1985, s. 87. In *Waltham Forest LBC* v. *Thomas* (1992), the House of Lords held that it does not matter whether the successor and the tenant reside together in one or more houses or whether the residences were all council houses, provided that the successor and tenant resided together in a council house at the moment of death and provided that they resided together during the period of 12 months prior to the death of the tenant.

(c) *Right to buy.* The secure tenant has a right to buy (at a discount) the freehold of a house of which L has a freehold interest, or the lease of a house or flat: HA 1985, ss. 118, 129. (For 'right of first refusal' on a disposal by L of premises containing two or more flats, *see* Landlord and Tenant Act 1987, Part I.)

(d) *Rent.* A local housing authority may make 'such reasonable charges' as they may determine for the tenancy of their houses and may review rents: HA 1985, s. 24.

18. The secure tenancy following HA 1988

A tenancy entered into after the commencement of the 1988 Act *cannot* be a secure tenancy *unless*, e.g.: it is entered into in pursuance of a contract made before the commencement of the Act; or it is granted to a person who, immediately before it was entered into, was a secure tenant and is so granted by the body which at the time was the landlord under the secure tenancy; or L's interest belongs to a local authority, a new town corporation, urban development corporation, housing action trust (*see* 9:4), or a housing co-operative: HA 1988, s. 35.

> NOTE: *See also* HA 1988, s. 38 (transfer of existing tenancies from public to private sector), and 9:8.

19. The statutory tenancy

Following the *termination of a protected tenancy of a dwelling house*, the person who, immediately before that termination, was the protected tenant, shall, if and so long as he occupies the dwelling-house as his residence, be the statutory tenant of it and, when there is a statutory tenant of a dwelling-house, that house is referred to as subject to a statutory tenancy: *see* RA 1977, s. 2(1)(a) *See Killick* v. *Roberts* (1991).

(a) The statutory tenancy, which is a purely personal right, can be brought to an end only by T's giving up possession, or by the court making a possession order. Effectively, T is given 'a status of irremovability': *See Jessamine Investments* v. *Schwartz* (1978). The tenancy binds L's successors in title: *see* LRA 1925, s. 70(1)(g).

(b) The four necessary conditions for a statutory tenancy are: there must have been a protected tenancy; it must have come to an end, e.g. by forfeiture; there must be a person who was a protected tenant immediately before the termination; the tenant must be in occupation of the dwelling-house as his residence. *See Lloyd* v. *Sadler* (1978); *Hampstead Way Investments* v. *Lewis-Weare* (1985); *Brickfield Properties* v. *Hughes* (1988).

(c) L will not be granted a possession order unless it is considered reasonable to make such an order *and* the court is satisfied concerning alternative accommodation for T, or circumstances exist as specified in RA 1977, Sch. 15. *See* RA 1977, s. 98.

 (*i*) In Sch. 15, Part I, there are *ten cases* where the court *may* order possession, e.g. as where T has failed to pay rent, or is in breach of some other obligation, or T has allowed the condition of the premises to deteriorate.

 (*ii*) In Sch. 15, Part II, as amended by Rent (Amendment) Act 1985, there are *11 cases* establishing *mandatory grounds* for possession, e.g. as where L let the dwelling prior to his retirement and seeks possession because he has retired and now requires it as his residence, or where L is a serviceman who requires the house as a residence (inserted by HA 1980, s. 67).

(d) It is possible for a tenancy to pass by *statutory succession* to members of the family of the deceased tenant. Generally, the surviving spouse who was residing in the house immediately before T's death becomes the statutory tenant. Two statutory successions were allowed. *See* RA 1977, Sch. 1, para 2 (substituted by HA 1980, s. 76(1)), para 3).

(e) For protection of lawful sub-tenants, *see* RA 1977, s. 137. *See Bromley Park Garden Estates* v. *George* (1991) — a head tenant's surrender of a non-statutory tenancy prior to the expiry of a regulated sub-tenancy deprived the sub-tenant of the protection, as against the head landlord, of the Rent Acts after the expiry of the sub-tenancy.

20. The statutory tenancy following HA 1988

The statutory tenancy continues, but *only one succession is now possible*: *see* HA 1988, s. 39. Note that under HA 1988, Sch. 4, Part I, para. 2, for the purposes of succession, 'a person who was living with the original tenant as his or her wife or husband shall be treated as the spouse of the original tenant.' *See also* 5:**46**.

Progress test 7

1. What is the general purpose of the Housing Acts of the 1980s? **(3)**

2. How does the Protection from Eviction Act 1977 deal with eviction? **(5)**

3. What is the essence of the 'protected tenancy'? **(8)**

4. Explain the nature of the 'secure tenancy' following the Housing Act 1988. **(18)**

5. Outline the concept of the 'statutory tenancy'. **(19, 20)**

Statutory protection of the residential tenant (2)

The 'new-style' assured tenancy under HA 1988

1. Meaning

A tenancy under which a *dwelling-house* is let as a *separate dwelling* is, for the purposes of HA 1988, an assured tenancy if and so long as the tenant is *an individual,* who occupies the dwelling-house as his *only or principal home,* and the tenancy is not one which under the Act cannot be an assured tenancy (*see* **2** below): s. 1(1).

(a) Where a dwelling-house is let together with other land for the purpose of providing a home for T, the other land is to be treated as part of the dwelling-house: s. 2(3).

(b) Where T has the *exclusive occupation* of any accommodation ('the separate accommodation'), and the terms between T and L on which the separate accommodation is held include the use of other accommodation in common with another person (not including L) and the separate accommodation would not, apart from this section, be a dwelling-house let on an assured tenancy, the separate accommodation is deemed to be a dwelling-house let on an assured tenancy: s. 3(1).

(c) While T is in possession of the separate accommodation, any term of the tenancy modifying or terminating his right to use any of the shared accommodation which is living accommodation is of no effect: s. 3(3).

2. Tenancies which cannot be assured tenancies

These are listed in HA 1988, Sch. 1, Part I.

(a) Tenancies entered into before commencement of the 1988 Act.

(b) Tenancies of dwelling-houses with high rateable values. (For ascertainment of rateable values, *see* Sch. I, Part II.)

(c) Tenancies at a 'low rent'.

(d) A (business) tenancy to which the Landlord and Tenant Act 1954, Part II, applies.

(e) Tenancies under which the dwelling house comprises 'licensed premises' (involving the sale of intoxicating liquors).

(f) Tenancies under which agricultural land, exceeding two acres, is let together with the dwelling-house.

(g) Tenancies of agricultural holdings.

(h) Lettings to students by their own or other specified educational institutions.

(i) Holiday lettings.

(j) Tenancies in which the dwelling-house forms part only of a building and, except in a case where the dwelling-house also forms part of a flat, the building is not a purpose-built block of flats and the tenancy was granted by a person who, at the time of the grant, occupied as his only or principal home another dwelling-house which also forms part of the flat or also formed part of the building. *See* Sch. 1, Part III.

(k) Crown tenancies.

(l) Local authority tenancies, etc.: as where L's interest belongs to, e.g. a local authority, Commission for the New Towns, Development Board for Rural Wales, development corporation, a housing action trust (*see* 9:4).

(m) Tenancies regarded under the 1988 Act as 'transitional cases', e.g. protected tenancy within the meaning of RA 1977, a housing association tenancy, a secure tenancy, a tenancy involving the Rent (Agriculture) Act 1976.

Security under the assured tenancy

3.   Essence of security of tenure

Under HA 1988, s. 5(1), L cannot end an assured tenancy *except by obtaining a court order* in accordance with the Act, or in the case of a fixed term tenancy which contains power for L to determine the tenancy in certain circumstances, by exercise of that power. Hence a notice to quit served by L will be ineffective in relation to a periodic fixed tenancy.

(a) If an assured tenancy which is a fixed term tenancy comes to an end otherwise than by a court order, or surrender or other action by T, then, in general, T is entitled to remain in possession: s. 5(2).

(b) A 'periodic tenancy' is one which takes effect in possession immediately on the ending of a fixed term tenancy, under which the premises which are let are the same dwelling-house as was let under the fixed term tenancy, and under which the periods of the tenancy are the same as those for which rent was last payable under the fixed term tenancy: s. 5(3). (For fixing of terms of a 'statutory periodic tenancy', which arises under s. 5(5), *see* s. 6.)

4.   Grounds for the issuing of an order for possession: the mandatory grounds

Under HA 1988, s. 7(1), the court will not make an order for possession of a dwelling-house let on an assured tenancy *except* on one or more of the grounds set out in Sch. 2: s. 7(1). (This does *not* affect proceedings for possession brought under LPA 1925 by a mortgagee: s. 7(1).) *Eight grounds* on which the court *must* order possession, irrespective of whether it considers it reasonable to do so, are set out below. (*See* Sch. 2, Part I.)

(a) *Ground 1*. L has given written notice to T, not later than the beginning of the tenancy, informing T that possession might be recovered on this ground, or the court is of the opinion that it is just and equitable to dispense with notice; and L occupied the dwelling-house as his only or principal home and requires it for his or his spouse's only or principal home, and neither L nor any other person deriving title under L acquired the reversion on the tenancy for money or money's worth.

(b) *Ground 2*. The dwelling-house is subject to a mortgage granted before the beginning of the tenancy and the mortgagee is entitled to exercise power of sale, and requires possession so as to dispose of the lease with vacant possession in exercise of that power.

(c) *Ground 3*. The tenancy is a fixed term tenancy for a period not exceeding eight months and L has given T written notice of the possibility of recovering possession; and at some time within the period of 12 months ending with the beginning of the tenancy, the house was let for holiday occupation.

(d) *Ground 4*. As for ground 3, except that the fixed term tenancy does not exceed twelve months, and the house was let at sometime within the period of twelve months, ending with the beginning of the tenancy, to students.

(e) *Ground 5*. The dwelling is held so as to be available for occupation by a minister of religion, and is now needed for that purpose.

(f) *Ground 6*. L is a registered housing association or charitable housing trust and a superior landlord intends to demolish or reconstruct the dwelling-house, and this cannot be carried out without T giving up possession.

(g) *Ground 7.* The tenancy is a periodic tenancy which has devolved under the former tenant's will or intestacy, and proceedings for possession are begun not later than 12 months after his death.

(h) *Ground 8.* At the date of service of notice under s. 8 (*see* **6** below) and the date of the hearing, rent is unpaid for a prescribed period.

> NOTE: Grounds 1–5 require L to have given written notice to T stating that possession might be recovered on a particular ground no later than the start of the tenancy.

5. **Grounds for the issuing of an order for possession: the discretionary grounds**

There are *eight grounds* on which the court *may* order possession if it considers it *reasonable* to do so. (*See* Sch. 2, Part II.)

(a) *Ground 9.* Suitable alternative accommodation is, or will be, available for T. (*See* Sch. 1, Part III.)

(b) *Ground 10.* Some rent lawfully due from T is unpaid on the date on which proceedings for possession are begun.

(c) *Ground 11.* T has persistently delayed paying rent which is lawfully due.

(d) *Ground 12.* T has broken some obligation other than that concerning payment of rent.

(e) *Ground 13.* T's default has resulted in the deterioration of the dwelling-house.

(f) *Ground 14.* T, or some other person residing in the dwelling-house, has been guilty of conduct which is a nuisance or annoyance to adjoining occupiers.

(g) *Ground 15.* T's ill-treatment of furniture provided for use under the tenancy has resulted in its deterioration.

(h) *Ground 16.* The dwelling-house was let to T in consequence of his employment by L, and T has ceased to be in that employment.

> NOTE: (1) The court will not make an order for possession to take effect at a time when the dwelling is let on an assured fixed term tenancy *unless* the grounds for possession are 2 or 8, or any ground in Sch. 2, Part II (other than Grounds 9 or 16) *and* the terms of the tenancy make provision for it to be ended on the ground in question: s. 7(6). (2) The court may adjourn a possession claim for such period as it thinks fit: s. 9(1).

6. **Procedure for possession of an assured tenancy**

Proceedings will not be entertained by the court unless L has served notice on T (but the court may consider it just and equitable to dispense with this requirement): s. 8(1). The notice must be in the prescribed form: s. 8(3). Execution of the order for possession may be suspended, or the date of possession postponed for such period as the court thinks just: s. 9(2). In the case of a postponement the court may impose conditions concerning payment of arrears of rent: s. 9(3); and where these conditions are complied with, the court may discharge or rescind the order for possession: s. 9(4). There are special provisions applicable to shared accommodation: *see* s. 10. *See also* Sch. 1, Part IV.

7.   Misrepresentation, etc.

Where L has obtained an order for possession of a dwelling-house let on an assured tenancy and it is shown subsequently that misrepresentation or concealment of material facts was used, the court may order L to pay T compensation for damage or loss sustained as a result of the order: s. 12.

Rent and other matters

8.   Increases in rent

For the purpose of securing an increase of rent under an assured periodic tenancy, L may serve on T a notice in prescribed form, proposing a new rent to take effect at the beginning of a new period of tenancy, not earlier than the minimum period after the date of service of the notice and (except in the case of a statutory periodic tenancy) the first anniversary of the date on which the first period of the tenancy began, and, if the rent under the tenancy has previously been increased by virtue of a notice under this section, or a determination of rent by an assessment committee, the first anniversary of the date on which the increase took effect: s. 13.

(a) The 'minimum period' referred to above is: yearly tenancy — six months; tenancy less than a month — one month; in any other case — a period equal to the period of the tenancy: s. 13(3).
(b) L and T have the right to vary by agreement any term of an assured tenancy (including a term relating to rent): s. 13(5).
(c) A rent assessment committee shall determine rent when a notice of increase is referred to it by T: s. 14. It shall consider the rent at which the dwelling-house concerned 'might reasonably be expected to be let in the open market by a willing landlord under an assured tenancy' which, e.g. is a periodic tenancy having the same periods as those of the tenancy to which the notice relates: s. 14(1)(a). The

committee will disregard, e.g. any increase in the value of the dwelling-house attributable to a relevant improvement carried out by T, if carried out otherwise than in pursuance of an obligation to his immediate landlord: s. 14(2)(b). *See N. & D.* v. *Gadsdon* (1992).

9. Assignment, etc. without consent

Under HA 1988, s. 15(1), it shall be an implied term of every assured periodic tenancy that, except with L's consent, T shall not assign the tenancy (in whole or part), or sub-let or part with possession of the whole or any part of the dwelling-house.

10. Access for repairs

Under HA 1988, s. 16, it shall be an implied term of every assured tenancy that T shall afford to L access to the dwelling-house for executing therein any reasonable repairs which L is entitled to execute.

11. Succession by spouse

Where the sole tenant (T) under an assured periodic tenancy dies and, immediately before T's death, T's spouse (S) was occupying the dwelling-house as his/her only or principal home, and T was not himself/herself a successor, then, on the death, the tenancy vests in S; it does *not* devolve under T's will or intestacy: s. 17.

The assured shorthold tenancy

12. Meaning

An assured shorthold tenancy (*ast*) (created by HA 1988) is an assured tenancy which is *a fixed term tenancy granted for a term certain of not less than six months*, and in respect of which there is no power for L to determine the tenancy at any time earlier than six months from the beginning of the tenancy, and in respect of which a notice is served in prescribed form, stating that the assured tenancy to which it relates is to be a shorthold tenancy: s. 20(1),(2). It should be noted that a new tenancy *cannot* be an *ast* where:

(a) immediately before a tenancy ('the new tenancy') is granted, the grantee was a tenant under an assured tenancy which was not a shorthold tenancy, *and*

(b) the new tenancy is granted by the person who, immediately before the beginning of the tenancy, was the landlord under the assured tenancy referred to in (a) above: s. 20(3).

(Essentially, almost all *new lettings* in the private rented sector are now *either* assured tenancies *or* assured shorthold tenancies.)

13. Recovery of possession
On the expiry or termination of an *ast* which was a fixed term tenancy, the court may order possession if satisfied that the tenancy has ended *and* no further assured tenancy (other than a statutory periodic tenancy) is in existence *and* L has given *at least two months' notice*, stating that he requires possession: s. 21.

14. Excessive rents
Under an *ast*, T may apply to a rent assessment committee for a determination of the rent which, in the committee's opinion, L might reasonably be expected to obtain under the *ast*: s. 22(1). (L can apply only after the lease has been in existence for 12 months: s. 22(4).)

(a) No application may be made if the rent payable has been previously determined under s. 22, or the tenancy is an *ast* in respect of which notice need not have been served under s. 20(2): s. 22(2).
(b) The committee will not make a determination of rent *unless* they consider that there is a sufficient number of similar dwelling-houses in the locality let on assured tenancies, *and* that the rent that has been paid is 'significantly higher' than the rent which L might reasonably be expected to be able to obtain under the tenancy: s. 22(3).

> NOTE: Business tenancies are covered, in general, by the Landlord and Tenant Act 1954, Part II. The premises covered are those occupied by the tenant for the purposes of a business carried on by him. 'Business' includes a trade, profession or employment (*see* s. 23). Where the tenant occupies through his servants, personal occupation is not required.

Progress test 8

1. Explain the 'new-style assured tenancy' under the Housing Act 1988. **(1)**

2. 'Not every tenancy can be an assured tenancy.' Explain. **(2)**

3. When *must* the court issue a possession order in the case of an assured tenancy? **(4)**

4.   Explain the procedure for obtaining possession of an assured tenancy.   **(6)**

5.   Outline the essential features of the 'assured shorthold tenancy'.   **(12)**

Housing associations, housing trust areas, and change of landlord

Housing associations

1. Meaning
Under the Housing Associations Act 1985, s. 1, a 'housing association' means a society, body of trustees or company which does not trade for profit and among whose objects are the providing, constructing, improving, managing, or encouraging the construction or improvement of housing accommodation. Registration of housing associations is at the discretion of the Housing Corporation: s. 5.

2. Additional purposes
Under the Housing Associations Act 1985, s. 4(3), substituted by HA 1988, s. 48(1), permissible additional purposes of housing associations include the provision of land and services for the benefit of the associations' residents, the conversion of property, the construction of houses for shared ownership, the managing of houses held on leases.

3. Guidance and grants
Under the Housing Associations Act 1985, s. 36A, inserted by HA 1988, s. 49, the Corporation may issue guidance concerning the management of accommodation. The Housing Corporation and Housing for Wales (the latter body was created under HA 1988, s. 46) may make grants to registered housing associations: HA 1988, s. 50.

Housing action trust areas

4. Designated areas
Under HA 1988, s. 60(1), the Secretary of State may designate areas of land for which, in his opinion, it is expedient that a housing

action trust (*hat*) be established. (The constitution of a *hat* is set out in the HA 1988, Sch. 7.) The designated area may comprise two or more parcels of land which need not be contiguous and need not be in the district of the same local housing authority: s. 60(3). The *objects of a hat* are: to secure the repair and improvement of housing accommodation held by the trust to secure the proper management and use of that accommodation, to encourage diversity in the identity of landlords, and to secure the improvement of living conditions in the area: s. 63(1). The *hat* may acquire, hold, dispose of land, carry out building operations and carry on any business or undertaking: s. 63(3). It must prepare a statement of its proposals for its area: s. 64(1).

5. Functions

The functions of a *hat* are based on HA 1985, Parts II, VI, VII, IX–XII, XVI (which include provision of housing accommodation, repair and improvement notices, slum clearance, overcrowding control, assistance for owners of defective housing, etc.). Additionally, under the HA 1988, it may exercise planning control (s. 67), give financial assistance (s. 71), acquire land adjacent to or outside the designated area (s. 77), dispose of land (s. 79 and Sch. 11). (*See* s. 79(1) for the rule prohibiting a *hat* in general, disposing of a house which is subject to a secure tenancy.) The Secretary of State may order the transfer of land from a local housing authority to a *hat* (s. 74).

6. Disposal of dwelling-houses subject to secure tenancies

Where a *hat* wishes to dispose of houses let on secure tenancies which could result in a person who, before the disposal, is a secure tenant of the trust, becoming the tenant of another person, the consent of the Secretary of State must be sought, and written notice must be served on the appropriate local housing authority and the secure tenant: s. 84.

7. Rents

A *hat* may make 'such reasonable charges as it may determine for the tenancy or occupation of housing accommodation for the time being held by it': s. 85(1). It may review and change rents 'as circumstances may require': s. 85(2).

(a) Where the tenancy is *not* 'secure', the rent may be increased with effect from the beginning of a rental period by written notice given by the *hat* to T: s. 86(2).

(b) Notice of an increase must be given at least four weeks before the first day of the rental period, or any earlier day on which payment of rent in respect of that period falls to be made; it should inform T of his right to terminate the tenancy if he wishes to do so: s. 86(3).

Public sector tenants' right to buy

8.   Right conferred by HA 1988, Part IV
    Under HA 1988, s. 93(1), a right is conferred on any 'approved person' (*see* **9** below) to acquire from a 'public sector landlord' (*see* **(b)** below) the fee simple estate in any buildings each of which contains one or more dwelling-houses occupied by 'qualifying tenants' (*see* **(c)** below) of the public sector landlord, *and* the fee simple estate in any other property reasonably required for occupation with those buildings.

(a) For 'fee simple estate', *see* 3:**2**.
(b) 'Public sector landlords' include: local housing authorities within HA 1985, s. 1; new town corporations within HA 1985, s. 4(b); *hat* (*see* **4** above); the Development Board for Wales.
(c) 'Qualifying tenants' include secure tenants of a public sector landlord whose secure tenancies are held directly from a landlord as owner of the fee simple estate: HA 1988, s. 93(4).

9.   Persons who may exercise the right
    The right is not exercisable *except* by a person approved by the Corporation; and neither a public sector landlord nor the council of a county 'nor any other body which the Corporation have reason to believe might not be independent of such a landlord or council' may be approved: s. 94(1).

10. Property excluded from a Part IV acquisition
    The following buildings are excluded from a Part IV acquisition.

(a) Those of which any parts are occupied otherwise than for residential purposes, and the internal floor area of those parts exceeds 50 per cent of the internal floor area of the building.
(b) Those which contain two or more dwelling-houses which are occupied by secure tenants who are not 'qualifying tenants' and the number of dwelling-houses which are occupied by such tenants exceeds 50 per cent of the total number of dwelling-houses in the building.
(c) Those dwelling-houses occupied by secure tenants who are

precluded from being qualifying tenants, or tenants who are not secure tenants: *see* s. 95.

11. Application to exercise the right

An application must be made in the prescribed form and accompanied by a plan: s. 96(1). An applicant has the right of access to the property proposed for acquisition: s. 97(2).

12. Determination of purchase price

The relevant provision is HA 1988, s. 99, as amended by the Local Government and Housing Act 1989, s. 174. Subject to s. 100(3) (relating to excluded houses) and s. 103(1) (relating to the value of covenants), the price payable for the property to be acquired shall be the price which on the relevant date the property to which the acquisition relates would realise if sold 'on the open market by a willing vendor on the following assumptions'.

(a) That it was sold subject to any tenancies subsisting on that date but otherwise with vacant possession.

(b) That it was to be conveyed with the same rights and subject to the same burdens as it would be in pursuance of the right of acquisition.

(c) That the only bidders in the market were persons who on that date either were approved under s. 94 (*see* **9** above) or fulfilled the criteria for approval under s. 94(3).

(d) That the applicant would, within a reasonable period, carry out such works as are reasonably necessary to put the buildings included in the acquisition into the state of repair required by the landlord's repairing obligations.

(e) That the applicant would not be required to grant any leases in pursuance of regulations made under s. 100.

13. Final procedures

Under s. 102, the applicant (the potential new landlord) is obliged to consult, in accordance with such provisions as may be prescribed, the tenants likely to be affected by the change of landlord. Under s. 103(1), the applicant may serve on L notice of his intention to proceed with the acquisition. But notice may not be served if less than 50 per cent of the tenants involved have given notice (in the prescribed manner) of their wishes, *or* the number of tenants who have given notice of their wish to continue as tenants of the landlord exceeds 50 per cent of the total number of tenants involved: s. 103(2). Following notice, L must make to the applicant a grant of the property included in the acquisition for an estate in fee simple absolute, but subject to any rights to be retained by L, and the applicant must grant to L leases of any flats which he is required to grant under s. 100: s. 104(1). *See* Local Government and Housing Act 1989, s. 174 (payment of disposal costs).

14. Subsequent disposals

The new landlord may not dispose of any property acquired under Part IV except with the consent of the Secretary of State: s. 105(1). But this does not apply to 'exempt disposals', as set out in s. 105(7); they include, e.g. disposal of an easement, or of an interest by way of security for a loan. References to 'disposing of property' include references to: the granting or disposing of any interest in property; entering into a contract to dispose of property or to grant or dispose of any such interest; granting an option to acquire property or any such interest: s. 105(8). *See* Local Government and Housing Act 1989, Sch. 11, para. 107.

Progress test 9

1.   What are the features of a 'housing action trust area'?   **(4)**

2.   Explain the rights conferred by the Housing Act 1988, Part IV. **(8)**

3.   What types of property are excluded from a 'Part IV acquisition'?   **(10)**

4.   Outline the principles relating to the subsequent disposal of property acquired under Part IV.   **(14)**

Part three

Strict settlements and trusts for sale

10

Strict settlements

The nature of a settlement

1. Essentials

A *settlement* involves a disposition of property, freehold or leasehold, (by deed or will) for persons so that a *succession of beneficial interests* in the property is created. Under such a settlement *one* person may be entitled *at any particular time* to possession and enjoyment of the land, e.g. 'to A for life, remainder to B in fee simple'. (The term 'settlement' includes 'strict settlements' and 'trusts for sale' (*see* Ch. 11).) Note that a settlement of *personalty* is possible; in this chapter we are concerned with settlements of *land*.

2. The problem

The modern settlement originated in an attempt to solve the following problem: assume that A wished to provide for his wife during her widowhood, for his eldest son, for his other children, and for members of his family who might be born in the future. Should A make a settlement, then there would then be no one person who could *sell the fee simple* if that were to become necessary in the interests of the family, e.g. for purposes of developing the property.

3. A solution

If there existed a person who had the power to convey the fee simple, *even though he did not own it,* the problem might be solved. Additionally, if that person were able to convey a fee simple unencumbered by the beneficial interests of members of the family, then a purchaser would be able to take free of the interests which could be transferred from the land to purchase money. The Settled Land Acts 1882, 1925, attempted to solve the problem in this way.

4. Strict settlements and trusts for sale

Settlements (which comprise 'strict settlements' and trusts for sale) are methods of settling land. The object of the *trust for sale* (*see* Ch. 11) is to sell the land, but the sale can be postponed indefinitely. The object of the *strict settlement* is to keep the land in the family, although, in fact, the tenant for life is empowered to sell. The strict settlement and the trust for sale are *mutually exclusive*: SLA 1925, s. 1(7). The strict settlement is governed by SLA 1925; the trust for sale by LPA 1925. The strict settlement is now obsolescent; the trust for sale has virtually replaced it.

Settled Land Act 1925

5.   Changes made by SLA 1925

The main changes in the law introduced by the 1925 Act were as follows:

(a)   Strict settlements had to be made by *two documents*. Prior to 1926 one document sufficed. In settlements made after 1925 a trust instrument *and* a principal vesting deed are essential (*see* **6–8** below).

(b)   Trusts for sale were excluded from the Act (*see* LP (Amendment) A 1926, s. 7) and are now regulated by LPA 1925.

(c)   The whole legal estate is *vested in the (statutory) tenant for life* (not to be confused with the 'life tenant', who has a mere equitable life interest in property: *see* **12:2**) except:

(*i*)   where there is no tenant for life (*see*, e.g. *Re Gallenga* (1938)), and in such a case the legal estate and statutory powers will vest in the *statutory owner* (i.e. the person of full age upon whom express powers are conferred by the settlement, or the trustees of the settlement);

(*ii*)   where the tenant for life is a minor, and in such case the legal estate and statutory powers will vest in the personal representative in whom the land is vested, or the trustees of the settlement: *see* ss. 23,117.

Creation of a strict settlement under SLA 1925

6.   SLA 1925, s. 4(1)

'Every settlement of a legal estate in land *inter vivos* shall, save as in this Act otherwise provided, be effected by *two deeds*, namely, a *vesting deed* and a *trust instrument* and if effected in any other way shall not operate to transfer or create a legal estate.' (The trust instrument (the so-called 'private document') states the beneficial interests of the tenant for life (*see* **18** below) and his successors. It is effectively 'behind the curtain', in that the purchaser is not entitled to see it. The vesting deed (the so-called 'public document') contains the information which the purchaser is entitled to see.) (Note *Ungurian* v. *Lesnoff* (1989) in which a strict settlement was *implied* although there was neither trust instrument nor vesting deed.)

7. The trust instrument

This instrument must, under s. 4(3):

(a) declare the trusts affecting the settled land (thereby creating equitable interests under the settlement);
(b) appoint the trustees of the settlement;
(c) contain the power, if any, to appoint new trustees of the settlement;
(d) set out the powers intended to be conferred by the settlement in extension of those conferred by the Act;
(e) bear any stamp duty payable in respect of the settlement.

8. The vesting deed

This instrument (referred to as the *principal vesting deed*) must contain, under s. 5(1):

(a) a general or specific description of the settled land;
(b) a statement that the settled land is vested in the person or persons to whom it is conveyed or in whom it is declared to be vested upon the trusts from time to time affecting the settled land;
(c) the names of the trustees of the settlement (since the purchase money must be paid to them);
(d) additional or larger powers conferred by the trust instrument;
(e) the name of the person entitled under the trust instrument to appoint new trustees.

> NOTE: Under s. 110(2) (the 'curtain principle') the purchaser of a legal estate in settled land is obliged to take the vesting deed at *face value* and to assume that the particulars are correct. Note also that, under s. 18, once a vesting instrument is executed, unauthorised dispositions of settled land become void. *See* **41**(b) below.

9. A strict settlement created by will

Where the settlement is created by will, the will is, for the purposes of the Act, a trust instrument: s. 6(a). The personal representatives of the testator, in whom the legal estate vests in the first place, must vest the legal estate in the tenant for life by a vesting instrument. The vesting instrument may be a vesting deed or a vesting assent, 'which shall contain the like statements and particulars as are required by this Act in the case of a principal vesting deed': s. 8(4)(b).

10. Subsidiary vesting deeds

Section 10 provides for the procedure whereby other land is brought into a settlement which is in existence. In such a case a subsidiary vesting deed is needed, and it must contain:

(a) particulars of the last or only principal vesting instrument affecting land subject to the settlement;
(b) a statement that the land conveyed is to be held upon and subject to the same trusts and powers as the land comprised in such last or only principal vesting instrument;
(c) the names of persons who are the trustees of the settlement;
(d) the name of any person for the time being entitled to appoint new trustees of the settlement.

11. When the disposition of the legal estate takes effect

When a tenant for life, or statutory owner, has become entitled to have a principal vesting deed, or a vesting assent executed in his favour, then any purported disposition of the legal estate before the execution of the vesting instrument will not take effect *except* in favour of a purchaser of the legal estate without notice of any settlement: s. 13. The exceptions to this rule are:

(a) where the settlement has ended before the execution of a vesting instrument: *Re Alefounder's WT* (1927);
(b) where there has been a disposition by a personal representative: s. 13. *See Re Cayley & Evans' Contract* (1930);
(c) under the provisions of LP (Amendment) A 1926: where a person of full age is beneficially entitled to land in fee simple which is charged voluntarily or in consideration of marriage, or by way of family arrangement, with rentcharges (see 16:**27**), portions, etc., he can convey the land subject to the charges as though it were not settled land, i.e. he can sell it as though he were an absolute owner and without having to execute a vesting deed.

What constitutes a strict settlement

12. Settled land

'Land which is or is deemed to be the subject of a settlement is for the purposes of the Act settled land, and is in relation to the settlement referred to in this Act as the settled land': SLA 1925, s. 2.

13. A settlement for the purposes of the Act
Under SLA 1925, s. 1(1), a settlement will be created by an instrument or instruments whereby land stands:

(a) limited in trust for any persons by way of succession (i.e. the usual express settlement); or

(b) limited in trust for any person in possession:
    (*i*) for an entailed interest, barrable or not; or
    (*ii*) for an estate in fee simple or for a term of years absolute subject to an executory limitation;
    (*iii*) for a base or determinable fee; or
    (*iv*) in the case of a minor, for an estate in fee simple or for a term of years absolute; or

(c) limited in trust for any person for an estate in fee simple or for a term of years absolute contingently on the happening of any event; or

(d) charged, voluntarily or in consideration of marriage or by way of family arrangement, with the payment of sums (portions, maintenance, etc.) for the benefit of persons: *see Re Austen* (1929).

> NOTE: This section has no application to land held on trust for sale: s. 1(7).

14. Examples of settlements under s. 1(1)
The following examples indicate the types of settlements which can be created in accordance with SLA 1925, s. 1(1).

(a) 'To John for life and then to Mary' (s. 1(1)(i)) — *see* **13(a)** above).

(b) 'To John for life and the first of his sons in tail male' (s. 1(1)(ii)(a) — *see* **13(b)**(*i*) above).

(c) 'To John for life, but then to Mary when John shall qualify as an architect' (s. 1(1)(ii)(b) — *see* **13(b)**(*ii*) above).

(d) 'To John until he qualifies as an architect' (s. 1(1)(ii)(c) — *see* **13(b)**(*iii*) above).

(e) 'To John in fee simple' (Note: John is 14) (s. 1(1)(ii)(d) — *see* **13(b)**(*iv*) above).

(f) 'To John when he shall marry' (s. 1(1)(iii) — *see* **13(c)** above).

(g) 'To John in fee simple, but subject to his charging the property with an annual payment of £10,000 for the maintenance of Mary' (s. 1(1)(v) — *see* **13(d)** above).

Other types of settlement

15. Referential settlements
These are settlements which incorporate earlier settlements by reference: SLA 1925, s. 32.

16. Compound settlements
Where new trusts are declared of land subject to a 'subsisting settlement', the land is held to be subject to a compound settlement. Under SLA 1925, s. 31(1), the trustees of the subsisting settlement (or, if none, the trustees of the resettlement: LP (Amendment) A 1926) shall be the trustees of the compound settlement. *See Re Ogle* (1927).

17. Ad hoc settlements
In the case of land which is not already settled land, a person of full age beneficially entitled in possession to a legal estate subject to equitable interests may by deed declare that the legal estate is vested in him on trust to give effect to those interests: SLA 1925, s. 21(1). Such a deed must be executed by two or more trustees appointed by the court, or by a trust corporation (*see* 11:**21**). He may then sell as a tenant for life, and the equitable interests are charged against the purchase money: *see* 11:**24**.

The tenant for life under SLA

18. Definition under SLA
Under s. 117(1)(xxviii), 'tenant for life' includes 'a person (not being a statutory owner) who has the powers of a tenant for life under this Act'. *See Re Jefferys* (1939).

19. Who is the tenant for life?
'The person of full age who is for the time being beneficially entitled under a settlement to possession of settled land for his life is for the purposes of this Act the tenant for life of that land and the tenant for life under that settlement': s. 19(1). He is, in general, the first person who is entitled under the settlement to the property. 'If in any case there are two or more persons of full age so entitled as joint tenants, they together constitute the tenant for life for the purposes of this Act': s. 19(2).

20. Limited owners having the powers of a statutory tenant for life

Under SLA 1925, s. 20(1), each of the following persons being of full age shall, when his estate or interest is in possession, have the *powers of a tenant for life* under this Act:

(a) a tenant in tail, including a tenant in tail after possibility of issue extinct;

(b) a person entitled to land for an estate in fee simple or for a term of years absolute with or subject to, in any of such cases, an executory limitation, gift or disposition over on failure of his issue or in any other event (*see also* LPA 1925, s. 134(1));

(c) a person entitled to a base or determinable fee, or to any corresponding interest in leasehold land;

(d) a tenant for years determinable on life, not holding merely under a lease at a rent (*see Re Catling* (1931) — definition excluded a person paying only a nominal rent);

(e) a tenant for the life of another, not holding merely under a lease at a rent;

(f) a tenant for his own or any other life, or for years determinable on life, whose estate is liable to cease in any event during that life, whether by expiration of the estate, or by conditional limitation, or otherwise, or to be defeated by an executory limitation, gift or disposition over, or is subject to a trust for accumulation of income for any purpose;

(g) a tenant by the curtesy (abolished by AEA 1925, s. 45(1) except as regards entailed interests (*see* also LPA 1925, s. 130(4), and 13:**34**));

(h) a person entitled to the income of land under a trust or direction for payment thereof to him during his own or any other life, whether or not subject to expenses of management or to a trust for accumulation of income for any purpose, or until sale of land, or until forfeiture, cesser or determination by any means of his interest therein, unless the land is subject to an immediate binding trust for sale;

(i) a person beneficially entitled to land for an estate in fee simple or for a term of years absolute subject to any estates, interests, charges, or powers of charging, subsisting or capable of being exercised under a settlement.

NOTE: The powers of a tenant for life are discussed at **27–33** below.

21. Where there is no tenant for life

See Re Frewen (1926). Where there is no tenant for life under a settlement (e.g. where the person entitled is a minor) nor a person having, by virtue of SLA, the powers of a tenant for life, statutory powers are to be exercised by the so-called *statutory owners*, who are either:

(a) any person of full age upon whom the powers are conferred: *or*
(b) in any other case, the trustees of the settlement: s. 23(1).

Trustees of the strict settlement and their duties

22. Trustees for the purpose of SLA

The following are trustees of a settlement for purposes of the Act, under s. 30(1):

(a) the persons, if any, who are for the time being under the settlement trustees with power of sale of the settled land; or, if none, then
(b) the persons, if any, for the time being, declared by the settlements to be trustees *for the purpose of the Settled Land Acts*; or, if none, then
(c) the persons, if any, who are for the time being under the settlement trustees with power of sale of any other land comprised in the settlement and subject to the same limitations as the land to be sold or otherwise dealt with; or, if none, then
(d) the persons, if any, who are for the time being under the settlement trustees with a future power of sale; or, if none, then
(e) the persons, if any, appointed by deed to be trustees of the settlement by all the persons who at the date of the deed were together able, by virtue of their beneficial interests or by the exercise of an equitable power, to dispose of the settled land in equity for the whole estate the subject of the settlement.

23. Lack of trustees under a settlement created by will or on intestacy

In the case of a settlement created by will or arising under an intestacy, and where there are no trustees, the *personal representatives* of the deceased act as trustees of the settlement until others are appointed. In the case of there being only one personal representative (not a trust corporation), he must appoint an additional trustee to act with him: SLA 1925, s. 30(3).

24. Appointment of trustees by the court

'If at any time there are no trustees of a settlement, or where in any other case it is expedient for the purposes of this Act that new trustees of a settlement be appointed, *the court* may, if it thinks fit, on the application of the tenant for life, statutory owner, or of any other person having, under the settlement, an estate or interest in the settled land, in possession, remainder or otherwise, or, in the case of an infant, of his testamentary or other guardian or next friend, *appoint fit persons to be trustees* of the settlement': SLA 1925, s. 34(1).

25. The duties of the trustees

In general, trustees under SLA must supervise the control of the settled land, for example:

(a) they must receive and hold capital money: SLA 1925, s. 18(1)(b);

(b) they must consent to transactions by the tenant for life, e.g. the compromising of claims: SLA 1925, s. 58(1);

(c) they must act as statutory owners in the absence of a tenant for life, or where the tenant for life is a minor;

(d) they must execute vesting deeds or deeds of discharge: SLA 1925, s. 17;

(e) they must exercise the power of the tenant for life if he wishes to acquire the settled land for his own benefit: SLA 1925, s. 68;

(f) where the tenant for life is a minor they must manage or superintend the management of the land, with full power to deal with the following matters, for example:

    (*i*) the felling of timber;

    (*ii*) the erection, rebuilding and repair of houses;

    (*iii*) the insuring of property against loss by fire;

    (*iv*) the determination of tenancies: SLA 1925, s. 102(2).

26. The liability of the trustees of the settlement

In general, the liability of the trustees does *not* extend to *all* the acts of the tenant for life. Their liability is restricted under SLA 1925. Thus:

(a) they are not liable for giving consent or for not bringing an action which they might have brought: s. 97(a);

(b) they are not liable for not investigating the propriety of a purchase of land with capital money arising under the Act: s. 97(b) (*see Wheelright* v. *Walker* (1883));

(c) they are not liable for investigation of title if the conveyance purports to convey the land in the proper mode: s. 97(c);

(d) they are not liable for the acts of an agent employed by the tenant for life, or for not employing an agent in the valuation of a proposed security or investment: s. 98(1);

(e) they are not liable for paying or applying capital money by the direction of the tenant for life: s. 98(2);

(f) each trustee is answerable only for what he actually receives, notwithstanding his signing any receipt for conformity; nor is he answerable for the acts and defaults of any other trustee: s. 96.

Powers conferred by SLA on tenant for life

27. The statutory powers

The extensive powers conferred upon the tenant for life have as their object 'to render the land a marketable article, notwithstanding the settlement': *per* Chitty LJ in *Re Mundy and Roper's Contract* (1899). In effect, the tenant for life has the fee simple which he can sell, lease or mortgage. They may be classified under the following headings:

(a) power of sale and exchange (*see* **28** below);

(b) power to grant and accept leases (*see* **30** below);

(c) power to borrow money (*see* **31** below);

(d) power to apply capital money (*see* **32** below);

(e) miscellaneous powers (*see* **33** below).

28. Power of sale and exchange

'A tenant for life may sell the settled land, or any part thereof, or any easement, right or privilege of any kind over or in relation to the land': SLA 1925, s. 38(i). He may also 'make an exchange of the settled land or any part thereof, or of any easement, right, or privilege of any kind. . .': s. 38(iii). (For power to sell the house occupied as the main residence, *see* s. 65.)

(a) A sale 'shall be made for the best consideration in money that can reasonably be obtained': s. 39(1).

(b) A sale may be made 'in consideration wholly or partially of a perpetual rent, or a terminable rent consisting of principal and interest combined, payable yearly or half yearly to be secured upon the land sold': s. 39(2).

(c) The rent 'shall be the best rent that can reasonably be obtained': s. 39(3).

(d) In the case of a sale in consideration of a rent, 'the conveyance shall contain a covenant by the purchaser for payment of the rent, and the statutory powers and remedies for the recovery of the rent shall apply': s. 39(4)(i). (The powers referred to are contained in LPA 1925, s. 121.)

(e) Where land is sold to a company incorporated by Act of Parliament the consideration on sale may 'with the consent of the tenant for life, consist, wholly or in part, of fully-paid securities of any description of the company': s. 39(5).

(f) A sale may be made in one lot or in several lots, and either by auction or by private contract: s. 39(6).

29. Notice to trustees of intention to sell or exchange

A tenant for life when intending to make a sale, exchange, lease, mortgage or charge or to grant an option must give notice to the trustees, not less than one month before the transaction, of his intention. 'Any trustee, by writing under his hand, may waive notice either in any particular case, or generally, and may accept less than one month's notice': SLA 1925, s. 101(4).

30. Power to grant and accept leases

A tenant for life may lease the settled land for any purpose for any term not exceeding: in the case of a building lease, 999 years; mining lease, 100 years; forestry lease, 999 years; in any other lease, 50 years: SLA 1925, s. 41. (He should give written notice to the trustees of his intention to grant a lease.)

(a) The lease must be by deed (*see Re Morgan's Lease* (1972)), to take effect in possession not later than twelve months after its date, or in reversion after an existing lease, not having more than seven years to run at the date of the new lease, must reserve the best rent obtainable and must contain a covenant for re-entry: s. 42(1).

(b) A lease at the best rent obtainable, whereby the lessee is not exempted from punishment for waste, may be made without notice to the trustees if the term does not exceed twenty-one years: s. 42(5).

(c) In the case of a binding lease a nominal rent may be made payable for the first five years, or any less part of the term: s. 44(2).

(d) In the case of a mining lease (*see* LPA 1925, s. 205(1)(xiv); SLA 1925, s. 117(1)(xv)), the rent may be made to vary according to the acreage worked or according to the quantities mined: s. 45(1)(i). Part of the rent is to be set aside as capital money: three-fourths where the tenant for life is impeachable for waste, one-fourth where he is unimpeachable for waste: s. 47.

(e) In the case of a forestry lease, the rent may be nominal for the first ten years: s. 48(1)(i).

(f) The tenant for life 'may accept a lease of any land or of any mines and minerals or of any easement, right or privilege, convenient to be held or worked with or annexed in enjoyment to the settled land': s. 53(1).

> NOTE: For the power to grant options, *see* ss. 51, 90(1)(i). An option must be made exercisable within an agreed number of years not exceeding ten: s. 51(2).

31. Power to borrow money

The tenant for life may raise money on the security of the settled land, or of any part thereof, by a *legal mortgage,* and the money so raised shall be capital money for that purpose and may be paid or applied accordingly. The power to raise money by mortgage applies in nine specified cases: SLA 1925, s. 71(1). These cases include:

(a) discharging an incumbrance on the settled land or part thereof;
(b) paying for any improvement authorised by SLA or the settlement;
(c) equality of exchange;
(d) commuting an additional rent made payable on the conversion of a perpetually renewable leasehold interest into a long term;
(e) payment of the costs of any transaction authorised by ss. 69-71.

32. Power to apply capital money

Capital money is that which results from the exercising of a statutory power, as in the case of a mining rent (*see* **30(d)** above) or in the case of damages received by the tenant for life for breach of a covenant by a lessee: SLA 1925, s. 80(1). Twenty-one modes of investment or application of capital money are stated, and include the following:

(a) *Investment in securities*: s. 73(1)(i). Investment may be made in Government securities, or in other securities in which the trustees of the settlement are by the settlement or by law authorised to invest trust money. A wide category is permitted under the Trustee Investments Act 1961, as amended. *See* the Agricultural Holdings Act 1986, Sch. 14; *Steel* v. *Wellcome Custodian Trustees Ltd* (1988) (approval of power to delegate investment of funds).
(b) *Purchase of land*: s. 73(1)(xi), (xii). Capital money may be used to purchase land in fee simple, or leasehold land held for sixty years or more unexpired at the time of purchase, or to purchase, either in fee simple or for a term of sixty years or more, mines and minerals convenient to be held or worked with the settled land.

(c) *Payment for authorised improvements*: s. 73(1)(iii). If the capital money is with the court, the court may, if it thinks fit, 'on a report or certificate of the Minister, or of a competent engineer or able practical surveyor approved by the court, or such other evidence as the court may think sufficient', make an order for the application of the money towards payment for the improvements: s. 84(3). The SLA 1925 enumerates over thirty specified improvements: Third Schedule:

    (i) *Part I improvements*: e.g. drainage, bridges, reclamation. In this case the costs *need not* be replaced by instalments.

    (ii) *Part II improvements*: e.g. restoration of damaged buildings, structural alterations to buildings. The costs of these improvements *may be* replaced by instalments.

    (iii) *Part III improvements*: e.g. heating or electric power apparatus for buildings, machinery for farming purposes. The costs of these improvements *must be* replaced by instalments.

33. Miscellaneous powers

The Act includes a number of miscellaneous powers of the tenant for life, some of which are as follows:

(a) Power to sell heirlooms, under order of the court: s. 67. The money received becomes capital money.

(b) Power to make a grant or lease at a nominal price or rent for a public or charitable purpose: s. 55(1).

(c) Power, with the consent of the trustees, to compromise claims concerning the settled land: s. 58(1).

NOTE: (1) The court may sanction any transaction (which includes any sale, exchange, grant, lease) which is not otherwise authorised by the Act or settlement if it considers the transaction to be 'for the benefit of the settled land... or the persons interested under the settlement': s. 64(1), (2). *See Re Rycroft's Settlement* (1962); *Raikes* v. *Lygon* (1988) — trustees had power to transfer part of settled land to a maintenance fund so as to ensure that the overall fund was managed in a tax-efficient manner. *See also* SLA 1925, s. 46; Trustee Act 1925, s. 57; Variation of Trusts Act 1958. (2) The settlement may grant powers additional to those conferred under the Act: s. 109(1). (3) Any limitation on the exercise of powers by a tenant for life is void: s. 106(1). *See Re Aberconway's ST* (1953). In *Re Ames* (1893) it was held that a provision which took from the tenant for life the right to a financial benefit in the event of the land being sold was void, because it discouraged sale of the land. (4) Where a tenant surrenders his life interest to the reversioner or remainderman, 'the statutory powers shall thenceforth become exercisable as if he were dead': s. 105(1). *See Re Acklom* (1929); *Re Maryon-Wilson's Instruments* (1971). (5) Any disposition by the tenant for life other than one authorised by the Act is void: s. 18(1).

34. The beneficiaries and the tenant for life

'A tenant for life or statutory owner shall, in exercising any power under this Act, have regard to the interests of all parties entitled under the settlement, and shall, in relation to the exercise thereof by him, be deemed to be in the position and to have the duties and liabilities of a trustee for those parties': s. 107(1).

(a) The tenant for life 'must come to what, in his judgment, is the right thing to do under the circumstances — not the best thing, but the right thing to do': *per* Lord Esher in *Re Earl of Radnor's WT* (1890). **(b)** Where a power is exercised by the tenant for life solely to acquire a benefit for himself, he will be liable: *Chandler* v. *Bradley* (1897) — tenant for life accepted a bribe from lessee in return for reduced rent.

35. Dealings as between the tenant for life and the estate

Where a life tenant wishes to exercise a power in his own favour, s. 68(1) allows land to be bought from him, or exchanged with him, or the advancement of capital money on mortgage to him. *See Re Pennant's WT* (1970).

NOTE: A tenant for life cannot contract *not* to exercise his statutory powers: s. 104.

Overreaching under SLA

36. SLA 1925, s. 72(2)

'Overreaching' involves *detaching equitable interests from the land and attaching them to the purchase money*. The purchaser then takes the land free of those interests. Where the tenant for life effects a disposition concerning the settled land by deed, such a deed conveys the land discharged from 'all the limitations, powers, and provisions of the settlement, and from all estates, interests and charges subsisting or to arise thereunder...' *Such a conveyance is subject, however, to the following*:

(a) all legal estates and charges by way of legal mortgage having priority to the settlement;
(b) all legal estates and charges by way of legal mortgage which have

been conveyed or created for securing money actually raised at the date of the deed;

(c) all leases and grants at fee-farm rents, i.e. perpetual rents issuing out of lands held in fee simple, reserved on grant of the lands, or otherwise, and all grants of easements, rights of common, or other rights which:

> (*i*) were before the date of the deed granted or made for value in money or money's worth, or agreed so to be, by the tenant for life or statutory owner, or by any of his predecessors in title, or by any trustees for them under the settlement, or under any statutory power, or are at the date otherwise binding on the successors in title of the tenant for life or statutory owner;
>
> (*ii*) are at the date of the deed protected by registration under the Land Charges Act, if capable of registration thereunder: SLA 1925, s. 72(2)(i–iii).

37. Overreaching

Registration under the Land Charges Acts (*see* Ch. 18), does *not* prevent the overreaching of the following interests:

(a) an annuity (*see* LCA 1972, s. 1(1), (4));

(b) a limited owner's charge, or a general equitable charge.

38. Capital money received

See SLA 1925, s. 75. The capital money received as the result of a conveyance must be paid into the court or to the trustees, who must be at least two in number, or a trust corporation. *Interests overreached by the conveyance are enforceable against the money held by the trustees.*

> NOTE: 'Capital' is not defined in SLA 1925; *see*, however, ss. 79, 80, and *Re Pelly's WT* (1957). Capital money includes proceeds of sale or mortgage paid by a tenant for breach of covenant, etc. Such money, and investments representing it, are treated as land, and will be subject to the same trusts as the land: s. 75(5).

Change of ownership and protection of purchasers under SLA

39. Procedure

This is governed by SLA 1925, s. 7(1)–(5).

(a) On the death of a tenant for life or statutory owner, the personal representatives hold the settled land on trust, and, when required to do so, must convey it to the person who, under the trust instrument, or by virtue of SLA, becomes the tenant for life or statutory owner (and, if more than one, as joint tenants).

(b) A person who becomes a tenant for life for the purposes of the Act, by attaining full age, is entitled to require the trustees of the settlement, or personal representatives, to convey the land to him.

(c) If, by reason of forfeiture or surrender the estate owner of settled land ceases to have the statutory powers of a tenant for life, he will be bound forthwith to convey the land to the person who under the trust instrument, or by virtue of the Act, becomes the tenant for life or the statutory owner.

(d) If a person of full age becomes absolutely entitled to the settled land free from all limitations, powers and charges taking effect under the settlement, he is entitled to require the trustees or personal representatives to convey the land to him.

40. Mode of conveyance
This is based on SLA 1925, s. 8.

(a) A conveyance by personal representatives (under s. 6, which deals with a settlement created by the will of an estate owner, or s. 7, for which *see* **39** above) may be made by assent in writing signed by them, which shall operate as a conveyance: s. 8(1).

(b) Where the land is or remains settled land, a conveyance under s. 6 or s. 7 shall, if by deed, be a principal vesting deed, and, if by an assent, shall be a vesting assent, which must contain the particulars required by the Act in the case of a principal vesting deed (*see* **8** above): s. 8(4). *See* SLA 1925, Sch. 1.

41. Protection of purchasers
The situation is governed by SLA 1925, s. 110. (*See* also, SLA 1925, ss. 13, 39(4)(iii), 112(2); LPA 1925, s. 152.)

(a) On a disposition, a purchaser who deals in good faith with a tenant for life, or statutory owner, shall, as against all those entitled under the settlement, be conclusively taken to have given the best price, consideration, or rent that could reasonably be obtained by the life tenant or statutory owner, and to have complied with all the requisitions of the Act: s. 110(1). *See Re Morgan's Lease* (1972).

(b) The purchaser of a legal estate from a tenant for life may not generally see or call for the trust instrument, and is entitled to assume that the statements made in the vesting deed are correct: s. 110(2) (the so-called 'curtain' principle).

(c) The purchaser of a legal estate from a personal representative is entitled to assume that if capital money arising under the transaction is paid to the personal representative, he is acting under his statutory or other powers and requires the money for purposes of administration: s. 110(3)(i).

(d) If a conveyance of or an assent relating to land formerly subject to a vesting instrument does not state who are the trustees of the settlement for the purposes of the Act, a purchaser of a legal estate is entitled to assume that the person in whom the land was thereby vested was entitled to the land free from limitations and charges taking effect under that settlement, and that the facts in the conveyance are correct: s. 110(5).

Determination of a settlement

42. Duration of a settlement
Under SLA 1925, s. 3:

'Land which has been subject to a settlement shall be deemed for the purposes of this Act to remain and be settled land, and the settlement shall be deemed to be a subsisting settlement for the purposes of this Act so long as:

(a) any limitation, charge, or power of charging under the settlement subsists, or is capable of being exercised; or
(b) the person who, if of full age, would be entitled as beneficial owner to have the land vested in him for a legal estate is an infant.'

NOTE: Under LP (Amendment) A 1926, s. 7, a settlement ends once the land is held on trust for sale.

43. Deed of discharge
A deed of discharge, on the termination of a settlement, must be executed in accordance with SLA 1925, s. 17(1). The court may make an order discharging the trustees: s. 17(2). A deed of discharge is not necessary where no vesting instrument has been executed: *see Re Alefounder's WT* (1927).

Progress test 10

1. 'Strict settlements require two documents.' Explain. **(5–8)**

2.   Explain the nature of an *ad hoc* settlement.   **(17)**

3.   Who is the 'tenant for life' under the Settled Land Act 1925?
(19, 20)

4.   Who are the trustees of a strict settlement?   **(22)**

5.   Outline the nature of the duties of the trustees of a strict
settlement.   **(25)**

6.   'The liability of the trustees of a settlement does not extend to
all the acts of the tenant for life.' Explain.   **(26)**

7.   What are the 'powers of sale and exchange' conferred by the
Settled Land Act 1925 upon the tenant for life?   **(28)**

8.   Discuss the powers of the tenant for life to apply capital money.
(32)

9.   Outline the problem of overreaching in relation to the Settled
Land Act 1925.   **(36)**

10. How are purchasers protected under the Settled Land Act
1925?   **(41)**

11
Trusts for sale

Nature of a trust for sale

1. The strict settlement and the trust for sale

The strict settlement (*see* Ch. 10) had as one of its principal objects the retention of land within a family. But where land was considered merely as an investment, the purpose of which was to ensure a regular income to the beneficiaries, a procedure was adopted which differed from that involved in a strict settlement. The purpose of this procedure was *to vest the legal estate in trustees upon trust to sell the land and to hold proceeds of the sale, together with rent and profits, upon stated trusts*. The trustees could be empowered to postpone the sale at their discretion. Settlements of land are, therefore, of *two types*: the strict settlement and the trust for sale.

2. The equitable doctrine of conversion

Under the equitable doctrine known as *conversion*, the rights of the beneficiaries behind a trust for sale are assumed to be converted from rights in land to *rights in money* from the beginning.

(a) Conversion in equity is a *notional change*, under certain circumstances, of land into money, or money into land, which occurs *as soon as the direction to convert is given*.

(b) The doctrine rests upon the equitable principle: 'Equity looks on that as done which ought to be done.' Therefore, where a person is under an obligation to sell land and convert it into money, or to employ money in the purchase of land, equity will look upon the property as being, for all purposes, in its converted state from the particular time when that obligation commenced. *See Perry* v. *Phoenix Assurance* (1988); Charging Orders Act 1979.

(c) 'Nothing is better established than this principle that money directed to be employed in the purchase of land, and land directed to be sold and turned into money, are to be considered as that species of property into which they are directed to be converted; and this in whatever manner the direction is given, whether by will, by way of contract, marriage articles, settlement or otherwise; and whether the money is actually deposited, or only covenanted to be paid, whether the land is actually conveyed, or only agreed to be conveyed, the owner of the fund, or the contracting parties, may make land money or money land': *per* Sewel MR in *Fletcher* v. *Ashburner* (1779).

(d) Thus, under the trust for sale the beneficiaries had rights in the purchase money, but *not* in the land which was the subject of the trust for sale.

(e) In *Re Kempthorne* (1930), T made a will in 1911 and died in 1930, owning, at his death, an undivided share in freehold land. T left all his personalty to X and all his realty to Y. It was held that the undivided share was to be considered as personalty, so that it passed to X.

(f) Note the comments of Cross LJ in *Irani Finance Ltd* v. *Singh* (1971):

> 'The whole purpose of the trust for sale is to make sure, by shifting the equitable interests away from the land and into the proceeds of sale, that a purchaser of land takes free from the equitable interests. *To hold these to be equitable interests in the land itself would be to frustrate this purpose.* Even to hold that they have equitable interests in the land for a limited period, namely, until the land is sold, would, we think, be inconsistent with the trust for sale being an "immediate" trust for sale working an immediate conversion, which is what LPA 1925 envisages.'

3. The essence of a trust for sale

A trust to sell is not merely a power to sell. In the latter case a *power* may be exercised in accordance with a *discretion*. But a *trust is obligatory*, i.e. it is based on an instruction by the settlor to sell the land, and the trustees must carry it out in accordance with its terms. The form of the instrument purporting to create a trust or power is not decisive; the terms must be considered: *Re Newbould* (1913): *see* Ch. 10.

4. Failure of conversion

Where A devises property to B and C as trustees to sell and hold proceeds of sale for D and E, and E predeceases A, there is a *partial failure*. In that case if the conversion was directed by deed, the property reverts to the settlor in its converted form: *Griffiths* v. *Ricketts* (1849). If the conversion was directed by will, the property passes in its converted form to the person entitled to it in its unconverted form: *Re Walpole* (1933). Where A devises property to B and C as trustees to sell and hold proceeds of sale for D, and D predeceases A, there is a *total failure*. In that case there is no conversion, whether directed by will or deed: *Re Grimthorpe* (1908).

5. LPA 1925, and trusts for sale

Trusts for sale are *not* governed by SLA 1925, and are excluded expressly: LP (Amendment) A 1926. They are regulated by LPA 1925.

Definition of a trust for sale

6. LPA 1925, s. 205(1)(xxix)

'"Trust for sale" in relation to land means an immediate binding trust for sale, whether or not exercisable at the request or with the consent of any person, and with or without a power at discretion to postpone the sale; "trustees for sale" mean the persons (including a personal representative) holding land on trust for sale; and "power to postpone a sale" means power to postpone in the exercise of a discretion.' (For 'personal representative' *see* LPA 1925, s. 205(1)(xviii).)

> NOTE: 'Where a disposition or settlement coming into operation after the commencement of this Act contains a trust either to retain or sell land the same shall be construed as a trust to sell the land with power to postpone the sale': LPA 1925, s. 25(4).

7. Interpretation of s. 205(1)(xxix)

The phrase 'immediate binding trust' is particularly important, since only a trust of this nature will be considered as a trust for sale. The practical significance is this: assume that P is buying land from T_1 and T_2, and that T_1 and T_2 claim to be conveying the land as trustees for sale, and, as such, claim that the legal estate is vested in them. If, in fact, the land is merely settled land and not subject to a trust for sale (in which case the legal estate will be vested in the tenant for life), T_1 and T_2 will be unable to convey title to P.

(a) The trust must be *immediate*. This is not interpreted as a direction that the land must be sold without delay. (The necessity of immediacy relates to the *trust* rather than to the *sale*.) (Note the power to postpone sale under LPA 1925, s. 25; *see* **16** below). But in the case of a *future* trust for sale, the trustees are not considered as trustees for sale, and the land will be regulated by SLA 1925: *Re Jackson's Settled Estates* (1902); SLA 1925, s. 30(1)(iv); *Re Herklot's WT* (1964).

(b) The trust must be *binding*. Several interpretations of 'binding' have been put forward, e.g:

(*i*)   the trustees' power to convey the land so that all equitable interests prior to the trust are overreached: *Re Leigh's Settled Estates (No.1)* (1926);

(*ii*) the excluding of a mere revocable trust: *Re Parker's Settled Estates* (1928);

(*iii*) an imperative trust of the entire legal estate: *Re Norton* (1929).

Creation of a trust for sale

8.   General

A trust for sale may arise in two ways:

(a) *expressly*, i.e. where land is limited on trust for sale;

(b) *by operation of statute*.

9.   Express trust for sale

An express trust for sale may be created *inter vivos*, or by will.

(a) Where the trust for sale is created *inter vivos*, two documents are often, although not always, used:

(*i*)   a *conveyance* passes the legal estate to the trustees;

(*ii*) a *trust instrument* states the beneficial interests which it is intended shall be created.

(b) Where the trust for sale is created by *will*, the will may be considered as the trust instrument. A written assent by personal representatives is necessary so as to vest the legal estate in the trustees for sale: AEA 1925, s. 36(4).

10. The statutory trust for sale

In some cases the trust for sale will arise as the result of statute, e.g. where an estate owner dies intestate: AEA 1925, s. 33(1); or where any property, vested in trustees by way of security, becomes, by virtue of the statutes of limitation, or of an order for foreclosure or otherwise, discharged from the right of redemption: LPA 1925, s. 31(1). *See also* LPA 1925, s. 35, at **12:15(b)**.

11. Duration of the trust

Under LPA 1925, s. 23, a trust for sale shall 'so far as regards the safety and protection of any purchaser thereunder, be deemed to be subsisting until the land has been conveyed to or under the direction of the persons interested in the proceeds of sale.' Where the beneficiaries are of full age and absolutely entitled, they may end the trust by a conveyance to themselves. Should a trust for sale end prior to the sale of the land, the interest held by the beneficiaries is reconverted to an interest in realty: *Re Cook* (1948).

Beneficiaries under a trust for sale

12. Powers of the beneficiaries

The beneficiary under a trust for sale does not have the powers of a tenant for life (*see* Ch. 12) since the powers are vested in the trustees for sale. For the beneficiaries' right to occupy, *see*, e.g. *Re Bagot's Settlement* (1894); *Bull* v. *Bull* (1955).

13. Delegation of powers to the beneficiary

Under LPA 1925, s. 29, the powers of leasing, accepting surrenders of leases, and management, may, until sale of the land, be *revocably* delegated from time to time, by the trustees for sale, in writing, 'to any person of full age (not being merely an annuitant) for the time being beneficially entitled in possession to the net rents and profits of the land during his life or any less period.'

(a) Powers so delegated may be exercised 'only in the names and on behalf of the trustees delegating the power.'
(b) The trustees who delegate under the section are not liable for the acts or defaults of the person to whom the power is delegated.

14. Consultation in the case of a statutory trust for sale

Under LPA 1925, s. 26(3): 'The trustees for sale shall, so far as practicable, give effect to the wishes of the persons of full age for the time being beneficially interested in possession in the rents and profits of the land until sale, or, in the case of dispute, of the majority (according to the value of their combined interests) of such persons, but a purchaser shall not be concerned to see that such wishes are complied with.' Under LP (Amendment) A 1926, this section was limited to a trust for sale created by statute, and to a trust in which it was intended that such a provision was to have application.

Trustees for sale

15. General

'Trustees for sale shall ... have the powers of a tenant for life and the trustees of a settlement under the Settled Land Act 1925, including in relation to the land the powers of management conferred by that Act during a minority': LPA 1925, s. 28(1); LP (Amendment) A 1926, s. 7; *Re Wellsted's WT* (1949).

16. Power to postpone

'A power to postpone a sale shall, in the case of every trust for sale of land, be implied unless a contrary intention appears.' 'Where there is a power to postpone the sale, then (subject to any express direction to the contrary in the instrument, if any, creating the trust for sale) the trustees for sale shall not be liable in any way for postponing the sale, in the exercise of their discretion for any definite period; nor shall a purchaser of a legal estate be concerned in any case with any directions respecting the postponement of a sale': LPA 1925, s. 25(1), (2).

(a)   In *Re Rooke* (1953) a testator gave directions to trustees to sell his farm 'as soon as possible after my death', proceeds from such sale to fall into residue. It was held that this direction constituted a 'contrary intention' under s. 25(1), which prevailed over the wish of the trustees to delay the sale.

(b)   In *Re Mayo* (1943) land was held on trust for sale. The trustees were unable to agree whether to execute the trust and sell the land or postpone sale. It was held that the land had to be sold since, although the majority wished to postpone sale, *all* had to agree to exercise a power to postpone, whereas the trust was to sell the land.

17. Consents

Where the consent of more than two persons is, by the disposition, made requisite to the execution of a trust for sale, then, in favour of a purchaser, the consent of any two of such persons will suffice: LPA 1925, s. 26(1). Where the person whose consent is required is under a disability or is not *sui juris* (i.e. of full legal capacity) his consent is not required in favour of a purchaser, but the consent of the parent or other appropriate persons is required: LPA 1925, s. 26(2). The court may dispense with a requisite consent which cannot be obtained, or is refused: LPA 1925, s. 30; *Stevens* v. *Hutchinson* (1953). Note *Re Herklot's WT* (1964) in which a will had imposed a trust for sale upon a residence; X was allowed a right to remain there as long as she wished and Y was given the right to acquire the residence upon the death of X. The court held it to be implicit that a sale in the lifetime of X could not occur save with the consent of X and Y.

18. Refusal of trustees for sale to exercise powers

If trustees for sale refuse to sell or to exercise powers, or requisite consents cannot be obtained, any person interested may apply to the court for a vesting or other order for giving effect to the proposed transaction or for an order directing the trustees for sale to give effect thereto, and *the court may make such order as it thinks fit*: LPA 1925, s.30.

(a) The problem of exercise of the court's discretion ('to make such order as it thinks fit') was discussed in *Re Buchanan-Wollaston's Conveyance* (1939). 'The power of the court to enforce the trust for sale must be exercised in regard to the statutory trust for sale according to well-known and ordinary principles': *per* Lord Greene. All the circumstances of the case should be examined so as to ascertain whether it is 'right and proper that such an order shall be made.' *See Jones* v. *Challenger* (1961).

(b) Where the trustees are in dispute as to the necessity for a sale, the court may order a sale even though the majority of the trustees are not in agreement; discharge of the primary purpose of the trust for sale should prevail: *Re Mayo* (1943).

(c) Where the trustees have covenanted among themselves not to sell the land without their unanimous concurrence, the court is unlikely to order a sale under s. 30: *Re Buchanan-Wollaston's Conveyance* (1939).

(d) Where persons have become co-owners for a specific purpose which continues, a sale under s. 30 is unlikely to be ordered: *Bedson* v. *Bedson* (1965). But where the purpose has ended (as where a marriage has ended in fact), a sale will be ordered: *Rawlings* v. *Rawlings* (1964). *See* also *Jones* v. *Jones* (1977) — court refused to order execution of implied trust for sale on grounds of estoppel rendering such a sale inequitable.

(e) *See* also *Bernards* v. *Josephs* (1982); *Chhokar* v. *Chhokar* (1984).

19. Power to apply the income

Income from land held under trust for sale is applied until its sale 'in like manner as the income of investments representing the purchase money would be payable or applicable if a sale had been made and the proceeds had been duly invested', subject to any directions to the contrary: LPA 1925, s. 28(2). *See Re Wellsted's WT* (1949).

Overreaching under a trust for sale

20. General
See LPA 1925, s. 2. Where there is a conveyance under a trust for sale:

(a) the equitable rights of the beneficiaries under the trust for sale *will* be overreached (so that a purchaser will have good legal title free from any beneficial claims);
(b) the rights which were in existence prior to the creation of the trust for sale *will not* be overreached;
(c) legal estates *will not* be overreached.

21. Payment of purchase money
Money arising from a sale of land under trust for sale must *not* be paid to or applied by the direction of fewer than two persons as trustees *except* where the trustee is a trust corporation: LPA 1925, s. 27(2). *See* LP(Am.)A 1926, Schedule.

> NOTE: A 'trust corporation' includes the Public Trustee, Treasury Solicitor, Official Solicitor, and certain companies entitled to act as 'custodian trustees', i.e. incorporated under the Companies Acts in the UK, or in any other member state of EC, with an issued capital of at least £250,000, of which a minimum of £100,000 should have been paid up in cash.

22. *City of London Building Soc.* v. *Flegg* (1988)
In this case, the House of Lords considered, *inter alia*, the effect of a disposition by trustees for sale.

(a) *The facts.* The registered title in a family home was purchased in the names of A and B; nearly half of the purchase money was provided by B's parents, X and Y. The conveyance to A and B contained an express trust for sale and a statement that the joint trustees (A and B) had the mortgaging powers of an absolute owner. X and Y were not referred to in the conveyance, but it was clear that they were beneficiaries behind the trust for sale. X and Y jointly occupied the house with A and B.
  Later, without the knowledge of X and Y, A and B executed a

charge on the property in favour of the CLBS to secure a loan. Subsequently, A and B were made bankrupt and the CLBS attempted to recover possession of the house, under the belief that the mortgage executed by the two trustees for sale overreached all equitable interests.

(b) *The judge's decision.* The judge found that the parents, X and Y, were equitable tenants in common with A and B and had an overriding interest. But under LPA 1925, s. 2(1)(ii), that interest *was overreached* by execution of the legal charge in favour of the CLBS by the two trustees for sale. The parents, X and Y, appealed.

(c) *Court of Appeal.* The appeal was *allowed*. It was held that X and Y, as beneficiaries in actual occupation, had an interest in the house (within LPA 1925, s. 14) which *was not overreached* under s. 2(1)(ii) by the execution of a legal charge on the property by the two trustees for sale. No enquiry had been made of X and Y prior to execution of the charge, so that the CLBS took its mortgage subject to the overriding interests of X and Y.

(d) *House of Lords.* The decision of the Court of Appeal was unanimously *reversed*. The interests of X and Y *were overreached* by the legal charge in favour of the CLBS because their beneficial interest was transferred to the equity of redemption (*see* 14:**10**) held by A and B; when A and B defaulted, X and Y could *not* set up an overriding interest under LRA 1925, s. 70(1)(g) (*see* 20:**12**), capable of defeating the claim of the CLBS to possession. (As a result, there now seems little doubt as to the payment of purchase money to at least two trustees for sale overreaching any equitable claims of any beneficiary under a trust for sale.)

The *ad hoc* trust for sale

23. Creation of an *ad hoc* trust for sale

Where the trustees for sale are either two or more persons approved or appointed by the court, or successors in office of such persons, or a trust corporation, a sale shall overreach certain prior interests: LPA 1925, s. 2(2). Such a sale is generally known as an *ad hoc*, or special, trust for sale.

24. Effect of a conveyance under an *ad hoc* trust for sale

A conveyance under an *ad hoc* trust (and an *ad hoc* settlement — *see* 10:**17**) will overreach rights prior to the trust for sale or settlement, with the *exception* of the following:

(a) equitable interests protected by deposit of documents;

(b) equitable easements;

(c) estate contracts;

(d) restrictive covenants;

} which cannot be represented in monetary terms

(e) an equitable interest registered under the Land Charges Acts, with the *exception* of:

(*i*) annuities created and registered prior to 1926;

(*ii*) general equitable charges;

(*iii*) limited owner's charges.

} which are sufficiently protected if enforceable against the money rather than the land

NOTE: The Law Commission Working Paper No. 94 (1985), suggests the replacement of the trust for sale ('no longer suitable for modern conditions') by a 'new trust of land' under which co-owned land would be held by trustees empowered to retain and sell. A purchaser would derive title from trustees; the interests of beneficiaries would be overreached, on condition of payment to two trustees.

Progress test 11

1. Outline the equitable doctrine of conversion.   **(2)**

2. 'The trust for sale must be immediate.' Discuss.   **(7)**

3. How may a trust for sale arise?   **(8–11)**

4. May powers be delegated to beneficiaries under a trust for sale?   **(13)**

5. Comment on *Re Rooke* (1953).   **(16)**

6. What events may follow on a refusal by trustees for sale to exercise their powers?   **(18)**

7. Comment on *City of London BS* v. *Flegg* (1988).   **(22)**

8. What is the effect of a conveyance under an *ad hoc* trust for sale?   **(24)**

Part four

Life, concurrent, and other interests

12
Life and concurrent interests

The essence of life interests

1. The life estate
An interest in land 'for life', e.g. arising from a grant to X 'for his life', existed before the 1925 legislation as a *legal estate*. Following the LPA 1925, s. 1(3), it exists only as an *equitable interest* and is known today as a *life interest*. *See* LPA 1925, s. 205(1)(x) for definitions of 'legal estates' and 'equitable interests'.

2. Estate 'for the life of the tenant'
See 1:15(a). This arose where there was an express limitation (e.g. grant 'to X for life') or by operation of law, as in the case of the rights accruing to a surviving spouse under the doctrine of curtesy (based upon an old rule which states that where an entail is owned solely by a married woman who dies intestate after a child who could have inherited under that estate has been born alive, the husband ('tenant by the curtesy') is entitled to a life interest). The estate ended on X's death; it did not constitute an interest which could be claimed by X's heirs. *See* LPA 1925, s. 205(1)(xxvi).

3. Estate pur autre vie
See 1:15(a). Where a grant was made in express terms 'to X for the life of Y', X became *tenant pur autre vie* (tenant for the term of another's life), and Y was known as *cestui que vie* (he whose life is the measure of the duration of the estate). X's interest lasted only for as long as Y's life.

4. After 1925
A life interest may now be created *only* under a strict settlement (*see* Ch. 10) *or* behind a trust for sale (*see* Ch. 11).

Some general rights and liabilities of the tenant for life at common law

5.   Right to emblements
(*See* 5:5.) The tenant for life is entitled at common law to the profits from the land. Where the life interest ends during the life of the tenant, and the tenant is in no way responsible for this, he may re-enter and reap any annual fruit-bearing crop which he has sown.

6.   Liability of the tenant for waste
The doctrine of waste is discussed at 5:7(a). A tenant for life may be either impeachable (i.e. liable) or unimpeachable at common law for waste.

(a)   Where a tenant for life is impeachable for waste, he will be liable in the case of voluntary waste (*see* 5:7(a)(*i*)).
(b)   Where a tenant for life is unimpeachable for waste, he is not liable for permissive or for voluntary waste (*see* 5:7(a)(*i*),(*ii*)).
(c)   He is liable for equitable waste unless an intention to confer the right to commit such waste is given expressly by the instrument conferring the right: LPA 1925, s. 135 (*see* 5:7(a)(*iv*)).
(d)   The tenant for life may cut timber as estovers (*see* 5:5(b)) in the following cases: if the land is a timber estate; in accordance with local custom: *Dashwood* v. *Magniac* (1891).
(e)   A tenant *pur autre vie* has the liability for waste which attaches to a tenant for life.
(f)   A tenant in tail after possibility is not liable for permissive or voluntary waste.

7.   Mineral rights
The tenant for life may work mines unless he is impeachable for waste and the mine has been opened since the starting of his tenancy. He may work a mine which was open before the starting of his tenancy: *Re Morgan* (1914); *Viner* v. *Vaughan* (1840).

The nature of concurrent interests

8.   When concurrent interests arise
Where two or more persons have *simultaneous, and not consecutive interests* in the same land at any one time, they are said to be entitled to *concurrent interests*, and the land is said to be subject to *co-ownership*.

Examples: _____

Grants 'to A and B in fee simple', or 'to A and B equally', create concurrent interests. A grant 'to A for life, remainder to B in fee simple' does *not* create concurrent interests; their interests are consecutive.

_____

9. Types of co-ownership

Prior to 1926 there were four types of co-ownership in land:

(a) the joint tenancy (*see* **10–19** below);

(b) the tenancy in common (*see* **20–28** below);

(c) the tenancy by entireties (*see* **29–32** below);

(d) coparcenary (*see* **33–36** below).

Today, only **(a)** and **(b)** are of significance. Both involve the holding of interests behind a trust for sale (*see* Ch. 11).

Essence of the joint tenancy

10. Fundamental features

A joint tenancy exists where an entire estate or interest in land is vested simultaneously in the two or more co-owners. Each of the joint tenants (i.e. the co-owners) is possessed of the entire joint property 'by every part and by the whole', i.e. no single joint tenant holds a specific share in the land himself. *The total interest in the land is vested in each and all of the tenants.* As between themselves, joint tenants possess separate rights: but as against others they constitute *a single, composite owner.* (Note that 'tenant', 'tenancy', in this context, do not relate to a tenant or tenancy under a lease; the terms as used here derive from 'tenant' in a general relationship to 'tenure' (*see* **1:13**).) The joint tenancy is the only kind of co-ownership existing *at law.* The principal features of the joint tenancy are:

(a) the presence of 'the four unities'; *and*

(b) the right of survivorship; *and*

(c) no words of severance.

These are discussed at **11** and **12** below.

11. The four unities

These must be present if a joint tenancy is to be created.

(a) *Unity of possession.* Each of the tenants is entitled to possession of every part *and* the whole of the land. The land is *not* divided into parts, with each part belonging, separately, to a tenant. Where X, Y and Z are constituted joint owners of land, X may not describe any part of the land as 'mine'; nor may Y, for example, bring an action for trespass against Z. *See Bull* v. *Bull* (1955). (For an example of the setting-aside of unity of possession under statute, *see Davis* v. *Johnson* (1979) — exclusion of a joint tenant under the Domestic Violence and Matrimonial Proceedings Act 1976, ss. 1(2),2(1),(2); the House of Lords held that such exclusion *was possible*, irrespective of the property right vested in the person excluded).

(b) *Unity of interest*. The nature, duration and extent of the estate of each joint tenant must be the same (since the tenants hold one and the same estate). There can be no joint tenancy, therefore, where one person holds a term of years while the other holds an estate for life: *Kenworthy* v. *Ward* (1853). Hence, a conveyance of land in co-ownership of this nature involves the consent of *all* the joint tenants, and the purchaser need investigate *one title only*.

(c) *Unity of title*. The title of each joint tenant must be created by the same document or act, e.g. the same conveyance.

(d) *Unity of time*. In general, the interest of each joint tenant must vest at the same time (e.g. 'to X and Y in fee simple').

12. The right of survivorship (*jus accrescendi*)

The general principle is: on the death of one joint tenant, his interest will pass to the surviving joint tenants. This procedure continues until there is only one survivor; he will hold as *sole owner*.

(a) Note that, because the joint tenant 'holds nothing and yet holds the whole', he cannot pass his interest under his will (nor will it pass on intestacy).

(b) Assume X, Y and Z to be joint tenants. On the death of X, his entitlement is extinguished; he owns no *specific* interest which can be passed on his death. The entire estate is now vested in Y and Z. When, eventually, it passes 'to a single hand', the joint tenancy comes to an end. Should Y pre-decease Z, Z will hold the interest as sole owner.

Creation of a joint tenancy

13. At common law

Where land was conveyed or devised to two or more persons, without the use of words of severance (i.e. words which demonstrated an intention to give a separate share to each tenant, such as 'to A and B equally', or 'three-fifths to X and two-fifths to Y') *and* the four unities were present (*see* **11** above), a joint tenancy was impliedly created.

14. In equity

In general, equity tended to lean *in favour of a tenancy in common* (*see* **25** below) and *against a joint tenancy*. (Law has leaned in favour of a joint tenancy.) The concept of *jus accrescendi* (*see* **12** above) was not favoured in equity, which aimed, in general, at equality. Because equity 'followed the law', wherever there was a tenancy in common at law, there would be a tenancy in common in equity. The existence of a joint tenancy in equity demanded the presence of the four unities, appropriate, express words in the conveyance, absence of words of severance indicating that the property was to be shared, and construction of the document as a whole so as to reveal the grantor's appropriate intention. Note, additionally, the following four presumptions in favour of a tenancy in common.

(a)   Where land was bought by *partners* they were presumed to hold it as beneficial tenants holding in common: *Lake* v. *Craddock* (1732).
(b)   Where X and Y purchased property as *joint purchasers with money in unequal shares*, they were presumed to be tenants in common: *Lake* v. *Gibson* (1729). *Jus accrescendi inter mercatores pro beneficio commercii locum non habet* — the right of survivorship among merchants, for the benefit of commerce, does not exist.
(c)   Where X and Y advance money *on mortgage*, a tenancy in common between the mortgagees (X and Y) is presumed. *See Steeds* v. *Steeds* (1889).
(d)   Where X and Y, joint purchasers of land, held it for their *several individual business purposes*, a tenancy in common was presumed: *Malayan Credit* v. *Jack Chia MPH* (1986).

15. Following LPA 1925

Under s. 1(6) a legal estate is *not* now capable of subsisting or being created in an undivided share in land. After LPA 1925, co-ownership at law takes the form of a joint tenancy only. A joint tenancy of a legal estate may *not* be converted by severance (*see* **19** below) into a tenancy at common law: *see* s. 36(2).

(a)   Where land is expressed to be conveyed to any persons in undivided shares and those persons are of full age, the conveyance operates as if the land had been expressed to be conveyed to the grantees (if more than four, then to the first four named in the conveyance) as *joint tenants upon the statutory trusts*: *see* s. 34(2).

(b) The statutory trusts are set out in s. 35. They refer to land held upon a trust to sell the same and stand possessed of the net proceeds of sale, after payment of costs, and of the net rents and profits until sale upon the trusts and subject to the powers and provisions requisite for giving effect to the rights of the persons beneficially interested in the land.

(c) For details concerning the trust for sale, *see* Ch. 11; for power to postpone sale, consents, refusal of trustees to exercise powers, *see* 11:16–18.

(d) A disposition purporting to make a settlement of an undivided share in land operates only as a settlement of a corresponding share of the net proceeds of sale and of the rents and profits until sale of the entirety of the land: s. 34(4).

(e) 'The legislature in putting an end to the system of land-holding in law in undivided shares was aiming at a real mischief. Where land had been split into undivided shares, those shares, developing independently, became subdivided through devolutions and dispositions, so that ultimately the making of title to the entirety became a difficult matter, to the mutual detriment of all the co-owners. The legislative method of dealing with that mischief was to prohibit the creation of undivided shares in land in the future, and to make every future conveyance, devise or settlement purporting to create undivided shares operate as creating a trust for sale': *per* Tomlin J in *Re Robins* (1928).

(f) Where a legal estate (not being settled land) is beneficially limited to or held in trust for any persons as joint tenants, the same shall be held on trust for sale, in like manner as if the persons beneficially entitled were tenants in common, but not so as to sever their joint tenancy in equity: s. 36(1).

(g) Nothing in LPA 1925 affects the right of a *survivor* of joint tenants, who is solely and beneficially interested, to deal with his legal estate as if it were *not* held on trust for sale: s. 36(3).

> NOTE: A conveyance to two or more minors as joint tenants will take effect as a settlement under the SLA 1925 (*see* Ch. 10). The legal estate will be held under LPA 1925, s. 19(1), by a statutory owner.

Determination of a joint tenancy

16. Partition

This involves a physical 'division' of the land among joint tenants so that each becomes the *sole owner* of the plot of land allocated to him. Partition could be voluntary, e.g. as where co-owners agreed to divide the property into separate shares, or compulsory, as where, under the Partition Acts 1539, 1540, a joint tenant could insist on a partition. Under the Partition Act 1868 (repealed by the LPA 1925, Sch. 7) sale could be ordered instead of partition.

(a) Under LPA 1925, s. 28(3), trustees for sale, in whom the legal estate has been vested may 'with the consent of the persons, if any, of full age, not being annuitants, interested in possession in the net rents and profits of the land until sale', partition the land or any part thereof and provide by way of mortgage or otherwise for the payment of any equality money.

(b) Where trustees for sale refuse to exercise their power to partition, an interested person may apply to the court for an order directing them to do so: LPA 1925, s. 30.

17. Union in sole tenant

Where the land in its entirety (i.e. all the legal and beneficial interests) vests in a sole tenant, the joint tenancy is determined. Note also LPA 1925, s. 72(4).

18. Sale

Where the trustees for sale sell the legal estate, the interests of the beneficiaries are overreached (*see* 2:**19**) so that the purchaser takes free from them. The joint tenancy terminates.

(a) Under LP (Amendment) A 1926, a surviving joint tenant who is entitled to the land solely and beneficially may deal with the legal estate as though it were not held on trust for sale.

(b) LP (Joint Tenants) A 1964, s. 1(1), states that the survivor of two or more tenants shall be deemed 'to be solely and beneficially interested if he conveys as beneficial owner or the conveyance includes a statement that he is so interested.'

19. Severance

'The process of separating off the share of a joint tenant, so that the concurrent ownership will continue but the right of survivorship will no longer apply. The parties will hold separate shares as tenants in common': *per* Dillon LJ in *Harris* v. *Goddard* (1983).

(a) Severance results from destruction of any of the four unities (*see* **11** above), or from an act of a joint tenant which excludes the operation of the rule of survivorship (*see* **12** above).

(b) Pre-1926 modes of severance (which remain relevant today) were reviewed in *Williams* v. *Hensman* (1861). They include the following.

(i) 'The act of any one of the persons interested operating upon his own share may create a severance as to that share': *per* Page-Wood VC. The act must be 'final' so that the joint tenant is unable to claim by survivorship any interest arising from the joint tenancy: *see Re Wilks* (1891). Example: where a joint tenant alienates his interest. (But alienation by will does *not* sever a joint tenancy.)

(ii) Mutual conduct, i.e. 'any course of dealing sufficient to intimate that the interests of all were mutually treated as constituting a tenancy in common': *per* Page-Wood VC. It requires no more than joint acceptance of a course of action which, for example, excludes the operation of the survivorship rule. *See Re Wilford's Estate* (1879).

(iii) *Mutual agreement of all the joint tenants.* In *Burgess* v. *Rawnsley* (1975) the Court of Appeal held that an oral agreement by one joint tenant to buy another's share was a 'course of dealing' which sufficed for the act of severance. 'The thing to remember is that equity leans against joint tenants and favours tenancies in common ... It is sufficient if there is a course of dealing in which one party makes clear to the other that he desires that their shares should no longer be held jointly but in common. Similarly it is sufficient if both parties enter on a course of dealing which evinces an intention by both of them that their shares shall henceforth be held in common and not jointly': *per* Lord Denning.

(c) Under LPA 1925, s. 36(2), *written notice* of a tenant's desire to sever the joint tenancy must be given. He is then entitled as tenant in common to share in the profits and the net proceeds of sale.

(d) The following recent decisions are of interest.

(i) In *Re Draper's Conveyance* (1969) it was held that the issue of a summons in proceedings to have property vested in the sole name of the wife (suggesting a separation of the joint interest) constituted 'notice in writing'.

(ii) In *Re 88 Berkeley Road NW9* (1971), A and B, joint tenants, occupied premises. A served notice on B by means of a registered letter sent to the premises. It was received and signed for by A (who had posted it); the notice of severance, contained within the letter, was never handed to B. It was held, nevertheless, to constitute good service, so that the joint tenancy was severed. *See also* LPA 1925, s. 196(3).

(*iii*) In *Harris* v. *Goddard* (1983) it was held that a prayer in a divorce petition for an adjustment order concerning the matrimonial home and property did *not* operate of itself so as to sever the spouses' joint tenancy.

(*iv*) In *Goodman* v. *Gallant* (1986) the Court of Appeal held that where a conveyance into joint names contained an express declaration that the parties were to hold proceeds of sale on trust for themselves as joint tenants, then, on severance, there is created a tenancy in common in equal shares, and the declaration is conclusive of the position unless and until the conveyance is rectified or set aside.

(*v*) In *Re Gorman* (1990) it was held that the beneficial joint tenancy of a matrimonial home is severed by operation of law when one party becomes bankrupt and his interest is vested in the trustee. They hold thereafter as tenants in common.

NOTE: For severance in consequence of a homicide, *see Cleaver* v. *Mutual Reserve Fund Life Assoc.* (1892). *See* now the Forfeiture Act 1982, and *Re K.* (1985).

Essence of the tenancy in common

20. Fundamental features
The tenancy in common exists where land is limited to two or more persons *and* appropriate words of severance are used. The result is that the co-owners hold *distinct, undivided shares* (i.e. the shares have not been divided up). Examples: as where land was granted 'to A and B equally' or 'to X and Y in equal moieties'. The tenancy in common exists only in equity: LPA 1925, s. 1(6). It cannot be created except behind a trust for sale: SLA 1925, s. 36(4).

21. The tenancy in common and the joint tenancy
The tenancy in common differs from the joint tenancy in the following important ways.

(a) *Jus accrescendi* (*see* **12** above) does *not* apply to the tenancy in common. Thus, in the case of a tenant in common who dies, his share will pass in accordance with his will or the rules of intestacy. (Tenants in common hold in *undivided* shares.)

(b) The only 'unity' (*see* **11** above) which is required in the tenancy in common is unity of *possession*. Tenants in common may hold under different titles and may hold different types of interest. *See Jacobs* v. *Seward* (1872); *Jones* v. *Jones* (1977).

Creation of a tenancy in common

22. Absence of unities

Unity of possession (*see* **11(a)** above) is essential; indeed, it is present in all forms of co-ownership. An absence of one or more of the other unities (time, title, interest) will create a tenancy in common. It should be noted that an absence of unity of possession will result in the parties taking as separate owners. *See Grant* v. *Edwards* (1986).

23. Words of severance

Where words are used which suggest clearly that the parties are intended to take *distinct shares*, the words are words of severance, and a tenancy in common is created. Examples: 'to be divided among'; 'between'; 'in equal shares'; 'share and share alike'.

(a) 'A joint interest in equal shares is a contradiction in terms; the words of severance create a tenancy in common': *per* Bagnall J in *Cowcher* v. *Cowcher* (1972).

(b) In the absence of words of severance, it might be possible to show, considering the grant *in its entirety*, that there was an intention to create a tenancy in common: *Surtees* v. *Surtees* (1871).

(c) In *Martin* v. *Martin* (1987), the court considered the effect of the phrase 'beneficial joint tenants in common in equal shares' in a conveyance. It was held that the words 'in equal shares' constituted words of severance or provided a controlling context for 'joint', and created, therefore, a tenancy in common and not a joint tenancy. If the court applied the general rule that, where two inconsistent expressions existed which could not be reconciled, the first in time would prevail, then the first expression in the present case would create a beneficial joint tenancy. But the second of the inconsistent phrases would then constitute a severance of the equitable joint tenancy and *the creation of a beneficial tenancy in common*.

24. Existence of any of the presumptions in equity

See **14** above.

25. Following LPA 1925

The tenancy in common can no longer exist in a legal form:

s. 1(6). Under s. 34, where a legal estate has been limited to tenants in common, it will vest in them as joint tenants upon the statutory trusts for sale (*see* **15(b)** above). The tenancy in common continues in equity for 'giving effect to the rights of persons interested in the land.'

> NOTE: A conveyance to two or more minors as tenants in common will take effect as a trust for sale. *See* SLA 1925, ss. 1(1)(ii), 36. *See also* **19:6–7.**

Determination of a tenancy in common

26. Partition
See **16** above. Trustees for sale may partition with the consent of the beneficiaries. *See* LPA 1925, ss. 28(1),30 (application to court for order where trustees or beneficiaries will not agree to partition).

27. Union in sole tenant
The tenancy in common ends when the land becomes vested in a sole tenant. *See* **17** above.

28. Sale
Co-ownership ends when the tenants convey the property to a single third party.

The tenancy by entireties

29. Nature of the tenancy by entireties
Where an estate was conveyed or devised to a husband and wife so that they would have taken as joint tenants had they not been married, they were considered to be tenants by entireties.

(a) Each was considered as the tenant of the entire estate.
(b) Their interests could not be severed.
(c) On the death of one, the survivor took absolutely.

30. Married Women's Property Act 1882
Where a limitation was made to husband and wife jointly without words of severance, they became joint tenants and *not* tenants by entireties: *Thornley* v. *Thornley* (1893).

31. LPA 1925, s. 37
'A husband and wife shall, for all purposes of acquisition of any

interest in property, under a disposition made or coming into operation after the commencement of this Act, be treated as two persons.' *See Re Draper's Conveyance* (1969).

32. LPA 1925, Sch. 1, Part VI

'Every tenancy by entireties existing immediately before the commencement of this Act shall, but without prejudice to any beneficial interest, as from such commencement be converted into a joint tenancy.' *See Bedson* v. *Bedson* (1965).

Coparcenary

33. Nature of coparcenary

Coparcenary existed where two or more persons together constituted a single heir, e.g. as where a tenant in tail died intestate, leaving female heirs only.

(a) They had unity of possession, interest and title.
(b) They held in undivided shares.
(c) *Jus accrescendi* did not apply (*see* **12** above).

34. AEA 1925, s. 45(1)

Descent to coparceners was virtually abolished, except in the case of a tenant in tail who dies without having barred the entail. Where coparcenary arises as in **33** above, the interests of the coparceners are equitable, and the land will be held on trust for sale. *See* AEA 1925, s. 33(1); LPA 1925, s. 36(1),(2).

> NOTE: In the case of *the matrimonial home*: 'where a husband or wife contributes in money or money's worth to the improvement of real or personal property in which, or in the proceeds of sale of which, either or both of them has or have a beneficial interest, the husband or wife so contributing shall if the contribution is of a substantial nature . . . be treated as having then acquired by virtue of his or her contribution a share or an enlarged share, as the case may be, in that beneficial interest': Matrimonial Proceedings and Property Act 1970, s. 37. *See Stokes* v. *Anderson* (1991); *Sherry* v. *Sherry* (1991).

Party-walls

35. Meanings of the term

In *Watson* v. *Gray* (1880), Fry J gave the term the following alternative meanings:

(a) a wall of which two adjoining owners are tenants in common;
(b) a wall divided vertically into two strips, one half of the thickness of each belonging to each of the neighbouring owners;
(c) a wall belonging entirely to one owner, but subject to an easement (*see* 17:2) in the other to have it maintained as a dividing wall;
(d) a wall divided vertically into two equal strips, each being subject to a cross-easement in favour of the owner of the other.

36. LPA 1925, s. 38, Sch. 1, Part V
'Where under a disposition or other arrangement which, if a holding in undivided shares had been permissible, would have created a tenancy in common, a wall or other structure is or is expressed to be made a party wall or structure, that structure shall be and remain severed vertically as between the respective owners, and the owner of each part shall have such rights to support and user over the rest of the structure as may be requisite for conferring rights corresponding to those which would have subsisted if a valid tenancy in common had been created.'

37. Result of the legislation
Most party-walls in this country fall within category **(a)** at **35** above, and would have been subject to a trust for sale (because they were held under a tenancy in common — *see* **20** above). Following the 1925 legislation they are now considered to be in category **(d)** at **35** above.

Progress test 12

1. How may a life interest be created today?   **(4)**

2. What are the fundamental features of the joint tenancy?   **(10)**

3. Explain the 'right of survivorship' in relation to the joint tenancy.   **(12)**

4. 'Equity leans against the joint tenancy.' Discuss.   **(14)**

5. How is a joint tenancy determined by 'partition'?   **(16)**

6. Comment on *Burgess* v. *Rawnsley* (1975).   **(19)**

7.   Explain the significance of 'words of severance' in relation to a tenancy in common.   **(23)**

8.   How may a tenancy in common be determined?   **(26–28)**

9.   Explain how the Law of Property Act 1925 deals with the general problem of party-walls.   **(36, 37)**

Future, determinable and conditional interests

The nature of future interests

1. Definition

A future interest is one which is limited so that it confers a right to the enjoyment of land *at some time in the future*: *see* 1:15(c).

Examples:
_____
'To A for his life, and then to the first of his sons who shall attain the age of 21'; 'To A for life with remainder to B in fee simple'.
_____

2. Vested and contingent

An interest may be vested or contingent.

(a) An interest is *vested* where the person who is entitled to the interest has been *ascertained and* where the interest is limited so that it will take effect in possession *as soon as the prior estate is determined*.

Example:
_____
'To X for his life and, upon his death, to Y in fee simple.' Y is ascertained, and his interest will take effect in possession upon the death of X.
_____

(b) An interest is *contingent* where the person who is entitled to the interest *has not been ascertained* (i.e. his identity is not known) *or* where the interest is limited so that it will take effect in possession *upon the happening of some future uncertain event*.

Examples:
_____
'To A and B for their lives, and, upon the death of one of them, to the survivor in fee simple.' The survivor is *not yet ascertained* and the event which will vest the fee simple in the survivor is in the future and is uncertain. 'To B when he qualifies as a surgeon.' The grant remains contingent until B qualifies; until then it is unfulfilled. *See Evans* v. *Walker* (1876); *Pearson* v. *IRC* (1981).
_____

Categories of future interests

3.   General
Before 1926, the following types of future interest existed:

(a) reversions (*see* **4** below);
(b) legal remainders (*see* **5** below);
(c) future trusts (*see* **6** below);
(d) legal executory interests (*see* **7** below).

4.   Reversions
A reversion is an interest which remains in a grantor after he grants a *particular estate* (i.e. less than a fee simple). (Note: 'particular' is derived from *particula* = a part.) 'A reversion is where the residue of the estate always doth continue in him who made the particular estate, or where the particular estate is derived out of his estate': Coke. 'Reversion cometh of the Latin word *revertor* and signifieth a returning again': Coke. *See* 1:15(c)(*i*). So where L grants a lease to T, L retains the reversion. *A reversion is, by its nature, a vested interest.*

(a) *Before 1926* a reversion could have been legal or equitable.
(b) *After 1925* a reversion in the case of a life estate or entail is equitable; a reversion in the case of a term of years may exist as a legal estate.

> NOTE: For problems of interpretation of LPA 1925, s. 3(3) ('Where, by reason of a statutory or other right of reverter, or of an equitable right of entry taking effect, or for any other reason, a person becomes entitled to require a legal estate to be vested in him, then and in any such case the estate owner whose estate is affected shall be bound to convey or create such legal estate as the case may require') and s. 7(1) (*see* 3:5), *see* Re Clayton's Deed Poll (1980) and *Re Rowhook Mission Hall* (1985). The Reverter of Sites Act 1987 attempts to solve conflicting interpretations. When a site ceases to be used for the purposes for which it was originally granted, the charitable trustees shall continue to hold the legal estate *on trust for sale* for the revertee: s. 1. The trustees must attempt to ascertain the identity of the revertee: s. 3. The trustees may apply to the Charity Commissioners to have the revertee's interests extinguished: s. 2. In some circumstances the revertee whose rights are extinguished can apply for compensation: s. 2(4). *See* Charities Act 1992, s. 31.

5.   Legal remainders
'A residue of an estate in land depending upon a particular estate

and created together with the same': Coke. Example: 'To X for life, remainder to Y in fee simple': *see* 1:**15(c)**(*ii*). A remainder is *vested* where the remainderman is ascertained and his interest is limited so as to take effect at once upon the determination of the prior estate, e.g. 'To X for life, remainder to Y in fee simple'. Here Y is *ascertained*, and his interest will take effect at once upon the death of X. A remainder is *contingent* where the remainderman is *not ascertained* or where the interest of a remainderman will take effect upon the occurrence of some designated event, e.g. 'To B for life, remainder to his son' (where B is unmarried). The common law rules affecting legal remainders were strict.

(a) A remainder was *void* unless preceded by a particular freehold estate created under the same instrument: *Barwick's Case* (1597). A limitation of a remainder which would emerge by itself in the future was impossible. Hence, 'To X when he shall attain the age of 21' was void.

(b) A remainder was *void* if limited after a fee simple: *Musgrave* v. *Brooke* (1884). (There was an exception in the case of a remainder after a base fee. (For 'base fee', *see* 3:**12**.))

(c) A remainder was *void* if limited so that it took effect by defeating the particular estate: *Cogan* v. *Cogan* (1596). 'The remainder must wait for the regular ending of the precedent estate.' Thus, in a grant 'to X for life, but should he become bankrupt, to Y', the limitation would be void and the reversion would be in the grantor.

(d) A remainder was *void* unless limited so that it could, and did, vest either during the continuance of the particular estate or at the very instant of its determination: *Corbet* v. *Stone* (1653). There must be no abeyance of seisin (i.e. no interruption in physical possession). Thus, in a grant 'to X for life, and one year after his death to Y', the remainder was void.

6. Future trusts

In the case of *equitable interests*, the common law remainder rules, stated at **5** above, had *no application*.

7. Legal executory interests

The common law remainder rules had no application in the case of *legal executory interests*, e.g. *springing uses*, which were interests limited *by way of use* so that they would take effect at some time in the future without their affecting any prior freehold estate.

Future interests following the legislation of 1925

8.   LPA 1925

By LPA 1925, it became *impossible to create legal future interests in real property*.

9.   Results of the legislation

Legal remainders and legal executory interests ceased to exist; *future interests became equitable*. Those legal remainders and legal executory interests which existed before 1926 were converted into *equitable interests*: LPA 1925, Sch. 1.

Rules concerning remoteness

10.   General

The general policy of the law has been one of opposition to tying up of property in perpetuity. In *The Duke of Norfolk's Case* (1681), Lord Nottingham referred to 'perpetuities [which] fight against God. . . and are utterly against the reason and policy of the common law'. Rules relating to the creation of interests in perpetuity are:

(a) the rule against accumulations (see **11–14** below);
(b) the rule against perpetuities (see **15–28** below).

Rule against accumulations

11.   Application of the rule

The rule has application to directions to accumulate income, e.g. a direction that for a stated number of years income from investment shall be used for the purchase of certain shares.

12.   Statutory rules

The Accumulations Act 1800 was replaced by LPA 1925, ss. 164–6, amended by the Perpetuities and Accumulations Act 1964.

(a) Under LPA 1925, s. 164(1), *no person may direct the accumulation of income for any longer period than one of the following*:
    (*i*) the life of the grantor or settlor;
    (*ii*) a term of 21 years from the death of the grantor, settlor or testator;
    (*iii*) the duration of the minority or respective minorities of any

person or persons living or *en ventre sa mère* at the death of the grantor, settlor or testator;

(*iv*) the duration of the minority or respective minorities only of any person or persons who under the limitations of the instrument directing the accumulations would, for the time being, if of full age, be entitled to the income directed to be accumulated.

(b) Under P & AA 1964, s. 13(1), the periods, in the case of a disposition which takes effect on or after 16 July 1964, include the following additions:

(*i*) a term of 21 years from the date of the making of the disposition, and

(*ii*) the duration of the minority or respective minorities of any person or persons in being at that date.

NOTE: 'Minority' denotes an age less than 18 years of age: Family Law Reform Act 1969, s. 1.

13. Exceptions to the rule

LPA s. 164(1), does not extend to the following:

(a) provisions for the *payment of the debts* of any grantor, settlor, testator or other person; but the exception does *not* extend to debts which did not exist when the instrument directing accumulation became effective (*see Re Rochford's ST* (1965));

(b) provisions for the *raising of portions* for any children or remoter issue of a person taking any interest under any settlement or other disposition directing the accumulations or to whom any interest is thereby limited; *and*

(c) provisions concerning the *accumulation of the produce of timber or wood*: LPA 1925, s. 164(2).

NOTE: A corporate settlor is not a 'person' under s. 164, so that a settlement made by a corporation is outside the rule against accumulations: *Re Dodwell & Co.'s Trust Deed* (1979).

14. Breach of the rule

Where a direction to accumulate is for a period which is in excess of the general perpetuity period (i.e. life or lives in being, plus twenty-one years), *such a direction is void in toto: Curtis* v. *Lutkin* (1842). Where a direction does not infringe the general perpetuity rule, but exceeds the appropriate statutory period, such a direction is not void *in toto*, but is void only so far as it exceeds that statutory period: *Griffiths* v. *Vere* (1803); *Re Ransome's WT* (1957).

(a) The 'appropriate statutory period' is determined by the court on the basis of *the facts* of the particular case and *the language* used in the instrument containing the direction.

(b) Under the rule in *Saunders* v. *Vautier* (1841), beneficiaries of full age who hold an absolute beneficial interest in a trust fund may, at any time, and notwithstanding any direction to accumulate, terminate that accumulation and require the trustees to transfer the property to them. *See Berry* v. *Green* (1938).

Rule against perpetuities

15. General

The policy of the law in relation to the tying up of property in perpetuity is exemplified in the common law rule against perpetuities. The Perpetuities and Accumulations Act 1964 introduced important changes into the law concerning perpetuities, but it applies only to those limitations coming into effect *on or after 16 July 1964.*

16. Essence of the common law rule

Where there is a possibility that a future interest in property might vest after the expiration of the perpetuity period, such an interest is void. The perpetuity period at common law consists of the lives in being at the time the instrument creating the interest becomes effective, *plus* a period of 21 years and any gestation period.

(a) The rule is concerned with *possibilities,* not probabilities and actual events. Hence, if, at the date of the limitation, it is *possible* that the gift might vest at a date beyond the perpetuity period, the gift is void *ab initio* under the common law rule.

(b) 'Vest' means ceasing to be contingent, that is, vesting in interest. Vesting requires that the person(s) entitled should be ascertained, that the interest can take effect in possession at once, and that the size of the interest is known: *Re Cassel* (1926); *Beachway Management Ltd* v. *Wisewell* (1971); *Re Drummond* (1988) (*see* **23(e)** below).

17. Examples of the rule

The following examples illustrate the rule.

Examples: ————————————————————————————————

(a) Grant 'to Z for life, remainder to his children who attain 21'. Since Z is alive, and all of his children must attain 21, if they attain that age at all, within Z's life plus 21 years, the remainder is *good.*

(b) Grant 'to A for life, remainder to his first grandchild who shall attain 21' (A is a bachelor). The only 'person living' when the grant takes effect is A, and no one else is referred to explicitly or implicitly in the grant. It is not certain that the first grandson to attain 21 will be ascertained during the life of A plus 21 years. Hence the remainder is *void ab initio*.

(c) Gift 'to X for life, remainder to the first of his sons who shall become a Master of Arts of Redbrick University'. When the gift comes into force X has no children. The remainder will be *void* at common law.

The rule in operation

18. Perpetuity period

(The common law period is stated at **16** above.) Under P & AA 1964, s. 1(1), the perpetuity period may be a fixed period of years *not exceeding 80*. See e.g. *Re Green's WT* (1985).

19. 'Lives in being'

The common law rule was that the lives in being selected by the donor could be stated expressly or by implication. There is no restriction as to the number of lives selected: *Re Villar* (1928) — period of restriction 'ending at the expiration of 20 years from the day of the death of the last survivor of all the lineal descendants of Her late Majesty Queen Victoria who shall be living at the time of my death' was held *valid*.

(a) A person is not considered to be a 'life in being' unless alive (or *en ventre sa mère*) at the date of an instrument under which a gift *inter vivos* was made, or at the date of the testator's death, in the case of a will.

(b) The lives must be human lives.

(c) The changes introduced by P & AA 1964, are considered at **21** below.

20. Possibility of vesting

The common law rule was applied rigidly. Where there was even a highly remote chance that the interest might vest outside the perpetuity period, the limitation was held to be void.

(a) In *Jee* v. *Audley* (1787) T gave a sum to his niece M 'and the issue of her body lawfully begotten, and to be begotten, and in default of such issue, I give the same sum to be equally divided between the daughters then living of my kinsman John Jee, and his wife Elizabeth'. M was 40, John and Elizabeth, who had four daughters, were 70. The gift was held void because, among other matters, the court presumed that further children might be born to the Jees. *See also Ward* v. *Van der Leoff* (1924).

(b) Under P & AA 1964, s. 2(1), it shall be presumed 'that a male can have a child at the age of 14 years or over, but not under that age, and that a female can have a child at the age of 12 years or over, but not under that age or over the age of 55 years'. In the case of a living person evidence may be given to show that he or she will or will not be able to have a child at the time in question.

21. The 'wait and see' principle

Under the common law rule there was no 'wait and see'; a limitation was void if it could *possibly* fail to vest during the perpetuity period.

(a) Under P & AA 1964, s. 3, the 'wait and see' principle applies in *three cases*, to instruments which become effective after July 1964.

(*i*) An interest capable of vesting after the perpetuity period will not be treated as void under the perpetuity rule until it is established that it will vest (if at all) after the perpetuity period has ended.

(*ii*) In the case of a general power of appointment which could possibly be exercised after the end of the perpetuity period, such a power will be treated as valid 'until such time (if any) as it becomes established that the power will not be exercisable within the perpetuity period'.

(*iii*) In the case of a disposition consisting of the conferring of any power, option or other right which might be exercised after the end of the perpetuity period, such a disposition will be void 'only if, and so far as, the right is not fully exercised within that period'.

(b) The waiting period (which must not exceed 80 years) is that specified by the settlor, or a period of lives plus 21 years. But the lives (i.e. the so-called *statutory lives*) are enumerated under P & AA 1964, s. 3(5), as follows:

(*i*) the person who made the disposition;

(*ii*) the person to whom, or in whose favour, the disposition was made;

(*iii*) parents and grandparents of beneficiaries, in certain cases;

(*iv*) any person on the failure or determination of whose prior interest the disposition is limited to take effect.

NOTE: (1) The lives of those mentioned at (*ii*) and (*iii*) above should be disregarded if the number of persons of that description is such as to render it impracticable to ascertain the date of death of the survivor: P & AA 1964, s. 3(4)(a). (2) Payments out of income may be made during the period of waiting. (3) Where there are no lives as in **21(b)** above, the waiting period is 21 years: P & AA 1964, s. 3(4)(b).

22. Age contingencies

Assume a gift to A, who is a bachelor, 'for life, remainder to the first of his sons who shall attain the age of 21'. The remainder is *void* at common law, as it is in breach of the perpetuity rule.

(a) Under LPA 1925, s. 163(1), where the vesting of property was made to depend on the attainment by a beneficiary or members of a class of an age exceeding 21 and thereby the gift would be void for remoteness, the age of 21 was to be substituted for the age stated in the instrument.

(*i*) The limitation must be in an instrument executed after 1925, or in the will of a testator who dies after 1925.

(*ii*) Thus, in a gift to A (who is a bachelor) 'for life, remainder to his first son who shall reach the age of 28', the remainder is void at common law, but was validated by s. 163, which substituted 21 for 28.

(b) Under P & AA 1964, s. 4, s. 163 of LPA 1925, was *repealed,* and there is now substituted the age nearest to that which would have prevented the disposition from being void.

23. Class gifts

In the case of a class gift (e.g. 'to all my sons who shall live to the age of thirty') the composition of the class and the share of each member of that class must be known within the perpetuity period.

(a) 'A gift is said to be to a class of persons when it is to all those who shall come within a certain category or description defined by a general or collective formula, and who, if they take at all, are to take one divisible subject in proportionate shares; and the rule is that the vice of remoteness affects the class as a whole, if it may affect an unascertained number of its members': *per* Lord Selborne in *Pearks* v. *Moseley* (1880).

(b) Thus a class gift is contingent until the identity of every member is ascertained. The gift is void if there is even a possibility that ascertainment will be impossible until after the perpetuity period. A class gift is wholly valid, or wholly void.

(c) Under the rule in *Andrews* v. *Partington* (1791), where the numbers in a class of potential beneficiaries are not certain, the class will close as soon as the first member becomes entitled to take his share. Such a rule can be excluded by the expression of a contrary intention.

(d) In the case of a class gift made after P & AA 1964, 'Where the inclusion of any persons, being potential members of a class or unborn persons who at birth would become members or potential members of the class, prevents the foregoing provisions of this section from operating to save a disposition from being void for remoteness, those persons shall thenceforth be deemed for all the purposes of the disposition to be excluded from the class, and the said provisions shall thereupon have effect accordingly.' *See* s. 4.

(e) In *Re Drummond* (1988), the settlor (S) created trust funds giving him a life interest, and, after his death, a trust of income in favour of his three daughters and to the issue of any daughter who predeceased him. There was to be a contingency distribution stated thus: 'In case there shall be no such child who shall live to take a vested interest in such share upon trust to pay transfer and divide such share equally amongst such of my daughters who shall be living and the issue of any of them who may then be dead such issue taking their parents' share on attaining the age of 21 years or marrying under such age.'

    (*i*)   All three daughters survived, attained 21 and survived S, but only the second daughter had children.

   (*ii*)   It was held, on a summons for determination, that the clause (*see above*) was void for remoteness.

  (*iii*) The Court of Appeal *reversed* the decision. The words 'shall then be living' referred to the date of the daughters' deaths. Therefore the gift to 'the issue of any of them who may be dead' was effective as a gift to the issue then living. Hence the clause did *not* offend the perpetuities rule.

Exceptions to the perpetuity rule

24. Interests following an entailed interest

A remainder following an entailed interest will *not* be void under the perpetuity rule: *Heasman* v. *Pearse* (1871).

25. Charities

In general, in the case of a gift to a charity which is followed by a gift over to another charity on a certain event, the gift over will *not* be void merely because the event may take place after the end of the perpetuity period: *Re Tyler* (1891).

26. Mortgages and leases

The rule does *not* apply to covenants for renewal which are contained in a lease. Nor does it apply to the postponement of a mortgagor's right to redeem (*see* 14:**13**) beyond the perpetuity period: *Knightsbridge Estates Trust Ltd* v. *Byrne* (1940).

27. Options relating to land

In the case of an option to buy a leasehold reversion, such an option does *not* come within the rule if it is exercisable not later than one year after the determination of the lease and if it is exercisable only by the lessee or by his successors in title: P & AA 1964, s. 9(1).

28. Rights of entry

The right of a lessor to enter and terminate a lease on breach of covenant does *not* come within the rule. The right of entry to enforce a rentcharge (*see* LPA 1925, s. 121(3)) is also outside the rule. But the right of entry in the case of a fee simple (in respect of a broken condition) may not be exercised outside the perpetuity period. *See also* LPA 1925, s. 162.

Determinable interests

29. Nature of a determinable interest

A determinable interest is one which may end on the happening of some contingency before its natural termination, e.g. a limitation to X 'until his bankruptcy': *In Re Leach* (1912) — freehold devised upon trust, rents to be paid to X until he should assign or charge, or become bankrupt. It was held that X took an equitable fee simple, determinable should one of those events occur, and which would ripen into an absolute fee, if, at his death, none of the events had occurred.

30. Determinable fee

Under SLA 1925, s. 1, an instrument under which a determinable fee is created constitutes a *settlement*, so that the person who is entitled to possession has the powers of a tenant for life, and may convey the land by sale, lease or mortgage.

(a) In *Hopper* v. *Liverpool Corporation* (1944) it was held that the possibility of reverter in the case of a determinable fee simple (i.e. possibility that the determining event will happen and the fee will revert to the grantor and his heirs) came within the rule against perpetuities.

(b) Under P & AA 1964, s. 12, this ruling is given statutory force: 'In the case of a possibility of reverter on the determination of a determinable fee simple, or a possibility of a resulting trust on the determination of any other determinable interest in property, the rule against perpetuities shall apply. . .'.

Conditional interests

31. Nature of conditional interests

A *condition precedent* is one which delays the vesting of an interest until a stated event takes place. A *condition subsequent* is one which results in the defeating of an interest when a stated event takes place, e.g. *Re Macleay* (1875) — devise of land to X 'on condition that he never sells out of the family'.

32. Difference between conditional and determinable interests

In essence, the main difference is that a determinable interest involves a grant which is *less than the interest specified*, while a conditional interest involves a grant of the interest *subject to the possibility of its being defeated*.

(a) The perpetuity rule applies to a condition subsequent and to reverter of a determinable fee.

(b) In the case of a condition subsequent which is void (*see* **33** below), the limitation will take effect as though the condition did not exist. In the case of a determinable interest which is invalidated, the grant will fail entirely.

(c) A determinable interest *ends automatically* upon the happening of a stated event. In the case of a conditional interest, such interest will become *voidable* when the condition is breached; it does not terminate automatically.

(d) The conditional fee continues in existence until the grantor exercises his right of entry (which is subject to the rule against perpetuities).

33. Conditions subsequent which are void

The following are examples of such conditions.

(a) *Conditions which are contrary to public policy: In Re Sandbrook* (1912) — condition was that property was divested if the donees (the donor's grandchildren) lived with their father.

(b) *Conditions which are uncertain: Re Jones* (1953) — condition was that donee should not have a social or other relationship with a certain named person.

(c) *Conditions in restraint of marriage.* If the conditions are attached to *personalty* they are void where the restraint is total, but may be valid if the restraint is partial, provided that there is a gift over on breach of the stated condition. If the conditions are attached to *realty*, they are void if the restraint is total, but may be valid if the restraint is partial: *Re Bathe* (1925).

(d) *Conditions against alienation.* Total restraint is void. A partial restraint may be valid: *Ware* v. *Cann* (1830).

(e) *Conditions excluding bankruptcy laws: Graves* v. *Dolphin* (1826) — condition that an annuity should not be subject to any debts or charges of testator's son.

A note on entailed interests

34. Essentials

The word 'entailed' or 'tail' is derived from *feudum talliatum* (i.e. a fee which had been 'cut down'). Whereas the fee simple can pass to the general heirs of the holder, in the case of a fee tail the land descended neither to an ancestor nor to a collateral relative, but only to *the lineal descendants of the first tenant in tail.* The estate endured for as long as the original tenant or his lineal descendants survived. 'He who has land in tail has ... the land for time as long as he has issues of his body': *Walsingham's Case* (1573). Under LPA 1925, an entailed interest (the correct title for an equitable entail) exists only as *an equitable interest behind a trust.* The legal estate tail does *not* now exist.

35. Examples of the fee tail

The following examples should be noted: 'to John and the heirs of his body'; 'to John and the heirs male of his body'; 'to John and the heirs female begotten by him upon Mary'.

36. Creation by deed and will after 1925

'An interest in tail may be created by way of trust in any property, real or personal, but only by the like expressions as those by which before the commencement of this Act a similar estate tail could have been created by deed (not being an executory instrument) in freehold land ...': LPA 1925, s. 130(1). Creation by will is governed also by

s. 130. For the barring of an entailed interest, *see* Fines and Recoveries Act 1833.

Progress test 13

1. Explain and illustrate 'vested' and 'contingent' interests.   **(2)**

2. What are 'legal remainders'?   **(5)**

3. Give an account of the effect of the Law of Property Act 1925, s. 164(1) on the problem of accumulation of income.   **(12)**

4. What are the exceptions to the rules of the Law of Property Act 1925, s. 164(1)?   **(13)**

5. Outline the essence of the common law rules against perpetuities.   **(16)**

6. How has the rule against perpetuities been affected by the Perpetuities and Accumulations Act 1964?   **(18–21)**

7. Explain the nature of a 'determinable' interest.   **(29)**

Part five

Incumbrances on land

Mortgages (1)

Fundamentals

1. Terminology

Assume that A borrows money from B and that he later conveys property to B as a security for the repayment of the loan.

(a) *Mortgage.* A mortgage is *the transfer of an estate or interest in land or other property* in order to *secure* the repayment of a debt or the discharge of some other obligation. *See Santley* v. *Wilde* (1899). In the above example it is the conveyance of property by A to B. *See* LPA 1925, s. 205(1)(xvi).

(b) *Mortgagor.* The person who has *mortgaged his property* so as to provide security for a debt — A in the above example.

(c) *Mortgagee.* The person to whom property has been mortgaged — B in the above example (i.e. *the lender of money*).

(d) *Mortgage debt.* The *debt* for which security has been created.

(e) *Legal (or contractual) date of redemption.* The date which is *specified in the mortgage deed* on which the mortgagor will repay the principal plus interest.

(f) *Legal mortgage.* (*See* **3** below.) *The transfer of a legal estate or interest* to act as security for the repayment of a debt.

(g) *Equitable mortgage.* (*See* **6** below.) A transfer for mortgage purposes which passes *only an equitable estate or interest.*

(h) *Redemption.* (*See* **8** below.) The *recovery of mortgaged property* on payment of the debt.

(i) *Incumbrance. A liability which burdens property. See* LPA 1925, s. 205(1)(vii).

2. Nature of a mortgage

(*Mort gage*=dead pledge.) In essence the mortgage arises *where property is conveyed* so that repayment of a debt or the discharge of some other obligation is assured. Its creation *brings into existence duties and rights* affecting mortgagor and mortgagee. The mortgage has developed from common law, equity and statute.

(a) In Anglo-Saxon times land could be pledged as security for a loan. By the twelfth century such a pledge might have been in the form of a *vivum vadium* (living pledge), by which the lender took possession of the land and took rents and profits as discharge of the principal and interest on the loan, or *mortuum vadium* (dead pledge), by which the lender took rents and profits as a discharge of the interest only.

(b) By the fifteenth century a mortgage involved a conveyance of property in fee simple, on condition that repayment of the loan on an agreed day would defeat the conveyance. The mortgagor forfeited his interest in the property on failure to repay on the agreed day.

(c) Equity intervened, guided by the principle: 'Once a mortgage, always a mortgage.' Equity did not consider that a mortgagor's failure to repay promptly justified the extinction of his interest in the mortgaged property. 'In natural justice and equity the principal right of the mortgagee is to the money, and his right to the land is only as a security for the money': *per* Lord Nottingham in *Thornborough* v. *Baker* (1675); *see* **10** below.

(d) The law of mortgages was reformulated under LPA 1925. *See* ss. 85–120.

The legal mortgage

3. Definition
A legal mortgage is the transfer of a legal estate or interest in land or other property so as to secure the repayment of a debt or the discharge of some other obligation. *See* LPA 1925, Part III.

4. Creation after 1925
The following changes were introduced.

(a) *In the case of a freehold.* It became possible, after 1925, to create a mortgage of an estate in fee simple at law by either of the following methods:
   (*i*) a demise (i.e. transfer) for a term of years absolute (usually 3,000) subject to a provision for cesser on redemption (i.e. that the term shall cease on repayment of the loan made on a stated day);
   (*ii*) a charge by deed expressed to be by way of legal mortgage: LPA 1925, s. 85(1); *see also* **20:16**.

(b) *In the case of a leasehold.* After 1925 a mortgage of a leasehold can be created by either of the following:

    (*i*) grant of a sublease for a slightly shorter period;

    (*ii*) charge by way of legal mortgage made by deed: *See* LPA 1925, ss. 86(1), 87(1).

5. The charge by deed by way of legal mortgage

A charge on the land made by deed *will not confer any estate in the property on the mortgagee.* Advantages of this charge are that it enables a mortgagor to effect a *compound mortgage,* i.e. of freeholds and leaseholds, and a mortgagor of a leasehold can create a mortgage, using this method, without the consent of the lessor, in the case of a lease which contains a covenant forbidding underletting without such consent. A mortgage of this nature gives the mortgagee the same protection, powers and remedies as if the mortgage had been made by lease or sub-lease: s. 87.

> NOTE: (1) A mortgagee may use an existing mortgage term as security for a loan which he wishes to raise; in this way sub-mortgages can be created. (2) After 1925 a purported mortgage of a freehold by conveyance of the fee simple operates as a grant of a term of 3,000 years. (3) Almost any type of property may be mortgaged. There are some exceptions, however, e.g. charity estates (unless permission of the Commissioners has been granted). (4) In general, any adult may create a mortgage. The exceptions to this general rule include: patients under the Mental Health Act 1983; trustees, in the case of trust property, unless under trust for sale or under authority conferred by the trust instrument. (5) For mortgage of registered land, *see* 20:**16**.

The equitable mortgage

6. Definition

An equitable mortgage is one which *transfers an equitable interest only,* either because the mortgagor's interest is equitable, or because the conveyance or mode of transfer is equitable.

7. Creation after 1925

The following methods are used.

(a) *Deposit of title deeds.* Where the borrower delivers to the lender the title deeds of his (the borrower's) property, without other formalities, intending that the property shall be regarded as security: *Russel* v. *Russel* (1783). (Where a legal mortgage is not accompanied by deposit of title deeds it is known as a *puisne mortgage*.) This now requires consideration within the context of LP (Misc. Provs.) A 1989, s. 2 (*see* 3:**15**).

(b) *Creation of an equitable charge.* In this case property is charged with payment of the debt, but there is no transfer of possession or ownership of the property: *Matthews* v. *Goodday* (1861). *See Swiss Bank Corp.* v. *Lloyds Bank* (1982).

(c) *Equitable mortgage of an equitable interest.* An equitable interest (such as a life interest under a settlement) is transferred to the mortgagee, with a proviso for redemption. Such a mortgage must be in writing and signed by the mortgagor or his agent: LPA 1925, s. 53(1)(c). *See Thames Guaranty Ltd* v. *Campbell* (1985).

(d) *Agreement to create a legal mortgage.* 'Equity looks on that as done which ought to be done.' Thus, where one person, in consideration of money advanced to him, agrees to execute a legal mortgage in favour of another person, an equitable mortgage is created immediately. When the appropriate deed is executed the agreement is converted into a legal mortgage. *See Tebb* v. *Hodge* (1869); *Walsh* v. *Lonsdale* (1882) — *see* 4:**20**. *See* LP (Misc. Provs.) A 1989.

The equity of redemption

8. Definition

Immediately a mortgage is created, the mortgagor acquires a *contractual right to redeem* (i.e. to recover the mortgaged property) on the contractual date of redemption, and, after that date has passed, an *equitable right to redeem*, on tender of principal, any arrears of interest and expenses of discharge of the mortgage. *The mortgagor's equity comprises all those rights of redemption, signifying that he remains, essentially, the owner of the mortgaged property.* (Hence the equity of redemption includes the equitable right to redeem.) 'The equity to redeem, which arises on failure to exercise the contractual right of redemption, must be carefully distinguished from the equitable estate, which, from the first, remains in the mortgagor, and is sometimes referred to as an equity of redemption': *per* Lord Parker in *Kreglinger* v. *New Patagonia Meat Co.* (1914). (The equitable right to redeem applies to the mortgage of a fee simple *and* the mortgage of leases.)

9. The equity of redemption as a proprietary interest (an equitable interest in land)

'An equity of redemption has always been considered as an

estate in the land, for it may be devised, granted, or entailed with remainders, and such entail and remainders may be barred by a fine and recovery, and therefore cannot be considered as a mere right only, but such an estate whereof there may be a seisin; the person therefore entitled to the equity of redemption is considered as the owner of the land ... The interest of the land must be somewhere and cannot be in abeyance, but it is not in the mortgagee, and therefore must remain in the mortgagor': *per* Lord Hardwicke, in *Casborne* v. *Scarfe* (1738). *See Re Sir Thomas Spencer Wells* (1933): the equity passes on intestacy to the person entitled under that intestacy.

10. Importance of the doctrine

Since equity considers as a vital principle, *'Once a mortgage, always a mortgage'* (*per* Lord Eldon in *Seton* v. *Slade* (1802)), the equitable right to redeem can be exercised in any transaction which is, *on its proper construction*, a mortgage: *Samuel* v. *Jarrah Timber and Wood Paving Corp. Ltd* (1904). (It should be remembered that equity is concerned with the *substance* of the transaction and not necessarily with its form: *Grangeside Properties* v. *Collingwood Securities* (1964).)

11. The right of redemption is inviolable

'There is great reason and justice in this rule, for necessitous men are not, truly speaking, free men, but to answer a present exigency will submit to any terms that the crafty may impose on them': *per* Lord Henley in *Vernon* v. *Bethell* (1762). No agreement which *clogs the equity*, i.e. which makes the mortgage irredeemable, will be recognised by the courts. 'You cannot by contract between the mortgagor and mortgagee clog, as it is termed, the equity of redemption so as to prevent the mortgagor from redeeming on payment of principal, interest and costs': *per* Romer J in *Biggs* v. *Hoddinott* (1898). (A 'clog' or 'fetter' is in the nature of a repugnant condition: *Santley* v. *Wilde* (1899).)

(a) In *Fairclough* v. *Swan Brewery Co. Ltd* (1912), a mortgage of a term of 20 years contained a clause which purported to postpone the right to redeem for 19 years and 46 weeks. It was held that this clause rendered the property *virtually irredeemable*, and that the mortgagor had a right to redeem at an earlier date. *Per* Lord Macnaghten: 'Equity will not permit any device or contrivance being part of the mortgage transaction or contemporaneous with it to prevent or impede redemption.'

(b) In *Lewis* v. *Frank Love Ltd* (1961), L mortgaged property to A so as to secure a loan, and after A's death the personal representatives demanded repayment. L agreed to repay by means of two documents, which contained an agreement whereby in consideration of defendants agreeing not to demand repayment of the mortgage for a period of two years, L would grant them an option to purchase a part of the mortgage property. It was held that the option was *void*, since it was a clog on the equity of redemption. *Per* Plowman J:

> 'I am quite satisfied that the loan . . . and the grant of the option were all part and parcel of one transaction. In my view, the principle on which the courts have held that a clog on the equity of redemption is void applies just as much to a transfer of a mortgage which is arranged between the mortgagor and the transferees, where one of the terms of that arrangement is that the transferees in return for parting with their money shall have an option to purchase part of the mortgaged property.'

12. The right of redemption may not be restricted unduly

Where an agreement seeks to restrict in any undue sense the mortgagor's right to redeem, it will not be upheld: *Davis* v. *Symons* (1934) — refusal to uphold an agreement by which some of the mortgaged property was to be considered irredeemable; *Salt* v. *Northampton* (1892) — refusal to uphold covenant by which mortgaged property would belong absolutely to the mortgagee in the event of the borrower dying before his father. 'A mortgagee can never provide at the time of making the loan for any event or condition on which the equity of redemption shall be discharged': *Samuel* v. *Jarrah Timber* (1904).

13. The right of redemption may be postponed

An agreement may be made whereby the contractual date of redemption is postponed. Where such an agreement does not make the right of redemption impossible, and where it is not oppressive, it may be upheld: *Knightsbridge Estates Trust Ltd* v. *Byrne* (1940) — the mortgagors had agreed to repay a loan of £310,000 by instalments over 40 years. The mortgagors later wished to redeem before the end of the term, in order to borrow elsewhere at a reduced rate of interest. They claimed that the postponement of the right to redeem was unreasonable. It was held that they were bound by the agreement and could redeem only under its terms. *Per* Greene MR: '... Equity does not reform mortgage transactions because they are unreasonable. It is concerned to see two things — one that the essential requirements of a mortgage transaction are observed, and the other that oppressive or unconscionable terms are not enforced. Subject to this, it does not, in our opinion, interfere.' The agreement was referred to by Greene MR as 'a commercial agreement between two important corporations experienced in such matters, and has none of the features of an oppressive bargain where the borrower is at the mercy of an unscrupulous lender'. (For an example of an 'irredeemable mortgage', *see* the Companies Act 1985, s. 193, for details of the 'perpetual debenture'.)

14. Collateral advantages after redemption

A mortgagee may be granted a collateral advantage which gives him rights in addition to the payment of principal, interests and costs. Such an agreement will generally be upheld *unless it is oppressive or seeks to violate the right of redemption*.

(a) In *Noakes* v. *Rice* (1902) the mortgagor of a public house covenanted that the premises would be a 'tied house' for a period which might have continued *after* redemption. It was held that the covenant was a clog on the equity. The premises, which were free when mortgaged, would have been tied to the mortgagee when redeemed.

(b) In *Bradley* v. *Carritt* (1903) X mortgaged shares in a tea company and agreed to use his best endeavours to secure that the plaintiff's firm 'shall always hereafter have the sale of all the company's tea as broker'. It was held that the agreement was repugnant to X's equity of redemption.

(c) In *Kreglinger* v. *New Patagonia Meat Co.* (1914) an agreement provided that a loan to the NP Meat Company was to be secured by a floating charge. There was a stipulation that for a period of five years from the date of the loan the Company would not sell sheepskins to persons other than the lenders, provided that the lenders paid the best price obtainable. It was held that the agreement was *valid*, the stipulation being regarded as a collateral contract which did not form a part of the *main* mortgage transaction. 'There is now no rule in equity which precludes a mortgagee, whether the mortgage be made upon the occasion of a loan or otherwise, from stipulating for any collateral advantage, provided such advantage is not either (1) unfair and unconscionable, or (2) in the nature of a penalty clogging the equity of redemption, or (3) inconsistent with or repugnant to the contractual and equitable right to redeem': *per* Lord Parker.

(d) In *Cityland and Property Holdings* v. *Dabrah* (1968), a term in the mortgage necessitated immediate repayment of the entire balance of the premium and loan on default. The term was considered by the court to be *oppressive and unreasonable*, particularly in view of the very high premium. The court allowed the mortgagor to redeem on payment of the loan together with interest at a rate to be approved by the court.

(e) In *Multiservice Book Binding Ltd* v. *Marden* (1978), the mortgagor borrowed money on terms which allowed, *inter alia,* for interest to be payable at 2 per cent above minimum lending rate, and the value of capital and interest to be index-linked to the Swiss franc. It was held that the terms of the mortgage were *valid*. A collateral stipulation in a mortgage which does not clog the equity is objectionable *only* if unfair and unconscionable, i.e. if imposed in a morally reprehensible manner and not merely if it is unreasonable. *Per* Browne-Wilkinson J: 'I consider that it was unreasonable both for the debt to be inflation proofed by reference to the Swiss franc and at the same time to provide for a rate of interest 2 per cent above bank rate — a rate which reflects at least in part the unstable state of the pound sterling. On top of this, interest on the whole sum was to be paid throughout the term. The defendant made a hard bargain. But the test is not reasonableness.'

> NOTE: The Courts and Legal Services Act 1990, ss. 104—107, controls the 'tying-in' of services with residential property loans. 'Residential property loans' are defined as loans secured on land in the UK, and made in respect of the acquisition of land for residential use.

15. The right of redemption may be lost
The right to redeem is lost in the following ways.

(a) *Release of the equity.* A mortgagee may purchase the equity of redemption from the mortgagor, but only by a separate and independent transaction once the mortgage has been made: *Reeve* v. *Lisle* (1902).

(b) *Foreclosure decree.* In such a case the mortgagee will take the mortgaged property free from the equity of redemption: *see* 15:**9**.

(c) *Sale of land by the mortgagee: see* 15:**10**.

(d) LA 1980, s. 16. 'When a mortgagee of land has been in possession of the mortgaged land for a period of *12 years,* no action to redeem the land of which the mortgagee has been so in possession shall be brought after the end of that period by the mortgagor or any person claiming through him.' *See also* LA 1980, s. 17. In such a case, where a mortgagee obtains title free of the mortgage, he may, under LPA 1925, ss. 83(3), 153, enlarge the term of years into a fee simple, where the term was created originally for not less than 300 years, and a period of at least 200 years remains to run at the date of the proposed enlargement.

NOTE: (1) On the death of the mortgagor the equity will pass to his personal representatives, and from them to his devisee, or to those entitled on intestacy. (2) Where the terms of a mortgage are in restraint of trade, the mortgage may be invalid: *Esso Petroleum Co. Ltd* v. *Harper's Garage Ltd* (1968). 'The mere designation of a transaction as a mortgage, however true, does not, *ipso facto*, protect the entire contents of the arrangements from examination, however fettering of trade these arrangements': *per* Lord Wilberforce. *See also Esso Petroleum Co. Ltd* v. *Kingswood Motors Ltd* (1974); *Alec Lobb (Garages) Ltd* v. *Total Oil Ltd* (1985).

Priorities of mortgages

16. The general problem
There may be several mortgages on one piece of land; the mortgagor defaults and the land, when placed on the market, is not valuable enough to repay the outstanding mortgage debts. One or more of the mortgagees may lose money. The rules of mortgage priorities will apply. *See*, e.g. *Equity and Law Home Loans* v. *Prestidge* (1991). Three questions must be asked initially and answered;

(a) Does the situation involve the mortgage of a legal or equitable interest?
(b) Is the land registered or unregistered? (*See* 19:**1.**)
(c) Has there been, on the part of a mortgagee, any suggestion of fraud, misrepresentation or negligence? If so, priority may be lost.

17. Borrower mortgages legal interest in unregistered land
The following rules apply.

(a) If the borrower deposits title deeds, the mortgage he is granting will take priority over all other mortgages *except* any earlier mortgage properly registered. The *order of creation* of the mortgages is vital.
(b) If the borrower does not deposit title deeds, the mortgage is subject to any earlier mortgage with deposit of title deeds, and to any other mortgage properly registered as a land charge (*see* Chapter 18).

18. Borrower mortgages legal interest in registered land
'Subject to any entry to the contrary on the register, registered charges on the same land shall as between themselves rank according

to the *order in which they are entered on the register*, and not according to the order in which they are created: LRA 1925, s. 29. (For details of land registration, *see* Ch. 20.)

(a) If, therefore, the mortgage has been protected on the register, it defeats all later mortgages and any earlier non-protected mortgages.
(b) Hence, the first mortgage entered on the register ranks first; the remainder rank according to the date of registration (not creation), unless an entry in the register provides otherwise.

19. Borrower mortgages equitable interest in registered or unregistered land
The following rules apply.

(a) Mortgages generally rank according to the order in which written notice was received by persons appropriate to receive it, and this applies whether or not title to the land is registered or unregistered. *See Dearle* v. *Hall* (1828) (at **20** below); LRA 1986, s. 5(1).
(b) The following persons are entitled to receive notice: equitable interest is in settled land — *trustees of settlement*; equitable interest is in land held on trust for sale — *trustees for sale*; equitable interest is in neither of these categories — *estate owner*.

20. A note on *Dearle* v. *Hall* (1828)
The rule in *Dearle* v. *Hall* concerns successive mortgages of an equitable interest in *any kind* of property.

(a) The rule was that where the owner of an equitable interest in *pure personalty* created more than one incumbrance on it, the priority of the incumbrances was determined by the dates on which notice of those incumbrances was received by trustees. The rule was qualified, so that a later incumbrancer who at the time of taking the security had actual or constructive notice (*see* 1:20) of the earlier incumbrance, did not obtain priority merely by being the first of the incumbrancers to give notice to the trustees: *Re Holmes* (1885).
(b) After 1925 the rule has application to *all* transactions involving equitable interest in pure personalty, land, and capital money representing land. The rule applies *only* to dealings with equitable interests already created.

21. The doctrine of tacking
The general rules of priority may be modified where there is a

possibility of tacking. *Tacking allows a subsequent mortgagee to insist on repayment of his loan before repayment of a prior mortgagee, in certain cases.*

(a) *The tabula in naufragio (plank in a shipwreck).* Before 1926, where a legal mortgage to X was followed by an equitable mortgage to Y and then by an equitable mortgage to Z, Z could obtain priority of payment over Y if he paid off X and acquired the legal estate from him. The legal estate here was regarded as a 'plank in a shipwreck', allowing one mortgagee to 'save himself' while the other 'was drowned'. This had application only where Z did not know of the earlier mortgage to Y when he made the loan; if Z did know of this, the equities were not equal. This doctrine was *abolished* by LPA 1925, s. 94.

(b) *Tacking of further advances.* Before 1926, where a legal (but not an equitable) mortgagee made a further loan to a mortgagor, he was allowed to tack together both loans and to recover them prior to any intervening mortgagee, always provided that he had not received any notice of the intervening mortgage at the time of the further loan, or that the first mortgage had allowed for a further advance: *Hopkinson* v. *Rolt* (1861).

(c) LPA 1925, s. 94(1). 'After the commencement of this Act, a prior mortgagee shall have a right to make further advances to rank in priority to subsequent mortgages (whether legal or equitable) — if an arrangement has been made to that effect with the subsequent mortgagees; or if he had no notice at the time when the further advance was made by him; or whether or not he had such notice as aforesaid where the mortgage imposes an obligation to make such further advances.'

(d) LPA 1925, s. 94(3), (4). 'Save in regard to the making of further advances as aforesaid, the right to tack is hereby *abolished*. Provided that nothing in this Act shall affect any priority acquired before the commencement of this Act by tacking, or in respect of further advances made without notice of a subsequent incumbrance or by arrangement with the subsequent incumbrancer.' 'This section applies to mortgages of land made before or after the commencement of this Act, but not to charges registered under the Land Registration Act 1925, or to any enactment replaced by that Act.'

Discharge of mortgages

22. Modes of discharge

A mortgage may be discharged: by a mortgagee exercising his power of sale (*see* 15:10); by foreclosure (*see* 15:9); by redemption (*see*

23 below); by merger (*see* **24** below); under LPA 1925, s. 115(1) (*see* **25** below); under the LA 1980, s. 16 (*see* **26** below).

23. Redemption

The right to redeem may be exercised by any person who has an interest in the equity of redemption, e.g. the mortgagor, his personal representatives, trustees in a bankruptcy. Redemption will involve repayment of the principal, interest and any appropriate costs (e.g. any costs of litigation relating to the debt). *See Holmes* v. *Cowcher* (1970): mortgagee was entitled to receive all principal and interest due, including statute-barred interest at the time of redemption.

(a) Reasonable intention to redeem must be given by the mortgagor to the mortgagee. The usual notice is six months. But no notice is required where a mortgagee has attempted to enforce payment.
(b) Under LPA 1925, s. 95(1), the mortgagor has a right, where he is entitled to redeem, to require that the mortgagee shall convey the mortgaged property to a third person.
(c) 'Redeem up, foreclose down.' Assume that M has mortgaged property to L_1, L_2, L_3, L_4, L_5, in that order of priority. L_4 wishes to redeem L_2.

> (*i*) L_4 must also redeem those mortgages between him and the prior mortgage he wishes to redeem. He must also foreclose any subsequent mortgagees and the mortgagor.
> (*ii*) L_3, L_5 and M must be made parties to the action.
> (*iii*) L_3 must be redeemed.
> (*iv*) L_5 and M must be foreclosed and allowed an opportunity to pay off the prior mortgage.

> NOTE: The rule has no application in the case of redemption out of court.

24. Merger

The rule *at law* was that where two estates or interests in property vested in one person by virtue of the same right, there was an automatic merger. *In equity* the rule was that merger depended on intention. In the absence of expressed intention, there was a presumption in equity against merger. Under LPA 1925, s. 185: 'There is no merger by operation of law only of any estate the beneficial interest in which would not be deemed to be merged or extinguished in equity.' The determining factor in merger at law and in equity is, therefore, *intention*.

25. LPA 1925, s. 115(1)

The money owed to the mortgagee is paid. Under this section, a receipt indorsed on or annexed to a mortgage, signed by the mortgagee and stating the name of the person who has paid the money, operates so as to extinguish a mortgage of *unregistered land*. For the discharge of a mortgage of *registered land*, the registered charge is cleared off the register: *see* LRA 1925, s. 35, and LRR 1925, r. 151.

26. Limitation Act 1980, s. 16

See **15(d)** above for wording of the section. 'Possession' referred to in the section must be possession *qua* mortgagee and not under some other guise: *Hodgson* v. *Salt* (1936).

NOTE: (1) For discharge of building society mortgages, *see* the Building Societies Act 1986, Sch. 4, para. 2. (2) For the protection available to mortgagors based on the doctrine of undue influence, *see National Westminster Bank* v. *Morgan* (1985) (in which the House of Lords noted the importance of the need to establish victimisation of one party by another and a dealing in which an unfair advantage had been taken of another); *Avon Finance* v. *Bridger* (1985); *Kingsnorth Trust* v. *Bell* (1986); *Coldunell* v. *Gallon* (1986).

Progress test 14

1. How may a legal mortgage be created today?   **(4, 5)**

2. Explain how an equitable mortgage may be created today.   **(7)**

3. What is the 'mortgagor's equity of redemption'?   **(8)**

4. 'You may not clog the right of redemption.' Explain.   **(11)**

5. Comment on *Multiservice Book Binding Ltd* v. *Marden* (1978). **(14)**

6. Are there any circumstances in which the right of redemption can be lost?   **(15)**

7. What are the rules relating to the priority of mortgages in relation to registered land?   **(18, 19)**

Mortgages (2)

Rights of the mortgagor

1. **General**
    The rights of the mortgagor considered here and in Ch. 14 are:

(a) the right to redeem (*see* 14:**8**);
(b) the right to enjoyment of the property (*see* **2** below);
(c) the right to grant leases (*see* **3** below);
(d) the right to accept surrender of leases (*see* **4** below);
(e) the right to bring actions (*see* **5** below);
(f) miscellaneous rights (*see* **6** below).

2. **Right to enjoyment of the property**
    A mortgagor in possession has a right to enjoyment of the property. There is no obligation on him to account to the mortgagee for rents or profits which accrue during the period of possession.

3. **Right to grant leases**
    Both parties to a mortgage have a common law right to create leases which are not binding on each other. The statutory power by which the mortgagor and mortgagee in possession may grant leases is contained in LPA 1925, s. 99.

(a) The leases authorised by this section are:
    (*i*) agricultural or occupation leases for any term not exceeding 21 years, or, in the case of a mortgage made after the commencement of the Act, 50 years;
    (*ii*) building leases for any term not exceeding 99 years, or, in the case of a mortgage made after the commencement of the Act, 999 years.
(b) The lease must be made so as to take effect in possession not later than twelve months after its date, and it must reserve the best rent

that can reasonably be obtained, regard being had to the circumstances of the case, but without any fine being taken.

(c) The lease must contain a covenant by the lessee for payment of the rent, and a condition of re-entry on the rent not being paid within a time therein specified not exceeding 30 days. *See Rhodes* v. *Dalby* (1971).

(d) Section 99 applies only if and as far as a contrary intention is not expressed in the mortgage deed, or otherwise in writing.

(e) The mortgagor and mortgagee may, by agreement in writing, whether or not contained in the mortgage deed, reserve to or confer on the mortgagor or mortgagee, or both, any further or other powers of leasing, and such powers so reserved or conferred shall be exercisable as if conferred by the Act.

> NOTE: Power of leasing may be excluded in the mortgage deed. But such exclusion is *prohibited* in the case of agricultural land by the Agricultural Holdings Act 1986, Sch. 14, para. 12.

4.   Right to accept surrender of a lease

Under LPA 1925, s. 100, a mortgagor in possession, or a mortgagee who is in possession or has appointed a receiver, may accept surrender of a lease, but such surrender will be valid only if:

(a) an authorised lease is granted of the whole of the land, or mines and minerals comprised in the surrender, to take effect in possession immediately or within one month after the date of surrender;

(b) the term granted is no shorter than the unexpired term of the lease surrendered;

(c) where the rent reserved by the new lease is not less than the rent which would have been payable under the original lease if it had not been surrendered.

> NOTE: The section may be excluded by contrary intention expressed in the mortgage deed or otherwise in writing.

5.   Right to bring actions

Under LPA 1925, s. 98, a mortgagor for the time being entitled to possession or receipt of rents and profits of land, as to which the mortgagee has not given notice of intention to take possession or to enter into receipt of rents and profits, may sue for possession, or for recovery of rents and profits, or to prevent or recover damages in respect of trespass, in his own name only, unless the cause of action arises upon a lease or other contract made by him jointly with any other person.

NOTE: The section does not prejudice the mortgagor's power independently of the section to take proceedings in his own name only, either in right of any legal estate vested in him or otherwise.

6. Miscellaneous rights
The mortgagor also has the following rights:

(a) to inspect and make copies or abstracts from the documents of title: LPA 1925, s. 96(1);
(b) to require the mortgagee to transfer the mortgage to a third party: LPA 1925, s. 95(1); *see* 14:**23(b)**.

Rights of the legal mortgagee

7. General
The following are considered here and in the previous chapter:

(a) action on personal covenant (*see* **8** below);
(b) right to foreclose (*see* **9** below);
(c) right of sale (*see* **10** below);
(d) right to take possession (*see* **11** below);
(e) right to appoint a receiver (*see* **12** below);
(f) right to tack (*see* 14:**21**);
(g) right to consolidate (*see* **14** below);
(h) right to grant and accept surrender of leases (*see* **15** below);
(i) miscellaneous powers and rights (*see* **16** below).

8. Action on the personal covenant
The legal mortgagee may sue on the mortgagor's personal covenant to repay principal and interest. The mortgagor is liable on that covenant even though he has transferred his interest in the property: *Kinnaird* v. *Trollope* (1889). *See Bolton* v. *Buckenham* (1891).

(a) An action to recover the principal sum will be barred if brought *after 12 years* from the date of the accrual of the right to receive it: LA 1980, s. 20(1). *See* 21:**7**.
(b) Only *6 years' interest* is recoverable: LA 1980, s. 20(5).

9. Right to foreclose
This is a *right to acquire the land free from the mortgagor's equity of redemption*. A right to foreclosure arises after the date for redemption has passed, or, in the case of a mortgage which requires that payment shall be due on any breach of a term of the mortgage, on any such

breach, e.g. failure to pay interest. Where no redemption date has been stated, a right to foreclosure will arise when the mortgagee has demanded repayment, and no such repayment has been made after a reasonable time has elapsed: *Brighty* v. *Norton* (1862). Proceedings generally take place in the High Court. An action for foreclosure must be brought *within 12 years* from the date on which the right to foreclose accrued. But if the mortgagee was in possession of the mortgaged property after that date, the right to foreclose on the property which was in his possession shall not be treated as having accrued for the purposes of this subsection until the date on which his possession discontinued: LA 1980, s. 20(2). *See* Administration of Justice Act 1970, s. 36, as amended by Administration of Justice Act 1973, s. 8 (power to stay possession and foreclosure proceedings: *see* **11** below).

(a) 'Foreclosure is done by order of the court, not by any person': *per* Warrington J in *Re Farnol Eades Irvine & Co. Ltd* (1915). *See Ness* v. *O'Neill* (1916).

(b) A first or subsequent mortgagee may bring an action for foreclosure: *Rose* v. *Page* (1829).

(c) All those interested in the equity of redemption must be made parties to the action: *Westminster Bank Ltd* v. *Residential Properties Improvement Co. Ltd* (1938).

(d) A *foreclosure order nisi* will be granted by the court. Accounts are then taken, and it is provided that the mortgage shall be discharged if the money due is paid by a stated date (usually within 6 months), but that it shall be foreclosed if the money is not paid by that date.

(e) Under LPA 1925, s. 91(2), the court on the request of any person interested in the mortgage money or the right of redemption, may direct a sale of the property 'on such terms as it thinks fit, including the deposit in court of a reasonable sum fixed by the court to meet the expenses of sale and to secure performance of the terms' (rather than order a foreclosure). *See China & South Sea Bank Ltd* v. *Tan Soon Gin* (1990); *Palk* v. *Mortgage Services Funding plc* (1992) (the court has an unfettered discretion to enable it to order a sale of mortgaged property against the wishes of the lender, despite the fact that the mortgage would not thereby be redeemed, where it would be unfair to the borrower to postpone a sale).

(f) A *foreclosure order absolute* will end the mortgagor's equity of redemption and will vest in the mortgagee the entire estate held by the mortgagor: LPA 1925, ss. 88, 89. A foreclosure may be re-opened, e.g. where some unforeseen accident has prevented the mortgagor from making payment: *Campbell* v. *Holyland* (1877).

NOTE: Notwithstanding that construction of a mortgage deed may result in the mortgagee's being deprived of the statutory right of sale upon default in payment of interest, he may nevertheless retain the right to foreclose, in particular where the deed does not include an express proviso for early redemption: *Twentieth Century Banking Corp.* v. *Wilkinson* (1977).

10. Right of sale

Provided that a mortgage has been made *by deed*, a statutory power of sale arises, under LPA 1925, s. 101(1), when the legal date for redemption has passed (usually *six months* from the date of mortgage), *and* no contrary intention appears in the mortgage deed.

(a) *The power of sale may be exercised* only if *any one* of the following circumstances is applicable:

(*i*) interest has fallen in arrear and is unpaid for at least two months (s. 103(ii)); *or*

(*ii*) notice has been served on the mortgagor and has been followed by 3 months' default (s. 103(i)); *or*

(*iii*) there has been a breach of some covenant (other than the covenant to repay capital and interest) in the mortgage deed (s. 103(iii)).

(b) *Mode of sale.* The sale can take place by auction, tender or private treaty. Under the Building Societies Act 1986, Sch. 4, para. 1(1), a building society must exercise *reasonable care* so as to get the *best price* reasonably obtainable. Other mortgagees should take *reasonable care* to secure the *correct market value: Cuckmere Brick Co. Ltd* v. *Mutual Finance Ltd* (1971). The selling mortgagee must behave as a reasonable man would in the realisation of his own property: *McHugh* v. *Union Bank of Canada* (1913); *Bishop* v. *Bonham* (1988). *See also Standard Chartered Bank* v. *Walker* (1982); *Parker-Tweedale* v. *Dunbar Bank* (1990) (the duty of care owed by the mortgagee to the mortgagor arises under the rules of equity, not negligence, and does not extend to a beneficiary).

(c) *Effect of sale.* The entire estate vested in the mortgagor is conveyed to the purchaser, subject to any prior mortgage, but free from the mortgagor's equity of redemption (which is effectively extinguished). *See* LPA 1925, ss. 88, 89, 104.

(d) *Proceeds of sale.* After prior mortgages have been paid off, the money is held by the mortgagee on trust to pay expenses incidental to the sale, to repay principal, interest and costs, and to pay the surplus 'to the person entitled to the mortgaged property' (i.e. the next subsequent mortgagee, or, if none, the mortgagor): LPA 1925, s. 105. *See Palmer* v. *Barclays Bank* (1971).

(e) *Sale to associated person.* Such a sale will not necessarily be put aside, but the burden of proof rests on the selling mortgagee to show that the sale was in good faith and that *reasonable precautions were taken* to obtain the best price reasonably obtainable at the time: *Tse Kwong Lam* v. *Wong Chit Sen* (1983). In that case, the mortgagor (M) had exercised his power of sale through a public auction. M's wife was the only bidder; she was representing the company of which she and M were directors and shareholders. No competitive bids were received at the auction, with the result that the property was purchased at a reserve price which had been fixed by M. The Privy Council held that M had been unable to demonstrate that 'in all respects he had acted fairly to the borrower and used his best endeavours to obtain the best price reasonably obtainable for the mortgaged property'. *See also* LPA 1925, s. 104(2).

> NOTE: Exercise of the mortgagee's power of sale (unlike foreclosure) does *not* require leave of the court.

11. Right to take possession

A legal mortgage entitles the mortgagee to take possession immediately the mortgage is made. 'The right of the mortgagee to possession in the absence of some contract has nothing to do with default on the part of the mortgagor. The mortgagee may go into possession before the ink is dry on the mortgage unless there is something in the contract, express or by implication, whereby he has contracted himself out of that right. He has the right because he has a legal term of years in the property': *per* Harman J in *Four-Maids Ltd* v. *Dudley Marshall (Properties) Ltd* (1957). *See Western Bank* v. *Schindler* (1977), in which an immediate order for possession was granted to the mortgagee to protect his security, although there had been no default under the terms of the mortgage.

(a) A mortgagee may covenant not to take possession before the end of an agreed period of time.

(b) He may be restricted by injunction from taking possession where that would involve a breach of such a covenant.

(c) The mortgagee must account strictly for money received while in possession, and for what he would have received had he acted with diligence: *White* v. *City of London Brewery* (1889).

(d) After deducting costs of management, the mortgagee must use any rents and profits received to satisfy his claim against the mortgagor. *See Chaplin* v. *Young* (1864).

(e) The mortgagee in possession has the power, where the mortgage was made by deed, 'to cut and sell timber and other trees ripe for cutting, and not planted or left standing for shelter or ornament, or to contract for any such cutting and sale, to be completed within any time not exceeding 12 months from the making of the contract': LPA 1925, s. 101(1)(iv).

(f) Where a mortgagee has remained in possession for 12 years without receiving payment from the mortgagor, or without acknowledging the mortgagor's title, he acquires title to the land and the mortgagor loses his right to redeem. *See* LA 1980, s. 16; 21:4.

(g) Where the mortgagee claims possession of a *dwelling house* and it appears that the mortgagor is likely to be able to pay the sum due within a reasonable period, the court may stay, suspend, or postpone an order for possession, *or* adjourn the proceedings: Administration of Justice Act 1970, s. 36, amended by the Administration of Justice Act 1973, s. 8. *See Town and Country BS* v. *Julien* (1991).

(h) 'Where by a mortgage of land *which consists of or includes a dwelling-house*, or by any agreement between the mortgagee under such a mortgage and the mortgagor, the mortgagor is entitled or is to be permitted to pay the principal sum secured by instalments or otherwise to defer payment of it in whole or part, but provision is also made for earlier payment in the event of any default by the mortgagor or of a demand by the mortgagee or otherwise, then for purposes of the Administration of Justice Act 1970, s. 36 . . . a court may treat as due under the mortgage on account of the principal sum secured and of interest on it only such amounts as the mortgagor would have expected to be required to pay if there had been no such provision for earlier payment': Administration of Justice Act 1973, s. 8.

> (*i*) In *Habib Bank* v. *Taylor* (1982), 'to defer payment' was construed to mean 'to defer payment of the principal sum beyond its due date'.
>
> (*ii*) *See also Centrax Trustees Ltd* v. *Ross* (1979) — the court has to take into account not merely the legal stipulations in the mortgage, but also their practical effect in equity; *Bank of Scotland* v. *Grimes* (1985) — the provisions of the 1970 and 1973 Acts empower the court to grant relief against orders for possession made against mortgagors under 'endowment mortgages' (i.e. where the principal sum is left outstanding

during the duration of the mortgage term); *Citibank Trust* v. *Agivor* (1987).

(*iii*) Orders for the suspension or stay of a possession order under s. 36 must not be made where there is no prospect of the instalments being met: *First National Bank* v. *Syed* (1991). S and his wife had obtained a loan from F which was secured on their home; they fell into arrears and possession proceedings began. They sought an order staying or suspending the warrant for possession. The Court of Appeal refused a stay because S was unemployed and was able to make only modest repayments.

(i) The Court is entitled to look behind the formal relationship of parties, so that a mortgagee will not be granted possession of property unless sought bona fide for the purpose of enforcing a security: *Quennell* v. *Maltby* (1979).

(j) Note that where a mortgage deed has been signed as a result of undue influence or a misrepresentation, the mortgagee's right to take possession may be restricted: *see National Westminster Bank* v. *Morgan* (1985); *Goldsworthy* v. *Brickell* (1987). The presumption of undue influence was considered in *Midland Bank* v. *Shephard* (1988). The Court of Appeal held that the relationship between husband and wife does not, in itself, give rise to such a presumption; but even where such a presumption does exist a transaction will not be set aside unless it can be shown that it was manifestly to the disadvantage of the person influenced.

(k) For the right of the mortgagor's spouse to be joined as a party in possession proceedings, *see* the Matrimonial Homes Act 1983, s. 8.

12. Right to appoint a receiver

Under LPA 1925, s. 101(1)(iii), a mortgagee has a power 'when the mortgage money has become due, to appoint a receiver of the income of the mortgaged property, or any part thereof; or, if the mortgaged property consists of an interest in income, or of a rentcharge or an annual or other periodical sum, a receiver of that property or any part thereof'. *See Chatsworth Properties Ltd* v. *Effiom* (1971). The receiver is deemed to be the agent of the mortgagor; the mortgagor is solely responsible for the receiver's acts unless the mortgage deed provides otherwise: LPA 1925, s. 109(2). *See American Express Corporation* v. *Hurley* (1985) — mortgagee is not responsible for receiver's actions unless he directs or interferes with them. (In the case of *registered land* (*see* Ch. 20) the mortgagee should be registered as the proprietor of a charge prior to the appointment of a receiver: *Lever Finance Ltd* v. *Needleman's Trustee* (1956).)

(a) The power may be exercised only in one of the circumstances enumerated at **10(a)** above.

(b) The appointment must be made in writing: LPA 1925, s. 109(1).

(c) The receiver may be removed, and a new receiver appointed, by the mortgagee by writing under his hand: LPA 1925, ss. 109(1),(5).

(d) Money received by the receiver must be applied, under LPA 1925, s. 109(8), in the following order:

> (*i*) in discharge of all rents, rates, taxes and outgoings affecting the mortgaged property;
>
> (*ii*) in keeping down all payments having priority to the mortgage;
>
> (*iii*) in paying his own commission, insurance premiums, and cost of executing necessary or proper repairs directed in writing by the mortgagee;
>
> (*iv*) in payment of interest accruing due in respect of any principal due under the mortgage;
>
> (*v*) in or towards discharge of the principal if so directed in writing by the mortgagee.

(e) Any residue is to be paid to the person who, but for the possession of the receiver, would have been entitled to receive the income, or who is otherwise entitled to the mortgaged property.

(f) A mortgagee owes no duty of care to the mortgagor in deciding whether or not to appoint a receiver to protect its interests: *Shamji* v. *Johnson Matthey* (1991).

13. Right to tack
This is discussed at 14:**21**.

14. Right to consolidate
The doctrine of consolidation is based on the equitable principle: 'He who comes to equity must do equity.' Where one person creates at least two separate mortgages in favour of one mortgagee, that mortgagee has a right to require that the mortgagor, on seeking to exercise his equitable right to redeem one of the properties, shall redeem both of the properties or neither of them: *Jennings* v. *Jordan* (1880). (The rule also has application in a case of more than two mortgages.)

(a) *Consolidation is allowed* only where the legal date for redemption of both mortgages (which must have been made by one mortgagor) has passed, and where the right to consolidate has been reserved (*see* **(b)** below) by at least one of the mortgages, and where the equities of redemption are vested in one person and the mortgages in another, or where that position has existed at some time in the past: *Pledge* v. *White* (1896).

(b) Under LPA 1925, s. 93, *consolidation is restricted* unless the mortgages were made before 1882, or unless 'a contrary intention is not expressed in the mortgage deeds or one of them'. The right may be preserved by a provision in the mortgage deed(s) that s. 93 is excluded.

(c) The rules concerning consolidation apply to legal and equitable mortgages of personal and real property.

(d) In *Re Salmon* (1903) it was held that the doctrine applied to two mortgages on the same property.

15. Right to grant and accept surrender of leases
See **3–4** above.

16. Miscellaneous powers and rights
The following are of importance.

(a) *Right to possession of title deeds*. A first mortgagee is entitled to possession of the title deeds, even though he may not have the fee simple: LPA 1925, s. 85(1).

(b) *Right to insure the property*. Under LPA 1925, s. 101(1)(ii), where the mortgage is made by deed, the mortgagee has the power 'at any time after the date of the mortgage deed, to insure and keep insured against loss or damage by fire any building, or any effects or property of an insurable nature, whether affixed to the freehold or not, being or forming part of the property which or an estate or interest wherein is mortgaged, and the premiums paid for any such insurance shall be a charge on the mortgaged property or estate or interest, in addition to the mortgage money, and with the same priority, and with interest at the same rate, as the mortgage money'.

  (*i*) The amount of insurance shall not exceed the amount specified in the mortgage deed, or, if no amount is specified, two third parts of the amount that would be required, in case of total destruction, to restore the property insured: LPA 1925, s. 108(1).

  (*ii*) An insurance shall not be effected by the mortgagee if there is a declaration in the mortgage deed that no insurance is required, or where an insurance is kept up by the mortgagor or on his behalf in accordance with the mortgage deed, or where the deed contains no stipulation respecting insurance and the mortgagor keeps up an insurance with the consent of the mortgagee to the amount to which the mortgagee is authorised to insure under the Act: LPA 1925, s. 108(2).

(*iii*) Money received on an insurance shall, if the mortgagee so requires, be applied by the mortgagor in making good the loss or damage in respect of which the money is received: LPA 1925, s. 108(3).

(*iv*) A mortgagee will have no rights to money received under an insurance policy entered into by a mortgagor on his own account: *Halifax Building Society* v. *Keighley* (1931).

(c) *Right to fixtures. See* 1:**24**.

Rights of the equitable mortgagee

17. Right to sue for money due

The mortgagor may be sued *personally* for recovery of the money. In the case of an equitable mortgage created by deposit of title deeds, they may be retained by the mortgagee until payment is made: *Re Molton Finance Ltd* (1968).

18. Right to foreclose

An equitable mortgagee may foreclose in the same manner as a legal mortgagee. *See* **9** above. The foreclosure involves a court order conveying title into the mortgagee's name.

19. Right of sale

Where the equitable mortgage was made *by deed*, the mortgagee has the statutory power of sale under LPA 1925, s. 101 (*see* **10** above). In *Re Hodson and Howe's Contract* (1887), in which an equitable mortgagee attempted to exercise his right of sale, it was held that, as an equitable mortgagee, he could not vest the legal estate in a purchaser from him. But note the comments of Lord Denning MR in *Re White Rose Cottage* (1965): 'I see no reason why an equitable mortgagee, exercising his power of sale, should not be able to convey the legal estate. I do not regard *Re Hodson* as authority under LPA, s. 104(1).' *Per* Harman LJ: 'An equitable mortgagee, under a deed in the terms of the memorandum of deposit can, by virtue of the power of attorney contained in it, convey to a purchaser the legal estate in the mortgaged property without first going through the form of calling for the execution by the mortgagor of a legal mortgage.' *See* LPA 1925, s. 91(7).

20. Right to appoint a receiver

The statutory power exists (*see* **12** above) only if the equitable mortgage was made *by deed*. In other cases a receiver can be appointed by the court: *Meaden* v. *Sealey* (1849). *See* LPA 1925, s. 101(1)(iii); Supreme Court Act 1981, s. 37(1), (2).

> NOTE: The equitable mortgagee has no right to take possession, or to collect rents and profits, in the absence of a special provision to this effect in the mortgage agreement. (It has been argued, however, that the *Walsh* v. *Lonsdale* doctrine, which is noted at 4:**20**, gives the equitable mortgagee the same right as a mortgagee under a legal mortgage; hence he should have the same right to take possession.) The court, however, may award him possession.

Mortgages and the Consumer Credit Act 1974

21. Mortgages within the 1974 Act

A mortgage comes within the 1974 Act if it is a 'regulated consumer agreement', i.e. a personal credit arrangement by which a creditor provides a debtor with a credit not exceeding (currently) £15,000 (*see* SI 1983/1878).

(a) The 1974 Act does *not* regulate a consumer credit agreement where the creditor is a local authority or building society or a body specified in an order made by the Secretary of State, being, for example, an insurance company or a land improvement company. Further, this exemption applies only where the agreement is a debtor-creditor-supplier agreement *financing the purchase of land or the provision of dwellings on any land,* and secured by a mortgage on that land or a debtor-creditor agreement secured by any land mortgage: s. 16, as amended by HA 1988, Sch. 17. *See* the Consumer Credit (Exempt Agreements) Order 1989, as amended.

(b) Under the 1974 Act s. 93, interest cannot be increased on default. Under s. 94 a debtor has the right at any time to complete payments ahead of time.

22. Withdrawal from mortgage arrangements

The matters in this paragraph and the next *do not apply to non-commercial agreements* (defined under s. 189(1) as follows: '"Non-commercial agreement" means a consumer credit agreement or a consumer hire agreement not made by the creditor or owner in the course of a business carried on by him').

(a) Before sending to the debtor for his signature an unexecuted agreement in a case where the prospective regulated agreement is to be secured on land, the creditor shall give the debtor a copy of the agreement containing a notice in prescribed form indicating the debtor's right to withdraw from the prospective agreement: s. 58(1). **(b)** This has no application to a restricted-use credit agreement to finance the purchase of the mortgaged land or an arrangement for a bridging loan in connection with the purchase of the mortgaged land: s. 58(2).

23. Signing of the agreement

A regulated agreement will not be properly executed unless the document contains the prescribed terms and embodies all the terms of the agreement and is in such a state that all its terms are legible: s. 61(1). An agreement which is improperly executed can be enforced against the debtor only by court order: s. 65.

24. Mortgagor's rights

Under ss. 137–140 the court can open a credit agreement if it is considered extortionate, i.e. if it requires the debtor or a relative to make payments which are 'grossly exorbitant' or otherwise contravene any principles of fair dealing: s. 138(1). In determining whether an agreement is extortionate, regard shall be had to interest rates prevailing at the time it was made, the debtor's age, experience, business capacity and the degree to which he was under any financial pressure. In relation to the creditor, regard shall be had to the degree of risk accepted by him and his relationship to the debtor, and any other relevant matters. *See Davies* v. *Direct Loans Ltd* (1986); 14:**14(e)**.

(a) Under s. 139(1), if the court considers a mortgage to be, in effect, an extortionate bargain, it may re-open the agreement and relieve the debtor from payment of sums in excess of what is fairly due and reasonable. It can order direct accounts to be taken; it can set aside the whole or any part of any obligation; it can alter the terms of the mortgage agreement.
(b) It is important to note that: 'If in proceedings ... the debtor ... alleges that the credit bargain is extortionate it is for the creditor to prove to the contrary': s. 171.
(c) In *Ketley Ltd* v. *Scott* (1981) the court held that a rate of 48 per cent was *not* extortionate (i.e. grossly exorbitant) within the meaning of s. 138. The court took into account: interest rates prevailing, S's age, experience and business capacity ('S knew exactly what he was doing'), financial pressure, other relevant considerations (in the short time available it had not been possible to investigate the financial

standing of S, and, had such investigations been made, K would never have made the loan), degree of risk accepted by K (considerable, in that the loan was 80 per cent of the value of the property and, had there been sale on default, the sum realised would have been well below open market valuation).

(d) In *Woodstead Finance* v. *Petrou* (1986), defendant had charged her home in an effort to prevent her husband's impending bankruptcy. An interest rate of 42 per cent was charged. The court held that the rate was not excessive, given the husband's poor record in relation to payments, and given the couple's parlous financial situation.

25. Mortgagee's rights

A security cannot be enforced by reason of the breach of a regulated agreement until a default notice has been served: s. 87. A land mortgage securing a regulated agreement is enforceable only on order of the court. A mortgagee's rights of foreclosure ought now to be read in the light of s. 113, under which the creditor shall not secure any direct or indirect benefit greater than would be derived from enforcement of a regulated agreement if the security had not been provided. Note s. 129, giving the court power to make a 'time order', i.e. an order for payment of arrears, in an action brought to enforce possession of land to which a regulated arrangement applies, by instalments and payable at such times as the court, having regard to the means of the debtor, considers reasonable.

NOTE: For mortgage interest relief at source, *see* Finance Act 1982, Sch. 7, para. 14, as amended by Finance Act 1983, s. 17.

Proposals for reform of mortgage law

26. Law Commission Report No. 204 (1991): 'Transfer of land — Land Mortgages'

The Law Commission published, in 1986, a working paper (No. 99) in which major defects in the present law of mortgages of interests in land were examined. Its conclusion was that the law was in need of simplification and modernisation, having 'achieved a state of artificiality and complexity that is now difficult to defend'. In 1991 the Commission presented a Report comprising proposals for a radical reform of mortgage law together with the draft of a Bill 'to amend the law relating to mortgages of interests in land'.

(a) The Report is concerned with 'consensually created securities over interests in land', i.e. all mortgages, charges and other security interests voluntarily created or protected by the mortgagor.

(b) 'Mortgage' is defined in the draft Bill to include all agreements by which an interest in land is made security for the performance of an obligation. 'Interest in land' includes all legal and equitable estates and interests in land. 'Mortgagors' and 'mortgagees' are defined to include successors in title to the original mortgagor and mortgagee.

27. Defects in the present law
The Report emphasised the following current problems.

(a) *Multiplicity of types of mortgage.* Different security interests in land, such as the legal mortgage, the equitable mortgage of a legal estate, the equitable mortgage of an equitable interest, constitute a proliferation which no longer serves any useful purpose.

(b) *Inappropriateness of form.* The methods used to create security interests in land are considered by the Commission to 'give rise to inappropriate relationships between the parties', e.g. as in the case of the mortgagor's duty to the mortgagee to keep the property repaired, ... yet this is a duty more usually imposed by a landlord upon a tenant, rather than by a tenant on a landlord'.

28. Formal and informal land mortgages
The guiding principle to be adopted in defining the nature of the new type of mortgages envisaged by the Commission is that 'the only function of the mortgaged property is to provide security for the performance of the mortgagor's payment obligations. It follows from this that the nature and extent of the mortgagee's interest ought to be dictated by the need to preserve the value of the security and, where necessary, to enforce it.'

(a) *The formal land mortgage* will be made by deed and has application to the mortgage of a legal estate or an equitable interest. No particular form of words will be necessary, other than those needed to constitute a deed. The formal land mortgage will be a legal interest as the result of an amendment to the LPA 1925, s. 1(2) — *see* 2:**15**.

(b) *The informal mortgage* will be created by deed or an instrument which is not a deed but which satisfies the requirements of the LP (Misc. Provs.) A 1989, s. 2 (*see* 3:**15**).

29. Protected mortgages
These should consist of all formal and informal land mortgages of any interest in land *which includes a dwelling house* (whether or not

it also includes premises used for other purposes) *except where* the mortgagor is a body corporate, or enforcement of the mortgage would not affect the occupation of the dwelling house, or the dwelling house is occupied under a service tenancy. The form and content of protected mortgages would be subject to regulations made by the Secretary of State.

(a) Any term of a protected mortgage would be *void* if it purports to provide: that the mortgagor shall pay interest on amounts unpaid in breach of the terms of the mortgage at a rate exceeding the rate at which it would fall to be paid if there had been no breach; that the mortgagor is to give notice of intention to redeem the mortgage; or that the mortgagee is entitled to charge interest in lieu of notice to redeem.

(b) Any term of a protected mortgage which postpones the right to redeem or otherwise impedes redemption will be void unless the land in which the mortgaged interest subsists includes non-residential premises.

(c) If the court is satisfied on an application by the mortgagor that the mortgagee has unreasonably varied or failed to vary the interest rate under the mortgage, it may order that interest shall be paid at such a rate as it considers reasonable.

30. Other matters

The Report also includes the following recommendations.

(a) A mortgagee's rights, remedies and powers shall be available to him only for use in good faith and to protect or enforce his security.

(b) It shall be an implied provision of a formal land mortgage that the mortgagee shall have power to sell the mortgaged property in such manner and on terms and conditions he thinks fit. The power of sale is to be exercisable only where the mortgagor has failed to comply with an obligation for payment and has not remedied that failure, or where the mortgagor, by failing to comply with an obligation (other than for payment) has substantially reduced the value or availability of the property as a security and has not remedied that failure.

(c) The court may re-open a mortgage with a view to doing justice between the parties if it appears: that the principles of fair dealing were contravened when the mortgage terms were being settled; that the effect of the mortgage terms, at the time when the question of re-opening falls to be determined, is to give the mortgagee rights substantially greater than or different from those necessary to make the mortgaged property adequate security for the liabilities secured by the mortgage; that the mortgage requires exorbitant payments to be made; that the mortgage includes terms which postpone the right to redeem or otherwise impede redemption.

(d) A mortgage is to be considered discharged if the mortgagor discharges all his liabilities under it.

(e) The Secretary of State may by regulations prescribe a standard form of discharge of a formal land mortgage.

(f) It shall be an overriding provision of a formal or informal land mortgage that the consolidation of mortgages (*see* **14** above) shall be prohibited.

Progress test 15

1.   What rights are granted to a mortgagor under the Law of Property Act 1925, s. 99?   **(3)**

2.   Explain the nature of the legal mortgagee's right to foreclose. **(9)**

3.   Discuss the mortgagee's right to appoint a receiver?   **(12)**

4.   What is the 'right to consolidate'?   **(14)**

5.   How does the Consumer Credit Act 1974 affect mortgages? **(21–25)**

6.   Consider the concept of 'protected mortgages' suggested in the Report of the Law Commission (1991).   **(29)**

Restrictive covenants

Nature of restrictive covenants

1. Terminology

Assume that X owns and occupies Blackacre. He sells part of Blackacre in fee simple to Y. X and Y agree that Y shall not use his part of Blackacre for, say, any purposes connected with business.

(a) Y is the *covenantor* (i.e. he has given an undertaking).

(b) X is the *covenantee* (i.e. an undertaking has been given to him).

(c) The contract (usually contained in a deed) is in the nature of a *restrictive covenant,* i.e. a contract whereby one owner of land (Y) undertakes to *restrict the use of his land* for the benefit of another owner of land (X). (Where Y undertakes to *perform some specified act,* the covenant is *positive.*)

(d) The part of Blackacre retained by X is known as the *dominant land.*

(e) The part of Blackacre bought by Y is known as the *servient land.*

NOTE: For covenants in leases, *see* 5:**2.**

2. The problem

In the example at **1** above there is a contract under which X and Y are bound. But to what extent can the covenant be enforced between persons who were not original parties to it?

(a) Assume that X later assigns Blackacre to A. Can the *benefit* of the covenant be assigned to A, and can A restrain an attempted breach of the covenant by Y (the covenantor)?

(b) Assume that Y assigns his part of Blackacre to B. Does the *burden* of the covenant pass to B?

3. The different rules

The problem of restrictive covenants is complicated by the following matters.

(a) There are different rules in the case of the *running of a benefit* and in the case of the *running of a burden.*

(b) *The rules at common law differ from the rules in equity concerning covenants.* The general rule at common law was that only the benefit of a covenant would run. But as a result of developments in equity some restrictive covenants now have the nature of equitable interests, and are protected accordingly.

General position at common law

4.   The benefit of a covenant

At common law the general rule was that *the benefit* of either a positive or a negative covenant could be enforced by an assignee of the original covenantee. Assume, in the example given at **1** above, that X had assigned to A. *At common law A would be entitled to enforce the covenant.* This common law rule operated, however, *only* if the conditions enumerated at **5–7** below existed. *See also Shaw* v. *Applegate* (1977). Note that there must be an *intention* that the benefit should run with the land owned by the covenantor at the date the covenant was made. *See* LPA 1925, ss. 78(1), 136.

5.   The covenant must 'touch and concern' the land of the covenantee (or have reference to the subject matter of the lease: LPA 1925, s. 141)

For a discussion of 'touch and concern' *see* 5:**41**. (A covenant which 'touches and concerns' the land of a covenantee 'must either affect the land as regards mode of occupation, or it must be such as *per se*, and not merely from collateral circumstances, affects the value of the land': *per* Tucker LJ in *Smith and Snipes Hall Farm Ltd* v. *River Douglas CB* (1949).) The covenant must enable the land of the covenantee to be benefited in some way: *Rogers* v. *Hosegood* (1900).

(a)   In that case, four partners in a building firm owned the fee simple of land in Kensington, subject to a mortgage. In 1869 a plot was sold to the Duke of Bedford, who entered into a covenant 'with intent that the covenants might so far as possible bind the premises conveyed and every part thereof and might enure to the benefit of the vendors, their heirs and assigns and others claiming under them to all or any of their lands adjoining or near to the said premises . . . that no more than one messuage or dwelling house should at any one time be erected or be standing on the plot'. In 1872, a plot nearby was sold, and conveyed a year later to X, who had no knowledge of the covenant. The Duke's successors in title intended to build, in breach of the covenant, a building on this and adjoining plots, to be occupied as residential flats. The trustees of X's will sought an injunction to restrain the defendants from building the flats. *It was held that the plaintiffs were entitled to enforce the covenant.*

(b) '[The] authorities establish the proposition that, when the benefit has been once clearly annexed to one piece of land, it passes by assignment of that land, and may be said to run with it, in contemplation as well of equity as of law, without proof of special bargain or representation on the assignment. In such a case, it runs, not because the conscience of either party is affected, but because the purchaser has bought something which inhered in or was annexed to the land bought. This is the reason why, in dealing with this burden, the purchaser's conscience is not affected by notice of covenants which were part of the original bargain or on the first sale, but were merely personal and collateral, while it is affected by notice of those which touch and concern the land. The covenant must be one that is capable of running with the land before the question of the purchaser's conscience and the equity affecting it can come into discussion. When, as in *Renals* v. *Cowlishaw* (1878), there is no indication in the original conveyance, or in the circumstances attending it, that the burden of the restrictive covenant is imposed for the benefit of the land reserved, or any part of it, then *it becomes necessary to examine the circumstances under which any part of the land reserved is sold, in order to see whether a benefit, not originally annexed to it, has become annexed to it on the sale,* so that the purchaser is deemed to have bought it with the land, and this can hardly be the case when the purchaser did not know of the existence of the restrictive covenant. But when, as here, it has been once annexed to the land reserved, then it is not necessary to spell an intention out of surrounding facts, such as the existence of a building scheme ... and the presumption must be that it passes on a sale of that land, unless there is something to rebut it, and the purchaser's ignorance of the existence of the covenant does not defeat the presumption. We can find nothing in the conveyance to [X] in any degree inconsistent with the intention to pass to him the benefit already annexed to the land sold to him. We are of opinion, therefore, that [X's] assigns are entitled to enforce the restrictive covenant against the defendants': *per* Collins LJ.

6. The covenantee must have the legal estate in the land to be benefited

Webb v. *Russell* (1789) — the covenantees were equitable owners (mortgagors) and the benefit did *not* run.

7. The person wishing to enforce the covenant should have the same legal estate as that possessed by the original covenantee

Westhoughton UDC v. *Wigan Coal and Iron Co. Ltd* (1919). The rule *does not apply*, however, *after 1925*. 'A covenant relating to any land of the covenantee shall be deemed to be made with the covenantee and his successors in title and the persons deriving title under him or them, and shall have effect as if such successors and other persons were expressed ... "Successors in title" shall be deemed to include the owners and occupiers for the time being of the land of the covenantee intended to be benefited': LPA 1925, s. 78(1). *See Shelfer* v. *City of London Electric Lighting Co.* (1895), applied in *Federated Homes* v. *Mill Lodge Properties* (1980). *See also* LPA 1925, s. 79 (at 5:**43**).

(a) In *Federated Homes*, a restrictive covenant not to build more than 300 dwellings was imposed when D bought land from P's predecessor in title. The covenant was not expressed as being for the benefit of any land, but merely 'so as not to reduce the number of units which the vendor might eventually erect on the retained land under the existing planning consent'. Consent had been granted for the sold land and the retained land (described in the conveyance as being 'any adjoining or adjacent property retained by the vendor'). P, now owner of part of the retained land, claimed that he was entitled to enforce the covenant.

(b) The Court of Appeal found that P *could* enforce the covenant. *Per* Brightman LJ: '. . . If the condition precedent of s. 78 is satisfied, that is to say, there exists a covenant which touches and concerns the land of the covenantee, that covenant runs with the land for the benefit of his successors in title, persons deriving title under him or them and other owners or occupiers.' Further, the covenant would run with any part of the benefited land without the need for words specifying the whole or any part or parts.

(c) It would seem that the effect of this judgment is that s. 78 is 'more than the mere provision of a shorthand form for the saving of words in a conveyance'; and that where there is a restrictive covenant relating to, or touching and concerning the covenantee's land, s. 78(1) effectively annexes the benefit of the covenant to the covenantee's land.

(d) Note *Roake* v. *Chadha* (1984), relating to a covenant stating that

P covenanted with V 'but so that the covenant shall not enure for the benefit of any owner or subsequent purchaser ... unless the benefit of the covenant shall be expressly assigned.' It was held that s. 78 could *not* have effect irrespective of the terms of the covenant.

> NOTE: The benefit of a covenant may be expressly assigned as a chose in action under LPA 1925, s. 136(1), if in writing, and express written notice is given to the covenantor.

8. The burden of a covenant

In general, *the burden of a covenant which affects land does not run with that land — this is the common law rule*. The principle is derived from the concept of *privity of contract*, whereby a person who is not a party to a contract may not generally sue and may not be sued upon that contract. In *Austerberry* v. *Oldham Corp.* (1885) the Court of Appeal held that the burden of a covenant *never* runs with the land at law, *except* as between landlord and tenant.

> NOTE: It is possible to circumvent some of the difficulties of enforcing positive covenants in a number of ways, some of which were noted in the Report of the Committee on Positive Covenants Affecting Land (1965): by chains of indemnity covenants whereby a covenant is taken by successive purchasers; by the enlargement of long leases into freeholds, under LPA 1925, s. 153 (*see* 4:**39**); by covenants against the sale of registered land without the consent of the developer; by right of entry reserved on the breach of a covenant; by leasing instead of selling land and enforcing covenants between lessor and lessee. Note also the principle whereby he who claims the benefit of a grant must accept the burdens: *see* e.g. *Halsall* v. *Brizell* (1957) ('. . . a man cannot take a benefit under a deed without subscribing to the obligations thereunder': *per* Upjohn J); *Tito* v. *Waddell (No. 2)* (1977).

General position in equity

9. *Tulk* v. *Moxhay* (1848)

In 1808, Tulk, who owned houses and vacant ground in Leicester Square, London, sold the ground in fee to Charles Elms. The deed included a covenant by Elms that 'the said Charles Elms, his heirs and assignees shall and will from time to time and at all times hereafter ... keep and maintain the said piece or parcel of ground and square garden ... in its present form, and in sufficient and proper repair, as a square garden and pleasure ground, in an open state and uncovered with any buildings, in a neat and ornamental order ...' Elms devised the land to A, and as the result of further conveyances, it passed in

1848 to Moxhay. The conveyance to Moxhay did not contain a restrictive covenant, but he admitted that he took with notice of the covenant of 1808.

(a) Tulk sought, and was granted, an injunction to restrain Moxhay from erecting buildings upon the square garden.

(b) *Per* Lord Cottenham LC: 'It is said that, the covenant being one which does not run with the land, this court cannot enforce it; but the question is, not whether the covenant runs with the land, but whether a party shall be permitted to use the land in a manner inconsistent with the contract entered into by his vendor, and with notice of which he purchased.'

10. The doctrine in *Tulk* v. *Moxhay*
Tulk v. *Moxhay* established the following doctrine.

(a) A purchaser of land *who has notice* of a restrictive covenant affecting that land may be restrained from use of the land which is not consistent with that covenant.

(b) Where the vendor of land covenants with the purchaser so that the use of the land is restricted in some way, the vendor may seek an injunction restraining a breach of that covenant against parties other than the original covenantor.

(c) The right to seek such an injunction is an equitable right enforceable against all *except a bona fide purchaser of the legal estate for value without notice of the covenant.*

(d) Hence it may be said that, in some circumstances *the burden of a restrictive covenant runs with the land in equity.* (As a consequence, equitable remedies are available and these are discretionary.)

11. The application of the doctrine in *Tulk* v. *Moxhay*
The equitable doctrine of *Tulk* v. *Moxhay* is applied *only* where certain conditions exist:

(a) the covenant must accommodate the dominant tenement;

(b) the covenant must be restrictive or negative in substance (*see* **12** below);

(c) the covenantee must have retained land which was intended to be protected by the covenant (*see* **13** below);

(d) the assignee of the dominant land must show that he has acquired the benefit of the covenant (*see* **14** below).

NOTE: (1) Provided the appropriate conditions are fulfilled, the benefit of a covenant can be annexed to and run with the land despite the absence of express words to that effect: *Shropshire CC* v. *Edwards* (1983). (2) For a recent consideration of the Leicester Square covenant in the light of the Local Government Act 1972, ss. 123(1), 131(1), *see R.* v. *Westminster CC ex. p. Leicester Square Coventry Street Association* (1989).

12. The covenant must be negative in substance

A covenant by R to build a house on Blackacre is a *positive covenant*; a covenant by R not to use Blackacre for business purposes is a *negative covenant*.

(a) A covenant may be stated in positive terms although its substance may be negative, e.g. a covenant by P that he will use a house only as a dwelling house is worded in positive terms, but in essence it is a negative covenant, since it forbids the use of the house except as a dwelling house.

(b) Where the performance of a covenant involves expenditure of money by the covenantor, the covenant cannot be negative in substance: *Haywood* v. *Brunswick Building Society* (1881).

13. The covenantee must have retained land which was intended to be protected by the covenant

The following points are of importance.

(a) Where the dominant land is not retained by the covenantee, the benefit will not pass to another person. In *Formby* v. *Barker* (1903) Formby sold, in 1888, all the land he owned to a land company, the sale being subject to covenants which restricted the user. The defendant, an assignee of the land company of part of the land, had taken with notice of the covenants. The plaintiff, Formby's widow, to whom Formby had given the property by will, sued in order to restrain Barker's building shops, alleged to be in breach of covenant. The covenant was held to be *unenforceable. Per* Romer LJ:

> 'If restrictive covenants are entered into with a covenantee not in respect of or concerning any ascertainable property belonging to him, or in which he is interested, then the covenant must be regarded, so far as he is concerned, as a personal covenant — that is, one obtained by him for some personal purpose or object. It appears to me that it is not legally permissible for him to assign the benefit of such covenant to any person or persons he may choose, so as to place the assign or assigns in his position.'

(b) The nature of the covenant must be such that it touches and concerns the dominant land: *Kelly* v. *Barrett* (1924) — 'Covenants binding land in Hampstead will be too remote to benefit land in Clapham.'

(c) The benefit of the covenant may be annexed to the dominant land, and the benefit will run with the land on conveyance where the whole of the dominant land is capable of benefiting. The court will not make a severance so as to allow a covenant to be annexed to a part of the land capable of benefiting: *Re Ballard's Conveyance* (1937) — annexation of a covenant to the whole of an estate of 1,700 acres held to be ineffective since the covenant could not directly benefit the whole of that estate, and the court would not sever the covenant.

(d) Where there is an intention to annex the benefit of a covenant to the whole or to any part or parts of the estate, the benefit will be annexed to any part which is in fact benefited: *Marquess of Zetland* v. *Driver* (1939).

> NOTE: For the grant of an injunction relating to a restrictive covenant not to erect any new building on a plot of land save with the consent of an adjoining owner, *see Windsor Hotel* v. *Allan* (1981). (For injunctions, *see* **26** below.)

14. The assignee of the dominant land must show that he has acquired the benefit of the covenant

An assignee must prove that he has acquired the dominant land, and *additionally*, that he has acquired the benefit of the restrictive covenant. This may be done in the following ways:

(a) by showing the existence of a *building development scheme* (*see* **15** below);

(b) by showing that the benefit of the covenant was *assigned* to him (*see* **16** below);

(c) by showing that the benefit of the covenant was *annexed* to the land which he has acquired (*see* **17** below).

15. Scheme of development

'Scheme of development is the genus; building scheme a species': *per* Megarry J in *Brunner* v. *Greenslade* (1971). Where land is developed (as in the case of a *building scheme*, e.g. a housing estate) the developer can require that the purchaser of *any plot* shall enter into a restrictive covenant so as to maintain the character of the estate. A purchaser or his assignees may sue for breach of the covenant by another purchaser or his assignees. In *Elliston* v. *Reacher* (1908) Parker J stated the conditions under which such covenants would be enforced. It would have to be shown:

(a) that both the plaintiff and defendant derived title under a common vendor;

(b) that previously to selling the lands to which the plaintiff and defendant are respectively entitled, the vendor laid out his estate, or a defined portion thereof, for sale in lots subject to restrictions intended to be imposed on all the lots, and that such restrictions are consistent only with a general scheme of development;

(c) that the restrictions were intended by the vendor to be for the benefit of all the lots intended to be sold;

(d) that both the plaintiff and defendant, or their predecessors in title, purchased their lots from the common vendor on the footing that the restrictions were to inure for the benefit of the other lots included in the general scheme. *See Re Wembley Park Estate Co. Ltd's Transfer* (1968).

NOTE: (1) There must be evidence of a *scheme* : *see Lund* v. *Taylor & Co.* (1975). (2) The area of the scheme must be clearly defined: *see Baxter* v. *Four Oaks Properties Ltd* (1965). Note *Reid* v. *Bickerstaff* (1909). *Per* Cozens-Hardy MR: 'In my opinion there must be a defined area within which the scheme is operative. Reciprocity is the foundation of the idea of a scheme. A purchaser of one parcel cannot be subject to an implied obligation to purchasers of an undefined and unknown area. He must know both the extent of his burden and the extent of his benefit. Not only must the area be defined, but the obligation to be imposed within that area must be defined.' (3) The fact that some, though not all, of the plots which are subject to a building scheme fall into common ownership, will not mean that the restriction of the scheme can never thereafter be enforced on those particular plots *inter se*: *Texaco Antilles* v. *Kernochan* (1973).

16. Assignment of benefit of the covenant

The express assignment of the benefit, and the conveyance of the land must take place at the same time, and it must be possible to ascertain the dominant land: *Newton Abbot Co-op. Society* v. *Williamson & Treadgold Ltd* (1952). Assignment may also be implied: *Earl of Leicester* v. *Wells UDC* (1973).

17. Annexation of the benefit of the covenant to the land acquired by the covenantee

The wording of the restrictive covenant may make it clear that the benefit was intended to be taken by the original covenantee *and by subsequent owners*. In such a case the benefit will pass without any express assignment. The dominant land must be described so that it may be ascertained.

(a) Where a purchaser of the dominant tenement acquires the whole of the land, the benefit of the covenant will pass to him.

(b) Where he acquires part only of the dominant tenement, he must establish the annexation of the covenant to the part he has purchased or to every part of the whole: *Reid* v. *Bickerstaff* (1909).

> NOTE: 'A person may take an immediate or other interest in land or other property, or the benefit of any condition, right of entry, covenant or agreement over or respecting land or other property, although he may not be named as a party to the conveyance or other instrument': LPA 1925, s. 56(1). The section applies if the person was identified in the agreement and existed at the date of the covenant: *see Re Ecclesiastical Commissioners for England's Conveyance* (1936). *See also Beswick* v. *Beswick* (1968).

Restrictive covenants after 1925

18. Effects of the 1925 legislation

As a result of the legislation of 1925, the general effect of a restrictive covenant is now determined by the date of its creation, i.e. whether created prior to, or following, that legislation.

19. Restrictive covenants created before 1926

Such covenants bind those who acquire the land, *except* a purchaser for value of the legal estate without notice of the covenants.

20. Restrictive covenants created after 1925

In the case of *unregistered land*, such covenants (but *not* those created between lessor and lessee) will be *void* against a purchaser of the legal estate for money or money's worth *unless registered* as a class D(ii) land charge under the Land Charges Act 1972 (*see* 18:**21**). *See Dartstone Ltd* v. *Cleveland Petroleum Co. Ltd* (1969). In the case of *registered land*, the situation is as follows:

(a) 'Subject to any entry to the contrary on the register, and without prejudice to the rights of persons entitled to overriding interests (if any) and to any incumbrances entered on the register, who may not concur therein, the proprietor may in any registered disposition or other instrument by covenant ... impose or make binding, so far as the law permits, any obligation or reservation with respect to the building on or other user of the registered land or any part thereof ...': LRA 1925, s. 40(1).

(b) 'Entries shall be made on the register in the prescribed manner of all obligations and reservations imposed by the proprietor ... and of all obligations and reservations acquired by him for the benefit of the registered estate': s. 40(3). *See also* s. 50(1).

Modification and discharge of restrictive covenants

21. General

Restrictive covenants may be discharged, e.g. by the covenantee's disregarding a breach, or acquiescing in its continued breach (*Hepworth* v. *Pickles* (1900)), or under LPA 1925, s. 84, as subsequently amended. The courts will not enforce a covenant which, clearly, has been abandoned: *see Chatsworth Estates* v. *Fewell* (1931) (in which a covenantee had continued to disregard breaches in a manner which would justify a reasonable person assuming that future breaches would be disregarded). Each case turns on its own facts. Where the fees simple of land benefited by and of land burdened by restrictive covenants are vested in one person, the restrictive covenants are extinguished unless re-created by the common owner: *Re Tiltwood* (1978). *See also Price* v. *Bouch* (1986). A covenant may also be extinguished by statute (*see* **22–24** below).

22. LPA 1925, s. 84(1)

The section provides that application may be made for the *discharge or modification* of a restrictive covenant. The section has application to *freehold estates*; it has no application to a leasehold, *except* where the lease has been made for a period of more than 40 years, and 25 years have expired: LPA 1925, s. 84(12) as amended by the Landlord and Tenant Act 1954, s. 52. Application is made to the Lands Tribunal. *See Re Purnell* (1988); *Re Martin* (1989); *Re Beech* (1990); *Holdom* v. *Kidd* (1991); *Re Sheehy's Application* (1992).

23. Conditions for the making of an order

Under LPA 1925, s. 84(1), as amended by LPA 1969, the tribunal must satisfy itself:

'**(a)** That by reason of changes in the character of the property or the neighbourhood or other circumstances of the case which the Lands Tribunal may deem material, the restriction ought to be deemed obsolete (*see Balchin* v. *Buckle* (1982)); *or*
(aa) that the continued existence thereof would impede some reasonable user of the land for public or private purposes or,

as the case may be, would unless modified so impede such user (*see Stannard* v. *Issa* (1987)); *or*

(b) that the persons of full age and capacity for the time being or from time to time entitled to the benefit of the restriction, whether in respect of estates in fee simple or any lesser estates or interests in the property to which the benefit of the restriction is annexed, have agreed, either expressly or by implication, by their acts or omissions, to the same being discharged or modified; *or*

(c) that the proposed discharge or modifications will not injure the persons entitled to the benefit of the restriction.' *See Abbey Homesteads* v. *Northamptonshire CC* (1986).

24. Further amendments under LPA 1969

See Gilbert v. *Spoor* (1983). LPA 1969 extends the scope of LPA 1925, s. 84(1) by introducing the following additional subsections:

'**(1A)** Subsection 1(aa) above authorises the discharge or modification of a restriction by reference to its impeding some reasonable user of land in any case in which the Lands Tribunal is satisfied that the restriction, in impeding that use, either

(a) does not secure to persons entitled to the benefit of it any practical benefit of substantial value or advantage to them; or

(b) is contrary to the public interest;

and that money will be an adequate compensation for the loss or disadvantage (if any) which any such person will suffer from the discharge or modification.

(1B) In determining whether a case is one falling within subsection 1(A) above, and in determining whether (in any such case or otherwise) a restriction ought to be discharged or modified, the Lands Tribunal shall take into account the development plan and any declared or ascertainable pattern for the grant or refusal of planning permission in the relevant areas, as well as the period at which and context in which the restriction was created or imposed and any other material circumstances.'

For an application to succeed on the ground of public interest it must be shown that the interest is so important and immediate as to justify a serious interference with private rights and the sanctity of contract: *Re Collins' Application* (1975) (application to erect houses at a density of 3.2 per acre upon land upon which only one to the acre was permitted under restrictive covenants).

25. Town and Country Planning Act 1990, s. 237

This section authorises the overriding of private rights such as covenants and easements (*see* Chs. 16, 17) which affect the use of land held for planning purposes in circumstances in which development is carried out in accordance with planning permission. The power to override extends to 'any person deriving title' under the local authorities. For an explanation of 'deriving title', *see* s. 336(8).

26. Injunctions

An injunction for breach of covenant may be granted at the discretion of the court. Damages in lieu of an injunction may be awarded.

(a) An injunction will *not* be granted where enforcement of the covenant would be inequitable: *Wrotham Park Estate Co. Ltd* v. *Parkside Homes Ltd* (1974). In this case X had acted in breach of covenant by building houses, and damages were awarded in lieu of a mandatory injunction requiring X to demolish the houses. The demolition would have been 'an unpardonable waste of much-needed houses': *per* Brightman J.

(b) In *Wakeham* v. *Wood* (1981) P bought land from X, with benefit of a covenant binding X and his successors in title not to build in a manner which would obstruct P's view of the sea on X's adjoining land. P sought a mandatory injunction to force Y, X's successor in title, to demolish a building which did obstruct the sea view. The Court of Appeal held that Y had committed a breach of a negative covenant 'with his eyes open', and an injunction would be granted in the case of an express negative covenant. Y was ordered to demolish as much of the building as was interfering with P's view.

> NOTE: The Law Commission Report on Restrictive Covenants (1967) recommended the creation of a new interest in land, to be called a 'Land Obligation', which would be available to regulate the matters now dealt with by covenants. It would be capable of creation in respect of freehold or leasehold interests, but would not apply to rights between lessor and lessee in respect of the demised land. The burden and benefit would run automatically with the land until released, modified, discharged or ended by the effluxion of time. It would be enforceable only by and against persons concurrently concerned with the land as occupiers or owners of interests.

A note on rentcharges

27. Definition

'Any annual or other periodic sum charged on or issuing out of land except rent reserved by a lease or tenancy or any sum payable by way of interest': Rentcharges Act 1977, s. 1. For example, X charges Blackacre with a payment of £1,000 p.a. to Y.

28. Creation and discharge

Rentcharges could be created by will, by deed or by statute, e.g. SLA 1925. They could be extinguished by release (*see* LPA 1925, s. 70(1); by lapse of time; by merger; or by statute (*see* LPA 1925, s. 191). (*See now* **29** below.)

29. Present position

The creation of new rentcharges is *prohibited* under the 1977 Act, s. 2(1) save in the case of, for example, a rentcharge having the effect of making the land on which the rent is charged settled land by virtue of SLA 1925, s. 1(1)(v), *or* an 'estate rentcharge' for the purpose of making covenants to be performed by the owner of the land affected by the rentcharge enforceable by the rent owner against the owner for the time being of the land. Rentcharges are *extinguished* at the expiry of sixty years beginning with the passing of the 1977 Act or the date on which the rentcharge first became payable, whichever is the later. For apportionment, *see* the Rentcharges Act 1977, ss. 4, 5. For the discharge of a rentcharge by payment to the owner of the rentcharge of a lump sum representing capital value, *see* the 1977 Act, ss. 8–10, replacing LPA 1925, s. 191.

Progress test 16

1. Outline the nature of restrictive covenants. **(1)**

2. Consider *Rogers* v. *Hosegood* (1900). **(5)**

3. Comment on *Federated Homes* v. *Mill Lodge Properties* (1980). **(7)**

4. What was the essence of the doctrine established by *Tulk* v. *Moxhay* (1848)? **(9–11)**

5. How may restrictive covenants be discharged under the Law of Property Act 1925, s. 84(1)? **(22, 23)**

6. What is the situation today concerning the creation of rentcharges? **(29)**

17
Easements and profits

Terminology

1. General

Easements and profits are examples of rights which one person may have against the land of another (*in alieno solo*). Such rights, for example a right of way, or a right to cut turf, are *incorporeal hereditaments* (i.e. rights of property to which the law of real property applies).

(a) Easements and profits are examples of *servitude*s (a term derived from Roman law). In essence, a servitude is an incumbrance consisting of a right to the restricted use of land without the possession or ownership of it.

(b) Note the graphic description of servitudes in Adam Smith's *Lectures on Jurisprudence* (1762): 'Servitudes... are precisely the giving up some part of the full right of property. As if a man's farm lies betwixt me and the public road or any market town, I may by agreement or by law. . . obtain a servitude (that is, relaxation of his exclusive right) by which I am allowed to travel on horse or foot or drive carriages through his farm.'

2. Easements: definitions

An easement is an incorporeal hereditament comprising a right capable of forming the subject matter of a grant which is appurtenant to the land of one person and exercisable over the land of another, for example where A, owner of Blackacre, grants B, owner of the adjoining Whiteacre, the right to walk across Blackacre.

(a) In the above example the right of way granted to B is in the nature of an *easement*. *See*, e.g. *London and Suburban Land Co.* v. *Carey* (1991).

(b) Blackacre is the *servient tenement*; Whiteacre is the *dominant* *tenement* (i.e. the land which should benefit from creation of the easement). (*Tenement* means property held by tenure.)

(c) A is the *servient owner*; B is the *dominant owner*.

(d) The easement is an *affirmative easement,* i.e. A must allow B to perform a certain act (i.e. walking across Blackacre) upon the servient tenement.

(e) An easement is a *negative easement* where the servient owner can be compelled by the dominant owner not to perform certain acts.

3. Profits à prendre: definitions

A *profit à prendre* (known also as a 'profit') is a right to enter and 'a right to take something off another's land': *per* Lindley LJ in *Duke of Sutherland* v. *Heathcote* (1892), for example where X has a right to cut and take turf on Y's land, or to take Y's crops.

(a) A *profit in gross* is granted to the grantee personally and is exercised by the grantee irrespective of his occupation or ownership of land. (It may be exhaustive of the product of the servient tenement.)

(b) A *profit appurtenant* is one which is attached to and is limited to the needs of a dominant tenement by act of the parties. *See Anderson* v. *Bostock* (1976).

(c) A *profit appendant* is one which is attached to land by operation of the law.

(d) A *profit pur cause de vicinage* is a right enjoyed by commoners of adjoining commons, for example where the cattle on one common are allowed to stray on the other common.

(e) A *several profit* is a right to take something from another's land to the exclusion of all others, including the servient owner.

(f) A *profit in common* is a right exercised in common with others to take something from another's land. *See further* at **14** below.

Nature of an easement

4. General

A right over the land of another is not necessarily an easement. A right is an easement only where it has the following qualities (the name given by the parties to the right is not decisive):

(a) there must be a dominant and a servient tenement (*see* **5** below);

(b) the dominant and servient tenements must be owned or occupied by different persons (*see* **6** below);

(c) the easement must accommodate the dominant tenement (*see* **7** below);

(d) the right must lie in grant (*see* **8** below).

> NOTE: An easement subsists as a *legal estate* (and, therefore, binds the world) if held for an interest equivalent to an estate in fee simple absolute in possession or a term of years absolute (*see* LPA 1925, s. 1) and created by deed, statute, or prescription (*see* **22** below). Where either of these requirements is not satisfied it may be an *equitable easement*, e.g. where it is created informally for value, or 'for life'. A legal easement may be enforced against 'all the world'; an equitable easement, against 'all the world', save the bona fide purchaser for value of the legal estate without notice (*see* 1:**19**).

5.   There must be a dominant and a servient tenement

See Ackroyd v. *Smith* (1850). An easement must be attached to land (i.e. it must be appurtenant; it cannot exist in gross). Hence, it cannot be given to a grantee personally. In the example at **2** above, the right (easement of way) is attached to Whiteacre and is a right against Blackacre. The burden of the easement of way is attached to Blackacre for the benefit of Whiteacre: *Rangeley* v. *Midland Railways* (1868). (Note that, in general, an easement should not necessitate expenditure by the servient owner: *see Regis Property* v. *Redman* (1956); *Crow* v. *Wood* (1971) — exception to the rule. This case concerned a right to have a fence maintained by an adjoining owner. *Per* Lord Denning: 'It is not an easement strictly so-called because it involves the servient owner in the expenditure of money. It was described by Gale as a "spurious kind of easement". But it has been treated in practice by the courts as being an easement ... It seems to me that it is now sufficiently established, or at any rate, if not established hitherto, we should now declare — that a right to have your neighbour keep up the fences is a right in the nature of an easement which is capable of being granted by law so as to run with the land and to be binding on successors. It is a right which lies in grant.')

6.   Dominant and servient tenements must be owned or occupied by different persons

A person cannot have an easement over his own land (*see* **1** above). *See Morris* v. *Edgington* (1810).

(a) Two tenements may be owned by the same person who does not own them *in the same capacity*, for example where X owns Whiteacre as an executor, and owns Blackacre beneficially. In such a case the tenements are now owned by the same person in the same right.

(b) Where a person owns two separate but adjoining properties, he may exercise rights over one of them which, if that property were owned and occupied by another, would be classified as easements. Such rights are known as *quasi-easements*: *Wheeldon* v. *Burrows* (1879).

7. The easement must accommodate the dominant tenement

An easement 'must have some natural connection with the estate as being for its benefit': *per* Byles J in *Bailey* v. *Stephens* (1862).

(a) The right must exist for the benefit of the dominant tenement: *Moody* v. *Steggles* (1879). It must be a 'better tenement' as a result of the easement.

(b) Both tenements must be near (although not necessarily adjoining) each other ('propinquity, not necessarily contiguity'): *Todrick* v. *Western Nat. Omnibus Co.* (1934); *Pugh* v. *Savage* (1970).

(c) In *Hill* v. *Tupper* (1863) the proprietors of the Basingstoke Canal Navigation Company leased land on the bank of the canal to Hill, a boat proprietor. The lease gave him 'the sole and exclusive right or liberty to put or use boats on the said canal, and let the same for hire for the purpose of pleasure only'. Tupper, landlord of an inn which adjoined the canal, put boats on the canal without permission, and Hill claimed that this was an interference with his rights. It was held that Hill did not own an easement, his right being a purely personal licence which did not exist for the purpose of the land as such. It was acquired so as to exploit his business. 'It is not competent to create rights unconnected with the use and enjoyment of land, and annex them to it so as to constitute a property in the grantee': *per* Pollock CB.

8. The right must lie in grant

The right must be capable of being granted by a grantor to a grantee by deed: LPA 1925, s. 51.

(a) The right should be reasonably definite. An uncertain or vague right (e.g. right of privacy) will not constitute an easement.

  (*i*)   'The passage of undefined air gives rise to no rights': per Bowen LJ in *Harris* v. *De Pinna* (1886).

  (*ii*) Passage of air along a defined channel (as in a ventilation shaft) can form an easement: *Bass* v. *Gregory* (1890).

  (*iii*) The mere right to a view cannot form an easement: *Aldred's Case* (1610).

(*iv*)   *Jus spatiandi* (right of perambulation) may form an easement, as in the right to use a garden (*see* **11(b)** below).

(*v*)   A right to possession of other land cannot form an easement: *Copeland* v. *Greenhalf* (1952).

(*vi*)   An easement of unlimited storage within a defined space is probably not capable of existing as a matter of law, e.g. storage in a cellar: *Grigsby* v. *Melville* (1973).

(b)   There must be a capable grantor and grantee. An easement can be *acquired* only by a person who has the capacity to acquire a grant: *National Guaranteed Manure Co. Ltd* v. *Donald* (1859). It can be *granted* only by one who has the capacity to make the grant: *Mulliner* v. *Midland Railway Co.* (1879).

(c)   Note *IDC Group Ltd* v. *Clark* (1992) in which the Court of Appeal held that a deed purporting to grant a licence to use adjoining premises as a fire escape route was *not* to be construed as creating a legal easement that bound successors in title and assigns of the grantors. It granted merely *personal rights* not binding on an under-lessee who was not a party to the deed.

Examples of easements

9.   General examples
The following are examples of easements:

(a)   rights of way, e.g. a right to walk across the servient tenement: *Cousens* v. *Rose* (1871); *Scott* v. *Martin* (1987);

(b)   rights of water, e.g. a right to pollute a stream, or a right to take water from a pump: *Baxendale* v. *McMurray* (1867); *Rance* v. *Elvin* (1985);

(c)   rights of air: *see* **8(a)**(*ii*) above;

(d)   rights of light: *see* **28** below;

(e)   rights of support. A landowner has a so-called natural right of support for his land: *Lotus Ltd* v. *British Soda Ltd* (1972). A right to support of buildings may exist as an easement: *Dalton* v. *Angus & Co.* (1881).

(f)   rights of fencing: *see Crow* v. *Wood* (1971) at **5** above.

> NOTE: A 'right of entry' (i.e. the right to enforce forfeiture of the subject-matter of a lease) is *not* an easement. See LPA 1925, s. 146.

10. Miscellaneous examples
The following rights have been held to be easements.

(a) The use of a letter box, a kitchen: *Goldberg* v. *Edwards* (1950); *Heywood* v. *Mallalieu* (1883).

(b) The use of a wall for fixing a sign, or for supporting a creeper: *Moody* v. *Steggles* (1879); *Simpson* v. *Weber* (1925).

(c) The use of coal sheds and the storage of trade materials on the servient tenement: *Wright* v. *Macadam* (1949); *A.-G. of S. Nigeria* v. *James Holt* (1915).

11. The creation of new easements

'It must not therefore be supposed that incidents of a novel kind can be devised and attached to property at the fancy or caprice of any owner': *per* Lord Brougham in *Keppell* v. *Bailey* (1834). 'The owner of land [cannot] render it subject to a new species of burden, so as to bind it in the hands of an assignee': *per* Cresswell J in *Ackroyd* v. *Smith* (1850).

(a) *The categories of easement, however, are not closed.* 'The category of servitudes and easements must alter and expand with the changes that take place in the circumstances of mankind': *per* Lord St Leonards in *Dyce* v. *Lady James Hay* (1852).

(b) *It is possible for new easements to arise.* Thus, a *jus spatiandi* (*see* 8(a)(iv) above) was held as being not capable of forming an easement in *International Tea Stores Co.* v. *Hobbs* (1903); but it was accepted as forming an easement in *Re Ellenborough Park* (1956).

(c) In *Re Ellenborough Park* (1956), owners of residential properties enjoyed a park enclosed by those properties; each owner contributed to the maintenance costs of the park. Later the park was acquired from the original owners by the plaintiff who wished to build on it. Owners of the residential properties claimed a right to use the park. The Court of Appeal held that the park was, effectively, 'a communal garden for the benefit and enjoyment of those whose houses adjoined it or were in its close proximity'. The park satisfied the requirement 'of connection with the dominant tenements to which it was appurtenant'. The use of the park was clearly beneficial to the premises to which it was attached. 'A tendency in the past to freeze the categories of easements has been overtaken by the defrosting operation in *Re Ellenborough Park*': *per* Russell LJ in *Dowty Boulton Paul Ltd* v. *Wolverhampton Corporation (No. 2)* (1976) (right to use an airfield).

(d) The recognition of new easements will not be unlimited. If the criteria set out in *Re Ellenborough Park* are satisfied *and* if it can be shown that the nature of the right claimed is essentially similar to an established type of easement, the claim might be justified. But recognition may be *unlikely* in the following circumstances:

   (*i*) where the easement claimed is negative (*see Phipps* v. *Pears* (1965));

  (*ii*) where, if the easement were recognised, the servient owner would be excluded from his land (*see Copeland* v. *Greenhalf* (1952));

 (*iii*) where the servient owner would be obliged to spend money (*see Regis Property Co.* v. *Redman* (1956)).

Easements and other rights

12. General

There are differences between easements and other similar rights over land. Easements may be differentiated from so-called natural rights, restrictive covenants, customary rights, public rights, licences.

(**a**) *Easements and natural rights.* The so-called natural rights which attach to property (*see* 3:**19**), e.g. the right to support, arise automatically from ownership. Easements do not arise automatically, and must be created, e.g. by grant (*see* **18** below).

(**b**) *Easements and restrictive covenants.* Both require the existence of dominant and servient tenements, and both may be negative in substance. But restrictive covenants exist only as equitable interests, unlike easements, which exist in equity *and* at law.

(**c**) *Easements and local customary rights.* A customary right, e.g. the right of parishioners to cross another person's land on their way to church (*Brocklebank* v. *Thompson* (1903)), is not the same as an easement, since the latter can lie in grant and an indefinite body, e.g. parishioners, cannot take by grant. Additionally, a customary right may be exercised without ownership of a dominant tenement. *See*, e.g. *Mercer* v. *Denne* (1905) — custom of drying fishing nets.

(**d**) *Easements and public rights.* Public rights, e.g. a right of way, may be exercised by any member of the public, unlike an easement, which may be exercised only by the owner of a dominant tenement. *See*, e.g. *R* v. *Welwyn Hatfield DC* (1982).

(**e**) *Easements and licences.* (*See* 6:**4**.) A licence exists where X merely allows Y the use of X's land for certain purposes without conveying to Y any estate or interest in that land. A licence may be coupled with an interest, for example where X sells standing timber to Y on condition that Y is to sever the timber: *Jones & Sons Ltd* v. *Tankerville*

(1909). In this case the sale implies a grant of a licence to Y to enter X's land. This licence will be irrevocable while the interest to which it is coupled endures. A bare licence is one granted gratuitously, for example where X gives Y permission to enter X's house. Such a licence is revocable at any time with reasonable notice: *Armstrong* v. *Sheppard and Short Ltd* (1959). Easements and licences differ in the following ways:

(*i*) a licence is an equity; an easement may be a legal or equitable interest;

(*ii*) no dominant tenement is necessary in the case of a licence; a dominant tenement is necessary in the case of an easement;

(*iii*) a licence does not require a deed of grant; an easement requires a grant for its creation;

(*iv*) an easement, unlike a licence, may not be revoked unilaterally.

Nature of *profits à prendre*

13. General

(See **3** above.) A profit involves a right to enter and take something capable of ownership from the land of another, e.g. the right to take sand or gravel: *Constable* v. *Nicholson* (1863). In general, that which is taken must form a part of the land, e.g. crops, or wild animals. (The right to take water from the spring on the land of another is not a profit, but an easement, since such water is considered as not being in the ownership of any person.)

14. Types of profit

Profits à prendre may exist as *several profits* or *profits in common* (*see* **3(e)**, **(f)** above). (Note: Profits in common are also known as *commons*, or *rights of common*.) Profits may be of the following types.

(a) *Profit in gross.* (*See* **3(a)** above.) Such a profit may be several, or in common, and does *not* require that its owner shall have ownership of a dominant tenement: *Lord Chesterfield* v. *Harris* (1908). (Note: 'several' means 'separate', as opposed to 'joint'.)

(b) *Profit appurtenant.* (*See* **3(b)** above.) Such a profit will run with the dominant tenement to which it is attached. It may be acquired by prescription (*see* **27** below), or by grant. The necessary conditions required for an easement (*see* **4** above) must exist in the case of a profit appurtenant. *See Anderson* v. *Bostock* (1976).

(c) *Profit appendant.* (*See* **3(c)** above.) Such a profit exists in one form only — common of pasture. Creation of this type of profit was not possible after *Quia Emptores* 1290. *See Re Ilkley and Burley Moors* (1984); **2:6**.

(d) *Profit pur cause de vicinage.* (*See* **3(d)** above.) Such a profit may exist only where the commons adjoin each other: *Commissioners of Sewers* v. *Glasse* (1874). Claim to such a profit will not be upheld if the cattle have been driven off one of the commons by the commoners: *Heath* v. *Elliot* (1838). *See Newman* v. *Bennett* (1981).

(e) *Commons of pasture, estovers, turbary and piscary.* These are ancient in their origins.

> (*i*)   *Common of pasture.* This exists where an owner of cattle has the right with others to pasture cattle on another's land. The number of cattle which may be pastured is determined by the needs of the dominant tenement.

> (*ii*) *Common of estovers*: *see* **5:5(b).** Such a right can be attached to land or to a house.

> (*iii*) *Common of turbary.* This right allows the owner to cut turf for use as fuel on another's land.

> (*iv*) *Common of piscary.* The right to fish in another's lake or pond may be a common of fishery (where it is exercised in common with others) or a several fishery (where the owner of the lake or pond is excluded): *Foster* v. *Wright* (1878).

Profits and other rights

15. General
> Profits may be differentiated from certain other rights over land.

(a) *Profits and easements.* A profit is a right to take something from another's land (e.g. soil, minerals, natural produce); an easement is a right over or against another's land. A profit may exist in gross; an easement cannot. There are different periods for the prescribing of profits and easements under the Prescription Act 1832 (*see* **27** below).

(b) *Customary rights.* A fluctuating body of persons cannot generally claim a profit by custom: *Gateward's Case* (1607). *See* note at **28** below.

> NOTE: Like easements, profits may be legal or equitable: *Mason* v. *Clarke* (1955); *Lowe* v. *Ashmore Ltd* (1971). *See* **4** above.

The creation and acquisition of easements and profits

16. General
> Easements and profits may be created and acquired by Act of

Parliament, or by grant (by deed or will). Grants may be express, implied or presumed ('prescription'). *See also* **27** below.

17. Act of Parliament

Inclosure Acts, for example, may create legal easements (and profits): *Adeane* v. *Mortlock* (1839). Public utilities may be granted easements by statute.

18. Express grant

At common law profits could be created by express grant, in the form of a deed. In equity an agreement for the grant of a profit may be enforced in the absence of a deed: *Mason* v. *Clarke* (1955). In the case of an easement the position is as follows.

(a) At common law a grant of an easement had to be made by deed. *See* LPA 1925, s. 52 (all conveyances to be by deed).

(b) 'Equity looks on that as done which ought to be done'; hence an oral agreement for valuable consideration to grant an easement was considered in equity as a grant of an easement: *McManus* v. *Cooke* (1887). But *see now* LP(Misc. Provs.)A 1989, s. 2.

19. Express reservation

A vendor who sells a part of his land may reserve *expressly* for himself easements (and profits) over the land sold. *See Johnstone* v. *Holdway* (1963).

(a) At common law this was not possible. But under LPA 1925, s. 65(1): 'A reservation of a legal estate shall operate at law without any execution of the conveyance by the grantee of the legal estate out of which the reservation is made, or any regrant by him, so as to create the legal estate reserved, and so as to vest the same in possession in the person (whether being the grantor or not) for whose benefit the reservation is made.' In *St Edmundsbury and Ipswich Diocesan Board of Finance* v. *Clark (No.2)* (1973) it was held that an easement reserved in favour of a vendor in a conveyance will be construed against him as grantor thereof. *See Lady Dunsany* v. *Bedworth* (1979); *Wiles* v. *Bank* (1985).

(b) Under LPA 1925, s. 62(1), a conveyance executed after 1881 operates (subject to an expressed contrary intention) to convey with the land all easements and rights appertaining or reputed to appertain to the land or any part thereof.

(c) There are limitations to the operation of s. 62.

    (i) There must be a 'conveyance' of land, and this will include a

mortgage, charge, lease, assent, vesting declaration, etc., and every other assurance of property or of an interest therein by any instrument, except a will: LPA 1925, s. 205(1)(ii). Thus, a contract for a lease would not be included. Further, the section has no application to future rights: *Nickerson* v. *Barraclough* (1981).

(ii) The right must be known to the law, i.e. it must be capable of constituting an easement. See *International Tea Stores Co* v. *Hobbs* (1903).

(iii) There must be diversity of ownership or occupation of the tenements prior to the conveyance. 'When land is under one ownership one cannot speak in any intelligible sense of rights, or privileges, or easements being exercised over one part for the benefit of another. Whatever the owner does, he does as owner, and until a separation occurs of ownership or at least occupation, the condition for the existence of rights does not exist': *per* Lord Wilberforce.

20. Implied grant

Where the owner of land grants part of it to another person, certain rights exercisable over the retained land are implied in favour of the *grantee* (i.e. the purchaser of the land). These rights are: easements intended to be created by grantor and grantee; easements of necessity; easements reasonably necessary for the enjoyment of a right expressly granted; easements arising from the doctrine of *Wheeldon* v. *Burrows* (1879) — *see* (c) below. (The doctrine does *not* apply to *profits*.)

(a) *Easements intended to be created by grantor and grantee*. Such easements will be implied, even though not stated expressly in the terms of the conveyance. 'The law will readily imply the grant or reservation of such easements as may be necessary to give effect to the *common intention* of the parties to a grant of real property, with reference to the manner or purposes in and for which the land granted ... is to be used': *per* Lord Parker in *Pwllbach Colliery Co. Ltd* v. *Woodman* (1915) (the mining of coal and the implied easement to deposit coal dust in the neighbourhood of the mine). See *Duke of Westminster* v. *Guild* (1985) (implied right of drainage).

(b) *Easements of necessity. See Wong* v. *Beaumont Property Trust Ltd* (1965), in which L granted the lease of a basement to T for use as a restaurant and refused permission to T to construct a duct necessary under the Food Hygiene Regulations 1955; it was held that, because of the terms of the lease, there had been an *implied grant of an easement of necessity*. (*Per* Lord Denning: 'In order to use this place as a restaurant, there must be implied an easement, by the necessity of the case, to carry a duct up the wall.') *See also Liverpool CC* v. *Irwin* (1977) (easements giving tenants right to use rubbish chutes, etc.). In *Nickerson* v. *Barraclough* (1981) the Court of Appeal held that a way of necessity could exist only in association with a grant of land and depended on the intention of the parties and an implication from the circumstances that unless some way was implied, the land in question would be inaccessible. *See London Surburban Land Co.* v. *Carey* (1991) (express grant of right of way did not carry implied right to park).

(c) *Easements arising from the doctrine of Wheeldon* v. *Burrows* (1879). 'On the grant by the owner of a tenement of part of that tenement as it is then used and enjoyed, there will pass to the grantee all those continuous and apparent easements (by which, of course, I mean quasi-easements), or, in other words, all those easements which are *necessary to the reasonable enjoyment of the property granted*, and which have been and are at the time of the grant used by the owners of the entirety for the benefit of the part granted': *per* Thesiger LJ.

    (*i*) 'Continuous.' Such an easement is one which has been enjoyed without interruption (i.e. permanently, not just temporarily), and without the owner's having had to assert that right. *See Suffield* v. *Brown* (1864).

    (*ii*) 'Apparent.' Such an easement is one whose existence may be discovered by careful inspection of the land by a person ordinarily conversant with the subject, e.g. the existence of a track across the servient tenement and leading to the dominant tenement may make visible a right of way. *See Hansford* v. *Jago* (1921); *Horn* v. *Hiscock* (1972).

NOTE: The doctrine in *Wheeldon* v. *Burrows* has been superseded to a large extent by LPA 1925, s. 62 (*see* **19(b)** above). But s. 62, unlike *Wheeldon* v. *Burrows*, applies only to a conveyance executed after 1881. Additionally, s. 62 applies to 'a conveyance', and this does *not* include a contract. *Wheeldon* v. *Burrows* would apply to a conveyance *and* a contract. Note that neither s. 62 nor *Wheeldon* v. *Burrows* can confer a benefit on a third party. *Wheeldon* v. *Burrows* relates only to easements; s. 62 relates to easements *and* profits.

21. Implied reservation

Where the owner of land grants part of it to another person, certain rights over the land granted are implied in favour of *the grantor*.

(a) The general rule is that a grantor may not derogate from his grant. Where he wishes to retain an easement, an express reservation must be made.

(b) Easements of necessity, e.g. easements necessary to carry out the common intention of the parties, will be implied in the grantor's favour: *Re Webb's Lease* (1951). *See Barry* v. *Hasseldine* (1952).

22. Presumed grant (prescription)

Prescription means, in its general sense, the acquisition or extinction of rights *by lapse of time. See Ironside & Crabb* v. *Cook & Barefoot* (1981).

(a) The word derives from the Roman legal concept of *praescriptio,* by which those who retained provincial land or some kinds of movables for an uninterrupted period of 10 or 20 years acquired ownership.

(b) The basis of prescription in English law is the presumption that, where a person is in undisturbed enjoyment of a right, he is not in possession as the result of some unlawful act.

(c) *Omnia praesumuntur rite et solemniter esse acta.* (All acts are presumed to have been done rightly and regularly.) Hence, long user may, in certain circumstances, give rise to a presumed grant of an easement or a profit.

23. The principles of prescription

There are some general principles of prescription.

(a) The claim must be based upon *actual and continuous user. See Dare* v. *Heathcote* (1856). 'Continuous' means here not incessant, but rather an absence of long periods of non-user.

(b) Enjoyment must be *as of right,* i.e. *nec vi, nec clam, nec precario* (without force, without secrecy, without permission). The claimant must establish that the servient owner has acquiesced in the exercise of the right. *Vi* could refer, for example, to user allowed under continuing protest. *Clam* could refer to the permissive exercise of a right, e.g. following an agreement or payment. *See Healey* v. *Hawkins* (1968).

(c) User must be by or on behalf of *a tenant in fee simple* against another tenant in fee simple who has acquiesced in that user. *See Pugh* v. *Savage* (1970). Two exceptions to this general rule are:

    (i) in the case of profits in gross, claim to the right is made on behalf of the claimant; it is not made concerning a dominant tenement;

    (ii) under the Prescription Act 1832, easements of light may be

acquired by T^1 (a lessee) against L (his lessor) or against T^2 (another lessee of L) (*see* **28(b)** below).

24. Modes of acquisition by presumed grant
There are three modes:

(a) prescription at common law (*see* **25** below);
(b) lost modern grant (*see* **26** below);
(c) the Prescription Act 1832 (*see* **27–28** below), which *supplements* the common law rules, but does not supersede them.

25. Prescription at common law
At common law a claimant to an easement or profit had to establish the following.

(a) *User since time immemorial* ('from time whereof the memory of men runneth not to the contrary': Coke). The Statute of Westminster I 1275 fixed it as 1189 (the first year of the reign of Richard I). Hence, a claimant had to show that the right had been enjoyed since 1189. In such a case the court would *presume* that a grant had been made prior to 1189. The difficulties of establishing continuous enjoyment since 1189 were formidable, and user for a long period (not less than *20 years*) led to a presumption by the court of continuous user since 1189: *Darling* v. *Clue* (1864). Such a presumption may be rebutted by proof that the right could not have existed, or, in fact, did not exist, in 1189 or at some period after 1189.
(b) *User nec vi, nec clam, nec precario*: see **23(b)** above.
(c) *Continuous user*. It is possible for a claimant to establish continuous user by successive owners. (Prescription of this nature is known as prescription in the *que estate* (derived from the phrase *ceux que estate il ad* — 'those persons whose estate he has').) The essence of this claim is that the easement was annexed in the past to a dominant tenement of which the claimant is now the owner.

26. Lost modern grant
This doctrine is based on a fiction whereby the court will presume from long user (20 years) that a grant has been made at some time after 1189, but that it has now been lost: *Dalton* v. *Angus & Co.* (1881). *See also Diment* v. *NH Foot Ltd* (1974); *Bridle* v. *Ruby* (1988) — presumption of lost modern grant was not rebutted by a mistaken belief as to right of way over land.

(a) User as of right must be shown.
(b) The right claimed must be capable of being acquired by grant.

(c) A claim under this doctrine may be made only where prescription at common law is not possible in the circumstances. *See Tehidy Minerals* v. *Norman* (1971).

(d) A claim might be defeated by proof that during the period of time when it was possible to have made the grant there was no person who could lawfully have made it: *Neaverson* v. *Peterborough RDC* (1902) (as where the dominant and servient tenements were in common ownership at the relevant time).

(e) The defendant must plead whether the alleged lost grant was made before or after stated dates; but he may plead alternative grants covering the entire period: *Tremayne* v. *English Clays Co.* (1972).

(f) In *Mills* v. *Silver* (1991), the Court of Appeal held that in order to succeed in a claim to a vehicular right of way over a disputed track, there had to be established sufficient and open use such as would warrant the implication of a lost modern grant. Once proved, mere toleration without objection to it by the servient owners did not prevent the acquisition of such a right. (Further, as defendants held a prescriptive right of way, they were entitled to repair it, but not to effect improvements which would place a greater burden on the land over which the track ran. Putting down of stones went beyond mere repairs and constituted a trespass.)

(g) In *Simmons* v. *Dobson* (1991), the Court of Appeal stressed that one tenant cannot acquire an easement by prescription against another tenant of the same landlord, at common law or under the Prescription Act 1832, s. 2 (*see* **27** below).

The Prescription Act 1832

27. Easements other than light
The Act provides the following.

(a) A claim to a *profit* which has been enjoyed as of right and without interruption for a period of *30 years* cannot be defeated by proof that user began after 1189. Uninterrupted user for *60 years* will make such a claim absolute and indefeasible: s. 1. *See Newnham* v. *Willison* (1988).

> NOTE: The Act has application to a profit appurtenant, but not to a profit in gross (*see* **14** above).

(b) A claim to an *easement* (other than a right to light) which has been enjoyed as of right and without interruption for a period of *20 years* cannot be defeated by proof that user began after 1189.

Uninterrupted user for *40 years* will make such a claim absolute and indefeasible: s. 2.

(c) Periods of enjoyment are those immediately preceding the action: s. 4. *See Goldsmith* v. *Burrow Construction Co.* (1987).

(d) No act will be deemed an interruption unless the dominant owner has acquiesced in it for one year after having notice of the interruption and of the person responsible for it: s. 4. ('Interruption' means active, overt obstruction and not merely non-user.) Acquiescence is a matter of fact: *Davies* v. *Du Paver* (1953).

(e) Where a claim is based upon the shorter periods of enjoyment, there must be deducted from those periods any time during which the servient owner has been an 'infant, idiot, or tenant for life': s. 7. A successful claim requires that there shall be a period of 20 years remaining after deductions.

(f) Where a claim is to a right of 'way or other convenient water-course or use of water' there shall be deducted from the period of enjoyment those periods when the servient tenement has been held under a tenancy for life or under a lease for a term of more than three years, provided that the claim is resisted by a reversioner within three years after the tenancy for life or the lease has ended: s. 8. ('Reversioner' does not include 'remainderman' (*see* 1:**15(c)**: *Symons* v. *Leaker* (1885).)

(g) In cases **(a)** and **(b)** above where oral consent was given at the beginning of the user, such consent will defeat any claim based on the shorter, but not the longer, periods. Written consents, or consents given regularly during the period of user, will defeat a claim based on the shorter or longer periods.

> NOTE: An agreement to move the position of a right of way on a servient tenement, which was made with the knowledge and acquiescence of the servient owner, and with the concurrence of all interested parties, will not break the prescription period so that time begins to run afresh: *Davis* v. *Whitby* (1973). *See also Pugh* v. *Savage* (1970).

28. Easements of light

Under s. 3, claim to such an easement may be based upon proof of actual enjoyment, without interruption, for *20 years*. The section applies to a 'dwelling house, workshop or other building'.

(a) Consent in writing will defeat the claim.

(b) User as of right is not necessary. Hence it is possible for a tenant to acquire such an easement against his landlord, or against another tenant of that same landlord: *Morgan* v. *Fear* (1907).

(c) Rights of Light Act 1959. Under this Act a light obstruction could be registered as a local land charge. For the purpose of preventing the access and use of light from being considered as having been enjoyed without interruption, any person who is an owner of land over which light passes to a dwelling house, workshop or other building, may apply to the local authority in whose area the dominant building is situated for registration of notice: s. 2. Where notice is registered, access of light to the dominant building is treated as obstructed to the same extent as if an opaque structure of the dimensions stated in the application had been erected on the date of registration of notice: s. 3(1). The notice has effect for one year, unless cancelled during that year. A dominant owner can bring an action for a declaration that he has acquired an easement of light. An easement of light for a special degree of light (e.g. for lighting and heating a greenhouse) may be acquired: *Allen* v. *Greenwood* (1979). *See Colls* v. *Home and Colonial Stores Ltd* (1904); *Carr-Saunders* v. *McNeil* (1986) — the dominant owner is entitled to such access of light 'as will leave his premises adequately lit for all ordinary purposes for which they may reasonably be expected to be used': *per* Millett J.

(d) If an interruption to light is of a permanent nature, the onus is on the plaintiff to prove that, at the time of commencement of the action, the interruption has lasted for less than one year. Where the interruption has lasted for more than one year, the onus is on him to prove that he neither submitted to nor acquiesced in it. 'Submission to' and 'acquiescence in' involve a state of mind evidenced by conduct: *Dance* v. *Triplow* (1992).

> NOTE: A fluctuating group of persons, e.g. the inhabitants of a parish, may acquire *quasi-easements* by custom, where that custom is certain and reasonable, has continued without interruption from time immemorial, and applies to a definite district. Such a group may claim profits *by custom* where the group has acted since time immemorial as a corporation and the court presumes a (lost) charter of incorporation from the Crown, and where claimants and local corporation have enjoyed the right since time immemorial and the court presumes a grant of the profit under a charitable trust to the corporation for itself and the claimants: *Goodman* v. *Mayor of Saltash* (1882). Note, however, *Beckett* v. *Lyons* (1967).

29. Creation of easements and rights over registered land

In general, easements and rights may be created over *registered land* (*see* Ch. 20) in similar fashion to unregistered land. The following points should be noted:

(a) In the case of a right created by *express grant*, there should be an entry upon the property register (*see* 20:**5**) of title to the dominant tenement and/or on the charges register (*see* 20:**5**) relating to the servient tenement. *See* LRA 1925, s. 70(2). A legal easement will constitute an overriding interest (*see* 20:**11**): *see* LRA 1925, s. 70(1)(a). Note LRR 1925, r. 258.

(**b**) Easements and profits concerning registered land may be created by *implied grant*: *see* LPA 1925, s. 62. Only if the grantee has been registered as proprietor may a legal right be created.

(**c**) Under LRR 1925, r. 250(1), 'easements, rights and privileges adversely affecting registered land may be acquired in equity by *prescription* in the same manner and to the same extent as if the land were not registered'. If such an easement were to take effect at law, it would constitute an overriding interest (*see* 20:**11**): LRA 1925, s. 70(1)(a). The Registrar may enter notice on the dominant tenement's property register or the servient tenement's charges register.

Modes in which easements and profits may be extinguished

30. General

Easements and profits may be extinguished: by statute; by unity of possession and ownership; by express or implied release; by alteration of the dominant tenement.

31. Statute

Under the Inclosure Acts land may be discharged from rights of common. The Commons Registration Act 1965 stated that common land and rights of common must be registered with the local authority, and such registration was deemed conclusive evidence of the rights registered. *See Corpus Christi College* v. *Gloucestershire CC* (1982). Rights of common cannot be exercised unless registered under the Act, or under the Land Registration Act 1925. (Note that a statutory restriction does not extinguish a prescriptive right, neither does a mere increase of user during the period of prescription: *Cargill* v. *Gotts* (1981).) *See also Duke of Bedford* v. *Dawson* (1875); HA 1988, Sch. 10, Part II; TCPA 1990, ss. 236, 237 (extinguishment of rights over land compulsorily acquired and power to override easements affected by use of land for planning purposes).

32. Unity of possession and ownership

An easement or profit will be extinguished where the dominant tenement and the servient tenement pass into possession and ownership of one and the same person, provided that the tenements are held in the same capacity. *See White* v. *Taylor* (1969).

33. Release
Release may be express or implied.

(a) *Express release.* A deed of release is necessary at common law in relation to a legal easement or profit, but in equity an informal release (e.g. agreement to release) may be upheld: *Waterlow* v. *Bacon* (1866).

(b) *Implied release.* Mere non-user does not necessarily indicate an implied release; it must be considered with other circumstances. There must be some *intention* to abandon the right: *Cook* v. *Mayor & Corp. of Bath* (1868) — door had been bricked over for more than 30 years, and this was held not to constitute an abandonment of a right of way; *Moore* v. *Rawson* (1824) — plaintiff demolished wall containing windows and rebuilt wall with no windows, and this was held, 17 years later, to have shown an intention to abandon a right to light; *Re Yately Common* (1977) — to establish abandonment of a right of common, it must be established that the owner of the right has ceased to use it *and* that he never intends to use it again; *Benn* v. *Hardinge* (1992) — non-user, even for so long as 175 years was not sufficient by itself to indicate an intention by the owner to abandon a right of way (for 'such a right was a valuable property whose abandonment should not be lightly inferred').

34. Alteration in the dominant tenement
Where the dominant tenement is altered so that enjoyment of a profit appurtenant is no longer possible, the profit is extinguished. Where the dominant tenement is altered so that enjoyment of an easement becomes unnecessary, the easement is extinguished: *National Guaranteed Manure Co.* v. *Donald* (1859) — canal was converted to a railway and, as a result, an easement of water for the canal was extinguished.

> NOTE: (1) Remedies for an infringement of profits and easements are action for injunction, damages or declaration; and abatement, where no more force than is reasonably necessary may be used and no injury results to the public or to a third party. (2) The Law Reform Committee Report on the Acquisition of Easements and Profits by Prescription (1966) recommended the abolition of the prescriptive acquisition of easements and *profits à prendre*. All the existing methods of acquisition of easements and profits should be abolished, and the Prescription Act

1832 should be repealed. But if prescription is retained for easements, the prescription period should be a period of *12 years* in gross, and there should be no disabilities. An easement acquired by prescription should be lost after continuous non-user for *12 years*.

Progress test 17

1. What is the essence of an 'easement'? Is a right over the land of another invariably an easement? **(2, 4)**

2. 'An easement must accommodate the dominant tenement.' Explain. **(7)**

3. 'The categories of easements are not closed.' Comment. **(11)**

4. What types of *profit à prendre* exist? **(14)**

5. Consider the express reservation of easements and profits over land sold. **(19)**

6. Comment on *Wong* v. *Beaumont Property Trust Ltd* (1965). **(20)**

7. What are the general principles of prescription? **(23)**

8. Outline the principles of the Prescription Act 1832 in relation to easements of light. **(28)**

9. Outline the principles concerning the creation of easements and rights over registered land. **(29)**

10. What is the effect on profits and easements of an alteration in the dominant tenement? **(34)**

18
The registration of land charges

Preliminaries

1. A caveat

The word 'registration' in the phrase 'registration of land charges' must *not* be confused with 'registration of title', which is the essence of the procedures involving 'registered land' (*see* Ch. 20). The registration of land charges refers to a scheme of registering charges in *unregistered land*. Where these interests occur in the context of registered title, they can be protected by entry on the Land Register (*see* 20:2) as 'minor interests' (*see* 20:14).

2. Land Charges Register

This must *not* be confused with the register kept by the Land Registrar relating to registration of title: *see* 4 below.

The Land Charges Acts

3. LCA 1925; LCA 1972

LCA 1972 is a consolidating Act which repeals, but re-enacts, most of LCA 1925, with amendments. (Section references in this chapter are to the 1972 Act, unless otherwise stated.)

The object of the Land Charges legislation is the provision of a centralised scheme whereby *certain incumbrances on unregistered land may be registered*. The result of the workings of the scheme is:

(a) intending purchasers of land are enabled to *discover* the existence of incumbrances on that land;

(b) owners of incumbrances have some *protection* against a purchaser of the legal estate without notice, since registration of a registrable incumbrance may be equivalent to notice;

(c) where a registrable incumbrance is not registered it may be *defeated*, i.e. rendered ineffective in relation to a third party.

4. The registers

Under LCA 1972, s. 1, *five registers* in which incumbrances are recorded are kept by the Registrar at the Land Charges Department of the Land Registry at Plymouth. These registers record:

(a) pending actions (*see* **5–7** below);
(b) annuities (*see* **8–10** below);
(c) writs and orders affecting land (*see* **11–13** below);
(d) deeds of arrangement affecting land (*see* **14–16** below);
(e) land charges (*see* **17–24** below).

Searches can be made by a prospective purchaser in person, or by telephone or post. Official certificates of search, recording searches made by registry staff, are available and, in favour of a purchaser or an intending purchaser, are conclusive: s. 10(4).

Register of pending actions

5. Pending actions

These include any action or proceeding pending in court relating to land or any interest in or charge on land: s. 17(1). *See Taylor* v. *Taylor* (1968). A wife's application in matrimonial proceedings for transfer of property is registrable: *Whittingham* v. *Whittingham* (1979). *See Selim* v. *Bickenhall Engineering* (1981); *Haslemere Estates* v. *Baker* (1982); *Regan Ltd* v. *Rogers* (1985).

6. What may be registered

See s. 5. Pending actions, including petitions in bankruptcy may be recorded in this register. On the determination of proceedings the court, if it thinks fit, may make an order vacating a registration under s. 5: s. 5(10). An action in which an easement over land is directly in issue is a pending land action for purposes of LCA 1972: *Greenhi Builders* v. *Allen* (1979).

7. Registration and non-registration

The following points are important:

(a) a pending land action will not bind a purchaser without express notice of it, unless it is for the time being registered under s. 5: s. 5(7) (*see Perez-Adamson* v. *Perez-Rivas* (1987));
(b) a petition in bankruptcy will not bind a purchaser of a legal estate in good faith, for money or money's worth, unless it is for the time being registered under s. 5: s. 5(8).

Register of annuities

8. Annuities

An annuity, under the terms of LCA 1972, means 'a rentcharge or an annuity for a life or lives or for any term of years or greater estate determinable on a life or on lives and created after 25 April 1855, and before 1 January 1926, but does not include an annuity created by a marriage settlement or will': s. 17(1). (*See* 16:**27–29** in relation to rentcharges.)

9. What may be registered

No further entries shall be made in the register of annuities, and the register shall be closed when all the entries in it have been vacated or the prescribed evidence of the satisfaction, cesser or discharge of all the annuities has been furnished: LCA 1972, Schedule 1(1),(3).

10. Registration and non-registration

'An annuity which before 1 January 1926, was capable of being registered in the register of annuities shall be void as against a creditor or a purchaser of any interest in the land charged with the annuity, unless the annuity is for the time being registered in the register of annuities or in the register of land charges': Schedule 1(4). The fact that an annuity is registered will not prevent its being overreached (*see* **26** below).

Register of writs and orders affecting land

11. Writs and orders

Under this heading are included primarily those writs and orders concerning land issued by the court in order to enforce judgments.

12. What may be registered

There may be registered in this register:

(a) writs or orders affecting land issued for the purpose of enforcing a judgment or recognisance;
(b) any order appointing a receiver or sequestrator of land;
(c) any bankruptcy order, whether or not the bankrupt's estate is known to include land: s. 6(1) as amended.

13. Registration and non-registration

Entries of writs and orders of this nature must be made in the name of the estate owner or other person whose land is affected by the writ or order registered: s. 6(2).

(a) In general, such writs and orders are void as against a purchaser of the land unless the writ or order is for the time being registered under this section: s. 6(4).

(b) The title of a trustee in bankruptcy is void as against the purchaser of a legal estate in good faith for money or money's worth unless the bankruptcy order is registered under this section: s. 6(5) as amended.

(c) Where a petition in bankruptcy has been registered under s. 5 (*see* **6** above), the title of the trustee in bankruptcy is void as against a purchaser of a legal estate in good faith for money or money's worth claiming under a conveyance made after the date of registration, unless at the date of the conveyance either the registration of the petition is in force, or a receiving order on the petition is registered under s. 6: s. 6(6).

Register of deeds of arrangement

14. Deeds of arrangement

These involve documents under which a debtor makes an arrangement in favour of his creditors: *see* Deeds of Arrangement Act 1914, s. 1. They include, e.g. an assignment of property to a trustee for creditors, an agreement under seal or otherwise for a composition.

15. What may be registered

A deed of arrangement affecting land may be registered, in the name of the debtor, on the application of a trustee of the deed or a creditor assenting to or taking the benefit of the deed: s. 7(1).

16. Registration and non-registration

A deed of arrangement is void as against a purchaser of any land comprised in it or affected by it unless it is for the time being registered under s. 7: s. 7(2).

> NOTE: Registrations under ss. 5, 6, 7 shall cease to have effect at the end of *five years* from the dates on which they were made, but they may be renewed from time to time, and where so renewed, have effect for *five years* from the date of renewal: s. 8.

Register of land charges

17. General

The register of land charges records certain types of charges on, or obligations affecting land. *Registration is in the name of the estate owner whose estate is intended to be affected*: s. 3(1). The words 'name of the estate owner' mean the name as disclosed by the conveyance: *Standard Property Investment* v. *British Plastics Fedn* (1987). *See Oak Co-operative BS* v. *Blackburn* (1968) — a purchaser who makes a search against the wrong name in the register is bound, nevertheless, by any interests registered therein against the correct name: *Diligent Finance Ltd* v. *Alleyne* (1972).

(a) The registration is not altered when the estate changes hands; the name of the original estate owner remains.
(b) A search should include the names of all past estate owners.

There are *six classes of charge*, which are set out at **18–23** below.

18. Class A charges

A charge of this type is a rent or annuity or principal money payable by instalments or otherwise, with or without interest, which has not been created by deed, but is a charge upon land created *pursuant to the application* of some person under the provisions of an Act of Parliament. The object of a charge of this nature is usually the securing of money spent on land in accordance with statutes. *See*, e.g. Agricultural Holdings Act 1986, ss. 86, 87 (compensation rights of landlord).

19. Class B charges

These are statutory land charges *not* created pursuant to the application of some person, and *not* local land charges: s. 2(3). Such charges arise directly out of statute and automatically, in contrast to Class A charges which require statutory application. *See*, e.g. Legal Aid Act 1974, s. 9(6) (unpaid contribution to legal aid fund).

20. Class C charges

Four types of charge are included.

(a) *Puisne mortgages.* These are *legal* mortgages not protected by a deposit of documents relating to the legal estate affected: s. 2(4)(i). (Note that this is a *legal interest*, unlike most other land charges.)
(b) *Limited owner's charges.* These are equitable charges acquired by a tenant for life or statutory owner, under statutes such as the

Inheritance Tax Act 1984 and the Finance Act 1986, by reason of the discharge by him of any liabilities and to which special priority is given under statute: s. 2(4)(ii).

(c) *General equitable charges.* These are charges which:

    (*i*) are not secured by deposit of documents relating to the legal estate affected;

    (*ii*) do not arise or affect an interest arising under a trust for sale or a settlement;

    (*iii*) are not given by way of indemnity against rents equitably apportioned or charged exclusively on land in exoneration of other land and against the breach or non-observance of covenants and conditions;

    (*iv*) are not included in any other class of land charge: s. 2(4)(iii).

(d) *Estate contracts.* These are contracts by estate owners or persons entitled at the date of contract to have a legal estate conveyed to them to convey or create a legal estate, including contracts conferring valid options to purchase: s. 2(4)(iv). (For the difference between rights of *option* and rights of *pre-emption, see Pritchard* v. *Briggs* (1980). 'In the case of an option, the evolution of the relationship of vendor and purchaser may depend on the fulfilment of certain specified conditions and will depend on the volition of the option holder. In the case of a right of pre-emption, the evolution of the relationship of vendor and purchaser depends on the grantor, of his own volition, choosing to fulfil certain specified conditions and thus converting the pre-emption into an option': *per* Templeman LJ.) *See Georgiades* v. *Edward Wolfe & Co.* (1965); *Kitney* v. *MEPC* (1977); *Phillips* v. *Mobil Oil Ltd* (1989). (Contracts of sale, and agreements for a lease fall under this heading.)

(*See also* the Local Land Charges Act 1975, s. 17(1)(b), which excludes *local* land charges (*see* **28** below) from the scope of the 1972 provisions for registration.)

21. Class D charges

Three types of charge are included under s. 2(5):

(a) inland revenue charges (e.g. charges on land acquired by the Inland Revenue for any unpaid inheritance taxes) (s. 2(5)(i));

(b) restrictive covenants created after 1925 and *not* between lessor and lessee (s. 2(5)(ii));

(c) equitable easements, rights or privileges over or affecting land, created *after* 1925 (s. 2(5)(iii)). *See Shiloh Spinners Ltd* v. *Harding* (1973). (Note that easements acquired by estoppel are *not registrable*:

Ives Ltd v. *High* (1967).) The Report of the Committee on Land Charges has suggested the abolition of Class D(iii).

22. Class E charges

These are annuities created before 1 January 1926 and not registered in the register of annuities: s. 2(6).

23. Class F charges

These involve spousal rights of occupation which affect land by virtue of the Matrimonial Homes Acts 1967 and 1983. Under the 1983 Act, s. 1, where one spouse is entitled to occupy a dwelling house by virtue of a beneficial estate, interest, contract, or any enactment giving him/her a *right to remain in occupation,* and the other spouse is not so entitled, the spouse not so entitled has *certain rights of occupation,* e.g. a right not to be evicted save by leave of the court. *See,* e.g. *Hall* v. *King* (1987). *Such a right constitutes a charge on the estate*: 1983 Act, s. 2(1). It applies only to married couples, and the right ends on the death of the entitled spouse, or on the termination of the marriage: 1983 Act, s. 5. *The right is registrable* under LCA 1972, s. 2(7). It is valid against the other spouse, *whether registered or not. See* Insolvency Act 1986, s. 337(2) — right of occupation binds trustee in bankruptcy. For misuse, and setting aside, of a class F charge, *see Barnett* v. *Hassett* (1982). *See Richards* v. *Richards* (1984); *Kaur* v. *Gill* (1988) — wife's right defeated, when, unusually, the circumstances of the purchaser (a blind man who had purchased the house because of its convenience, but aware of the wife's rights) were taken into account.

> NOTE: For mortgages and other charges registered under the Companies Act 1985, ss. 395, 396, but not under LCA 1972, *see,* e.g. *Specialised Plant Services* v. *Braithwaite* (1987).

24. Effect of land charges and protection of purchasers

The following points apply.

(a) A land charge of Class A (other than a land improvement charge) or of Class B takes effect, when registered, as if it has been created by a deed of charge by way of legal mortgage, but without prejudice to the priority of the charge: s. 4(1).

(b) A land charge of Class A, created after 31 December 1888, shall be void as against a purchaser of the land charged with it or of any interest in such land, unless the charge is registered before completion of the purchase: s. 4(2).

(c) After the end of one year from the first conveyance occurring on or after 1 January 1889, of a land charge of Class A created before that date, the person entitled to the charge shall not be able to recover the charge or any part of it as against a purchaser of the land charged with it, or of any interest in the land, unless the charge is registered before completion of the purchase: s. 4(3).

(d) Land charges of Class B or C (other than estate contracts) created or arising on or after 1 January 1926, are void as against a purchaser of land charged with them, or of any interest in such land, unless they are registered before completion of purchase: s. 4(5).

(e) Estate contracts and land charges of Class D created or entered into on or after 1 January 1926, are void as against a purchaser for money or money's worth of a legal estate in the land charged with it, unless registered before completion of purchase: s. 4(6).

(f) After the end of one year from the first conveyance occurring on or after 1 January 1926, of a land charge of Class B or C created before that date, the person entitled to the charge shall not be able to enforce or recover the charge or any part of it as against a purchaser of the land charged with it, or of any interest in the land, unless the charge is registered before completion of the purchase: s. 4(7).

(g) Land charges of Class F are void as against a purchaser of the land charged, or of any interest in such land, unless registered before completion of the purchase: s. 4(8). (The term 'purchaser' means here a purchaser for value of a legal or equitable interest in the land.)

Priority notices, overreaching powers and general effect of registration

25. Date of effective registration and priority notice

Persons intending to make application for the registration of a charge, instrument or other matter in pursuance of the 1972 Act, or any rule made under it, may give a priority notice *before* the registration is to take effect, s. 11.

26. Overreaching

See 2:**19.** The registration of any charge, annuity or other interest under the Act shall not prevent its being overreached under any other Act, except as otherwise provided by that other Act: s. 13(1). The registration as a land charge of a puisne mortgage or charge does not operate to prevent its being overreached in favour of a prior mortgagee or a person deriving title under him where, because of sale or foreclosure, or otherwise, the right of the puisne mortgagee or subsequent chargee to redeem (*see* Ch. 14) is barred: s. 13(2). *See* Law Commission Working Paper No.106 (1988), '*Overreaching*'.

27. General effect of registration under LCA

'The registration of any instrument or matter under the provisions of the Land Charges Act ... in any register kept at the land registry or elsewhere, *shall be deemed to constitute actual notice* of such instrument or matter, and of the fact of such registration, to all persons and for all purposes connected with the land affected, as from the date of registration or other prescribed date and so long as the registration continues in force': LPA 1925, s. 198(1).

When the period of root of title was reduced to 15 years in 1969 it was realised that it would be impossible for purchasers to check *all* the land charges affecting the land they were buying because the charges are recorded against the name of the person(s) concerned, not against the property. By LPA 1969, s. 24, therefore, it is provided that *as against a purchaser* the provisions of LPA 1925, s. 198, will *not* apply, and the question of whether he knows of a land charge is determined solely on the basis of his *actual* knowledge. This special rule does not, however, apply to cases concerning *registered land*. A person who has lost his right to enforce a land charge as a result of the terms of LPA 1969, s. 24, can in some cases be compensated out of state funds under a scheme set out in LPA 1969, s. 25.

Local land charges

28. The local land charges register

Under the Local Land Charges Act 1975, s. 3, local authorities (including district councils, the City of London Corporation and London borough councils) must maintain a local land charges register (which may be computerised: Local Government (Misc. Provs.) Act 1982, s. 34). These charges are registered *against the land* and not against the estate owner's name (as in the case of land charges). Personal searches may be made (1975 Act, s. 8); official searches (1975 Act, s. 9) are conducted by the staff of the local authority concerned.

29. Divisions of the register

The register comprises twelve sections: general financial

charges; specific financial charges; planning charges; miscellaneous charges and prohibitions; charges for improvement of fenland ways; land compensation charges; new town charges; civil aviation charges; open-cast coal mining charges; listed buildings charges; light obstruction notices; drainage scheme charges. Note that, with the exception of light obstruction notices (enforced by private persons) and civil aviation and open-cast mining charges (enforced by statutory organisations), the charges are enforceable by local authorities. (Note, also, that under the Environmental Protection Act 1990, s. 143, local authorities at district level must maintain registers of land subject to contamination.)

30. Effect of registration of local land charges

It should be noted that these charges affect unregistered and registered land. *Failure to register will not affect enforceability*: s. 10. In effect, therefore, these charges 'bind the whole world' whether registered or not.

(a) If a personal search has been conducted, compensation may be paid for loss resulting from the local authority's failure to register the charge, or failure to insert it in the correct division of the register: 1975 Act, s. 10.

(b) Compensation may be claimed also where the local authority staff have erroneously given a certificate stating that there is no local land charge affecting the land, although a charge has been properly recorded.

(c) The right to compensation has application only if the search has been conducted *prior* to the exchange of contracts for the sale of land.

The problem of land charges registration and 'good faith'

31. *Midland Bank Trust Co. Ltd* v. *Green* (1981)

The question of 'dealing in good faith' emerged in this case, concerning failure to register a Class C(iv) charge. The facts were as follows. W owned land in fee simple and granted his son, G, an option to buy the land at a specified price of some £22,500. The son, G, failed to register the option as an estate contract under LCA 1972 (*see* **20** above). Some six years later W attempted to revoke the option. He discovered G's failure to register and 'quietly and swiftly' conveyed the land (which had doubled in price) to his wife, E, for a price of £500. G attempted to exercise his option. E refused to sell. Later, G commenced proceedings against W and E's executors (E having died). G later died and his executors (the bank) continued the action. (By this time the value of the land had risen to £400,000.) *At first instance,* the judge ruled that the unregistered option was *not binding* on E's estate. The judge stated that he had reached his decision 'with regret', but he could not allow his 'subjective moral judgment to stand in the way of the clear meaning of the statutory provisions'.

32. Court of Appeal

The lower court's ruling was *reversed* by the Court of Appeal. Lord Denning held that E had *not* given 'money or money's worth'; her payment was 'grotesquely small'. What was required was payment of a fair and reasonable value in money or money's worth, not an undervalue. Fraud unravels everything and 'no court in the land would allow unwary innocents to be deprived of their rightful dues'. W and E had 'hatched a plot' to deprive G of his unregistered option.

33. House of Lords

The House *reinstated* the lower court's ruling. Lord Wilberforce stated firmly that the omission of any requirement of good faith from the LCA was deliberate. The courts should not have to enquire into the purchaser's motives and state of mind, for this would be to re-introduce the concept of notice which the 1925 legislation had sought to avoid. 'The case is plain: the Act is clear and definite. Intended as it was to provide a simple and understandable system for the protection of title to land, it should not be read down or glossed: to do so would destroy the usefulness of the Act.'

34. Comment

Criticism was directed, in particular, to Lord Wilberforce's suggestion that it was not fraud to take advantage of legal rights. E was merely taking advantage of a situation created by the law, and the addition of a profit motive could not create an absence of good faith. Critics retort that this pragmatic approach seems to override claims of fairness. *See also* **1:19**. (It is of interest to note that in *Midland Bank* v. *Hett, Stubbs and Kemp* (1978), it was held that a solicitor who fails to register an estate contract may continue to be under a duty to do so until such time as a third party's transactions render registration ineffectual; and in *Midland Bank* v. *Green (No. 3)* (1982), it was held that a husband and wife can be liable for the tort of conspiracy.)

Progress test 18

1. Outline the general purpose of the registers kept in accordance with the Land Charges Act 1972.   **(3, 4)**

2. What may be registered as Class C land charges?   **(20)**

3. Outline the nature of the Class F land charge.   **(23)**

4. Comment on the problem of overreaching in relation to land charges.   **(26)**

5. What is the effect of a failure to register local land charges? **(30)**

6. Explain the decision of the House of Lords in *Midland Bank Trust Co. Ltd* v. *Green* (1981).   **(31, 33)**

7. Account for the general criticism of the decision in *Midland Bank Trust Co. Ltd* v. *Green* (1981). Do you consider the criticism to be justified?   **(34)**

Part six

Transfer of land, limitation of actions, and adverse possession

19
The transfer by sale of unregistered land

Preliminaries

1. Two systems of land transfer
Choice of one of the two systems of land transfer will depend on whether title to the land is or is not registered.

(a) *Registered land* is covered by the LRA 1925–88 and the LRR 1925. The system is outlined in Ch. 20.

(b) *Unregistered land* is covered by the old rules derived from common law and equity, amended and supplemented by a number of statutes such as LPA 1925 and LCA 1972. Although *all land* in England and Wales is now covered by compulsory registration (*see* 20:**3**), that system requires registration only upon *sale* (*see* 20:**7**), so that unregistered titles will continue to exist for years to come.

2. Conveyancing
'Conveyancing' is the technical term used to describe the principles and formal procedures involved in the creation and transfer of interests and estates in or over land, involving the use of a document designed for that purpose. Note LPA 1925, s. 205(1)(ii), under which 'conveyance' includes 'a mortgage, charge, lease, assent, vesting declaration, vesting instrument, disclaimer, release and every other assurance of property or of an interest therein by any instrument except a will'. (The relevant law and technical details may be found in *Conveyancing Law* by P. H. Kenny and C. M. Bevan (*M&E Handbook Series*).)

3. Contracts for the sale of land
The relevant law has been modified, following LP (Misc. Provs.) A 1989, s. 2.

(a) *Pre-September 1989.* The situation was covered by LPA 1925, s. 40(1): 'No action may be brought upon any contract for the sale or other disposition of land or any interest in land, unless the agreement upon which such action is brought, or some memorandum or note thereof, is in writing, and signed by the party to be charged or by some person thereunto by him lawfully authorised.' An oral contract was unenforceable in the courts. Part performance was a possible alternative to a written memorandum.

(b) *Post-September 1989*. The situation is now governed by LP (Misc. Provs.) A 1989, s. 2, which is set out at 3:**15**. Essentially a contract for the sale of an interest in land *must be made in writing*, and the relevant document must contain *all the terms* agreed on by the parties.

4.   Types of contract
Three types of contract relating to the sale of unregistered land should be noted.

(a) *Formal contract*. This type of contract involves a specific reference to National Conditions of Sale and Law Society's Conditions of Sale (1992 revision), for example.

(b) *Contract made by correspondence*. 'The Lord Chancellor may from time to time prescribe and publish forms of contracts and conditions of sale of land, and the forms so prescribed shall, subject to any modification, or any stipulation or intention to the contrary, expressed in the correspondence, apply to contracts by correspondence, and may, but only by express reference thereto, be made to apply to any other cases for which the forms are made available': LPA 1925, s. 46. *See Holland* v. *Tolley* (1952) (exchange of telegrams).

　(*i*) Note that the phrase 'contracts by correspondence' is not defined in the 1925 Act. In general it has been taken to imply a contract the terms of which are to be found in letters passing between P and V (or their agents), whether sent through the post or not.

　(*ii*) *See Stearn* v. *Twitchell* (1985) — the Court of Appeal held that a 'contract by correspondence' does *not* include a contract arising out of the acceptance by letter of an oral offer to buy or sell land; a single letter does *not* constitute 'correspondence'.

(c) *Open contract*. This is a contract in which some terms may be unspecified, but are *implied* by general law. Among the rights and obligations under such a contract are: V must make good title; he must show title for 15 years; he must deliver an abstract and produce deeds; recitals (*see* **23(b)** below) are deemed correct; V has the right to retain title deeds; V must get in any outstanding estate and prove the identity of the property.

NOTE: *See* Law Commission Working Paper (1985) No. 92, '*Transfer of Land — Formalities for Contracts*'; Working Paper (1988) No. 107, '*Implied Covenants for Title*', which concludes that sales of land should be treated in the same way as sales of goods and that an unqualified term should be implied automatically into a contract for the sale of freehold land, guaranteeing that V has power to sell, that the land is free from undisclosed incumbrances, that P will have quiet enjoyment and that V will co-operate if title difficulties arise.

5. Remedies

Where a party to the contract for sale fails to carry out his obligations under that contract, the following remedies are available: damages; specific performance; rescission (where *restitutio in integrum* is possible); rectification; injunction (to restrain a threatened breach of the contract); declaration.

Disabilities in relation to the transfer of interests in land

6. Minors

A minor (or 'infant') is now a person under the age of 18: Family Law Reform Act 1969, s. 1. By that Act, s. 9, a person attains a specified age at the commencement of the relevant anniversary of his birth, subject to a contrary provision in any instrument or statute. The general rules are as follows.

(a) 'A *legal estate* is not capable of subsisting or of being created in an undivided share in land or of being held by an infant': LPA 1925, s. 1(6).

(b) A minor may hold an *equitable interest* in land.

(c) 'The appointment of an infant to be a *trustee* in relation to any settlement or trust shall be void': LPA 1925, s. 20.

(d) A minor may not be a *legal mortgagee* after 1925.

(e) There is a presumption that parties to any conveyance shall, until the contrary is proved, be presumed to be of full age: LPA 1925, s. 15.

7. General provisions

The following points should be noted.

(a) *Conveyance of a legal estate to a minor*. A conveyance to a minor of a legal estate in land, or to two or more persons jointly, both or all of whom are minors, for his or their benefit, operates as an agreement for valuable consideration to execute a *settlement* in favour of the minor(s). The land must be held in trust for the minor(s) in the meantime: LPA 1925, s. 19; SLA 1925, s. 27. A purported conveyance of a legal estate to a minor jointly with one or more persons of full age will operate so as to vest the legal estate in the person(s) of full age on the statutory trusts: LPA 1925, s. 19(2). *See also* Minors' Contracts Act 1987, s. 3.

(b) *Conveyance of an equitable interest to a minor.* Such a conveyance is voidable at the option of the minor during his minority or during a reasonable period after he has attained his majority: *Whittingham* v. *Murdy* (1889). *See also Davies* v. *Benyon-Harris* (1931) — minor in possession may be sued successfully for non-payment of rent.

(c) *Conveyance by a minor.* A purported disposition of an interest by a minor is voidable at his option on attaining his majority or within a reasonable time after.

    (*i*) Where a minor dies, a disposition made by him can be avoided by his personal representatives within a reasonable time.

    (*ii*) A minor cannot generally make a valid will of real or personal property, unless on actual military service: *see* Wills Act 1837, s. 11.

    (*iii*) A settlement made by a minor in contemplation of marriage is voidable. It will bind him unless repudiated within a reasonable time after he has attained his majority.

(d) *Conveyance of a legal mortgage to a minor.* A purported grant or transfer of a legal mortgage of land to a minor operates only as an agreement for valuable consideration to execute a proper conveyance when the minor attains full age. Until then the beneficial interest in the mortgage debt is to be held *in trust* for those persons for whose benefit the conveyance was intended to be made: LPA 1925, s. 19(6).

(e) *Conveyance to a minor as trustee.* Where the conveyance is to the minor alone it will operate as a declaration of trust. Where the conveyance is to the minor and to a person of full age it will operate as if the minor had not been named therein, but without prejudice to the minor's beneficial interest: LPA 1925, s. 19.

(f) *Conveyance to a minor by will.* The legal estate will first vest in the personal representatives. They may retain the land until the minor attains his majority, *or* they may create a settlement for the benefit of the infant.

NOTE: Under AEA 1925, s. 51, where a minor is absolutely entitled under a settlement and where he dies unmarried, he is deemed to have had an *entailed interest* (*see* Ch. 13) in the property. As a result of this provision *the land will revert to the grantor* (in the case of a settlement made by deed), *or to the residuary devisee* (in the case of a settlement made by will).

8. Persons suffering from a mental disorder

Under the Mental Health Act 1983 a receiver may be appointed by the court to administer the affairs of a person who becomes incapable of administering his property as the result of a mental disorder. Such a person is known under the Act as a *patient*. While the receivership is in force a patient may not make a disposition *inter vivos* of his property. But a will made by him during a lucid interval may be valid. Under the Mental Health Act 1983, ss. 96(1)(e), 97, the court is empowered to make a will for a patient. *See Re D.* (1982). Where no receiver has been appointed the position is as follows:

(a) where the disposition is not made for valuable consideration it is *void*;
(b) where the disposition is made for valuable consideration and the other party has notice of the patient's disability, it is *voidable* at the option of the patient;
(c) where the disposition is made for valuable consideration and the other person does not have notice of the patient's disability, it is *valid*.

9. Corporations

The general rule was that unless a corporation was authorised by statute or by Crown licence in mortmain it could not hold land. Where land was acquired by a corporation which did not have authority or licence it was liable to be forfeited to the Crown: Mortmain and Charitable Uses Act 1888, s. 1. The law of mortmain was repealed under the Charities Act 1960, s. 38.

10. Charities

A 'charity' comprises trusts for the relief of poverty, for the advancement of education and religion, and for other purposes beneficial to the community: *Commissioners of Income Tax* v. *Pemsel* (1891). Under the Mortmain and Charitable Uses Act 1888, assurances *inter vivos* to a charity had to be made at least 12 months before the grantor's death. This, and other restrictions, disappeared under the Charities Act 1960, ss. 38, 48.

(a) Under the Charities Act 1992, amending the Charities Act 1960, no land held by or in trust for a charity shall be sold, leased or otherwise disposed of without an order of the court or the Commissioners: s. 32(1).

(b) The above subsection does *not* apply to a disposition of such land if the disposition is made to a person who is *not* a connected person (defined in Sch. 2 as including, e.g. a charity trustee, a person who is the donor of any land to the charity, an officer, agent or employee of the charity, etc.): s. 32(2). Other requirements concerning s. 32(2) are set out in s. 32(3), (5).

Sequence of events leading to completion

11. Prior to signature of contract

Prior to signature of the contract, P should make preliminary searches in the Local Land Charges Register and at the Land Registry for information relating to the property to be purchased. He should also make enquiries to the appropriate local authority concerning matters such as highways abutting on the property and charges relating to their upkeep. Preliminary enquiries from P to V should also be made. Note that an action in negligence may result from a wrong answer to this type of enquiry. *See Strover* v. *Harrington* (1988) — the knowledge of P's solicitor that a representation was false was imputed to P.

12. Exchange of contracts

Until this stage is reached, V or P can withdraw from negotiations. When this stage is reached, the beneficial interest in the property is considered to have passed to P; the legal estate remains in V, so that V is trustee for P. The property is now generally at P's risk.

> NOTE: In *Domb* v. *Isoz* (1980) the Court of Appeal held that, subject to contrary instructions, a solicitor has an implied authority to exchange contracts in any manner recognised as valid, including exchange by telephone.

13. Deposits

There is a customary rule requiring P to pay a deposit of 10 per cent of the purchase price on exchange of contracts. *See*, e.g. *Damon* v. *Hapag-Lloyd* (1983); *McGrath* v. *Shah* (1987) — forfeiture of deposit.

(a) 'The deposit serves two purposes — if the purchase is carried out it goes against the purchase money — but its primary purpose is this, a guarantee that the purchaser means business': *per* Lord Macnaghten in *Soper* v. *Arnold* (1889).

(b) Under LPA 1925, s. 49(2), the court has discretion to order the repayment of the deposit to P. In *Universal Corporation* v. *Five Ways Properties* (1979), the Court of Appeal held that s. 49(2) gave an unqualified discretion to order repayment of a deposit where the justice of the case so required, and with regard to all the relevant considerations. *See also Dimsdale Development* v. *De Haan* (1984).

(c) Note that under the Estate Agents Act 1979, s. 13, clients' money received by an estate agent is to be held on trust by him for the person who is entitled to call for it to be paid over to him or to be paid on his direction or to have it otherwise credited to him.

14. Delivery of abstract

V next supplies P with a perfect 'abstract of title', commencing with the deed forming 'root of title' and tracing all those events constituting the connecting links in the chain of ownership leading to and culminating in V. (In *MEPC* v. *Christian-Edwards* (1979) the House of Lords held that the court should declare a good title shown where, in its opinion, the circumstances and facts of the case are so compelling as to indicate beyond reasonable doubt that there is no risk of any successful assertion of an incumbrance.)

(a) V must generally show title for 15 years: LPA 1969, s. 23.

(b) V must, at his own expense, produce those documents showing and constituting the root of title. (For the case of lost title deeds, *see Re Stuart's Contract* (1896).)

    (*i*) But 'where title is shown to a legal estate in land, it shall be deemed not necessary or proper to include in the abstract of title an instrument relating only to interests or powers which will be overreached by the conveyance of the estate to which title is being shown; but nothing in this Part of the Act affects the liability of any person to disclose an equitable interest or power which will not be so overreached, or to furnish an abstract of any instrument creating or affecting the same': LPA 1925, s. 10(1).

    (*ii*) 'Under a contract to grant or assign a term of years, whether derived or to be derived out of freehold or leasehold land, the intended lessee or assign shall not be entitled to call for the title to the freehold': LPA 1925, s. 44(2).

(c) In *Faruqi* v. *English Real Estates* (1979) it was held that, in equity,

V is obliged to make full and frank disclosure of any known defects in title in language which would indicate those defects to P. *See Nottingham Brick Co.* v. *Butler* (1886): 'In honesty and law alike, V was bound to give P full and fair information what it was that he had for sale and, having failed to do so, he cannot insist upon the bargain procured by the suppression of material facts': *per* Wills J. *See also Rignall Developments* v. *Halil* (1987).

> NOTE: Under LPA 1925, s. 183, it is a criminal offence to conceal any instrument or incumbrance material to the title or to falsify a material pedigree, with intent to defraud.

15. Perusal of abstract

P now has the duty of perusing carefully and checking the matter comprising the abstract of title. Under LPA 1925, s. 45(6), statements in deeds *20 years old* at the date of contract, shall, unless proved inaccurate, be taken as sufficient evidence of the truth of those statements.

16. Requisitions on title

P's solicitor may raise 'written requisitions on title', i.e. enquiries directed to V's solicitor relating to matters concerning any defect in title appearing on the abstract or disclosed in any other way, e.g. by examination of deeds or inspection of the property. *See* LPA 1925, s. 45(1)(b) (preventing P from raising requisitions concerning pre-root of title documents); *Re Ford* (1879) — improper requisitions. Rescission of contract may be allowed where P insists on a requisition with which V will not or cannot comply: *see* Law Society Condition 16. *See Selkirk* v. *Romar Investments* (1963).

17. Answers to requisitions

V's solicitor will reply precisely to the requisitions raised by P's solicitor, within a reasonable time.

18. Drafting of the conveyance

P's solicitor will draft a conveyance (*see* example on p. 278) and send it to V's solicitor for approval. V's solicitor will make any necessary amendments and return the document to P's solicitor. Eventually, a fair copy will be prepared and sent to V for signature.

19. Completion

Completion is generally effected at the offices of V's solicitors. V's solicitor will deliver the conveyance, duly executed, to P. The deed of conveyance may be read over and explained to the parties. A completion statement is prepared by V's solicitor. P's solicitor will hand over the balance of the purchase money and any outgoings referred to in the completion statement. He will take over any relevant deeds in the possession of V, any insurance policies and, where necessary, keys of the property to be handed to P. It should be noted that in the absence of any condition to the contrary, it is V's duty to deliver vacant possession on completion: *Cook* v. *Taylor* (1942). *See Raineri* v. *Miles* (1980) (failure by party to complete contract on or before completion date stipulated, amounts to breach of contract in cases in which time was not and has not become, of the essence of the contract; *Carne* v. *Debono* (1988) (there is no legal requirement that V should furnish a completion statement in advance of the completion date; it is merely a matter of practice); *Newberry* v. *Turngiant* (1991); *Graham* v. *Pitkin* (1992) (unreasonable delay in completing contract). *See* Law Society's *General Conditions of Sale* (1980 edn.), condition 22, clause (2). (*See* the Law Commission Working Paper No. 109 (1988): '*Transfer of Land: Passing of risk from vendor to purchaser*', in which the Commission suggests a statutory provision to provide that, subject to any contrary agreement, the risk should pass on completion, and, further, there should be a statutorily implied open contract term that the vendor should convey the property in the physical condition that it was at the date of the contract.) *See Gran Gelato* v. *Richcliff* (1992) (a vendor's solicitor owes no duty of care to the purchaser in an ordinary conveyancing transaction).

NOTE: (1) Under the Administration of Justice Act 1985, ss. 11, 12, conveyancing services may now be provided by 'licensed conveyancers' whose standards shall be controlled by the Council for Licensed Conveyancers. *See also* Courts and Legal Services Act 1990, s. 119(1). (2) For measure of damages at common law for breach of contract of sale (difference between contract price and market value at date of judgment), *see Suleman* v. *Shahsavari* (1988) (however, this is not an absolute rule).

Essentials of deed of conveyance

20. General
Under LPA 1925, s. 52(1): 'All conveyances of land or of any interest therein are void for the purpose of conveying or creating a legal estate unless made by deed.' Under s. 52(2), however, this has no application to:

Party	{	THIS CONVEYANCE is made the day of BETWEEN VINCENT VIVIAN VERRILL of No. 3 Green Street Berkhamsted in the County of Hertfordshire, Engineer (hereinafter called "the vendor") of the one part, AND PAUL PATRICK PERRY of
Party	{	No. 12 Black Street Staplehurst in the County of Kent, Dentist (hereinafter called "the purchaser") of the other part.
Recitals	{	WHEREAS the vendor is seised of those hereditaments intended to be conveyed for an estate in fee simple absolute in possession free from all incumbrances and has agreed with the purchaser to sell him the said property for the sum of four hundred thousand pounds (£400,000).
Testatum	{	NOW THIS CONVEYANCE WITNESSETH that in consideration of the sum of £400,000 paid to the vendor by the purchaser (the receipt whereof the vendor hereby acknowledges) the vendor as Beneficial Owner
Operative Words	{	hereby conveys to the purchaser
Parcels	{	ALL that messuage or dwelling house with yard and gardens thereto belonging known as No. 3 Green Street Berkhamsted in the County of Hertfordshire
Habendum	{	TO HOLD the same unto the purchaser in fee simple.
Testimonium	{	IN WITNESS of which the vendor has executed this deed in the presence of the attesting witness the day and year first before written.
Attestation Clause	{	Signed and delivered as a deed by the said VINCENT VIVIAN VERRILL in the presence of: *Vincent Vivian Verill*

Wilfred Warlock

WILFRED WARLOCK
13 THE COVENS
WITCHFORD MAGNA
BROOMSHIRE
(PHARMACIST.)

Simplified form of conveyance

(a) assents by a personal representative;

(b) disclaimers;

(c) surrenders by operation of law;

(d) leases or tenancies not required by law to be made in writing;

(e) receipts not required by law to be under seal;

(f) vesting orders of the court;

(g) conveyances taking effect by operation of law.

> NOTE: 'A disposition of an equitable interest or trust subsisting at the time of the disposition must be in writing signed by the person disposing of the same, or by his agent thereunto lawfully authorised in writing or by will': LPA 1925, s. 53(1)(c).

21. Signature, etc.
See LP (Misc. Provs.) A 1989, s. 1, at 4:18.

22. Example of deed of conveyance
A much-simplified example is given on p.278 with an indication of its various types of clause.

23. Clauses in the conveyance
The following should be noted.

(a) *Parties*. This clause records all those persons who are essential to the transaction recorded in the deed — in the example, two in number. Every person whose concurrence is needed in order to vest in P the interest contracted to be sold has to be made a party. (The date in the heading is inserted on completion.)

(b) *Recitals*. The words in this clause introduce the conveyance and indicate the history of the property to be conveyed and the purpose of the deed. 'Narrative recitals' record the history; 'introductory recitals' record purpose. *See Re Duce's Contract* (1937); LPA 1925, s. 45(6).

(c) *Testatum*. This is the operative part of the deed. The term 'beneficial owner' when used in a deed of conveyance raises, in the case of freehold land, certain covenants for sale:

    (*i*) covenant that V has full power to convey the interest;

    (*ii*) covenant that P will have quiet enjoyment of the property to be conveyed;

    (*iii*) covenant that the property is free from all estates and incumbrances other than those to which it has been made subject in the deed;

    (*iv*) covenant that V will do all that is necessary to perfect the conveyance.

(d) *Operative words.* These words ('... hereby conveys ...') constitute the actual conveyance of the property to P.

(e) *Parcels.* The parcels clause describes the property and may be read in conjunction with any map attached to the deed. The description must be precise and clear. *See Toplis* v. *Green* (1992), in which the Court of Appeal held that, in construing a plan attached to the deed, the court must view it as a reasonable observer with all the facts the parties had before them. Under LPA 1925, s. 62(2), a conveyance of land is deemed to include, and operates to convey, with the land, all houses or other buildings, outhouses, fixtures, drains, ways, passages, easements, rights, etc., 'appertaining or reputed to appertain to the land, houses or other buildings conveyed'. *See Scarfe* v. *Adams* (1981); *MRA Engineering* v. *Trimster Co.* (1988).

(f) *Habendum.* This clause defines the precise nature of the interest to be taken by P. (Note that in the case of a lease, a clause (the *reddendum*) would be inserted next, specifying the rent and rent days.) *See May* v. *Platt* (1900); LPA 1925, s. 60.

(g) *Testimonium.* This clause indicates the signing of the deed.

(h) *Attestation clause. See* LP (Misc. Provs.) A 1989, s. 1(3)(a), at **4:18.**

Progress test 19

1. Outline the effects of a purported conveyance to a minor of **(a)** a legal estate, and **(b)** an equitable interest.   **(7)**

2. What is meant by 'delivery of an abstract'?   **(14)**

3. Explain 'requisitions on title'.   **(16)**

4. What is the significance in a conveyance of unregistered land of the 'recitals clause' and the 'habendum clause'?   **(23)**

20

The transfer of registered land

Preliminaries

1. Essence of this type of transfer

'Registered land' is land the title to which is entered, in accordance with statutory formalities, on the register of *title to land*. Transfer of the registered estate is complete only when the name of the transferee who has become the proprietor of the transferred estate has been entered formally on the register.

2. The Register

The Land Register is maintained centrally and at district land registries. It must *not* be confused with the registers kept by the Land Charges Department of the Land Registry which record incumbrances on unregistered land ('land charges'). It contained 13.9 million titles in 1992.

Nature of registration of title

3. Background

A system of registration of title, on an optional basis, was created under the Land Registry Act 1862. Under the Land Transfer Act 1897, registration of title was made compulsory for land in the City of London.

(a) The existing system is based upon the Land Registration Acts 1925–88 and the Land Registration Rules.

(b) The essence of compulsory registration is that after an area is declared to be an area of compulsory registration, any dealings in land within that area must be effected under this system of conveyancing.

(c) Registration of title now covers all England and Wales: *see* SI 1989/1347.

4.　Purpose of registration of title

The purpose of registration is *the simplification of the transfer of land and the better protection of purchasers and the owners of equitable interests.* Title is entered in an official register, and any transfer of the title results in such change being recorded in the register (which is in computerised form at district land registries).

(a) Accuracy of title is virtually guaranteed by the State.

(b) Financial compensation may be given by the State to those affected adversely by errors in the register.

(c) The processes involved in conveyancing are simplified, and the time needed for the effective transfer of title is reduced.

Registration

5.　The register

The register (*see* LRA 1925, s. 1) is supervised by the Chief Land Registrar and is based on an index, each entry containing information relating to the *three parts of the register* (*see* **(a)**–**(c)** below). The three parts of the register are as follows.

(a)　*The property register.* This is a 'land register', not a 'name register'. In this register will be stated where the land (freehold or leasehold) is situated, descriptions of the land and the estates comprised in the title and title number. In the case of leasehold land there are, in addition to a description of the property, a description of the parties, title number, statements of rent payable, premium paid, date and term of the lease (if any). Exceptions and reservations are also recorded: LRR 1925, rr. 3, 5.

(b)　*The proprietorship register.* In this register will be stated the nature of the title (*see* **8** below), the name, address and description of the registered proprietor of the land, and any cautions, inhibitions and restrictions (*see* **15** below) affecting his right of disposing thereof: LRR 1925, r. 6.

(c)　*The charges register.* This contains details of burdens on the land:

> (*i*)　incumbrances subsisting at the date of the first registration;
> (*ii*)　subsequent charges, and other incumbrances (including notices of leases and other notices of adverse interests or claims permitted by the Act);
> (*iii*)　such notices as have to be entered relating to covenants, conditions, and other rights adversely affecting the land;
> (*iv*)　all such dealings with registered charges and incumbrances as are capable of registration: LRR 1925, r. 7.

NOTE: *A Land Certificate* is issued to the current registered proprietor as a document of title: LRA 1925, s. 63(1). Proof of title is not the certificate, but the register. An intending buyer checks title with the Registry; he is bound by any interest on the register *and* by any overriding interest (*see* 11 below).

6. Inspection of the register

The register was not generally open to public inspection: LRA 1925, s. 112. But under LRA 1988, s. 1, which substitutes a new s. 112 in the 1925 Act, any person may inspect and make copies of and extracts from entries on the register and documents referred to in the register which are in the custody of the registrar (other than leases or charges or copies of leases or charges). This has been in force since December 1990. Procedure is now governed by the LR (Open Register) Rules 1990. *See* SI 1990/1359/1362.

7. What must be registered

The system does not involve the compulsory registration of *all* land. The general rule is as follows:

> 'Every conveyance on sale of freehold land and every grant of
> a term of years absolute not being less than forty years from
> the date of the delivery of the grant, and every assignment on
> sale of leasehold land held for a term of years absolute having
> more than 21 years to run from the date of delivery of the
> assignment, shall (save as hereinafter provided), *on the
> expiration of two months* from the date thereof or of any
> authorised extension of that period, become void so far as
> regards the grant or conveyance of the legal estate in the
> freehold or leasehold land comprised in the conveyance,
> grant, or assignment, or so much of such land as is situated
> within the area affected, unless the grantee (that is to say, the
> person who is entitled to be registered as proprietor of the
> freehold or leasehold land) or his successor in title or assign
> has in the meantime applied to be registered as proprietor of
> such land ...': LRA 1925, s. 123(1), as amended by LRA 1986,
> s. 2.

(a) Hence, initial registration is now *compulsory* in all areas upon the *conveyance on sale of a fee simple*, or upon the *assignment on sale* or the *grant of certain types of lease*. See LRA 1925, s. 8(1A), LRA 1986, s. 2(2). In the case of any subsequent transfer, that transfer *must* be recorded. Where first registration rules are not complied with, an *equitable title* only will pass.

(b) Registration of leases *must* take place if the new lease is to run for a period of 21 years or more, *or* if there has been an assignment of a lease which has at least 21 years to run, *or* title out of which the lease has been granted has been registered and the lease is to run for more than 21 years. *See* LRA 1925, s. 123(1), as amended. Leases *must not* be registered if the lease runs for a period of 21 years or less, or if its assignment is the subject of an absolute prohibition in the lease.
(c) A prohibition on alienation in a lease can be protected by entry on the register: LRA 1925, s. 8(2), as substituted by LRA 1986, s. 3(1).

Titles and conversion of titles

8.   The kinds of title

Grades of title are recorded in the Proprietorship Register. The following kinds of title exist:

(a) *Absolute title to freehold land.* This is 'the best possible title' and is registered after an investigation by the Registrar: LRA 1925, s. 4. The result of registration is the vesting in the first registered proprietor of the fee simple in possession *subject to the following rights and interests*:

  (*i*)   incumbrances and other entries appearing on the register;
 (*ii*)   overriding interests affecting the registered land, unless the contrary is expressed on the register;
(*iii*)   where the first proprietor is not entitled for his own benefit to the registered land subject, as between himself and the persons entitled to minor interests, to any minor interests of such persons of which he has notice: LRA 1925, s. 5.

NOTE: The Registrar has discretion to refuse grant of absolute title without appeal; but application for judicial review is possible: *see Dennis* v. *Malcolm* (1934).

(b) *Qualified title to freehold land.*

'Where an absolute title is required, and on the examination of the title it appears to the registrar that the title can be established *only for a limited period, or only subject to certain reservations,* the registrar may, on the application of the party applying to be registered, by an entry made in the register, except from the effect of registration any estate, right or interest arising before a specified date, or arising under a specified instrument or otherwise particularly described in the register, and a title registered subject to such excepted estate, right, or interest shall be called a qualified title'; LRA 1925, s. 7(1).

Where the registered land is a freehold estate, registration has the effect of registration *with absolute title*, save that such registration shall not affect or prejudice the enforcement of any estate, right or interest appearing by the register to be excepted.

(c) *Possessory title to freehold land.* Where an applicant is unable to establish title in the usual way by title deeds, etc., a title based on possession of land may be granted. The first registration of such title has the effect of registration of land with absolute title, but the title will not affect any rights or interests subsisting or capable of arising at the time of the first registration: LRA 1925, ss. 6, 11.

(d) *Absolute title to leasehold land.* The Registrar must approve title to the leasehold, and to the freehold. The vesting of absolute title to leasehold land is subject to:

- (*i*) implied and express covenants, obligations;
- (*ii*) incumbrances and other entries on the register;
- (*iii*) overriding interests affecting the registered land: LRA 1925, ss. 8, 9.

(e) *Qualified title to leasehold land.* Such title may be granted by the Registrar where title can be established only for a limited period, or subject to any reservations.

(f) *Possessory title to leasehold land.* Such title may be granted to an applicant in possession, or in receipt of rents and profits. *See Spectrum Investment Co.* v. *Holmes* (1981); LRA 1925, ss. 8, 11.

(g) *Good leasehold title.* No guarantee as to the lessor's right to grant the lease is given, but in other respects the title is equivalent to an absolute leasehold title: LRA 1925, ss. 8, 10.

9. Conversion (upgrading) of title
See LRA 1925, s. 77, as substituted by LRA 1986, s. 1(1).

(a) *Good leasehold title* may be upgraded to absolute *at any time*, and *must* be upgraded on application by the proprietor if the Registrar is satisfied 'as to the title to the freehold and the title to any intermediate leasehold'.

(b) *Possessory title* may be upgraded to absolute (if freehold) or good leasehold (if leasehold), and *must* be so upgraded on application by the proprietor, provided that *either* the Registrar is satisfied as to title *or* the land has been registered with possessory title for at least 12 years and the Registrar is satisfied that the proprietor is in possession.

(c) *Qualified title* may be converted to absolute (if freehold) or good leasehold (if leasehold) at any time and *must* be so converted on application by the proprietor, provided that the Registrar is satisfied as to title.

Rights against registered land

10. Classification

Rights against registered land may be classified as follows:

(a) *substantively registrable interests,* i.e. those which can be registered in their own right, e.g. fee simple absolute, terms of years (over 21 years);
(b) *overriding* interests (*see* **11–13** below);
(c) *minor* interests (*see* **14–15** below).

11. Overriding interests

These interests will bind a purchaser *whether or not they are entered on the register, and whether or not the purchaser has or ought to have had knowledge of them.* They are the types of right, the existence of which *should have become apparent to a purchaser who has inspected the land he intends to buy and has made appropriate enquiries.* ' "Overriding interests" means all the incumbrances, interests, rights and powers *not entered* on the register but subject to which registered dispositions are by this Act to take effect': LRA 1925, s. 3(xvi). These interests 'bind the world'; they override specifically the buyer's interest at the time of registration of a transfer of land. A list of such interests, under various headings, is set out in LRA 1925, s. 70(1):

(a) Rights of common, drainage rights, customary rights ... public rights, *profits à prendre*, rights of sheepwalk, rights of way, watercourses, rights of water, and other easements not being equitable easements required to be protected by notice on the register: s. 70(1)(a). In *Celsteel* v. *Alton House Holdings* (1985), it was held that some *equitable interests* (those exercised openly and enjoyed with the land in question) would be considered as of an overriding nature. *See also* LRR 1925, r. 258.
(b) Liability to repair highways by reason of tenure, etc.: s. 70(1)(b). (Now virtually obsolete.)
(c) Liability to repair the chancel of a church: s. 70(1)(c).
(d) Liability in respect of embankments, and sea and river walls: s. 70(1)(d).
(e) Tithe redemption annuities: s. 70(1)(e). (*See now* Finance Act 1977, s. 56.)

(f) Rights acquired or in course of being acquired under the Limitation Acts: s. 70(1)(f). This will include those rights arising through adverse possession (see 21:**13**). See *Bridges* v. *Mees* (1957).

(g) *See* **12** below.

(h) In the case of a possessory, qualified, or good leasehold title, all estates, rights, interests, and powers excepted from the effect of registration: s. 70(1)(h).

(i) Rights under local land charges unless and until registered: s. 70(1)(i).

(j) Rights of fishing, sporting, and manorial rights: s. 70(1)(j).

(k) Leases granted for a term not exceeding 21 years: s. 70(1)(k), substituted by LRA 1986, s. 4(1). See *City Permanent BS* v. *Miller* (1952).

(l) Mineral rights relating to land where title was registered before 1926: s. 70(1)(l).

> NOTE: The Land Registration Rules 1925, r. 258, states: 'Rights, privileges and appurtenances appertaining or reputed to appertain to land or demised, occupied, or enjoyed therewith or reputed or known as part or parcel of or appurtenant thereto, which adversely affect registered land', are considered to be overriding interests within s. 70.

12. LRA 1925, s. 70(1)(g)

The important category of rights under this heading has been analysed in considerable detail by the courts. It consists of '*the rights of every person in actual occupation of the land or in receipt of the rents and profits thereof, save where enquiry is made of such person and the rights are not disclosed.*' The *object of this provision* is 'to protect a person in actual occupation of land from having his rights lost in the welter of registration. He can stay there and do nothing. Yet he will be protected. No one can buy the land over his head and thereby take away or diminish his rights. *It is up to every purchaser before he buys to make enquiry on the premises. If he fails to do so it is at his own risk*': per Lord Denning in *Strand Securities Ltd* v. *Caswell* (1965).

(a) A person seeking to claim under s. 70(1)(g) must show: that there was a right subsisting in reference to the property; that the owner of that right was in actual occupation (or in receipt of rent and profits) at the material time; that no enquiry was made of that person.

(b) The date on which the overriding interest becomes effective is that on which the application for registration is lodged with the Land Registry: see LRR 1925, r. 83(2), substituted by LRR 1978, r. 8; *Re Boyle's Claim* (1961); *Lloyds Bank* v. *Rossett* (1988). (In *Abbey National BS* v. *Cann* (1990) it was held that the date of *creation* of the charge, not the date of registration, was significant.)

(c) It should be noted that the provision protects not only residential tenants, but also the non-residential landlord (who is 'in receipt of the rents and profits').

(d) The 'rights' referred to in the provision are those which subsist *in reference to the land,* 'which have the quality of being capable of enduring through different ownerships of the land, according to normal conceptions of title to real property': *per* Russell LJ in *National Provincial Bank* v. *Hastings Car Mart* (1964). Hence, what is protected is not the occupation, but the *rights* of those persons in actual occupation.

   (*i*) 'Actual occupation is not an interest in itself': *per* Lord Templeman in *City of London BS* v. *Flegg* (1987) (*see* 11:**22**).

   (*ii*) 'Actual occupation' in the sense of s. 70(1)(g) is a matter of fact, not a matter of law: *Hodgson* v. *Marks* (1971); *Williams & Glyn's Bank Ltd* v. *Boland* (1981) — 'The statute has substituted a plain factual situation for the uncertainties of notice, actual or constructive, as the determinant of an overriding interest': *per* Lord Scarman. In *Epps* v. *Esso Petroleum Ltd* (1973) it was held that the parking of a motor vehicle at night on an undefined piece of land was not 'occupation' for purposes of the section.

   (*iii*) In *Williams & Glyn's Bank* v. *Boland* (1981), the House of Lords decided that the equitable interest of a spouse in actual occupation of the matrimonial home legally owned by the other spouse, was an overriding interest, having priority over a legal charge created by the legal owner. In this case, the wife had an equitable interest in the matrimonial home of which the husband was the legal owner. The wife's interest, based on contribution towards the purchase price was not registered. After she had acquired the interest, the husband mortgaged the house by way of legal mortgage to the bank, who made no enquiry concerning the wife's status. The husband defaulted, the bank foreclosed and obtained a possession order, which was reversed on appeal. The bank's appeal was dismissed; the wife was a person 'in actual occupation' within s. 70(1)(g) and the bank's charge was subject to the wife's overriding interest. (*See City of London BS* v. *Flegg* (1987), 11:**22**.)

(e) 'Rights' within s. 70(1)(g) are of a *proprietary* nature. They include, e.g. an equitable lease (*Rymer Investments* v. *Waite* (1958)): a beneficiary's equitable interest under a bare trust (*Hodgson* v. *Marks* (1971)); option to purchase legal estate (*Webb* v. *Pollmount Ltd* (1966)).

(f) Some rights, of a purely personal or contractual nature, are excluded from the scope of the provision, e.g. a spouse's personal rights of occupation (*see* the Matrimonial Homes Act 1983, s. 2(8)(b)). For statutory exclusions, *see*, e.g. LRA 1925, s. 86(2), by which the equitable interests of beneficiaries under a strict settlement are minor interests only; Leasehold Reform Act 1967, s. 5(5), excluding from the category of overriding interests notice given by a tenant so as to uphold his right to purchase a freehold in property which he is occupying.

(g) Note *Paddington BS* v. *Mendelsohn* (1987) — where under general law the rights of a person in actual occupation do not give priority over a registered estate owner, nothing in s. 70(1) operates so as to change the right into something larger.

(h) *See Kling* v. *Keston Properties* (1985) — right of pre-emption became an option creating an equitable interest which is an overriding interest within s. 70(1)(g).

(i) In *Strand Securities Ltd* v. *Caswell* (1965), C had the lease of a flat in which he allowed his stepdaughter, D, to live free of charge. C kept some furniture and clothes at the flat but lived elsewhere. D occupied the flat merely as a licensee. It was held that C possessed no overriding interest under s. 70(1)(g). He was not in occupation and received no rent from D. D's rights were *not* included in those enumerated under s. 70(1)(g).

(j) In *Hodgson* v. *Marks* (1971), X, an elderly lady, was persuaded by her lodger, Y, to allow him to look after the legal title to her property. She transferred title to him for nothing and Y later sold the property to Z. It was held that X had a beneficial interest under a resulting bare trust; this was sufficient to establish a right under s. 70(1)(g). X had been in actual occupation of the property and no enquiry had been made of her. Z was obliged to convey the legal estate to X.

NOTE: 'Where the existence of any overriding interest mentioned in this section is proved to the satisfaction of the registrar or admitted, he may (subject to any prescribed exceptions) enter notice of the same or of a claim thereto on the register, but no claim to an easement, right, or privilege not created by an instrument shall be noted against the title to the servient land if the proprietor of such land (after the prescribed notice is given to him) shows sufficient cause to the contrary': LRA 1925, s. 70(3). (An overriding interest which is noted on the register is transformed into a minor interest.)

13. Notice of freedom from or existence of overriding interests

'Where any person desires to have an entry made in the

register of the freedom from or the existence of an overriding interest mentioned in s. 70 of the Act, the application shall be made in writing and shall state the particulars of the entry required to be made.' 'Any entry, showing that the registered land is free from any one or more of the liabilities, rights, or interest, mentioned in s. 70 of the Act, shall be made in the Property Register': LRR 1925, r. 197(1), (6).

NOTE: (1) 'Whether an entry of an overriding interest is or is not made, it does not affect the validity of the overriding interest if such it be': *per* Upjohn LJ, in *Re Dances Way* (1962). (2) In *Webb* v. *Pollmount Ltd* (1966) plaintiff held under a lease granted by defendant's predecessor in title. Under that lease plaintiff had an option to purchase the freehold. The option was not recorded on the register. It was held that the option *was* an overriding interest. *Per* Ungoed-Thomas J: 'As the definition of "overriding interests" expressly excludes matters entered on the register, it indicates that matters registrable, but not registered, are not excluded. Overriding interests may include registrable matters, provided they have not been entered on the register...' (3) *See* the Law Commission Third Report on Land Registration No. 158 (1987), recommending a reduction in the number of overriding interests to five and the payment of compensation from public funds to those who suffer loss as the result of an overriding interest which could not reasonably have been discovered.

14. Minor interests

'"Minor interests" mean the interests *not* capable of being disposed of or created by registered dispositions and capable of being overridden (whether or not a purchaser has notice thereof) by the proprietors unless protected as provided by this Act, and all rights and interests which are *not* registered or protected on the register and are *not* overriding interests, and include:

(a) in the case of land held on trust for sale, all interests and powers which are under the Law of Property Act 1925, capable of being overridden by the trustees for sale, whether or not such interests and powers are so protected;

(b) in the case of settled land, all interests and powers which are under the Settled Land Act 1925, and the Law of Property Act 1925, or either of them, capable of being overridden by the tenant for life or statutory owner, whether or not such interests and powers are so protected as aforesaid...': LRA 1925, s. 3(xv). *See Murray* v. *Two Strokes* (1973).

Essentially, therefore, minor interests are a 'residual' category. They are *equitable only*.

15. Protection of minor interests

A minor interest may be protected by a notice, inhibition, restriction or caution entered on the register.

(a) *Notice*. Notice consists of a note recorded by the Registrar on the charges register. It will protect the kind of land charge registered under LCA, e.g. a legal rentcharge, creditors' rights in the event of a petition in bankruptcy concerning the registered proprietor. Where notice is entered, a subsequent disposition of the land will be subject to the rights thus protected. *See* LRA 1925, ss. 48–52.

(b) *Inhibition*. An inhibition may be entered on the proprietorship register on the application of any person interested, e.g. as where a proprietor's land certificate has been stolen. 'The Registrar... may... issue an order to make an entry inhibiting for a time, or until the occurrence of an event to be named in such order or entry, or generally until further order or entry, the registration or entry of any dealing with any registered land or registered charge': LRA 1925, s. 57.

(c) *Restriction*. (This is particularly useful in the case of equitable interests arising under strict settlements or trusts for sale.)

> 'Where the proprietor of any registered land or charge desires to place restrictions on transferring or charging the land or on disposing of or dealing with the land or charge in any manner in which he is by this Act authorised to dispose of or deal with it, or on the deposit by way of security of any certificate, the proprietor may apply to the registrar to make an entry in the register that no transaction to which the application relates shall be effected unless the following things, or such of them as the proprietor may determine, are done: — unless notice of any application for the transaction is transmitted by post to such address as he may specify to the registrar; unless the consent of some person or persons, to be named by the proprietor, is given to the transactions; unless some other such matter or thing is done as may be required by the applicant and approved by the registrar... The registrar shall thereupon, if satisfied of the right of the applicant to give the directions, enter the requisite restriction on the register, and no transaction to which the restriction relates shall be effected

except in conformity therewith': LRA 1925, s. 58(1), (2). *See Weston* v. *Henshaw* (1950).

(d) *Caution.* Any person interested in the registered land may lodge a caution with the Registrar against any dealing with that land. *See* LRA 1925, ss. 53–57; LRR 1925, r. 215. It will be entered on the Proprietorship Register. Entry of a dealing with such land may not then be made unless the cautioner has received notice. Any person who claims an interest in land not registered may lodge a caution against a first registration. Lodging of a caution without reasonable cause can lead to a remedy in damages: LRA 1925, s. 56(3). The benefit of a caution cannot be assigned. A caution can be used to protect an interest in the proceeds of sale of registered land: *Elias* v. *Mitchell* (1972). *See also Clayhope Properties* v. *Evans* (1986); *Tucker* v. *Hutchinson* (1987). A spouse's rights of occupation (under the Matrimonial Homes Act 1967), whether or not they constitute a charge, do not entitle that spouse to lodge a caution under LRA 1925, s. 54. *See* Matrimonial Homes Act 1983, s. 2(9). Note *Clark* v. *Chief Land Registrar* (1992) ('a caution is essentially a procedure, not an interest in land') and Charging Orders Act 1979.

> NOTE: The Index of Minor Interests (*see* LRA 1925, s. 102(2)) was *abolished* by LRA 1986, s. 5(1)(a). Priority between dealings with equitable interests in registered land is now governed by the rule in *Dearle* v. *Hall* (1828) (i.e. the order in which trustees receive notices).

Modes of transfer of registered land

16. Mortgage

The situation is governed by LRA 1925, s. 106, as substituted by the Administration of Justice Act 1977, s. 26(1). 'The proprietor of any registered land may, subject to any entry to the contrary on the register, mortgage, by deed or otherwise, the land or any part of it in any manner which would have been permissible if the land had not been registered, and, subject to this section, with the like effect.'

(a) *Registered charge.* See LRA 1925, s. 25. The charge is made by deed, and the appropriate Land Certificate is deposited in the Registry. The mortgagee receives a Certificate of Charge, and the charge will then be entered in the charges register.

(b) *Deposit of land certificate.* See LRA 1925, s. 66. A lien on the registered land may be created by deposit of the land certificate with the mortgagee. Written notice must be given to the Registrar by the mortgagee, and a caution must be entered on the charges register. *See Barclays Bank* v. *Taylor* (1974).

> NOTE: 'Unless and until the mortgage becomes a registered charge it shall take effect *only in equity* and it shall be capable of being overridden as a minor interest *unless* protected by a notice under s. 49 or a caution under s. 54': LRA 1925, s. 106 (as substituted by the Administration of Justice Act 1977, s. 26). *See Mortgage Corporation Ltd* v. *Nationwide Credit Corporation Ltd* (1992).

17. Death

The personal representatives of a deceased sole registered proprietor, or of the survivor of joint proprietors, may apply for registration as proprietor on production to the Registrar of grant of probate or letters of administration: LRA 1925, s. 41. In the alternative, they may, without registration, transfer the land directly to a purchaser, devisee or legatee, who, in such a case, will be registered in place of the deceased proprietor.

18. Bankruptcy

In the event of a presentation of a bankruptcy petition concerning a registered proprietor, a creditor's notice will be entered by the Registrar: *see* LRA 1925, s. 61(1), (3). As a result the land may not be sold free from the claims of a creditor. Where a bankruptcy order is made, a bankruptcy inhibition order is entered; this prevents any dealing with the land. Where the proprietor is adjudicated bankrupt the estate vests in the trustee in bankruptcy, who can be registered as proprietor.

19. Transfer *inter vivos*, i.e. by sale

A transfer form and land certificate will be lodged at the Land Registry. Searches of the register may be made by anyone. The transfer is recorded on a form set out in LRR and is considered as containing those 'general words', i.e. descriptive terms, implied in LPA 1925, s. 62. The transfer is effected by deed; it is stamped and then forwarded with a Land Certificate to the registry. *Upon the registration of the transfer the transferee acquires the legal estate.* Registration takes effect from the date of delivery of the completed application. The transferee takes subject to the interests which bound the transferor; but if he is a purchaser for value he will take free of any minor interests other than those protected by entry in the register: LRA 1925, ss. 20, 23.

NOTE: Title to registered estate may also be acquired by *adverse possession* (*see* 21:**13**). But no legal estate to registered land is acquired by an adverse possessor *unless he has been registered as proprietor*. Until such registration the registered proprietor is considered as holding the land on trust for the adverse possessor: LRA 1925, s. 75(1), (2).

Rectification and indemnity

20. Rectification of the register

See Norwich and Peterborough BS v. *Steed* (1992). This is a discretionary remedy. Under LRA 1925, s. 82(1), the register may be rectified pursuant to an order of the court or by the Registrar, subject to an appeal to the court, where the court or Registrar is satisfied that any entry in the register has been obtained by fraud, or in any other case where by reason of any error or omission in the register, or by reason of any entry made under a mistake, it may be deemed just to rectify the register. *See,* e.g. *Argyle BS* v. *Hammond* (1985). (Note the so-called 'slip rule' (LRR 1925, r. 13) allowing the Registrar to correct a minor clerical error in the register, or any plan or document referred to therein. *See also* r. 14.) But 'the register shall not be rectified except for the purpose of giving effect to an overriding interest or an order of the court so as to affect the title of the proprietor who is in possession:

(a) *unless* such proprietor has caused or substantially contributed to the error or omission by fraud or lack of proper care;
(b) *unless* for any other reason, in any particular case, it is considered that it would be unjust not to rectify the register against him': LRA 1925, s. 82(3), amended by the Administration of Justice Act 1977, s. 24.

NOTE: A disposition of land will take effect subject only to those interests which have been registered and any subsequent correction of the register does *not* have a retroactive effect; *Freer* v. *Unwins* (1976).

21. Right to indemnity

See: Re Chowood's Registered Land (1933); *Re Boyle's Claim* (1961); *Hodgson* v. *Marks* (1971). LRA 1925, s. 83, states: '(1) Subject to the provisions of this Act to the contrary, any person suffering loss by reason of any rectification of the register under this Act shall be entitled to be indemnified. (2) Where an error or omission has occurred in the register, but the register is not rectified, any person suffering loss by reason of such error or omission, shall, subject to the provisions of this Act, be entitled to be indemnified. ...' (5) No indemnity is payable if 'the applicant or person from whom he derives title (otherwise than under a disposition for valuable consideration which is registered or protected on the register) has caused or substantially contributed to the loss by fraud or lack of proper care' [as amended by Land Registration and Land Charges Act 1971, s. 3](11) '. . . When a claim to indemnity arises in consequence of the registration of an estate in land with an absolute or good leasehold title, the claim shall be enforceable only if made within six years from the date of such registration.'

NOTE: (1) The amount of indemnity which is claimed must reflect the loss in monetary terms suffered by claimant. (2) Any money paid under an indemnity arising in the case of settled land is paid to the trustees of the settlement who will hold it as capital money: LRA 1925, s. 84.

Registration and notice: recent developments

22. General

The policy of the LRA 1925 was predicated on the fundamental importance of 'the state of the register.' Registration replaced, in general, the equitable doctrine of notice (*see* 1:**19–20**) in relation to land with registered title. A failure to register an equitable interest renders it *void* against a purchaser, *whether or not he had notice*.

(a) Under LRA 1925, s. 20(1), where X transfers, for valuable consideration, a legal estate in registered land to Y, Y takes subject to the incumbrances and other entries, if any, appearing on the register and to the overriding interests (*see* **11** above), if any, affecting the estate transferred. Y's title is declared free from all other estates and interests whatsoever.

(b) Under LRA 1925, s. 59(6), a purchaser acquiring title under a registered disposition shall not be concerned with any matter, document, or claim (which is not an overriding interest) which is not protected by a caution, or other entry on the register, whether he has or has not notice (express, implied or constructive) of it.

(c) The combined effect of ss. 20(1) and 59(6) seemed to be that notice was of *no relevance* in the case of an unprotected minor interest. 'Notice of something which is not on the register should not affect a transferee unless it is an overriding interest': *per* Cross J in *Strand Securities* v. *Caswell* (1965).

23. 'Notice' re-emerges

The following matter should be noted carefully.

(a) *Peffer* v. *Rigg* (1978). It was held that a purchaser for value of property which he knows to be held on trust for a third party is bound by that interest *either* under LRA 1925, s. 20 *or* as constructive trustee on general equitable principles, even though that interest is not protected by any entry on the register. Only a transferee who has given consideration *and acted in good faith* is protected. 'A purchaser cannot be in good faith if he has in fact notice of something which affects his title': *per* Graham J. (Note the definition of 'purchaser' for the purpose of LRA 1925: 'A purchaser in good faith for valuable consideration and includes a lessee, mortgagee, or other person who for valuable consideration acquires any interest in land or in any charge on land': LRA 1925, s. 3(xxi).)

(b) *Lyus* v. *Prowsa Developments Ltd* (1982). It was held that where land is sold 'subject to and with the benefit of a contract', the purchaser holds on constructive trust for the beneficiary of that contract; so does a second purchaser who buys with notice of the contract. *Per* Dillon J: 'The court may intervene to raise a constructive trust on appropriate terms if to leave defendant retaining the property free from all interests would be tantamount to sanctioning a fraud on the part of defendant.'

(c) It would seem, therefore, that the situation is now as follows: should a purchaser have express knowledge of an unprotected minor interest, he may, nevertheless, be bound should it be possible to impose a constructive trust.

> (*i*) Note, however, the statement of Lord Wilberforce (commenting on LRA 1925, s. 70(i)(g) — *see* **12** above): 'To have regard to the doctrine of notice... would run counter to the whole purpose of the Act... Above all the system is designed to free the purchaser from the hazards of notice, real or constructive, which in the case of unregistered land, involved him in inquiries, often elaborate... In my opinion, the law as to notice as it may affect purchasers of unregistered land has no application even by analogy to registered land' (*Williams & Glyn's Bank* v. *Boland* (1981)).

> (*ii*) *See also* LRA 1925, s. 74 ('references to trusts shall, so far as possible, be excluded from the register').

(d) The Law Commission Report No. 158 (1987), 'Property Law', criticises the decision in *Peffer* v. *Rigg* (1978) and recommends that a transferee or purchaser should *not* be deemed dishonest merely because he had actual knowledge of the unprotected minor interest in question.

Progress test 20

1. Explain the purpose of the property, proprietorship and charges registers. **(5)**

2. What must be registered under the system involving registered land? **(7)**

3. Explain the terms (a) 'absolute title to freehold land', and (b) 'good leasehold title'. **(8)**

4. What is the essence of 'overriding interests' in relation to registered land? **(11)**

5. Explain and illustrate the object of the Land Registration Act 1925, s. 70(1)(g). **(12)**

6. Outline the nature of 'minor interests'. How may they be protected? **(14, 15)**

7. Under what circumstances may the register be rectified? **(20)**

8. What is the significance of the decisions in *Peffer* v. *Rigg* (1978) and *Lyus* v. *Prowsa Developments Ltd* (1982)? **(23)**

Limitation of actions, and adverse possession

Preliminaries

1. General principle of limitation

'One of the principles of the Act is that those who go to sleep on their claims shall not be assisted by the courts in recovering their property. But another equally important principle is that there should be an end of these matters, and that there shall be protection against stale demands': *per* Streatfield J in *RB Policies at Lloyd's* v. *Butler* (1950). 'Long dormant claims often have more of cruelty than justice in them': *per* Best CJ in *A'Court* v. *Cross* (1825).

2. Limitation Act 1980

LA 1980 consolidates the Limitation Acts 1939 to 1980. It repeals LA 1939 and LA 1975 in their entirety. LA 1963 and L (Amendment) A 1980 have been repealed in substantial measure. *See also* the Latent Damage Act 1986, relating to negligence cases and latent damage to property. Note that the Limitation Acts apply to registered land in the same manner and to the same extent as to unregistered land: LRA 1925, s. 75(1).

Actions to recover land and rent

3. Time limit for actions to recover land

No action shall be brought for the *recovery of land* (e.g. by seeking the remedy of foreclosure) after the expiration of *12 years* from the date on which the right of action accrued: s. 15(1). (*See* Sch. 1 at **10–12** below.) Where the estate or interest claimed is an estate or interest in reversion or remainder or any other future estate or interest, and the right of action to recover accrued on the date on which the estate or interest fell into possession by determination of the preceding estate or interest, and the person entitled to the preceding estate or interest (not being a term of years absolute) was not in possession of the land on that date, no action shall be brought by the person entitled to the succeeding estate or interest after the expiration of *12 years* from the date on which the right of action accrued to the person entitled to the preceding estate or interest, or *six years* from the date on which the right of action accrued to the person entitled to the succeeding estate or interest, whichever period last expires: s. 15(2). *See BP Properties* v. *Buckle* (1987). (An action to recover Crown land may be brought within *30 years*: s. 15(7).)

4. Time limit for redemption actions
See 14:**15**. When a *mortgagee of land* has been in possession of any of the mortgaged land for a period of *12 years*, no action to redeem that land shall be brought after the end of that period by the mortgagor or any person claiming through him: s. 16.

5. Settled land and land held on trust
See Chs. 10 and 11. The provisions of LA 1980 apply to *equitable interests in land*, including interests in the proceeds of the sale of land held upon trust for sale, as they apply to legal estates: s. 18(1). Where the period prescribed by the Act has expired for the bringing of an action to recover land by a tenant for life (*see* **12**) or a statutory owner of settled land, his legal estate shall not be extinguished if and so long as the right of action to recover the land of any person entitled to a beneficial interest in the land either has not accrued or has not been barred by the Act, and the legal estate shall accordingly remain vested in the tenant for life or statutory owner and shall devolve in accordance with SLA 1925, but if and when every such right of action has been barred by the Act, his legal estate shall be extinguished: s. 18(2).

6. Time limit for actions to recover rent
No action shall be brought, or distress made, to recover *arrears of rent*, or damages in respect of arrears of rent, after the expiration of *six years* from the date on which the arrears became due: s. 19.

Actions relating to recovery of money secured by mortgage, charge, proceeds of sale of land

7. Time limits
No action shall be brought to recover any principal sum of money

secured by a mortgage or other charge on property or proceeds of the sale of land after the expiration of *12 years* from the date on which the right to receive the money accrued: s. 20(1). *See* 15:**8(a)(b)**.

(a) No foreclosure action in respect of mortgaged land is covered by this section, but the provisions of the Act relating to actions to recover land apply to such an action: s. 20(4). *See* 15:**9**.

(b) Subject to subss. (6),(7), no action to recover arrears of interest payable in respect of any sum of money secured by mortgage or other charge or payable in respect of proceeds of sale of land, or to recover damages in respect of such arrears, shall be brought after the expiration of *six years* from the date on which the interest became due: s. 20(5). *See Holmes* v. *Cowcher* (1970). The period runs from the date when, on a true construction of the loan agreement, the lender could first have brought an action to recover the interest, not from the date when, under the agreement, it was due to have been paid: *Barclays Bank* v. *Walters* (1988).

(c) Where a prior mortgagee or other incumbrancer has been in possession of the property charged, and an action is brought within *one year* of the discontinuance of that possession by the subsequent incumbrancer, the subsequent incumbrancer may recover by that action all arrears of interest which fell due during the period of possession by the prior incumbrancer, or damages in respect of those arrears, notwithstanding that the period exceeded *six years*: s. 20(6).

(d) Where the property subject to mortgage or charge comprises any future interest, and it is a term of the mortgage or charge that arrears of interest be treated as part of the principal sum of money secured by the mortgage or charge, interest shall not be treated as becoming due before the right to recover the principal sum of money has accrued or is treated as having accrued: s. 20(7).

Extension in case of disability, fraud, etc.

8. Disability

In the case of a person to whom a right of action accrues being under a disability, an action may be brought at any time before the expiration of *six years* from the date when he ceased to be under a disability or died (whichever first occurred) notwithstanding that the period of limitation has expired: s. 28(1). No action to recover land or money charged on land shall be brought by virtue of this section by any person after the expiration of *30 years* from the date on which the right of action accrued to that person or some person through whom he claims: s. 28(4).

9.   Fraud, etc.

In the case of fraud, concealment of a fact relevant to plaintiff's right of action, and mistake, the period of limitation will not begin to run until plaintiff has discovered the fraud, concealment or mistake, or could with reasonable diligence have discovered it: s. 32(1). But nothing in s. 32 enables any action to recover property, or its value, or to enforce any charge against property, to be brought against the purchaser of the property or any person claiming through him in any case where the property had been purchased for valuable consideration by an innocent third party since the fraud or concealment or the transaction in which the mistake was made took place: s. 32(3).

> NOTE: For fresh accrual of action on acknowledgment or part payment, *see* s. 29; recovery of foreshore by Crown, *see* Sch. 1, Part II, para. 11.

Accrual of rights of action to recover land

10.   Accrual of right of action in case of present interests in land

Where the person bringing an action to recover land, or some person through whom he claims, has been in possession of the land and has, while entitled to the land, been dispossessed or discontinued his possession, the right of action shall be treated as having accrued on the date of dispossession or discontinuance: Sch. 1, para. 1. Where a person brings an action to recover the land of a deceased person who was, on the date of his death, in possession of the land and was the last person entitled to the land to be in possession of it, the right of action shall be treated as having accrued on the date of death: Sch. 1, para. 2.

11.   Accrual of right of action in case of future interests

The right of action to recover land shall, in a case where the estate or interest claimed was in reversion or remainder, or any other future estate or interest, and no person has taken possession of the land by virtue of the estate or interest claimed, be treated as having accrued on the date on which the estate or interest fell into possession by determination of the preceding estate or interest: Sch. 1, para. 4.

12. Accrual in case of forfeiture or breach of condition

A right of action to recover land by virtue of a forfeiture or breach of condition shall be treated as having accrued *on the date on which the forfeiture was incurred or the condition broken.* But if any such right has accrued to a person entitled to an estate or interest in reversion or remainder and the land was not recovered by virtue of that right, the right of action to recover shall not be treated as having accrued to that person until his estate or interest fell into possession, as if no such forfeiture or breach had occurred: Sch. 1, para. 7.

Adverse possession

13. Essential features

Adverse possession is occupation of land in a manner inconsistent with the rights of the true owner. An *adverse possessor* is one who is in occupation in this manner. Thus, without having obtained Y's permission, but with Y's knowledge, X has occupied Y's land uninterruptedly for thirteen years, during which time he has carried out improvements, e.g. by draining and levelling. During that period Y has been effectively excluded from the land as a result of X's possession. In such a case, X is the adverse possessor; Y is the 'paper owner'.

(a) Essentially, Y cannot bring a successful action against X. By statute (*see* LA 1980) X is refused a remedy, so that, other things being equal, X cannot be removed from the land.

(b) 'At the expiration of the period prescribed by this Act for any person to bring an action to recover land (including a redemption action) the title of that person to the land shall be extinguished': LA 1980, s. 17.

(c) Exceptions to the general rule include the following:

   (*i*) Where the land in question is *settled land* (*see* **10**) or held on *trust for sale* (*see* **11**), the title of the trustee to the legal estate is not considered as extinguished until the rights of action of the beneficiaries have been barred. *See* LA 1980, s. 18(2)(3).

   (*ii*) In the case of *registered land* (*see* Ch. 20) where a person has been registered as owner of the land under LRA 1925 and is dispossessed for 12 years or more, his title is not immediately extinguished. He is considered to hold the land for the time being *in trust* for the adverse possessor: LRA 1925, s. 75(1). 'Any person claiming to have acquired a title under the Limitation Acts to a registered estate in the land may apply to be registered as proprietor thereof: s. 75(2). The register may be rectified in favour of the adverse possessor on his application, but this must be done without prejudice to any estate or interest where the right has not been extinguished by lapse of time: s. 75(3).

(d) The adverse possessor acquires, in effect, an independent and new title to the fee simple; it will prevail against every person *except* one who is able to rely on a better title. 'Whenever you find a person in possession of property, that possession is *prima facie* evidence of ownership in fee, and that *prima facie* evidence becomes absolute when once you have extinguished the right of every other person to challenge it': *per* Cozens-Hardy MR in *Re Atkinson and Horsell's Contract* (1912).

(e) Because the adverse possessor is not a 'purchaser' of the land, he is bound by any earlier interest in it, whether or not he had notice of it.

(f) LRA 1925, s. 70(1)(f) (*see* 20:**11**), relating to overriding rights, covers rights arising through adverse possession.

(g) Each case concerning adverse possession turns upon its own facts. *See*, e.g. *Hyde* v. *Pearce* (1982); *Williams* v. *Usherwood* (1983).

14. Fundamentals of adverse possession

Behind the concept of adverse possession is the importance of certainty of title and the general principle that long dormant, stale claims shall not be allowed to interfere with the occupation of land which has been unchallenged for a considerable period of time.

(a) The relevant period (12 years) is contained in LA 1980, s. 15(1): *see* **3** above.

(b) Continuous dispossession must be proved by the adverse possessor. Thus, in *Edgington* v. *Clark* (1967) a *written offer* by an adverse possessor to the paper owner's agent to buy the freehold was held to be an admission of the paper owner's right, so that adverse possession was interrupted. In *Browne* v. *Perry* (1991) an *oral acknowledgment* of the paper owner's title was held not sufficient to interrupt adverse possession.

(c) There must be no concealment and no fraud on the part of the adverse possessor. Should this be proved, the 12-year period will begin to run from the time when the paper owner, by the exercise of reasonable diligence, could have noticed the adverse possessor's actions.

(d) Note the comments of Lord O'Hagan in *Lord Advocate* v. *Lord Lovat* (1880): 'As to possession, it must be considered in every case with reference to the peculiar circumstances. The acts, implying possession in one case, may be wholly inadequate to prove it in another. The character and value of the property, the suitable and natural mode of using it, the course of conduct which the proprietor might be expected to follow with a due regard for his own interests — all these things, greatly varying as they must, under various conditions, are to be taken into account'.

15. 'Adverse'
The following rules are important:

(a) Possession of the land must be *real*; this question will be determined by consideration of 'the nature of the land and the manner in which land of that nature is commonly used or enjoyed': *per* Slade J in *Powell* v. *McFarlane* (1977). In *Treloar* v. *Nute* (1977), derelict land was improved by the adverse possessor filling in a wide gulley. It was held that this constituted 'possession'. In *Wimpey Ltd* v. *Sohn* (1967), the erection and maintenance of extensive fencing was held *not* to have been intended to exclude the owner; adverse possession was *not*, therefore, established.

(b) *Animus possidendi* (the intention to possess) must be shown. In *Powell* v. *McFarlane* (1977), the necessary 'compelling evidence' of *animus possidendi* was *not* proved where, at the age of 14, plaintiff had begun to use land for purposes of grazing a cow. The intention to exclude the paper owner as well as other people must be shown, and intent must be inferred from the act itself. In *Tecbild Ltd* v. *Chamberlain* (1969), adverse possession was *not* inferred from trivial acts of trespass committed by a claimant's children who had played on the land and tethered ponies there. In *Bucks CC* v. *Moran* (1989), the placing of a new lock and chain on a gate amounted to an 'unequivocal demonstration' to possess the land. (The case stressed, also, that the adverse possessor was *not* required to demonstrate an intention to acquire *ownership*; intention to *possess* would suffice.) *See also Morrice* v. *Evans* (1989); *R.* v. *Secretary of State for the Environment ex p Davies* (1990) (sufficient *animus possidendi* was *not* demonstrated by a trespasser who had offered to pay rent in respect of her occupation of caravans in a disused quarry); *Bladder* v. *Phillips* (1991).

(c) It is not necessary that the adverse possession be 'hostile'.

(d) The adverse possession must not be, in any way, the result of permission.

(e) It is not necessary to establish inconvenience to the owner in order to establish adverse possession: *Treloar* v. *Nute* (1977).

(f) There must be some action in the nature of ouster by the adverse possessor. In *Boosey* v. *Davis* (1988), the grazing of goats, clearing of scrub and the erecting of a fence were held insufficient to constitute dispossession of the owner.

16. Leases and adverse possession
The following general rules apply.

(a) A tenant (T) may not claim adverse possession against his landlord (L) during the currency of the lease, because T may not deny L's title, and, in any event, T's possession under a lease is not 'adverse'.

(b) T's possession may be considered adverse only on expiry of the period covered by T's last payment of rent. *See Hayward* v. *Challoner* (1968).

(c) Where T is dispossessed by A during the currency of the lease, A's adverse possession begins against T at once; but it does not run against L, for purposes of statutory limitation, until the end of the lease. *See* LA 1980, Sch. 1, para. 4.

(d) *See Colchester BC* v. *Smith* (1992) (estoppel and adverse possession).

17. Successive adverse possessors
It is not necessary that the twelve-year period shall be by one adverse possessor only. Where an adverse possessor, A_1, is dispossessed, the second adverse possessor, A_2, acquires the period of time which has run in favour of A_1. If, however, A_1 abandons possession *before* A_2 takes possession, the time period will commence anew. Note LA 1980, s. 15(6), Sch. 1, para. 8: 'Where a right of action to recover land has accrued and after its accrual, before the right is barred, the land ceases to be in adverse possession, the right of action shall no longer be treated as having accrued and no fresh right of action shall be treated as accruing unless and until the land is again taken into adverse possession'. *See Mount Carmel Investments* v. *Thurlow* (1988).

18. Recovery of possession
The following points should be noted:

(a) *See* the Criminal Law Act 1977, s. 7, as amended by HA 1988, Sch. 17, para. 101, making adverse possession of residential premises in some circumstances *an offence*. *See also* the Public Order Act 1986, s. 39, empowering police officers to direct persons to leave open land where they have entered as trespassers, in certain cases.

(b) *See* the remedy by common law action for *possession*, and the remedy by summons (RSCO 113 and CCRO 24, which allow the court to make an order for possession within five days, or, in urgent cases, a shorter period, after service of summons). *See* SI 1986/2289.

Progress test 21

1. What is the general rule relating to time limits for actions to recover land?   **(3)**

2. What are the time limits for **(a)** redemption actions, and **(b)** actions to recover rent?   **(4, 6)**

3. How is the rule concerning limitation of actions affected by **(a)** disability, and **(b)** fraud?   **(8, 9)**

4. Outline the general principles of adverse possession.   **(13, 14)**

5. *'Animus possidendi* is the key to adverse possession.' Explain. **(15)**

6. How is the problem of successive adverse possessors resolved? **(17)**

Appendix 1
Bibliography

In all cases only the most recent editions should be used.

Textbooks

Artis D. and Houghton J.   *Land Law* (Blackstone Press)
Burn E.H.   *Cheshire and Burn: Modern Law of Real Property* (Butterworths)
Chappelle D.   *Land Law* (Pitman)
Gray K.J.   *Elements of Land Law* (Butterworths)
Green K.   *Land Law* (Macmillan)
Henderson N.   *Land Law* (Sweet & Maxwell)
Mackenzie J. & Phillips M.   *Practical Approach to Land Law* (Blackstone Press)
Megarry Sir R.   *Manual of the Law of Real Property* (Sweet & Maxwell)
Megarry Sir R. & Wade H.W.   *The Law of Real Property* (Sweet & Maxwell)
Murphy W.T. & Roberts S.   *Understanding Property Law* (Fontana)
Riddall J.G.   *Introduction to Land Law* (Butterworths)

Specialist texts

Annand R. & Cain B.   *Modern Conveyancing* (Sweet & Maxwell)
Arden A.   *Manual of Housing Law* (Sweet & Maxwell)
Barnsley D.G. & Smith P.W.   *Conveyancing Law and Practice* (Butterworths)
Hayton D.J.   *Registered Land* (Sweet & Maxwell)
Jackson P.   *Law of Easements and Profits* (Butterworths)
Kenny P.H. & Bevan C.M.   *Conveyancing Law* (Pitman)
Male J.M.   *Landlord and Tenant* (Pitman)
Simpson A.W.   *An Introduction to the History of Land Law* (Clarendon Press)

Tyler E.L.   *Law of Mortgage* (Butterworths)
Yates D. & Hawkins A.J.   *Landlord and Tenant Law* (Sweet & Maxwell)
Storey I.R.   *Conveyancing* (Butterworths)

Cases and materials

Burn E.H.   *Maudsley and Burn: Land Law—Cases and Materials* (Butterworths)
Gravells N.P.   *Property Statutes* (Sweet & Maxwell)
Harwood M.   *Cases and Materials on English Land Law* (Professional Books)
Thomas T.   *Statutes on Property Law* (Blackstone Press)
Tyler E.L.   *Cases and Statutes on Land Law* (Sweet & Maxwell)

Appendix 2
Examination technique

1. The general purpose of examinations in land law

Professional examinations in land law have as their objective the testing of a student's awareness of the overall pattern, unity and uniqueness of this section of the law, his/her comprehension of the broad principles underlying its structure, and his/her ability to apply those principles with understanding and precision in the solution of problems.

2. Questions on land law

It is possible to classify the types of question set under three very broad headings, bearing in mind that overlap is common. The examples used are taken from Land Law papers set in the LL.B. examinations of the University of London, with whose permission they are printed.

(a) *The factual question.* Example: 'Explain the nature and effect of a covenant for quiet enjoyment in a lease'.

(b) *The discussion question.* Example: '"Under the system of registration of title to land the old idea of notice has no part to play: everything depends on the state of the register." Comment on this statement.'

(c) *The question requiring a solution to a problem.* Example: 'X and Y acquired adjoining houses on a country estate in 1963 and became firm friends. In 1970, X allowed Y to place a television aerial on his (X's) roof because it improved reception, and a year later X allowed Y to park his second car on a particular part of his (X's) land. X died last year and his house has been sold to Z who declines to allow Y to maintain the aerial or park the car. Advise Y whether he can claim easements to entitle him to keep the aerial and to park the car.'

3. The factual question

The required answer must be precise, relevant and free from side-issues. Principles and cases must be assembled in a methodical sequence. Where cases are cited, they must be outlined and their significance noted. The question at **2(a)** above requires a precise explanation of 'a covenant for quiet enjoyment', with particular reference to the interpretation of the phrase 'quiet enjoyment'. Cases, such as *Browne* v. *Flower* (1911) or *Sampson* v. *Hodgson-Pressinger* (1981), should be explained. Appropriate attention should be paid to the 'effect' of the covenant; in particular, the results of a breach which 'interferes with the tenant's freedom of action in exercising his rights as tenant' (*per* Lord Denning in *McCall* v. *Abelesz* (1976)) require consideration. A systematic answer is essential, with definitions, illustrations and explanations set out in logical style.

4.   The discussion question

The discussion must be based on a solid foundation of fact and must grow from fact. Mere assertion or speculation unsupported by fact should be avoided. The question at **2(b)** above demands an answer based upon knowledge of the system of registered land generally, and the concept of notice in particular. Attention should be given to the significance of the phrases 'no part to play' and 'everything depends on ...' Among matters requiring discussion will be the view that the policy of the LRA 1925 appears to have been based on the significance of the 'state of the register', with its content acting as a 'mirror' reflecting the essence of title. The old equitable doctrine of notice (which should be outlined briefly) would disappear. The discussion will include reference to the unexpected re-emergence of the doctrine of notice, as evidenced by *Peffer* v. *Rigg* (1978) and *Lyus* v. *Prowsa Developments Ltd* (1982). The comments of the Law Commission Report (No. 158) (1987) which criticised the decision in *Peffer* v. *Rigg*, would be of particular relevance. A considered conclusion to the discussion is essential and might take the form of agreement or disagreement with the perceived re-emergence of 'notice' in the area of land registration. Has it resulted in 'a crack in the mirror'?

5.   The question requiring a solution to a problem

This type of question is a searching test of powers of comprehension and analysis. The following pattern for dealing with questions of this nature is suggested. *See* **2(c)** above.

(a) Read the question very carefully indeed, paying attention to words and phrases of outstanding importance. What is the question seeking to test? What are the implications of the data?

(b) Identify the precise matters involved. (Creation of easements, essential qualities of easements, for example.)

(c) Identify the principles involved. (Are the essentials of an easement present? Licence or easement?)

(d) Recall the leading cases (*Re Ellenborough Park* (1956), for example).

(e) Apply principles and cases to the facts of the problem. Are the four characteristics of an easement present in the examples given (aerial, parking of car)? Does *Crow* v. *Wood* (1971) indicate the possibility of easements being acknowledged in these circumstances? What of the Prescription Act 1832, s. 2? LPA 1925, s. 62 (concerning the sale of the house to Z)?

(f) Present a clearly-argued answer based upon your understanding of the problem in the light of **(e)** above.

6. In the examination room

Once in the examination room, the following advice should be kept in mind.

(a) *Read the instructions with great care* — they are not always precisely the same from year to year.

(b) *Plan the use of your time*. Allow some time for a final check of your answers at the end of the three-hour examination period.

(c) *Plan each of your answers*. The trained mind displays an awareness of the need to plan carefully. Planning, within the context of this type of examination, involves making a preliminary sketch and outline of the intended answer. Time spent on planning is never wasted.

Appendix 3
Specimen test paper

(The questions are taken from papers in Land Law set by the University of London, whose kind permission to use them is acknowledged.)

Instructions:

1. The time allowed for the paper is *three hours*.
2. Answer *any four questions* from the paper.
3. In all cases the questions should be answered on the basis of the law as it is on the date when the test is taken.
4. In accordance with the regulations of the University of London, you are permitted to use a copy of Butterworth's *Property Law Handbook* or *Sweet & Maxwell's Property Statutes* or Blackstone's *Property Statutes*.

1. 'The purpose of section 70(1)(g) of the Land Registration Act 1925 was to make applicable to registered land the same rule for the protection of persons in actual occupation of land as had been applied in *Hunt* v. *Luck*.'

    Explain this statement and consider the extent to which it is accurate.

2. Distinguish a lease from a licence. To what extent is the distinction important today?

3. William owns a large house and garden, with an adjoining pony paddock. He sells the pony paddock to Vera, who covenants that she will not erect more than one building in the paddock. Vera also covenants that the paddock will not be used for any business without first erecting, and thereafter maintaining, a ten-foot fence round the paddock. The conveyance to Vera does not refer to any land that is benefited.

Three years later, William sells off part of the garden to Xerxes, who covenants with William that he will not erect more than one building in the garden and that he will not use the land for any business purposes whatsoever. William tells Xerxes that he will take similar covenants from anyone to whom he sells the rest of the land. Next year William sells the house and the rest of the garden to Yvonne, taking similar covenants.

Yvonne has opened a car-repair business; Vera has sold her land to Zuleika, who opened a craft workshop giving employment to herself and her handicapped twin sons. Xerxes did not object originally, but Zuleika has expanded the business and employs six part-time workers and Xerxes now objects. No fence has been erected.

Advise Xerxes.

4. 'No one can take pride in the present state of English law on forfeiture of leases and the rules for relief from forfeiture. The best plan would be to scrap it all and start afresh.'

Discuss this statement, and suggest what improvements could be made by a new system.

5. To what extent does the courts' treatment of mortgages, and willingness to modify the bargain reached by the parties, support Maitland's jibe that the English mortgage was 'one long *suppressio veri* and *suggestio falsi* (a suppression of the truth and a statement of falsehood)'? Do you agree with the policy of departing from the strict wording of mortgages in certain circumstances?

6. Samuel is consulting the family solicitor, and writes to him as follows:

'Ever since my wife and two dear boys died in that horrible accident, my two sisters, Eva, who is ten years older than me, and Florence, two years younger, have lived at Oddstone Manor with me. I want them both to be able to stay there, and then it can be divided between all my nieces and nephews. I was talking to one of them, Timothy, the other day and he said there are two ways to tie up property that way. It sounded a bit technical so I want you to explain that. My two sisters are not very business-like, but young Tim and his sister Una are both very good and they can keep an eye on things if you advise that.'

To which two methods of 'settling' land was Samuel referring? Describe each of them and indicate which you would recommend in the circumstances of this case.

7.   Mike, Pat, Rob and Saul formed a pop group and decided to buy a house together situated near the recording studios. All four of them contributed equally to the purchase price and the house was conveyed into the joint names of Mike, Pat and Rob; Saul was aged 17 at the time of the conveyance. The pop group was not a success and in 1990 Mike sold his interest in the house to Pat. Shortly afterwards Rob wrote to Pat offering to sell him his interest for a certain price; Pat replied that he would be happy to purchase Rob's interest, but that the price was too high. Before any negotiations took place Rob was killed in a motor accident. Saul now wishes the house to be sold whereas Pat wishes to continue living there.

Saul would like to know whether he can force a sale of the house and, if so, how the proceeds would be divided.

Advise Saul.

8.   **(a)**   Is it true to say that the Land Charges Act is a statute that has been used as an instrument of fraud?

(b)   In 1982, Elias agreed to sell Bluehectare (unregistered land) to Fiona. Elias did not complete the sale to Fiona, but conveyed the land to Gillian.

Advise Fiona. Do you need any further information?

Index

Absolute, meaning of, 38
Abstract of title, 275–6
Accumulations, rule against, 176–8
Actions by mortgagor, 203
Ad hoc settlements and trusts, 155–6
Adverse possession, 302–6
  features of, 302–3
  fundamentals of, 303–4
  leases and, 305
  possession, recovery of, 305–6
  rules of, 304–5
  successive possessors, 305
Agricultural fixtures, 23
Agricultural tenancies, 90
Air flow, right to, 237
Air space, right to, 46–7
Alienation of fee simple, 44
Animals, wild, 46
Annexation and chattels, 21–2
Annuities, register of, 256
Assignment of lease, 50, 119
Automatic determination of tenancy,
  67

Bankruptcy, 293
Barring of entailed interest, 186
Base fee, 40–1
Building scheme, 226–7

Capital money and application of,
  140–1, 143
Care, duty of, 76
Cautions, 292
Charges, land, 254–64
  local, 262–3
  priority notices and, 261
  protection of purchasers and, 260–1
  registers concerning, 255–61
  types of, 258
Charities, 182, 273–4
Chattels, 11, 46
  personal, 11
  real, 11
Choses in action and possession, 11
Class gifts, 181–2

Common,
  law, 7
  tenancy in, 167–9
Commons of pasture, 242
Concurrent interests, 160–71
  coparcenary, 170
  joint tenancy, 161–7
  nature of, 160–1
  tenancy by entireties, 169–70
  tenancy in common, 167–9
  types of, 161
Conditional interests, 184–5
Consolidation, doctrine of, 184–5,
  210–11
Consumer agreement, 213
Contracts, for sale of land, 269–71
Conversion, doctrine of, 147–9
Conveyancing, 269
  deed of, 277–80
  simplification of, 29
Co-ownership, types of, 161
Coparcenary, 170
Copyholds, 27
Corporations, 273
Covenants,
  affecting land, 71–89
    rules, 88
    touching and concerning land,
     87–9
  concerning assigning and
    underletting, 77–9
  personal, 204
  remedies relating to, 82–4
  restrictive, 219–32
  usual, 71–2
Crown,
  owner of land, 6
cujus est solum, 8–9, 45

Debts, 28–9
Deed,
  conveyance, of, 277–80
  clauses in, 279–80
  execution of, 57–8
  vesting, 131–2

Deeds of arrangement, register of, 257
Deposits, 274–5
Determinable interests, 183–4
Disabilities, in relation to transfer of land, 271–4
Discharge, deed of, 145
Disclaimer, 69
Distress, right of, 82–3, 107
Dominant land, 219, 225, 226

Easements, 234–53
  acquisition of, 242–51
  creation of new, 239–40
  definition of, 234–5
  examples of, 238–9
  extinguishing of, 251–3
  light of, 249–50
  nature of, 235–6
  other rights and, 240–1
  quasi-, 237
Emblements and estovers, 72, 160
Enfranchisement of leases, 90–1
Enlargement, 68
Entailed interests, 185–6
Equitable,
  interests, 16–20
    creation and disposition of, 17
    essence of, 16
    leasehold, 58, 59
    mortgage, 191–2
    notice and, 17–20
    registration, 31
  lien and charge, 16
Equity, 7, 83–4, 190
Equity's darling, 18
Estate contracts, 259
Estates, 13–15, 30
  fee simple, 14
  fee tail, 13, 14
  freehold, 13, 14
  future, 15
  leaseholds, 13, 15
  life, 15, 159
  pur autre vie, 13, 15, 159
  subsisting at law, 30
Eviction, protection from, 62, 107
Executory interests, legal, 175

Fee,
  simple, 14, 37–49
    alienation of, 44, 45
    conditional, 39–40
    creation of, 41–3
    determinable, 39, 183–4
    essence of, 39

  meaning of, 37–9
  rights of owner, 43–9
  types of, 39–41
  will, grant by, 42–3
Feudalism, 7, 28, 6
Fines, 50
Fishing rights, 48
Fixtures, 20–3
Foreclosure, 204–5, 212
Forfeiture, 66, 83, 84–5, 302
Frankalmoign, 12, 13, 27
Fraud and limitation of actions, 301
Freehold, 11, 13, 14, 27
Frustration of leases, 68–9
Future,
  estates, 15, 39
  interests, 6, 173–86, 176, 301
    categories of, 174–5
    contingent, 173
    nature of, 173
    vested, 173

Gavelkind, 12, 27
General equitable charges, 259
Grant,
  derogation from, 75–6
  express, 243
  implied, 244–5
  lost, 247
  presumed, 246

Habitation, premises fit for, 76–7
Harassment of tenant, 106–7
Homicide, and severance, 167
Housing,
  action trust areas, 122–4
    designated areas, 122–3
    functions, 123
    rents, 123–4
  association, 122

id certum est, 54
Incumbrances on land, 189–264
Indemnity, right to, 294–5
Inhibitions, 291
Injunctions, 231
Insurance, 81, 211–12
interesse termini, 26
Intestacy, descent of property on, 29

Joint tenancy, 161–7
  creation of, 162–5
  determination of, 165–7
  tenancy in common, and, 167–8
jus accrescendi, 162, 167
jus spatiandi, 238, 239

Knight service, 13

Land,
  certificate, 283
  characteristics of, 4
  charges, 254–64
    local, 262–3
  definition of, 7–8
  disposition of interest in, 42
  enjoyment of, 48–9
  incumbrances on, 189–264
  law,
    anachronisms in old, 25–6
    legal history in, 5–6
    legislation of 1920s, 25–32
    modern, 7
    province of, 3–4
    sources of, 6–7
    vocabulary of, 5
  legal concept, 7–8
  limitation of actions concerning,
    298–302
  transfer of, 269–96
Lease (*see also* Term of years, tenancy),
  agreement for, 56
  creation of, 55–8
  definition, 50
  duration of, 53–5
  enfranchisement of, 90–1
  enlargement of, 68
  equitable, 56, 58
  formalities, 53, 56
  frustration of, 68–9
  grant and acceptance of, 139–40
  grant of by mortgagor and
    mortgagee, 202–3
  licence and, 93–104
  long, 90–1
  regulation of, 89–91
  types of, 59–65
Leases, regulation of, 89–91
Lessor and lessee, rights and duties of,
  71–91
Licences, 93–104, 240–1
  bare, 94
  characteristics, 94
  contractual, 95
  easements and, 240
  equitable, 95
  exclusive possession and, 93, 97–8,
    99
  expressed intention and, 98
  grant of interest and, 94
  leases and, 97–104
  proprietary estoppel and, 95–6
Lien, equitable, 16–17

Life,
  estates, 15
  interests, 159–170
    essence of, 159
Light, easement of, 249–51
Limitation,
  actions, of, 298–302
    disability, fraud and, 300–1
    mortgages and, 299–300
    recovery of land and rent,
      298–300
    words of, 28, 41
Limited owners' charges, 258–9
Lodgers, 99
Lost modern grant, 247–8

Manorial incidents, 27
Mental disorders, sufferers, 273
Merger,
  lease of, 67
  mortgages, and, 200
Minerals, rights to, 45, 160
Minor interests, 290–2
Minors, 169, 176, 271–2
Mortgages, 28, 189–218
  consolidation of, 210–11
  consumer credit and, 213–15
  discharge of, 199–201
  equitable, 191–2
  equity of redemption and, 192–7,
    200
  fundamentals, 189–90
  legal, 190–1
  limitation of actions and, 299–300
  merger and, 200
  nature of, 189–90
  priorities of, 197–9
  puisne, 258
  reform of, 215–18
  registered land, 292–3
  tacking and, 198–9
  terminology, 189
Mortgagor and mortgagee,
  definitions, 189
  rights of, 202–18

Natural rights, 43–4
nec vi, 246
Notice, doctrine of, 17–20
  actual, 19
  constructive, 19
  imputed, 20
  minor interests and, 291
  purchaser without, 17–19
  registration and, 295–6
  statutory, 20

omnia praesumuntur, 246
Ornamental fixtures, 23
Overreaching, 31–2, 142–3, 154–5, 261–2
Overriding interests, 286–90

Partition, 164–5
Party-walls, 170–1
Pending actions, 255
Perpetuities, rule against, 178–85
  age contingencies and, 181
  class gifts and, 181–2
  essence of, 178
  exceptions to, 182
  lives in being and, 179
  vesting and, 178, 179–80
  wait and see principle, 180–1
Personal property, 10–11
Possession,
  order, 116–18
  recovery of, 120
  right to take, 207–9
  significance of, 38–9
Premises, defective, 76–7
  improvement notice, 77
Prescription, 246–51
Priority notice, 261
Profits à prendre, 235, 241–2
  creation and acquisition of, 242–8
  definition, 235
  extinguishing of, 251–3
  other rights and, 242
  types of, 241–2
Property, 9–12, 27
  concept of, 9
  damage to, 80–1
  definitions, 9
  legislation, 25–32
  personal, 10–12
  real, 10–11, 52
Public sector tenants' right to buy, 124–6
Puisne mortgages, 258
Purchase, words of, 41
Purchaser, 17, 18, 143–5
  without notice, 17–20

quia emptores, 26
quicquid plantatur, 20
Quiet enjoyment of land, 74
Quit, notice to, 66

Real property, concept of, 10–11
Receiver, appointment of, 209–10, 213
Rectification of register, 294
Redemption,
  actions, limitation of, 299
  definition, 192
  equity of, 192–7, 200
  loss of right, 196–7
  process of, 200
Registered land, 14, 228–9, 250
  mortgages and, 197–9
  nature of, 281–2
  rights against, 286–92
  transfer, modes of, 292–4
Release, 252–3
Remainders, 15–16, 174–5
Remoteness, rules concerning, 176–84
Rent,
  adjustment of, 11, 118–19
  assessment committee, 118–19
  covenant for, 81–2
  definition, 51
  excessive, 120
  fair, 108
  housing action trusts, and, 123–4
  increases, 118
  limitation of actions and, 299
  rates, obligation to pay, 74
  registration of, 108
Rentcharges, 30, 232
Repairs and improvements, 73–4, 79–81, 119
Requisitions on title, 276
Reservation, express, and implied, 243, 245–6
Restricted contracts, rents under, 109
Restrictions and minor interests, 291–2
Restrictive covenants, 219–32, 259
  burden of, 223
  easements and, 240
  general position at common law, 220–3
  general position in equity, 223–8
  modification and discharge of, 229–31
  terminology, 219
  touching and concerning land, 220–1
Reversions, 15, 50, 174
Rights,
  entry, of, 183
  in personam, 16
  in rem, 16
  natural, 43–4
  of way, 238
  riparian, 47–8

Sale, right of, 206–7, 212
Satisfied term, 68
Secure tenancy, 115–20

Seisin, 6
Serjeanty, 12, 13
Servient land, 219, 234–5
Settlements, 129–56
  ad hoc, 134
  compound, 134
  creation of, 130–2
  determination of, 145
  discharge, deed of, 145
  examples of, 133
  limitation of actions and, 299
  nature of, 129–30
  overreaching and, 142–3
  ownership, change of, and, 143–4
  referential, 134
  strict, 130, 132–3
  tenant for life and, 134–6
  trustees of, 136–8
  trusts for sale, and, 129–30
  vesting deed and, 131–2
  will and, 131–2
Several profits, 235
Severance, 165–7
  words of, 168
Shorthold tenancy, assured, 119–20
sic utere tuo, 45
Socage, 12, 13
Specific performance, 59
Spouse, rights and succession, 119, 260
Statute in land law, 7
Statutory owners under settlement, 136
Sufferance, tenancies at, 64
superficies solo cedit, 8
Support, right to, 43–4
Surrender of lease, 67, 203
Survivorship, right of, 162, 167

Tacking, 198–9
Tenancy,
  agricultural, 61
  assured, 109, 114–19
  assured shorthold, 119–20
  common, in, 167–9
  determination of, 62, 66–9
  entireties, 169–70
  estoppel, by, 65–6
  fixed period, 60
  future, 65
  housing association, 110
  joint, 161–7
  lives, for, 65
  periodic, 115–16
  protected and statutory, 107–13
  renewable, perpetually, 64–5

  secure, 115–20
  shorthold, 119
  sufferance, at, 64
  week to week, from, 62
  will, at, 62–4
  year to year, from, 60–1, 61–2
Tenant,
  for life, 134, 160
    beneficiaries and, 142
    definition of, 134
    limited owners and, 135
    powers and liabilities of, 138–42
  in fee simple, 37
  residential protection of, 105–20
    essence of, 105
    harassment, 106–7
    payments, unlawful, 107
Tenants' fixtures, 22
Tenures, 6
  estates, and, 12–14
  reduction in, 26–7
Term of years, 15, 50–104
  definition, 50, 51
  essence of, 53–5
  fee simple, and, 52
  historical origins, 52
  meaning, 50
  merger and, 67
  satisfied, 68
  surrender of, 67
  terminology, 50–1
Theft, fixtures, of, 23
Title,
  abstract of, 275–6
  conversion of, 285–6
  investigation of, 275
  kinds of, 284–5
  registration of, 32, 281–2
  requisitions on, 276
Trade fixtures, 23
Transfer,
  registered land, of, 281–96
    indemnity and, 294
    inter vivos, 293
    modes of, 292–4
    nature of title, 284–6
    notice and, 295–6
    rectification and, 294
    register, 281, 283
    registration details, 281–4
  unregistered land, of, 269–80
    contracts, completion of, 274–7
    contracts relating to, 269–70
    contracts, types of, 270–1
    disabilities in relation to, 271–4
Treasure trove, 45–6

Trustees, of strict settlement, 136–8
Trusts for sale, 147–56
  ad hoc, 155–6
  beneficiaries under, 151
  consents and, 152–3
  conversion and, 147–9
  creation of, 150–1
  definition of, 149
  essence of, 148
  overreaching under, 154–5
  postponement, power of, 152
  powers, refusal to exercise, 153
  settlements and, 147
  statutory, 150
  trustees and, 152–4

Unities, four, 161–2, 167–8
Unregistered land, sale of, 269–80

Vendor and purchaser, 23

Vesting, deed, 131–2
Villein tenure, 12

Wait and see rule, 180–1
Waiver, 84
Waste, 73–4, 160
Water, rights over, 47–8
Way, rights of, 238
Wear and tear, 80
Week to week tenancies, 62
Will, tenancy at, 62–4
Wills,
  fee simple, by, 42–3
  minor conveyance to, by, 272
  settlement created by, 131–2
Words of severance, 168
Writs and orders, register of, 256–7

Year to year tenancies, 60–1, 61–2